Political Thought in Modern India

Political Thought in Modern India

Edited by
THOMAS PANTHAM
KENNETH L. DEUTSCH

$SAGE www.sagepublications.com
Los Angeles • London • New Delhi • Singapore • Washington DC • Boston

First published in 1986 by

SAGE Publications India Pvt Ltd
B 1/I-1 Mohan Cooperative Industrial Area
Mathura Road, New Delhi 110 044, India
www.sagepub.in

SAGE Publications Inc
2455 Teller Road
Thousand Oaks, California 91320, USA

SAGE Publications Ltd
1 Oliver's Yard, 55 City Road
London EC1Y 1SP, United Kingdom

SAGE Publications Asia-Pacific Pte Ltd
3 Church Street
#10-04 Samsung Hub
Singapore 048483

Published by Vivek Mehra for SAGE Publications India Pvt Ltd, photocomposed at South End Typographics, Pondicherry and printed at Chaman Enterprises, New Delhi.

Third Printing 2015

Library of Congress Cataloging-in-Publication Data
Main entry under title:
Political thought in modern India.

    Includes bibliographies.
       1. Political science—India—Addresses, essays, lectures. I. Pantham, Thomas.
    II. Deutsch, Kenneth L.

JA84.I4P65   1986   320.5'0954   85-30301

ISBN 10: 0-8039-9503-2   ISBN 10: 81-7036-024-2
ISBN 13: 978-0-8039-9503-1   ISBN 13: 978-81-7036-024-7
ISBN 10: 0-8039-9504-0 (pbk.) [USA]   ISBN 10: 81-7036-025-0 (pbk.) [India]
ISBN 13: 978-0-8039-9504-8 (pbk.) [USA]   ISBN 13: 978-81-7036-025-4 (pbk.) [India]

Contents

Preface

All the essays included here have been specially written for this book, in response to our invitation which was sent out along with a statement of objectives and guiding considerations which are incorporated in the introductory chapter. The contributors are all university teachers having distinctive achievements in the research and/or teaching of modern political thought. What brings us together is our common awareness of the inadequacies of the existing books that are used for university-level courses in modern Indian political thought. As this is our collective work, we cannot thank our contributing authors. But we do wish to say as editors how much we have been helped and encouraged by their enthusiastic and generous fellowship all through the five years during which this book has been in preparation.

Our collaborative editorship of this book has been facilitated by our receipt, separately, of Senior Fulbright Visiting Fellowships. Although this work was only tangential to our individual programmes of research during our separate fellowship-tenures (Pantham at the universities of Massachusetts at Amherst and Princeton, and Deutsch at the universities of Rajasthan and Baroda), we would like to express our appreciation of the benefits we derived from this academic exchange programme between India and USA. We also acknowledge our indebtedness to our own universities—namely, The Maharaja Sayajirao University of Baroda and the State University of New York at Geneseo, respectively—for giving us leave and other facilities.

January 1986   T..P.
                                                                 K.L.D

1

THOMAS PANTHAM

Introduction: For the Study of Modern Indian Political Thought

This collection of essays is intended to stimulate and promote the serious study of modern Indian political thought. Such a study, we feel, has been hampered by the lack of any book offering a consistently high-level treatment of the subject. There are, indeed, excellent books dealing with particular thinkers or aspects, for instance, R. Iyer's book on Gandhi, D. Dalton's book on the idea of freedom in Indian political thought and V.C. Joshi's edited volume on Raja Rammohun Roy. There are also some good books on modern Indian philosophy.[1] But when it comes to a book dealing with the whole or nearly the whole of the political thought of modern India, the available books seem to be disappointing to us. They do not maintain a uniformly high level of treatment of all thinkers or movements in India. This is partly due to the single-authored nature of these books. It is also a reflection of the low level of development of this field. In fact, until recently, most Indian universities did not have a course on modern Indian political thought. The recent interest in indigenous political thinking has led to the introduction of courses on it in almost all Indian universities. Our book is intended to bring about a significant raising and expansion of the intellectual content of these courses.

Our interest has not been in simply documenting what the thinkers said or wrote on various occasions. Rather, our interest has been in analysing the socio-historical contexts in which ideas and theories emerged, and the socio-historical changes that those ideas and theories were intended to bring about. Some related questions are: Who were the theorists' addressees? What were the beliefs or actions that they were advocating or opposing and why? What arguments were made in favour of them, and with what socio-historical consequences? We have tried to provide a world-historical and, to some extent, a political economy perspective on the contributions of the major political thinkers and on the ideologies of some of the political movements in modern India. We have also tried to compare these ideas and theories with Western ideas and theories.

Acknowledgements: The author acknowledges the helpful discussions he had had with Kenneth L. Deutsch on some of the points raised in this chapter

[1] See V.S. Naravane, *Modern Indian Thought: A Philosophical Survey* (Bombay: Asia, 1964); D.H. Bishop, ed., *Indian Thought: An Introduction* (New Delhi: Wiley Eastern, 1975); D.H. Bishop, ed., *Thinkers of the Indian Renaissance* (New Delhi: Wiley Eastern, 1982); T.M.P. Mahadevan and G.V. Saroja, *Contemporary Indian Philosophy* (New Delhi: Sterling, 1981).

In the West, apart from those universities which have 'area study' programmes dealing with India, Indian political thought does not constitute a part of the academic study of political theories.[2] This is unfortunate in the sense that it leaves out of consideration not merely the extensions or adaptations of Western theories of politics by the Indian people who make up a significant portion of humanity but also the Indian critiques of, and alternatives to, the West-centred paradigms of politics. That this neglect of Indian political thought is a source of theoretical impoverishment in the West is argued by Alasdair MacIntyre:

> The Indian political theorist has a harder task than his Western counterpart. He first of all has to be a good deal more learned, for he is required to know the history of Western political thought as well as the history of Asian thought . . . . He has to possess an array of linguistic skills that are uncharacteristic nowdays of Western political theories.
>
> Second, he has to sustain a relationship with his Western colleagues in which he takes their concerns with a seriousness that they rarely, unless they are among the very few Western specialists in Indian politics, reciprocate. Thus, a genuine dialogue is for the most part lacking. It is we in the West who are impoverished by our failure to sustain our part in this dialogue.[3]

Similarly, in a review article on A. Appadorai's *Indian Political Thinking in the Twentieth Century*, W.H. Morris-Jones of the Institute of Commonwealth Studies, University of London, raises the question of the parochialism of Western teachers of political thought. He points out that they will find much of 'relevance' in the contributions of those Indian thinkers, most notably Mahatma Gandhi, who blended Indian and Western traditions of thought.[4]

Several modern Indian political thinkers had the whole of humanity (and not just the Indians) as their audience. They offered theories for the resolution not merely, of some exclusively Indian predicaments or problems but of world-historical problems, issues or 'isms' such as feudalism, capitalism, imperialism, fascism, communism, utilitarianism, materialism, scientism and technocracy. They gave their interpretations of history, conceptions of man, visions of the good life, views on freedom, state, democracy, violence, human unity, ecological problems, means-end relationship and political morality. For instance, a very forceful expression of the Indian concern for some of the global political problems

---

[2] In this connection, see Alasdair MacIntyre's review of *Beyond Marxism* by Vrajendra Raj Mehta (New Delhi: 1978), in *Political Theory*, Vol. 2, No. 4, November 1983.

[3] A. MacIntyre, *ibid.*, p. 623.

[4] W.H. Morris-Jones, 'Parochialism in Political Thought,' *Political Studies*, Vol. 20, No. 4, Dec. 1972, pp. 475–77.

of our times was made in the Congress Working Committee's Manifesto, drafted by Jawaharlal Nehru at the outbreak of World War II. On the question of India's support for Britain's war efforts, the Manifesto declared:

If the war is to defend the status quo, imperialist possessions, colonies, vested interests and privileges, then India can have nothing to do with it. If, however, the issue is democracy and a world order based on democracy, then India is intensely interested in it. The Committee are convinced that the interests of Indian democracy do not conflict with the interests of British democracy or of world democracy. But there is an inherent and ineradicable conflict between democracy for India or elsewhere and imperialism and Fascism. If Great Britain fights for the maintenance and extension of democracy, then she must necessarily end imperialism in her own possessions, establish full democracy in India, and the Indian people must have the right of self-determination by framing their own constitution through a Constituent Assembly without external interference, and must guide their own policy. A free democratic India will gladly associate herself with other free nations for mutual defence against aggression and for economic cooperation. She will work for the establishment of a real world order based on freedom and democracy, utilising the world's knowledge and resources for the progress and advancement of humanity.

The crisis that has overtaken Europe is not of Europe only but of humanity and will not pass like other crisis or wars leaving the essential structure of the present-day world intact. It is likely to refashion the world for good or ill, politically, socially and economically. This crisis is the inevitable consequence of the social and political conflicts and contradictions which have grown alarmingly since the last Great War, and it will not be finally resolved till these conflicts and contradictions are removed and a new equilibrium established. That equilibrium can only be based on the ending of the domination and exploitation of one country by another, and on a reorganisation of economic relations on a juster basis for the common good of all. India is the crux of the problem, for India has been the outstanding example of modern imperialism, and no refashioning of the world can succeed which ignores this vital problem. With her vast resources she must play an important part in any scheme of world reorganisation. But she can only do so as a free nation whose energies have been released to work for this great end. Freedom today is indivisible and every attempt to retain imperialist domination in any part of the world will lead inevitably to fresh disaster.[5]

[5] See M.K. Gandhi, *Non-violence in Peace and War* (Ahmedabad: Navajivan, 1942), Vol. 1, pp. 220–21.

Mahatma Gandhi complimented Nehru for drafting the Manifesto in such a way as to compel India 'to think not merely of her own freedom, but of the freedom of all the exploited nations of the world'.[6] He noted that the Manifesto was addressed 'not only to his [i.e., Nehru's] own countrymen, not only to the British government and the British people, but it is addressed also to the nations of the world including those that are exploited like India.'[7] In his writings, Gandhi (like his great contemporaries, Rabindranath Tagore, Aurobindo Ghose and Jawaharlal Nehru) expressed his deep concern with, and proposals for remedying some of the global political problems and civilisational predicaments of our times. As Norman D. Palmer has noted: 'The concepts of the essential unity of mankind and of the philosophical ties which bind East and West have never been more profoundly held or more eloquently voiced than by the seminal thinkers of modern India.'[8]

Several modern Indian critiques of, and alternatives to, West-centred paradigms of politics are based on metaphysical and epistemological assumptions that differ sharply from those of the West. As perceptive scholars have reminded us, the mainstream of classical Indian thought subscribed to a non-dialectical or non-dualistic epistemology and metaphysics, in contrast to the dualistic metaphysics and epistemology that have dominated the Western mode of thought.[9] As V.R. Mehta has noted, 'While Western thought works in terms of antagonisms, dichotomies and antinomies between spirit and matter, the individual and society, bread and culture, necessity and freedom, Indian thought has always considered such dichotomies as artificial and unreal.' Western philosophy, we are further told, serves to legitimise atomistic individualism, irreconcilable contradictions, mindless competition, amoral power-politics, and the dichotomisation of ends and means, elite and mass, the chosen and the damned, heaven and hell. A non-dualistic metaphysics and epistemology, by contrast, tends to foster and sustain community, cooperation, world unity, humanism, and the rupturing of the dichotomies between elite and mass, subject and object, friend and enemy, ends and means. Such a philosophy sustains a conception of the state not as a Leviathan or as 'the *terminus ad quem* of man's whole development' but as a means to the attainment by man of his self-realisation.[10]

 6   *Ibid.*, p. 224.

 7   *Ibid.*

 8   Norman D. Palmer, 'Indian and Western Political Thought: Coalescence or Clash?,' *American Political Science Review*, Vol. 59, No. 3, Sept. 1955, p. 761. For discussions of Tagore's internationalism, see R. Chakrabarti's chapter in this volume and Subrata Mukherjee, 'Tagore's Critique of Nationalist Political Discourse,' *Democratic World* (New Delhi), 15 and 22 April 1984.

 9   V.R. Mehta, *Ideology, Modernisation and Politics in India* (New Delhi: Manohar, 1983), p. 74. See also the concluding chapters of D.H. Bishop's two books (as referred to in Note 1 above) and the introductory chapter of Mahadevan and Saroja, *op. cit.*

 10 See Palmer, *op. cit.*, p. 756.

Our intention in referring to these two highly abstract modes of thought and their corresponding socio-political implications is not to make any extravagant claims for the classical tradition of Indian thought. We do not mean to suggest that the Indian tradition of social and political thought and action has been unblemished or that what the world needs today is a simple refashioning of its social and political practices in accordance with ancient Indian wisdom. We do not subscribe to any such naively revivalist or 'holier than thou' standpoint. We only mean to suggest that in trying to overcome the limitations of the modern, scientistic, positivist paradigm of governance, we are likely to find philosophical or epistemological help from the creative strands of Indian thought.[11] As noted by Palmer, 'from India may come influences which will widen the horizons of Western political thinkers and which will give political ideas a sounder foundation of philosophical and metaphysical speculation.'[12]

In this context, it must be noted that India—which had a high level of civilisation with its distinctive mode of thought and action—did experience (to use Nehru's words) 'a progressive deterioration during centuries' reaching a very low level by the eighteenth century.[13] At least some of the sources of that decline were indeed internal to the Indian tradition of thought and action. At the turn of the century, Tagore wrote:

Our country having lost its link with the inmost truth of its being, struggled under a crushing load of unreason, in abject slavery to circumstances. In social usage, in politics, in the realms of religion and art, we had entered the zone of uncreative habit, of decadent tradition, and ceased to exercise our humanity.[14]

Raja Rammohun Roy attributed India's social decadence to such factors as religious ritualism, idolatry, Brahmanic elitism and needless social discriminations. He wrote:

Many learned Brahmans are perfectly aware of the absurdity of idolatry and are well informed of the nature of the purer modes of divine worship. But as in the rites, ceremonies and festivals of idolatry they find the sources of their comforts and fortunes, they not only never fail to protect idol worship from all attacks but even advance and encourage it to the utmost of their power by keeping the knowledge of their scriptures concealed from the rest of the people.[15]

[11] In this connection, it is interesting to note that Alvin Toffler finds that 'First and Third Wave civilisations seem likely to have more in common with each other than with Second Wave civilisations.' Alvin Toffler, *The Third Wave* (New York: Bantam Books, 1980), p. 337.

[12] Palmer, *op. cit.*, p. 761.

[13] Jawaharlal Nehru, *The Discovery of India* (New York: John Day, 1946), p. 42.

[14] See N. Mehta and S.P. Chhabra, *Modern Indian Political Thought* (Jullundur: New Academic Publishing Co., 1976), p. 1.

[15] Preface to the translation of the Ishopanishad, in *English Works of Rammohun Roy* (Calcutta, 1947), Vol. 2, p. 44.

In his *Discovery of India*, written in prison in 1944, Nehru diagnosed the sources of India's decline as follows:

> She [i.e., India] fell behind in the march of technique, and Europe, which had long been backward in many matters, took the lead in technical progress. Behind this technical progress was the spirit of science and a bubbling life and spirit which displayed itself in many activities and in adventurous voyages of discovery. New techniques gave military strength to the countries of Western Europe and it was easy for them to spread out and dominate the East. That is the story not of India only but of almost the whole of Asia.
>
> .... A rational spirit of inquiry, so evident in earlier times, which might well have led to the further growth of science, is replaced by irrationalism and a blind idolatry of the past. Indian life becomes a sluggish stream, living in the past, moving slowly through the accumulations of dead centuries. The heavy burden of the past crushes it and a kind of coma seizes it. It is not surprising that in this condition of mental stupor and physical weariness India should have deteriorated and remained rigid and immobile while other parts of the world marched ahead.[16]

Some of the essays included in this volume provide variations on Rammohun Roy's and Nehru's diagnoses of, and prescriptions for, the Indian problematique. All the Indian thinkers recognise the indigenous as well as the extraneous sources of Indian degeneration. As to the cure or remedy, one group of thinkers (which is perhaps more numerous than the other groups) favour the 'imitative reproduction' of the modern Western modes of political action and organisation, be it of the liberal or Marxist variety. A second type of thinkers advocate the revival and asseveration of India's classical tradition of social and political thought and action. A third group of thinkers, best represented by Gandhi, attempt a creative blending of the traditional Indian and the modern Western paradigms of politics.[17] These creative universalists seem to suggest that what our times require is a post-liberal world society.

In the quest for such a new, global, political order, we feel that contemporary Indian thought has much to offer. The Hindu civilisation differs from the Western Christian civilisation as no other civilisation does.[18] And yet the latter has had the most intimate and far-reaching

---

[16] Nehru, *op. cit.*, p. 42.

[17] See W.H. Morris-Jones, *op. cit.*, and Deena H. Khatkhate, 'Intellectuals, Power and Change in India,' in K.S. Krishnaswamy *et al.*, eds., *Society and Change: Essays in Honour of Sachin Chaudhuri* (Bombay: Oxford University Press, 1977), pp. 186–208.

[18] See Arnold Toynbee, *The World and the West* (London: Oxford University Press, 1953), Chapter 3: 'India and the West'; D.E. Smith, 'The Political Implications of Asian Religions,' in Smith, ed., *South Asian Politics and Religion* (Princeton University Press, 1966), pp. 3–20; and Johan Galtung, 'Western Civilization: Anatomy and Pathology,' *Alternatives*, Vol. 7, No. 2, 1981.

impact on the former, which has however maintained an essential continuity with its own past. Islam, too, has had a powerful impact on Indian civilisation. 'The contemporary Orient,' writes Northrop, 'is the product of the traditional self and the influence of the West.'[19] Northrop goes on to ask:

> Need one wonder, with all these Hindu, Mohammedan, Jainist, Marxist, Lockean, Elizabethan and Mercantile ideas of the good for man and the state, contradicting each other at many points, and pushing and pulling her in opposite directions, from both within and without, that staid, intuitive, receptive, indeterminate Mother India finds it difficult to make up her contemporary mind?[20]

It is indeed difficult, we would grant, for 'Mother India . . . to make up her contemporary mind.' That difficulty, we would like to stress, is largely due to the fact that India's making up *her* contemporary mind is closely interlinked with the making up of the global political mind; the Indians have to take on the concerns of the Lockeans and the Marxists, the Hindus and the non-Hindus and all the others listed by Northrop. It is indeed a serious difficulty. But there is in that very difficulty some ground for hope: the persisting philosophical distinctiveness of Hindu civilisation and the extent of intimate relationship it has already developed with western Christian and Islamic civlisations may serve as a positive aid in our quest for a reconstructed world society. As pointed out by Rajni Kothari, India can play a distinctive role 'in working out a transition towards its own version of a postmodern postsecular society' as an alternative both to the paradigm of the centralised, technocratic state of the modern positivist age and to the nativistic-fanatic-religious modes of resisting western-style modernisation. Kothari writes:

> Steeped in the tradition of social pluralism . . . (as distinct from the mere political pluralism as found in western democracies) and in a conception of unity based on dispersed identities and shared values, endowed with a non-theological religious pedigree without a fixed doctrine or an official clergy, and given its high tolerance of ambiguity and a deeply ingrained tradition of scepticism, India may be better placed than most societies to carve out a niche for itself in a world undergoing great transformations.[21]

---

[19] F.S.C. Northrop, *The Meeting of East and West* (New York: The Macmillan Co.. 1946), p. 405.

[20] *Ibid.*, p. 416.

[21] Rajni Kothari, 'The Crisis of the Moderate State and the Decline of Democracy.' in Peter Lyon and James Manor, eds., *Transfer and Transformation: Political Institutions in the New Commonwealth* (Leicester: Leicester University Press, 1983), p. 45.

We referred earlier to an essential continuity between ancient and modern Indian thought. This continuity is clearly seen in the contributions of Dayananda Saraswati, Bankim Chandra Chatterjee, Vivekananda, Aurobindo and Gandhi. Their objective, as acknowledged by Aurobindo, was the development of forms of thought 'not contradictory of the truths of life which the old expressed, but rather expressive of those truths restated, cured of defect, completed'.[22] Similarly, Gandhi acknowledged that his practico-political experiments were meant 'to throw new light on many an old truth'. What he has done, he said, was 'to put a new but natural and logical interpretation upon the whole teaching of the Gita and the spirit of Hinduism.'[23]

Because of this essential continuity between the tradition of Hindu political thought and modern Indian political thought, we have felt that an analysis of the former constitues a *prolegomenon* to the study of the latter. Hence, before turning to the contributions of the modern Indian political thinkers, we shall, in the next chapter, consider some distinctive features of the Hindu tradition of political thought.

[22] Sri Aurobindo, *The Renaissance in India* (Pondicherry: Sri Aurobindo Ashram, 1951), p. 6.
[23] M.K. Gandhi, *Hindu Dharma* (Ahmedabad: Navajivan, 1950), p. 157.

2

BHIKHU PAREKH

Some Reflections on the Hindu Tradition of Political Thought

In this paper I will examine critically some of the distinctive features of the Hindu tradition of political thought.* To avoid misunderstanding, it would be useful to begin by making four points of clarification. First, as it forms a relatively coherent and analytically convenient subject of investigation, I shall concentrate on the Hindu tradition from its early Vedic beginnings to the arrival of the Muslims in the eight century A.D., and shall ignore its subsequent development altogether.

Second, I shall not summarise the ideas of individual Hindu political thinkers, but only explore the basic framework within which they thought about politics. India was subjected to several foreign invasions and experienced several social and economic changes during the period in question. In response to these, Hindu political thinkers of different periods had to deal with different problems and approach familiar problems from different angles. Despite these, however, their basic framework of thought—that is, their basic concepts, concerns and problems—retained a remarkable continuity. It is in this sense that one can legitimately talk about the Hindu *tradition* of political thought.

Third, I shall use the term politics and its derivatives rather widely to refer to the affairs of a territorially organised community held together by allegiance to a common authority. And, finally, I am concerned here with examining not the unarticulate beliefs and assumptions underlying and informing Hindu political institutions and practices, but rather the body of ideas Hindu political thinkers developed in their systematic treatises on politics.

I

Hindu political thinkers conceptualised political life in terms of two central concepts namely, *danda* and *dharma*. For them political life or ruling a territorially organised community ultimately consisted in using *danda* to maintain *dharma*. The term *danda* means discipline, force, restraint, constraint or punishment. Hindu political writers generally used it to refer to the punitive use of the coercive power of government.

---

* The Hindu political ideas discussed in this paper are outlined in several standard commentaries on the subject, such as those by Beni Prasad, U. Ghoshal, K.P. Jaiswal, R. Mazumdar, J. Spellman and H.N. Sinha. I have, therefore, felt it advisable not to clutter up the paper with footnotes

Dharma is a much more difficult concept. It comes from the Sanskrit root *dhr*, meaning to hold. *Dharma* is that which holds a society together. Since the Hindus thought a society was held together by each individual and group doing his or its specific duties, they used the term to mean duties. Some writers used it broadly to mean all duties, whereas others confined it to religious or religiously prescribed duties.

Hindu political thinkers described the systematic study of political life as *niti* or, more commonly *sastra*. *Niti*, which comes from the Sanskrit word meaning 'to lead,' refers to a study of policies. Thus *dandaniti*, a term sometimes used to describe a systematic study of political life, means a study of the best ways of using the coercive power of government. The term *sastra* means a systematic study of the general principles and detailed organisation of a specific form of human activity. Thus *dharma-sastra* refers to a systematic treatise on the general principles and detailed content of righteous conduct. Sometimes the term sastra is given the additional connotation of an authoritative text, and the principles and rules laid down in a treatise are given the status of injunctions. Thus the principles and rules of *dharmasastras* are not merely analytical and elucidatory but also authoritative and binding in nature. This additional connotation, however, is absent in other usages of the term. Thus the principles laid down in Bharat's *Natyasastra* and Kautilya's *Arthasastra* are largely elucidatory and, at best, recommendatory,

As we saw, the Hindu political thinkers regarded *dharma* and *danda* as the two most basic features of political life. Although the two features were accepted by them as complementary, different Hindu writers chose to concentrate on one or the other and explored political life in terms of it, thereby giving rise to two different trends or strands of political thought.

The *dharmasastra* writers concentrated on exploring the *dharma* of individuals and social groups, including the government. They discussed the sources of *dharma* as well as what was to be done when these conflicted. And they also provided a detailed prospectus of duties. They were not moral philosophers but law-givers, and generally didactic and prescriptive. Since they did not concentrate on the government and attempted to provide a code of conduct covering the entire human life, they did not write books specifically on politics. Political *dharma* was incidental to their main concern and did not form a distinct and autonomous subject of investigation.

In contrast to *dharmasastra* writers, the authors of *arthasastra* were interested in the organisation and mechanics of *danda*, that is, the way the government, the agent of *danda*, could be most effectively organised. They concentrated on the nature and organisation of government, the nature and mechanics of power, the way power is acquired, weakened and lost, the sources of threat to government and the best way to deal with them, and so on. Since the *arthasastra* writers were primarily concerned with the government, their works were specifically political. Further, since they concentrated on the government, they appreciated the autonomy of political life and its distinctive problems to a much greater degree than the authors of *dharmasastras*.

It would, however, be a mistake to draw too neat a contrast between the two strands of Hindu political thought. It is true that the authors of *dharmasastras* were rather moralistic, and those of *arthasastras* realistic to the point of sometimes bordering on cynicism. However, the former were not politically naive and freely acknowledged the political need to disregard moral principles and values under certain circumstances, even as the *arthasastra* writers acknowledged and indeed insisted on the observance of *dharma*. Again, it is true that the *dharmasastra* writers occasionally ignored the contingencies and frailties of human affairs; however, they were not nervous about the need to use force. Similarly, although the *arthasastra* writers occasionally tended to treat political power as an end-in-itself, they did not generally lose sight of the moral ends of government. It would also be wrong to suggest, as is sometimes done, that the two approaches represent totally different views of man and society for, as we shall see, their views on these subjects were basically the same.

The two approaches differed primarily in their subject matter, one choosing to explore political life from the standpoint of *dharma*, the other from that of *danda*. This naturally led to differences in emphasis and orientation. Since the *dharmasastras* were concerned to lay down *dharma*, they were legalistic and religious in orientation, whereas the *arthasastras*, concerned with analysing the structure and functions of government, concentrated on institutions and policies and were secular in orientation. Neither approach was complete by itself, and this was fully appreciated by its followers. The two together constitute the Hindu tradition of political thought. The commentators who equate it with one of them and contend that it is either wholly moralistic or wholly cynical, or either legalistic or institutional, offer a distorted account of it.

II

The Hindu tradition of political thought displays remarkable continuity. It did, of course, undergo important changes in response to new theoretical and practical problems posed by the rise of new religious movements (especially Buddhism), new philosophical movements (especially the *Lokayata*), new castes, guilds and corporations, waves of foreign invasions, settlements of foreigners, and so on. Amidst all these changes, however, its basic theoretical concerns remained more or less constant.

For the Hindu political thinkers the universe is an ordered whole governed by fixed laws. It is characterised by *Rta*, the inviolable order of things. Society replicates the order of the universe and becomes an ordered whole when held together by *dharma*. For the Hindus, society is not a collection of individuals but a community of communities. It consists of castes, each of which is engaged in the performance of certain common functions and is related to the others in a hierarchical manner. Its characteristic functions and place in the social hierarchy define the perimeter of its *dharma*. An individual's *dharma* is derived from the caste of his birth. For the Hindu, an individual's birth into a particular caste is not accidental but a result of his *karma* or actions in his previous life. *Dharma* and *karma* are integrally connected. An individual's *karma* determines his caste, and therefore his *dharma*, and his *dharma* defines his rightful *karma*. In addition to caste, an individual also occupies other social positions. He is a father or a son, a husband, a brother, an uncle or a nephew, a cousin, a neighbour, a subject or a ruler, and so on. As an incumbent of each of these roles, he has a specific *dharma*. The Hindu writers divided man's life into four distinct chronological stages or *āshrams*, and each stage was again characterised by a specific *dharma*.

For the Hindu writers, *dharma* is the basis of personal and social life. It alone holds society together; violation of it shakes the society to its very foundations and constitutes a mortal threat to its existence. As was to be expected in a society under constant foreign invasion and based on domination by the two highest castes, the Hindu thinkers were most fearful of social disintegration. Accordingly they laid down detailed rules governing almost every aspect of human conduct, and insisted that any deviation from them spelt disorder and chaos. Every Hindu was to adhere strictly to the *dharma* of his specific stage in life, his specific social positions and roles, and above all his caste. Doing things that pertain to another caste is *adharma* or immoral. The *Gita* observes that an individual who disregards *svadharma* courts unhappiness and destruction; and it is better to die doing one's *dharma* than to attempt to perform someone else's. According to Hindu law-givers, whoever deviates from his caste duties runs the risk of forfeiting his social status; he may be made an outcaste and deprived of his right to follow certain types of occupations.

According to Hindu political thinkers, each individual does his *dharma* in an ideal society. There is, therefore, no disorder, and hence no need for *danda* or force, and obviously no need for government. For some Hindu thinkers men were once in such a state; for others they have always had refractory impulses; for yet others human history is cyclical in nature and characterised by a regular and inexorable alteration of four distinct epochs representing different degrees of human corruption. In any case, once men become corrupt and incapable of *svaraj* or self-rule, they begin to ignore their *dharma*. This results in *varnasankara* or 'confusion of castes,' *arajakata* or lawlessness, *matsyanyaya* or the law of the sea (the Hindu equivalent of the Western law of jungle) according to which the big fish eat the small, and the eventual disintegration of the social order. For some Hindu political thinkers such a situation did once prevail; for others it is only a definite possibility haunting every society. In any case, it must at all cost be remedied or avoided, and hence the institution of government becomes necessary. Although Hindu thinkers were familiar with the republican and other non-monarchical forms of governments, they concentrated on monarchy.

The king's main function was to maintain the established social order. Since a society was believed to remain well-ordered only so long as each individual observed his personal and caste *dharma*, the king's *dharma* consisted in maintaining the rule of *dharma* in society at large. In concrete terms, this meant that he was to facilitate the study of the *Vedas* and philosophy, encourage the development of industry and commerce, maintain proper relations between different castes, ensure the observance of parental, filial, matrimonial and other duties, enforce *dharma* pertaining to different stages of individual life, and so on. The king derived his authority from the fact that he needed it to maintain *dharma*. He was, therefore, to use it only for that purpose and in a manner consistent with it. If he used it for other purposes, or to enforce *adharma*, or in a manner disallowed by *dharma*, he was considered a tyrant. Some Hindu thinkers urged that a tyrant should be disobeyed, and even killed. Some others authorised disobedience only if led by 'respectable' men of 'status'; while others proscribed it altogether.

The king's duty to enforce *dharma* raised the obvious question as to who determined the content of it. The Hindu writers generally pointed to the *Vedas*, the *smritis* and *vyavahara*. The *Vedas* were not moral treatises, and such moral principles as they contained were highly general. The *smritis* were largely digests of prevailing social practices. And thus *vyavahāra* or custom was the operative source of *dharma*. Each caste had been in existence for a long time, and had acquired a specific body of traditions and usages. So long as they were not in conflict with Vedic injunctions, they constituted its *dharma*. Similarly, each family had developed a body of usages over time, and these constituted its members' *kuladharma*. From time to time the Hindu law-givers made a study of the traditions and usages of different social groups and wrote detailed digests.

Over centuries the social and political structure of India underwent important changes and many different types of social groups began to appear. In the aftermath of successive foreign invasions, fairly large communities of foreign settlers came into existence. Heretical groups began to appear within the fold of Hindu society itself. New religious movements and communities—especially the Buddhists and Jains—appeared. With the development of commerce and trade, corporations and guilds of traders, artisans and craftsmen began to appear. New castes came into existence as a result of intermarriages or new occupations.

Large empires (especially those of the Mauryas and the Guptas) appeared on the scene, and they had to rule over far-flung territories within some of which rather different conceptions of caste *dharma* prevailed.

The Hindu writers dealt with the situation in terms of their traditional concept of *dharma*. Even as they had maintained that each caste had its traditional *dharma* which it had the authority to enforce, the king intervening only when necessary, the Hindu writers argued that the new social groups must be accepted as autonomous and self-governing communities entitled to have their traditions and customs upheld and to make their own rules. Thus the communities of foreign settlers, corporations, religious communities, heretics, even atheists, villages and districts, guilds and new castes, were recognised as having their own distinctive *dharma*, which they were free to enforce on their members and whose legitimacy was accepted by the king. The Vedic injunctions were not binding on those groups that either consisted of non-Hindus or were essentially economic in nature. The Hindu writers realised that the customs and traditions of various groups might be ambiguous, or harm public interest, or remain silent about certain aspects of social conduct. In such cases the king was to make appropriate laws. In short the Hindu political thinkers broadened their earlier theory and recognised *vyavahara* (traditions and customs), *caritam* (conduct of good man) and *rajsasan* (royal edicts and civil laws) as the legitimate bases of *dharma*.

The Hindu political thinkers did not invest the ruler with arbitrary and despotic power as the theorists of Oriental Despotism have maintained. They viewed society as an organic structure articulated in terms of social groups. Each group had its own *dharma* which was not laid down by the ruler and with which the ruler could not generally interfere. Further many of the groups were quite powerful. The castes were strong social groups, enjoying autonomy and their own distinctive structures of authority. Like the castes, many villages too had à long tradition of self-government. And many guilds and corporations consisted of powerful and wealthy men.

The ruler was therefore an integral part of a highly differentiated and uncentralised social order. He did not stand above the social order. He was one of its several parts, albeit an important part, but still only a part. His authority was hedged in by the relatively inviolable authority of the various autonomous centres of power, and regulated by his own specific *dharma*. Since he was never seen as outside of, let alone above society, the very conceptual framework required by the idea of Oriental Despotism was absent. The king did, of course, sometimes misuse his authority and interfered with the private lives of his subjects. However, his authority was considerably limited by the autonomous institutions which were not his creations and had independent sources of legitimacy; and the rise of trade and commerce from around the third century B.C. meant that the royal monopoly of land was no longer a formidable source of power. Not so much the government as the religiously sanctioned social structure, helped no doubt by the government, was generally the source of oppression in ancient India.

Having briefly discussed *dharma*, we will now turn to the Hindu examination of *danda*. In their exploration of the structure of government, Hindu political writers were guided by certain common considerations. The king's duty to maintain *dharma* meant that he was to rely on the advice of people well-versed in the *Vedas* and the *Sastras*. The Brahmans, therefore, enjoyed considerable power and prestige. Indeed Hindu polities were for centuries based on and run by a 'holy' (or unholy?) alliance of the Ksatriyas and the Brahmans. Not surprisingly, almost the entire Hindu tradition of political thought was based on the unquestioned assumption of a close alliance between the two highest castes. It analysed political life within the framework of the alliance, and rarely ventured to explore alternative modes of constituting the polity.

In India, political power never really shifted from the Brahmans and the Ksatriyas. The two did, of course, initially struggle for supremacy. However, over time, a *modus vivendi* was reached between them. The Brahmans acknowledged the Ksatriyas' right to rule; in return the Ksatriyas acknowledged the Brahmans' social superiority, gave them a share in the exercise of political authority and made generous donations of land and money. The Ksatriyas had the monopoly of state power, the Brahmans that of learning and teaching. The former were to specialise in *danda*, the latter in *dharma*. By and large the Brahmans were expected not to interfere with the use of *danda*, and the Ksatriyas with the interpretation of *dharma*. The Ksatriya kings upheld the social order that gave the Brahmans moral and religious authority and material wealth; the Brahmans, in turn, used their monopoly of 'intellectual production' to produce ideological systems justifying the established political order, including the king's power and wealth. The corporate spirit in each of the two castes was most developed, as also the spirit of identity of interests between them.

By contrast, the other castes were too fragmented and isolated to develop such a spirit. The Vaisyas and the Sudras could never unite, and the Vaisyas were too large and their range of occupations too varied to allow them to develop a sense of corporate identity and collective power.

Some Hindu political thinkers distinguished between authority and power. Authority implied an *adhikar*. *Adhikar*, a difficult and complex Hindu concept, meant a deserved right, a right one deserves to possess as judged by established social norms. A ruler acquired *adhikar* to power when he was judged to possess appropriate intellectual and moral qualifications and was duly crowned by the Brahmans in a ceremony known as *abhiseka*. In this ceremony the Brahmans annointed and blessed him, symbolically raised him to the status of a Brahman and identified him with the territory and its people, and declared him *satyaraja*, a true or rightful king. For most Hindu political thinkers, however, even an usurper acquired authority if he had appropriate qualifications and ruled his kingdom righteously.

Hindu political thinkers were constantly haunted by the fragility of political authority. It could not be based on *dharma* alone, for people's sense of *dharma* is generally weak and ambitious and powerful men would want to plot against the ruler. Nor could it be based on *danda* alone, for fear cannot sustain a society long. Accordingly, Hindu political thinkers insisted that political authority rested on the twin foundations of *dharma* and *danda* (that is, on the popular recognition of the fact that the king was devoted to the maintenance of *dharma* and would not hesitate to use *danda*). They did not say much about the nature and basis of political authority and legitimacy, and devoted considerable attention to political power.

The Hindu political thinkers suggested various ways in which political power could be acquired and maintained. They insisted that the king should be a man of great intellect and character and advocated his rigorous intellectual and moral training. They insisted also on him having reliable and competent counsellors and ministers. Most Hindu writers distinguished between *mantrins* and *amatyas*. The former were men of independent social status, attended public functions with the king and acted as his advisors; the latter were executive officers in charge of day-to-day administration. The Hindu political thinkers insisted that since there was nothing more dear to a man than his customs and usages, the king should not generally interfere with them. They also advocated the importance of efficient administration, constant checks on subordinate officials, programmes of welfare provision, and so on.

As for the exercise of *danda* and instilling fear in the subjects, the Hindu political writers relied on several devices of which two deserve some attention—namely espionage and punishment. Nearly all of them stressed the need for an all-pervasive network of spies. According to the *Mahabharata*, every kingdom has 'its roots in spies and secret agents'. Megasthenes found them so numerous that he referred to them as a special class of Hindu society. They were so pervasive and evoked such terror that they were referred to in a Pallava inscription as *Samcarantakas* (moving agents of death).

Kautilya assigned considerable importance to them and indeed thought that their importance was next only to that of the ministers. He offered a detailed description of the cunning ways in which they were to be planted in society and the techniques they were to deploy. They were to go out in such varied disguises as merchants, mendicants, classmates, prisoners and beggars, and were free to use all kinds of treachery, sacrilege, cruelty and immoral devices. According to Hindu thinkers, the spies reported to the king the activities of his officers, family members, foreigners, courtesans and potential trouble-makers; they also spread false information and created divisions among the subjects; and they also spied on the private lives of the citizens and reported on the trends in public opinion and feelings.

Even as the Hindu writers saw nothing wrong in an extensive network of spies, they saw nothing wrong in imposing gruesome forms of punishment on those found guilty of violation of their legal and moral duties. They did, no doubt, insist that the utmost care should be exercised in deciding whether a man was really guilty of the alleged crime, and provided elaborate rules for collecting and assessing evidence, cross-examination and arriving at a verdict. Once a man was found guilty, especially of the violation of caste and other religious duties, most hideous punishments were imposed on him, including some horrifying types of torture (of which Manu, Vasistha, Gautama, Brahaspati, Kautilya, Auguttara Nikaya and others offered vivid lists). For the Hindu writers punishment was designed to create fear, for without fear men do not act righteously. Brahaspati reflects the common view when he compared *danda* to a dark goddess with red eyes inflicting brutal death on evil-doers. The Hindu writers insisted that while inflicting punishment, a man's caste should be taken into account. The higher castes were to receive lighter punishment and were to be exempt from corporal punishment.

The Hindu political thinkers were also preoccupied with the possible conflict between *danda* and *dharma*. They knew that the king may sometimes have to be untruthful, cruel, deceitful and so on, and questioned if and how this was justified. They were all convinced that it was justified, largely on the ground that the preservation of society was the highest political value. The preservation of society meant not just the physical security of the subjects but also the maintenance of the social order and the preservation of *dharma*. In the *Mahabharata*, even Krishna, the Lord Himself, tells a few lies and practises deception on a few occasions. These were all justified on the ground that they were required to uphold *dharma*. As far as relations with foreign rulers were concerned, the Hindu writers generally emphasised the considerations of self-interest and saw little reason for moral restraint.

The Hindu tradition of political thought met its most radical critique at the hands of Buddhism. Buddhism was atheistic in the sense that it did not see the need to postulate the existence of God; it denied the divine origin and the authority of the *Vedas*; it rejected the caste system; it admitted women to the religious order; since it had originated under a republican (or rather semi-oligarchical) system of government, it had pronounced quasi-democratic sympathies; it founded monasteries, organised them along the lines of the republican assemblies and gave India the first experience of organised religion; and so on. More important, Buddhism attracted the loyalty and support of the economically powerful but socially inferior class of traders, cultivators, artisans, merchants and skilled craftsmen. It also welcomed and assimilated such foreign settlers as the Greeks, Shakas, Kushanas and Huns whom the caste-based Hindu society had kept out of its fold. Buddhism also attracted the Sudras, who could shed their low social status by joining a caste-free religion and improve their material circumstances by escaping the expensive religious rituals required by the Brahmans. Buddhism thus represented a mass movement consisting of the bulk of the Vaisyas, some Sudras, foreigners, women and the isolated tribal republics that had still managed to survive.

Buddhism developed a new political theory. It advanced a quasi-contractualist theory of the origin of the government. It postulated a peaceful and harmonious state of social existence when men had few desires and were at peace with themselves and with their fellow-men. Over time men began to develop limitless wants and desires, and the institutions of private property and family came into being. Disorder and discord set in, and the institution of the government became necessary. People elected one of the 'noblest' among them as a ruler and authorised him to rule over the rest. He was to exercise his authority in cooperation with the assembly of people's representatives, who were not generally elected but were heads of noble families and men of status. The Buddhist writers advocated legal and social equality, but did not extend it to the poor, the propertyless and the Sudras. They accepted the Hindu view that the king's principal duty was to maintain *Dhamma*, but rejected its cast-based definition and content. *Dhamma* for them largely meant the basic social morality as expounded by the Buddha. They stressed the autonomy of corporations, guilds and *sanghas*, and advocated religious tolerance.

The Buddhist challenge did not, however, lead to a radical reformulation of the Hindu tradition of political thought. The Buddhist political theory was not sufficiently radical and subversive. It continued to share such basic Hindu beliefs as, life is full of sorrow, desires are bad, a man's *karma* in his previous life determines his destiny in this life, and the ruler must maintain *dharma*. Furthermore, while it challenged the power and authority of the Brahmans, it upheld those of the Ksatriyas. Basically, Buddhism attempted to replace the Ksatriya-Brahman alliance with the Ksatriya-Vaisya alliance under the former's leadership.

Thus it did not involve a radical break with the traditional form of political domination, only its reconstitution. The Buddhists did, of course, challenge some Hindu beliefs, to which the Hindu writers typically responded by accepting some Buddhist criticisms, ignoring some others and putting up a strong defence against the rest. Hence, in response to Buddhist criticisms such Hindu authors of *dharmasastras* (as Yajnavalkya,

Narada, Brahaspati and Katyayana) accepted the autonomy of guilds and corporations, recognised *vyavahara* as a valid source of law, gave the Vaisyas a larger share of power, laid greater stress on the importance of *artha*, paid greater attention to the republican institutions than they had done so far, and so on. At the same time, however, the Hindu thinkers rejected the Buddhist criticism of the caste system and advocated an even more rigid version of it. They also took a leaf out of the Buddhist book and relied on the ruler to take an active part in fighting Buddhism and defending the Hindu social order. Naturally, this led them to glorify the role of the government and to invest the ruler with even greater power and majesty than he had enjoyed so far.

I have outlined in the foregoing some of the basic features of the Hindu tradition of political thought. Obviously, a tradition that has developed over several centuries is too rich and complex to permit an easy summary. Our account of the Hindu tradition is, therefore, bound to involve distortions and omissions. It was intended, however, to provide neither a detailed summary of all its ideas, nor an outline of all the important phases in its development, but only to sketch the broad outlines of the general framework of ideas within which the Hindu writers attempted to understand political life.

III

A careful examination of the Hindu tradition of political thought shows that it is distinguished by several important features. It would be useful to briefly spell out some of the more important ones in order that we can grasp its general character.

First, the Hindu tradition is basically inegalitarian. Although it developed the idea of the moral equality of all men, and indeed of all sentient beings, it never developed the idea of social, legal and political equality. It made caste the basis not only of society but also of the polity, and integrated it into its very structure. As we saw, only the members of higher castes were entitled to the rights of citizenship or to be appointed as royal advisors; different kinds and degrees of punishment were meted out to men of different castes; and so on. In the name of maintaining *dharma*, the Hindu political thinkers subordinated the polity to the demands of a hierarchical social structure. As a result, they were rendered incapable of grasping the polity as a qualitatively different kind of organisation from society, and the government as an agent of social change.

Second, the Hindu tradition of political thought is pluralist in orientation. As we saw, the Hindu political writers from the very beginning recognised the autonomy of social groups. Initially, of course, the castes alone enjoyed the autonomy. However, over time, several different types of social groups were recognised as autonomous and self-governing. This had become such a common feature of Hindu life and thought that it must not be regarded as accidental but a matter of deliberate policy growing out of the considerations of not just political expediency but a deeply held moral principle of respect for others. The policy had obvious advantages. It facilitated social harmony, encouraged diversity, developed habits of self-government, allowed the Hindu religion and moral values to survive in the midst of political upheavals, and so on. The policy, however, also had its drawbacks. It did not allow the institution of the state to grow; it left individuals at the mercy of groups, some of which were oligarchically constituted; it allowed so many different systems of law to flourish that a common legal system could not develop; it heightened the judicial role of the government and did not allow it to acquire a major legislative role; and so on.

Third, the Hindu tradition of political thought is largely uncritical and apologetic of the established social order. Most Hindu political thinkers justified (or rather simply took for granted) the caste system, the caste-based conception of *dharma*, the largely fatalist concept of *karma*, the degradation of the Sudras and the slaves, the extensive moral interference of the state, and so on. There were, no doubt, several exceptions, such as the Buddhist, Jain and Carvak writers. However, the first two were outside the mainstream Hindu tradition, and the last denied the value of any kind of organised society and were largely apolitical.

While the Hindu tradition of political thought, therefore, lacked variety and provided little more than an elaborate justification of the hierarchical social order, the Hindu philosophical tradition was very different. It threw up a remarkable variety of brilliant and imposing philosophical systems, some of which presented a formidable critique of the dominant Brahmanical tradition. The Hindu philosophers explored such areas as metaphysics, ontology, epistemology, logic, philosophy of language, linguistics and grammar, and developed several different and fascinating theories, some of which have stood the test of time. *Prima facie*, it appears paradoxical that a culture with a rich and critical tradition of philosophy should have a relatively poor and uncritical tradition of political thought.

The paradox, however, is only apparent. Highly general and abstract metaphysical theories have no direct social and political impact. They do, no doubt, have social implications, but these are rather general and cannot be easily chartered in the service of political movements. What is more, abstract philosophical discussions invariably have a limited audience, usually confined to the members of the privileged classes. One can, therefore, be radical, even revolutionary in one's metaphysical theories, knowing fully well that the social structure and one's own material and social conditions are not in the least likely to be affected by them.

Political theory is a very different form of inquiry. It is more directly related to the political realm, can be harnessed in the service of one or another group, has a wider audience and can become socially subversive. In short, radicalism in metaphysics is socially much less consequential than radicalism in political thought. It is not, therefore, necessary that a society rich in critical philosophical thought should also be radical in its political thought, or that a society hospitable to the former must also be hospitable to the latter.

Fourth, since the Hindu tradition of political thought was largely apologetic or hostile to change, it almost entirely ignored the whole area of social conflict. No Hindu thinker examined the nature of sectional interests, the reasons why social groups come into conflict, the way political conflicts arise from clashes of material interests and ideologies, how a group acquires political power and presents its interests as general interests, and so on. The Hindu writers did, of course, appreciate that no social order is or can ever be wholly free of disharmony. However, they traced disharmony to such *personal* desires as greed and ambition, and rarely to the objective conflicts of interest and ideology between social groups. In other words, they overlooked the very essence of political life (namely, latent and open conflicts between organised groups). Since they ignored social conflict, they were unable either to explore its basis or to develop an institutional structure for expressing, articulating and resolving it. Not surprisingly, they remained haunted by the frailty of political authority and felt compelled to rely on such methods as extensive espionage and harsh punishment.

Fifth, the Hindu tradition of political thought is largely didactic and practical. Many Hindu writers, whether they wrote *dharmasastras* or *arthasastras*, wrote mainly for the attention of the rulers, and their works are largely manuals of ethics or of administration. The authors of *dharmasastras* aimed to lay down authoritative statements of the duties of individuals and social groups; those of *arthasastras* were concerned with discussing the most effective manner of organising the government and maintaining power. Since their concerns were essentially didactic and practical, neither attempted to interpret, understand and explain political life—that is, to offer a systematic and comprehensive philosophical theory of it. It is, of course, true that no systematic discussion of political life is possible without some theorising. However the theorising in Hindu political texts is largely incidental, patchy, implicit and lacking in rigour. Kautilya, the greatest representative of the *arthasastra* tradition, is largely descriptive and classificatory; Manu, the best known representative of the *dharmasastra* tradition, is dogmatic and assertive and provides little by way of theoretical analysis. Neither analyses such basic concepts as *nyaya, rajan, rastra, svaraj, samrat* and *svamitva*, or examines the basic presuppositions of political life, the kind of knowledge it requires, the way conflicts between different views can be articulated and resolved, the very different ways in which nyaya can be defined, how one view can be judged better than the others, and so on. The Maurya empire was one of the most complex and intricate in human history, distinguished by different types of ascending centres of power wielding different degrees of authority. Kautilya, its greatest student, made little attempt to analyse and distinguish all these or to discuss some disturbing moral and political problems raised by the empire and in general to provide a theory capable of illuminating its rich political structure.

This is not to say that the Hindu writers did not engage in philosophical exploration of political life. While the *arthasastras* have little philosophical content, other writings such as the *dharmasastras* and the two epics contain some penetrating and profound philosophical discussions of several political themes. As we saw, the Hindu thinkers conceptualised political life in terms of the two basic concepts of *danda* and *dharma* and addressed themselves to three basic themes (namely, the nature and organisation of *danda*, the nature and basis of *dharma*, and the relation between the two). Each theme raises large philosophical questions, to some of which Hindu writers addressed their attention. They did not find anything philosophically problematic about *danda* and have little of philosophical interest to say about it. Most of them concentrated on *dharma* and its relation to *danda*. They have much to say about *dharma*— its nature and basis, how it is grounded in the social nature of man, why man cannot be dissociated from his social group, how *dharma* is a form of *yajna* (or sacrifice), how it integrates man into the universal order, and so on. They also have something to say about the relationship between *danda* and *dharma*; that is, how the two can conflict, how the conflict can be resolved, and if and when violence can be justified.

These and other discussions notwithstanding, it would not be inaccurate to say that the Hindus did not develop a tradition of political philosophy. The discussions referred to above are incidental, fragmentary and episodic; they are often designed to solve personal problems; they are scattered in various texts; they are not comprehensive and exclude several large questions; they are sometimes not critical and probing enough, as, for example, the discussion of the nature of castes and their *dharma*; they sometimes consist of simple assertions, some of which are penetrating and profound, but these are not backed by arguments; and so on. If we added up the philosophical discussions of various themes scattered in several Hindu texts, we could certainly reconstruct Hindu political *philosophy*. However, we would still be left with the conclusion that the Hindus did not have political *philosophers*. One is hard put to name even one who offered a systematic philosophical analysis of all (or at least most of) the important aspects of political life. And without a number of writers interested in philosophical exploration of political life over a period of time, there obviously cannot develop a tradition of political philosophy. Some thinkers may ask or stumble into philosophical discussions of political themes; however these discussions, in the absence of a well-established tradition, remain fragile, tentative, non-argumentative, items of intellectual curiosity which others admire but with which they do not engage in a dialogue, and which stimulate but do not satisfy the philosophical appetite.

Why the Hindus did not develop a systematic tradition of political philosophy is a large question which lies beyond the scope of this paper. The answer to it may perhaps be found in a critical examination of the social structure of classical Athens where the Western tradition of political philosophy first made its appearance. After all, political philosophy, like any other form of inquiry, does not grow in a social vacuum, nor is it produced by creative minds out of their heads. It comes into existence when the wider social structure requires and calls for it, that is, when it becomes a social necessity. We need to ask why and how the social conditions in ancient India made political philosophy neither possible nor necessary.

3

THOMAS PANTHAM

The Socio-Religious and Political Thought of Rammohun Roy

I

In 1933, at a meeting held to commemorate the centenary of Raja Rammohun Roy's death, several thinkers (e.g., Rabindranath Tagore, Sarvepalli Radhakrishnan and Bipin Chandra Pal) spoke of him as the 'Father of Modern India'. In his address, entitled 'Inaugurator of the Modern Age in India,' Tagore referred to Rammohun as 'a luminous star in the firmament of Indian history'.[1] By his numerous tracts, pamphlets memoranda and books and public activities for religious, social, educational, economic and political reforms, Raja Rammohun Roy inaugurated the age of enlightenment and liberal-reformist modernisation in India.

In doing this, he drew on his wide knowledge of Perso-Arabic, Classical Greek, Vedantic and modern Western thought. He had learnt as many as ten languages—Persian, Arabic, Sanskrit, English, Urdu, Hindi, Hebrew, Greek, Latin and French—and was influenced by such contemporary events as the French Revolution and the freedom movements in Naples, Spain, Ireland and Latin America. Hence, his concerns as a reformer and thinker were not confined to India. This has been acknowledged by, among others, Jeremy Bentham, C.F. Andrews, Brajendranath Seal and Rabindranath Tagore. Andrews called him the 'pioneer of the whole world movement,'[2] while Bentham, before he met Rammohun during the latter's visit to England, addressed him in a letter as an 'intensely admired and dearly beloved collaborator in the service of mankind'.[3] Tagore has assessed Rammohun's work in the following words:

There was a day when, all alone, Ram Mohun Roy took his stand on the common claim of humanity and tried to unite India with the rest of the world. His vision was not dimmed by obsolete conventions and customs. His generous heart, and his equally generous mind, prompted

---

[1] Rabindranath Tagore, 'Inaugurator of the Modern Age in India,' in *The Father of Modern India, Commemoration Volume of the Rammohun Roy Centenary Celebrations*, 1933, edited by Satish Chandra Chakravarti (Calcutta: 1935).

[2] C.F. Andrews at the Rammohun Roy Centenary Celebrations at Cuttack, Orissa, in 1933, as cited in D.R. Bali, *Modern Indian Thought* (New Delhi: Sterling, 1980), p. 7.

[3] J. Bowring, ed., *The Works of Jeremy Bentham* (Edinburgh: 1843), Vol. 10, p. 589.

him to accept the message of the West without belittling the East. He braved the wrath of his countrymen in his attempts to impart to them a knowledge of the universal rights of man as man. He taught us that truth belongs to all men, that we Indians belong to the whole world. Ram Mohun extended India's consciousness in time and space.[4]

Brajendranath Seal, the Brahmo philosopher, has explained the significance of Rammohun's contribution:

> For a right understanding and estimate of the Raja's thought and utterance, it is necessary to bear in mind the two essentially distinct but indispensable parts which the Raja played on the historic stage. There was Raja Rammohun Roy, the Cosmopolite, the Rationalist Thinker, the Representative Man with a universal outlook on human civilisation and its historic march . . . . But there was another and equally characteristic part played by the Raja—the Nationalist Reformer . . . the Renovator of National Scriptures and Revelations.[5]

II

Rammohun Roy was born on 22 May 1772 in an orthodox Brahman family at Radhanagar in Bengal, which was then beginning to come under the direct administration of the British East India Company. His father, Ramakanta Roy, was a revenue official and dependent land-holder under the Maharani of Burdwan. Soon after the 1793 Permanent Settlement of Land Revenue by the British (more about which we shall see later), he bought several *mahals* and became an independent zamindar.

Rammohun's early education included the study of Persian and Arabic at Patna, where he read the Koran, the works of the Sufi mystic poets of Persia and the Arabic translations of the works of Plato and Aristotle. After completing his Islamic studies at Patna, he went to Benares, where he studied Sanskrit and read the ancient Hindu scriptures, especially the *Vedas* and the Upanishads. Returning to his village at the age of sixteen, he wrote a rational critique of Hindu idol worship. This displeased his father greatly and Rammohun had to leave his home. His wanderings took him to, among other places, Tibet, where he secured a first-hand

[4] Rabindranath Tagore in *Bharatpathik Rammohun Roy*, as cited in V.S. Naravane, *Modern Indian Thought* (Bombay: Asia, 1964), p. 23.

[5] Translation of several Principal Books, Passages, and Texts of the Vedas, and of some Controversial Works on Brahmanical Theology by Rajā Rammohun Roy with an Introductory Memoir, *Memorial Education* (Calcutta: Society for the Resuscitation of Indian Literature, 1903), pp. lxxi–lxxii; as cited in A.K. Majumdar, 'Religion of Rammohun Roy' in V.C. Joshi, ed., *Rammohun Roy and the Process of Modernization in India* (Delhi: Vikas, 1975), pp. 69–70.

knowledge of Buddhism, and to Benares, where he undertook further studies of the Sanskrit texts of the Advaita-Vedanta school. From 1803 to 1814, he worked for the East India Company as the personal diwan first of Woodforde and then of Digby. The association with these English civil servants, especially Digby, was instrumental in Roy's study of modern Western thought.[6] In 1814, he resigned from his job and moved to Calcutta in order to devote his life to religious, social and political reforms. By that time he had acquired ownership of two *taluks* and four *patni taluks* under the 1793 Permanent Settlement. He also had a money-lending business in North Calcutta. After shifting to Calcutta in 1818, he came into close contact with the British free-traders and invested his money in the Agency House of Mackintosh and Company. He also renewed his interactions with the scholars of the Fort William College and the Sadr Diwani Adalat in Calcutta, with whom he had been in contact in the course of his business dealings in Calcutta prior to 1803. Notable among his English friends in Calcutta were James Young, a merchant and follower of Jeremy Bentham, David Hare, a philanthropist, and J.S. Buckingham, the radical editor of *Calcutta Journal*. The writings of Locke, Hume, Bentham and the Christian unitarians exerted much influence on Rammohun.

· We shall return later to Rammohun's Calcutta writings and activities as a liberal-reformist moderniser. To complete this life-sketch, it may be noted here that in November 1830, he sailed for England to be present there to counteract the possible nullification of the Act banning *sati* (widow-burning); powerful propaganda had been mounted by the orthodox Brahmans against the banning of *sati* in 1829 by William Bentinck, the British Governor-General of India. Incidentally, it may also be noted that Rammohun was given the title of 'Raja' by the titular Mughal Emperor of Delhi, whose grievances the former was to present before the British king. In England, Rammohun was well-received by the king and the Directors of the East India Company. Among his important activities in England was the presentation of a memorandum to the Select Committee of the House of Commons on the Revenue and Judicial Systems of India. He fell ill and died at Bristol on 27 December 1833.

III
Religious and Social Thought

Rammohun Roy's immediate *problematique* was the religious and social degeneration of his native Bengal. His biographer has given the following description of the then decadent condition of that society:

---

[6] While Digby was in England on leave in 1817, he published from London Rammohun Roy's translations of the *Kena Upanishad* and *Abridgment of the Vedanta*.

Thick clouds of ignorance and superstition hung over all the land; the native Bengalee public had few books and no newspapers. Idolatry was universal and was often of a most revolting character; polygamy and infanticide were widely prevalent and the lot of Bengalee women was too often a tissue of ceaseless oppressions and miseries while, as the crowning horror, the flames of the suttee were lighted with almost incredible frequency even in the immediate vicinity of Calcutta.[7]

Several of the degenerate features of Bengal society were singled out scornfully in Rammohun's first published work, *Tuhfat-ul Muwahhiddin* (*A Gift to Deists*), published in 1803–4 at Murshidabad, where he was living at that time. It was written in Persian with a preface in Arabic. In it, he exposed such irrational religious beliefs and corrupt practices of the Hindus as the belief in revelations, prophets and miracles, the seeking of salvation through 'bathing in a river and worshipping a tree or being a monk and purchasing forgiveness of their crime from the high priests' and the 'hundreds of useless hardships and privations regarding eating and drinking, purity and impurity, auspiciousness and inauspiciousness'.[8]

Rammohun was particularly concerned with sectarian religious dogmas and practices. He noted that in the name of their separate religious orthodoxies, people develop discord among themselves by 'giving peculiar attributes to that Being and . . . [by] holding different creeds consisting of the doctrines of religion and precepts of *Haram* (the forbidden) and *Halal* (the legal).'[9] In the introduction to his Bengali translation of the *Sama Upanishada*, he pointed out the need 'to correct those exceptionable practices which not only deprive Hindus in general of the common comforts of society but also lead them frequently to self-destruction.'[10]

Rammohun identified himself with the victims of religious orthodoxies, which, he wrote in *Tuhfat*, 'have become causes of injury and detrimental to social life and sources of trouble and bewilderment to the people, instead of tending to the amelioration of the condition of society.'

How is it that the irrational and corrupt religious beliefs and practices which militated against the social comforts and political unity of the people were actually followed by them? Rammohun's answer was that the priestly class which invented and perpetuated those dogmas and doctrines derived benefits from them. He wrote:

---

[7] Sophia Dobson Collet, *The Life and Letters of Raja Rammohun Roy*, edited by Dilip Biswas and Prabhat Gangopadhyay (Calcutta: Sadharan Brahmo Samaj, 1962), pp. 60–61.

[8] As cited by Sumit Sarkar in V.C. Joshi, ed., *op. cit.*, p. 50.

[9] See D.H. Bishop, ed., *Thinkers of the Indian Renaissance* (New Delhi: Wiley Eastern, 1982), p. 7.

[10] As cited in Radharaman Chakraborti, 'Rammohun Roy: His Vision of Social Change,' in A.K. Mukhopadhyay, ed., *The Bengali Intellectual Tradition* (Calcutta: K.P. Bagchi, 1979), p. 23.

Many learned Brahmans are perfectly aware of the absurdity of idolatry, and are well informed of the nature of the purer mode of divine worship. But as in the rites, ceremonies, and festivals of idolatry, they find the source of their comforts and fortune, they . . . advance and encourage it to the utmost of their power, by keeping the knowledge of their scriptures concealed from the rest of the people.[11]

From this diagnosis, Rammohun concluded that religious reform is both social reform and political modernisation. He conceived of reformist religious associations as instruments of social and political transformation. Accordingly, he founded the Atmiya Sabha in 1815, the Calcutta Unitarian Association in 1821 and the Brahmo Sabha in 1828, which later became the Brahmo Samaj. The original manifesto which he himself wrote for the Brahmo Samaj reads as follows:

No graven image shall be brought in the Samaj. No sermon, discourse, prayer or hymn shall be delivered except such as may have a tendency to promote the contemplation of the Author and Preserver of the Universe, to the furtherance of charity, morality, piety, benevolence; virtue, and the strengthening of the bonds of union between men of all religious persuasions and creeds.[12]

The significance of these religious *sabhas* or *samajs* for social reform is brought out by Charles Heimsath:

Secular reformist crusades, usually for legislative social enactments or caste reform, succeeded in drawing adherents, but alterations in personal and family lives in India required revising religious beliefs and practices. Roy foresaw this connection, as Gandhi did a century later.[13]

Rammohun came to the conclusion that for the emancipation of the people, the monopoly of the orthodox Brahmans over the sacred texts had to be undermined. In other words, their exclusive rights to read and interpret the books of knowledge had to be challenged. 'In order to vindicate my own faith and that of our forefathers,' he wrote, 'I have been endeavouring to convince my countrymen of the true meaning of our sacred books.'[14] Accordingly, he set himself the task of interpreting the Vedantic literature and translating them into the vernacular. During the

---

[11] *English Works of Rammohun Roy* (Calcutta: 1947), Vol. 2, p. 44.
[12] As cited in V.S. Naravane, *op. cit.*, p. 26.
[13] Charles H. Heimsath, 'Rammohun Roy and Social Reform,' in V.C. Joshi, ed., *op. cit.*, p. 154.
[14] *English Works of Rammohun Roy*, p. 90.

period 1815 to 1823, he published *Translation of an Abridgement of the Vedant* and translations of several of the *Upanishads* into Bengali, Hindi and English. In this respect, Rammohun was a modern Indian Luther. In fact, the former is reported to have said to the Scottish Presbytarian missionary, Alexander Duff:

> As a youth, I acquired some knowledge of the English language. Having read about the rise and progress of Christianity in apostolic times, and its corruption in succeeding ages, and then of the Christian Reformation which shook off these corruptions and restored it to its primitive purity, I began to think that something similar might have taken place in India, and similar results might follow here from a reformation of the popular idolatry.[15]

As a Reformation thinker and Enlightenment rationalist, Rammohun applied the criteria of reason and social comfort or utility to the sacred texts. In his *Tuhfat-ul*, he argued that each individual has an innate natural faculty to know the truth and falsity of various religions 'without the instrumentality of prophets, religious authority, and traditional revelation.' He wrote:

> There is always an innate faculty existing in the nature of mankind that in case any person of sound mind, before or after assuming the doctrines of any religion, makes an enquiry into the nature of the principles of religious doctrines, . . . without partiality and with a sense of justice, there is a strong hope that he will be able to distinguish the truth from untruth and the true propositions from the fallacious ones, and also he, becoming free from the useless restraints of religion . . . will pay attention to the good of the society.[16]

Again,

> [T]he fact of God's endowing each individual of mankind with intellectual faculties and senses implies that he should not, like other animals, follow the examples of his fellow brethren of his race, but should exercise his own intellectual power with the help of acquired knowledge, to discern good from bad, so that his valuable divine gift should not be left useless.[17]

[15] S.D. Collet, *op. cit.*, p. 280. There were, however, the following differences between Rammohun Roy and his Bengal society, on the one hand, and Reformation Europe and Luther, on the other. The incipient nationalism of Reformation Europe against the claims of the Papacy was absent in the colonised society of Bengal. Moreover, while Luther wrote his German Bible in the common language of the peasants, Rammohun Roy used the Sanskrit-based Bengali of the emergent urban *bhadralok*.

[16] Kissory Chand Mitter, *Rammohun Roy and Tuhfat-ul Muwahhiddin* (Calcutta: K.P. Bagchi, 1975), p. 7.   [17] As cited in D.H. Bishop, *op. cit.*, p. 11.

Rammohun adopted three approaches to socio-religious reform: (*i*) exposing and discrediting those religious dogmas and practices which are irrational and/or contrary to social comfort; (*ii*) the promotion of modern Western education; and (*iii*) state action in support of both these programmes.

Rammohun Roy's attitude to modern Western education and socio-religious reform was different from his conservative and radical contemporary Bengali intellectuals. The conservatives, led by Raja Radhakanta Deb (1784–1867), favoured modern Western education. However, they did so not for its scientific spirit or emancipatory ideas but merely for its instrumentality for career advances in the professions and services under the British. Their approach conformed to the Macaulayan scheme of English education. Far from regarding Western education as a means of social transformation, they vigorously defended the social and religious status quo. They fully endorsed the British colonial government's policy of non-interference in the socio-religious orthodoxies of the native peoples. In fact, as Radharaman Chakraborti has pointed out, the 'state-society interaction had long been under suspension as a result of recoiling of the Hindu society in the face of the consolidation of Muslim rule in India. For ages the social process not only remained truncated from the mainstream of politics but slowly stagnated into clusters of local orthodoxy.'[18] Rammohun Roy pioneered the movement for state intervention for social and religious reforms.

Rammohun's reformism was also opposed by the young radicals led by the Anglo-Indian teacher of the Hindu College, Henry Louis Vivian Derozio (1809–1831). Influenced by Voltaire, Hume, Jeremy Bentham and Thomas Paine, Derozio became a rationalist free-thinker and denounced Hindu religion. He called Rammohun and his group 'half-liberals' and opportunists. He wrote:

> What his [Rammohun Roy's] opinions are, neither his friends nor foes can determine. It is easier to say what they are not than what they are . . . . Rammohun, it is well-known, appeals to the Veds, the Koran, and the Bible, holding them all probably in equal estimation, extracting the good from each and rejecting from all whatever he considers apocryphal . . . . He has always lived like a Hindoo . . . . His followers, at least some of them, are not very consistent. Sheltering themselves under the shadow of his name, they indulge to licentiousness in everything forbidden in the shastras, as meat and drink; while at the same time they feed the Brahmans, profess to disbelieve Hinduism, and never neglect to have poojahs at home.[19]

[18]   Radharaman Chakraborti, *op. cit.*, p. 20.
[19]   As cited in A.F. Salahuddin Ahmed, 'Rammohun Roy and His Contemporaries,' in V.C. Joshi, ed., *op. cit.*, p. 100.

Derozio obviously did not grasp the emancipatory or progressive nature of Rammohun's synthesis of 'the Veds, the Koran, and the Bible'.

From his comparative study of religions, Rammohun concluded that there are three basic tenets in all religions: (*i*) belief in one Universal Supreme Being; (*ii*) belief in the existence of the soul; and (*iii*) belief in life after death. Rammohun accepts these beliefs on the basis of reason and/or social utility. Other than these basic tenets, he finds many false and many objectionable dogmas and doctrines in Hinduism as well as in other religions. These, he says, must be rejected, for which he offers the following justification:

> If mankind are brought into existence, and by nature formed to enjoy the comforts of society and the pleasure of an improved mind, they may be justified in opposing any system, religious, domestic or political, which is inimical to the happiness of society, or calculated to debase the human intellect.[20]

His attack was directed, in particular, against polytheism and idolatry. As a result of his studies of Perso-Arabic literature and interactions with the Muslim scholars of the Sadr Diwani Adalat, he was attracted to Islamic monotheism. Monotheism, he maintainéd, is also the fundamental message of the Vedanta. In his *Tuhfat*, he wrote: 'I travelled in the remotest parts of the world, in plains as well as in hilly lands, and I found the inhabitants thereof agreeing generally in believing in the existence of One Being Who is the source of creation and the governor of it.'[21]

Rammohun's idea of a single, unitarian God was his corrective to the polytheism of orthodox Hinduism and to Christian trinitarianism. He believed that monotheism supported one universal moral order for humanity, while polytheism justified sectarian moralities. The significance of this aspect of Rammohun's work was recognised by Bentham when he wrote 'Rammohun Roy has cast off thirty-five millions of gods and had learnt from us to embrace reason in the all important field of religion.'[22]

[20] See Bimanbehari Majumdar, *History of Indian Social and Political Ideas* (Calcutta: Bookland Pvt. Ltd., 1967), p. 27.

[21] D.H. Bishop, *op. cit.*, p. 7. In 1833, in a critique of Rammohun Roy's interpretation of the Upanishads, K.M. Banerjee wrote that the Upanishads teach monism and not monotheism. See K.M. Banerji, *Review of the Mudock Upanishad by Ram Mohan Roy* (Calcutta: Enquirer Press, 1833), pp. 9–10. According to V.P. Varma, however, the Upanishads 'tend to blur the distinction between a personal supreme god and the impersonal absolute'—V.P. Varma, *Modern Indian Political Thought* (Agra: Lakshmi Narain Agarwal, 3rd edition, 1967), p. 19. It may also be noted in this context that in the Vedanta literature, there is also a blurring of the distinction between ontology and ethics. See Indira Rothermund's chapter in this volume.

[22] J. Bowring, ed., *op. cit.*, p. 571. According to Rajat Ray, before Rammohun Roy was influenced by British utilitarianism, he was influenced by 'the secularist, rationalist and deistic trend in the Perso-Arabic literature of seventeenth and eighteenth century India'— Rajat Ray in V.C. Joshi ed., *op. cit.*, pp. 7–8.

Rammohun's conception of the fundamental unity of all religions has been endorsed by several subsequent thinkers of India (e.g., Vivekananda, Tagore, Gandhi and Radhakrishnan). What these thinkers advanced, it must, however, be noted here in passing, was not Benthamite or utilitarian internationalism but spiritual-universalist cosmopolitanism. Rammohun Roy was himself called a 'religious Benthamite'.

The ground of Rammohun's opposition to polytheism and idolatry was their underlying anthropomorphic conception of the One Supreme Being. Moreover, idol-worshippers and ritualists make idols and rituals the centre of their devotion and worship, and neglect the purification of their mind or the self. Those who rely on rituals and ceremonies do so in the expectation of this-worldly or other-wordly rewards. They are not done from a sense of duty or in a spirit of detachment and as such are a bad means to spiritual or moral ends. For the ritualists and ceremonialists what matters are such mundane considerations as the appearance of one's ritual robes or the lavishness of the feast that one hosts.[23] Rituals or ceremonies, he says, do not yield morality which according to him comes from spirituality. He says that just as the religious or spiritual degeneration of Hinduism generated and sustained bad moral norms, so also the morality-codes of the Christians were corrupted by orthodoxies. He, therefore, turned his attention to raising the moral level of orthodox trinitarian Christianity. He expressed his views on Christianity in his 1820 publication, *The Precepts of Jesus, A Guide to Peace and Happiness.* The controversy it generated among some Christian missionaries led Rammohun to write three tracts, each entitled *An Appeal to the Christian Public in Defence of the Precepts of Jesus.*

Rammohun rejected the divinity of Christ but admitted that his moral teachings, best summed up in his Sermon on the Mount, are a 'guide to peace and happiness' and 'best calculated to lead mankind to universal love and harmony.' Christ's central teachings, Rammohun noted, are love of God and of one's fellowmen. Rejecting the Christian doctrine of the trinitarian God, Rammohun said that by his prayer, 'Our Father,' Jesus indicated that he and God were not ontologically one. The original, pure unitarian Christianity, Rammohun maintained, became corrupt with the intermixture of polytheistic and idolatrous ideas and practices introduced by the Greek and Roman converts. Orthodox Christianity, he noted, had its 'idols, crucifixes, saints, miracles, pecuniary absolutions from sin, trinity, transubstantiation, relics, holy water, and other idolatrous machinery.'[24]

In 1821, Rammohun supported the founding of the Calcutta Unitarian Committee, of which he and his eldest son became members. He also set up a Unitarian Press in Calcutta. Although he believed that Indians

---

[23] In Rammohun's anti-ritualist views, he was influenced by Islam and Buddhism.
[24] As cited by David Kopf in V.C. Joshi, ed., *op. cit.*, p. 27.

would benefit from the moral teaching of unitarian Christianity, he did not become a Christian convert. Once believing that he had become a Christian, the Bishop of Calcutta congratulated him for 'embracing the purer faith'. To this, Rammohun's reply was: 'My Lord, you are under a mistake—I have not laid down one superstition to take up another.'[25] He believed that the original Vedantic message of the unity of God was superior to the anthropomorphic conception of God contained in the Judeo-Christian Bible. He held that while Christianity justifies the death of Christ, God's son, for the atonement of man's sin against God, the Vedanta teaches that the 'only means of attaining victory over sin is sincere repentence and solemn meditation.'[26] To Rammohun it seemed 'Heathenish and absurd' that for the crime of a person another person had to be killed. He said that each sinner must make restitution for his sins and it is to be done through self-purification and repentence, and not through sacrifices and rituals.

Arguing that Rammohun used 'Unitarianism in an Indian way,' David Kopf writes:

> [His] comparativist approach coupled with a modernist outlook placed the Hindu reformation movement on an Orientalist foundation by which indigenous traditions could be defended at the same time they were modified according to progressive values in contemporary Western societies. Though the foundation was a precarious one, it saved the Hindu reformation repeatedly from the snare of militant nationalism.[27]

Rammohun is well known for his pioneering thought and action on the emancipation of women and especially on the abolition of *sati* or widow-burning. He, to use the words of David Kopf, found Bengali Hindu women 'uneducated and illiterate, deprived of property rights, married before puberty, imprisoned in *purdah*, and murdered at widowhood by a barbaric custom of immolation known as *sati*.'[28] Unless women were freed from such inhuman forms of oppression, Rammohun felt, Hindu society could not progress. He characterised *sati* as 'the violation of every humane and social feeling' and as symptomatic of 'the moral debasement of a race'. Just as he opposed the orthodox Christian doctrine of Atonement, so he rejected the theory that the wife can, or has to, atone for the sins of her husband. He also cited the Sacred Texts to show that they permitted the wife to continue her life after her husband's death. Largely as a result of Rammohun's campaign, *sati* was banned by Lord

[25] As cited by A.F. Salahuddin Ahmed in V.C. Joshi, ed., *op. cit.*, p. 94.
[26] See note 24 above.
[27] David Kopf, 'Rammohun Roy and the Bengal Renaissance: An Historiographical Essay,' in V.C. Joshi, ed., *op. cit.*, p. 28.
[28] *Ibid.*, p. 37.

Bentinck in 1829. Rammohun also advocated widow remarriage, female education and the right of women to property.

Rammohun's attitude towards the caste system was somewhat ambivalent. While he practised some of the overt caste rules (e.g., the wearing of the sacred thread), he noted that God makes no distinction of caste and that 'our division into castes . . . has been the source of want of unity among us.'[29]

Rammohun was a pioneer of modern Western education, which, he believed, would enlighten the Indians against the superstitions and injustices of religious orthodoxies. The mere study of ancient, Sanskrit texts, he said, would only 'keep the country in darkness'. In his famous letter on education to Lord Amherst, he wrote:

> If it had been intended to keep the British nation in ignorance of real knowledge, the Baconian philosophy would not have been allowed to displace the system of the school-men which was the best calculated to perpetuate ignorance. In the same manner the Sanskrit system of education would be the best calculated to keep this country in darkness if such had been the policy of the British legislature. But as the improvement of the native population is the object of the Government, it will consequently promote a more liberal and enlightened system of instruction, embracing Mathematics, Natural Philosophy, Chemistry, Anatomy, with other useful sciences.[30]

In 1816, Rammohun founded an English school and some years later he lent support to the founding of the Hindu College. In 1825, he started the Vedant College, in which the study of Western knowledge was combined with that of Indian learning.

IV
Economic and Political Thought

In Rammohun Roy's economic and political thought, there are some ambivalences between liberal-capitalist and feudal-aristocratic values as well as between colonial and post-colonial orientations. These ambivalences in his thought had to do with the fact that he was a zamindar with investments in free-trade business in an emerging colonial political economy. As Rajat Ray has noted, Rammohun was a participant in a three-fold process of modernisation:

> the consolidation of the position of the traditional high caste rural gentry on the land, the transformation of a medieval literati into a modern intelligentsia, and the transition from Company monopoly to

[29] D.H. Bishop, *op. cit.*, p. 21.
[30] *The English Works of Rammohun Roy*, Vol. 4, p. 108.

free trade imperialism (this was ultimately to lead to the failure of Indian capitalist enterprise after its brief development in partnership with the European free-traders).[31]

The socio-historical changes that Rammohun was responding to did not permit any neat and simple theoretical and philosophical treatment or paradigmatic encapsulation. In the face of the unprecedented socio-historical changes that were unfolding before him, he, in his writings, advocated the cause of what he felt were the liberating and growth-promoting forces and opposed what seemed to him to be the oppressive and growth-inhibiting features of the emerging political economy.

Initially, as he himself has acknowledged, he had a 'great aversion' to British rule, but subsequently he became its admirer and responsible critic. He wrote:

When about the age of sixteen . . . I proceeded on my travels, and passed through different countries, chiefly within, but some beyond, the bounds of Hindoostan, with a feeling of great aversion to the establishment of the British power in India. When I had reached the age of twenty . . . I first saw and began to associate with Europeans, and soon after made myself tolerably acquainted with their laws and form of government. Finding them generally more intelligent, more steady . . . I gave up my prejudice against them, and became inclined in their favour, feeling persuaded that their rule, tl ough a foreign yoke, would lead more speedily and surely to the ame·ioration of the native inhabitants.[32]

Broadly speaking, there were two main reasons for Rammohun's favourable attitude towards British rule in India. First, he was persuaded that British rule, unlike the despotic and tyrannical rule of the Mughals or the Rajputs, provided security and other civil liberties to the Indian people. Second, and relatedly, he felt that the introduction of capitalist norms and principles by the British were contributing to India's economic development.

Rammohun's economic ideas were shaped by, and supportive of, two of the most important institutional measures through which the Indian economy was linked with the British colonial system, namely, the Permanent Settlement of 1793 and the Agency Houses of *private* British trade with India.

The Permanent Settlement introduced the system of private landed

---

[31] Rajat K. Ray, 'Introduction' to V.C. Joshi, ed., *op. cit.*, p. 11.
[32] *Rammohun Rachanabali* (Calcutta: Haraf Prakashani, 1973), p. 449, as cited in Tapan Chattopadhyay, 'Rammohun Roy: An Analysis in Historical Perspective,' *Calcutta Journal of Political Studies*, Vol. 2, No. 1, Winter 1981, p. 108.

property in India as part of a new system of land revenue. Prior to the Settlement, about a third of the cultivable land in Bengal, Bihar and Orissa lay waste. The British felt that by giving permanent land-tenures in return for a system of fixed revenue, private individuals could be induced to extend and improve cultivation. It was hoped that 'the magic touch of property would set a certain productive principle in operation,' from which would result a general increase in revenue.[33] The new class of secure landlords, it was also believed, would serve as property-defending supporters of the British empire, in addition to constituting a consumers' market for British manufactures.

The Permanent Settlement did contribute to the increase in the area under cultivation and to making the new middle class of landlords loyal supporters of the British empire. But these results were obtained at the expense of production principles and to the detriment of the actual cultivators—namely, the ryots and peasants. These were exploited by the zamindars, who 'became more and more pure rentiers and performed no economic functions towards the improvement of agriculture.'[34] The Permanent Settlement and subsequent enactments gave the zamindars over-exploitative powers over the ryots and the peasants. Thus Regulation VII of 1799 empowered the zamindars to dispossess the ryots of all their personal property and even to arrest them for arrears of rent. Similarly, the Patni Taluk Regulation of 1819 legalised a system of subinfeudation, which was severely hurtful to the actual tillers of the land. In short, the Permanent Settlement led to the setting up of a semi-feudal system of land-ownership which subserved imperial interests through the mediation of the semi-feudal, semi-capitalist zamindars.

As we saw earlier, Rammohun derived his income from the zamindari and money-lending business. He also made investments in a free-trade business house. Defending property rights, he wrote: 'Every man is entitled by law and reason to enjoy the fruits of his honest labour and good management.'[35] In his submissions on the revenue system of India before the Select Committee of the House of Commons in 1831, he maintained that the Settlement was advantageous to both the British rulers and the Indian landlords, 'though not perhaps in equal proportion.' He proposed some reduction in the extent of revenue-demand on zamindars. His greater concern and compassion, however, were expressed for the peasants, whose miserable plight he lamented. '[S]uch,' he wrote, 'is the melancholy condition of the agricultural labourers, that it always gives me the greatest pain to allude to it.' He bemoaned the fact that as the cultivators were left with no surplus for accumulation, they were

[33] See Asok Sen, 'The Bengal Economy and Rammohun Roy,' in V.C. Joshi, ed., *op. cit.*, p. 113.
[34] *Ibid.*, p. 115.
[35] See B. Majumdar, *op. cit.*, p. 43.

unable to improve the production system. He exhorted the 'enlightened Government' of Britain to follow standards of justice. He pleaded against the enhancement of rents and for the security of the tenants. The resulting loss in revenue, he said, could be made up by taxing luxury goods and effecting economy measures in the revenue administration.[36]

Rammohun Roy's ideas for reforming the Permanent Settlement were denounced by the spokesmen of the conservative association, the Dharma Sabha. To them Rammohun seemed to be too harsh on the zamindars. But the *Bengal Hurkaru* found Rammohun's views too supportive of the zamindars and of British colonial administration. To the *Hurkaru*, the Rammohun of the 1831 Evidence was a 'mere Zamindar'![37] To me, this seems to be an unfair criticism since Rammohun Roy pointed out the injustices of the revenue system and demanded their rectification.

During Rammohun Roy's life, there was a long, drawn-out conflict between those favouring the British East India Company's monopoly rights to trade with India and the British private free-traders. This conflict ended with the victory of the latter over the former. The opening of the East India trade to private enterprise was begun by the Charter Act of 1813 and culminated by the Act of 1833. In this long conflict, Rammohun sided with the free-traders and endorsed their ideology of utilitarian liberalism. He participated in the Calcutta Town Hall meeting of free-traders in December 1829, which petitioned Parliament 'to throw open the China and India trade, and to remove the restrictions against the settlement of Europeans in India.'[38]

In his political thinking, as we noted earlier, he admired the British system of constitutional government for the civil liberties it gave to the people. He wanted to extend the benefits of that system of government to the Indian people. He wrote: 'I am impressed with the conviction that the greater our intercourse with European gentlemen, the greater will be our improvement in literary, social and political affairs.'[39] He sympathised with the freedom struggles of the Greeks and the Neapolitans. The French Revolution gladdened him. He rejoiced at the passage of the Reform Bill of 1832 by the English Parliament and the successful revolt by the Spanish colonies in South America. Yet he welcomed British rule over India! Commenting on his philosophy, B. Majumdar writes:

> He was the first Indian who imbibed the spirit of the English constitution and demanded civil liberty with all its implications. Fully aware as he was of the limitations of the Indians of his age he never thought of demanding political liberty for them. He was conscious of the ignorance

[36] See V.C. Joshi, *op. cit.*, pp. 101–2 and 118.
[37] See Asok Sen in V.C. Joshi, *op. cit.*, pp. 119–21.
[38] S.D. Collet, *op. cit.*, p. 270.
[39] *The English Works of Raja Rammohun Roy*, p. 917.

and superstitions that enveloped the minds of his countrymen, who betrayed a deplorable lack of public spirit in their conduct. So he could not think them capable of exércising self-government. The great problem which confronted the well-wishers of India in the first half of the nineteenth century was not autonomy for India but the bare recognition of the principles of justice and security of life and property.[40]

Rammohun Roy attributed India's decline in the immediate pre-British period to the 'tyranny and oppression' of the Rajput rulers and the despotism of the Muslim rulers. In contrast, British rule appeared to him as providing to the Indians a God-sent opportunity of securing civil liberties. In his Appeal to the King-in-Council against the 1823 Press Regulation, he noted that 'under their former Muhammadan Rulers, the natives of this country enjoyed every political privilege in common with Mussalmans, being eligible to the highest offices in the state.' But, he added, 'their property was often plundered, their religion insulted, and their blood wantonly shed,' till 'Divine Providence at last, in its abundant mercy, stirred up the English nation to break the yoke of those tyrants and to receive the oppressed Natives of Bengal under its protection.'[41] Rammohun Roy believed that the British rulers, who enjoyed civil and political liberties in their country, could 'also interest themselves in promoting liberty and social happiness, as well as free inquiry into literary and religious subjects, among those nations to which their influence extends.'[42]

Rammohun Roy believed that in his time, Indians could derive the advantages of the liberal spirit of British public or political life if the laws for India were made by the British Parliament rather than by an Indian Legislative Council located on Indian soil. If such a legislative council was set up, he feared that it would be controlled by the British Governor-General of India and his Council. That would be in contravention of the principle of separation of powers, of which Rammohun was an ardent supporter. 'In every civilised country,' he wrote, 'rules and codes are found proceeding from one authority, and their execution left to another. Experience shows that unchecked power often leads the best men wrong and produces general mischief.'[43] He maintained that if legislation for India was left to the British Parliament, it would benefit from the liberal public opinion in England. He was aware of the difficulties involved in making liberal legislation for a distant land. He, therefore, proposed three measures to ensure that the British Parliament makes good laws for the Indian people: (*i*) a free press; (*ii*) commissions of inquiry; and

[40] B. Majumdar, *op. cit.*, pp. 27–28.
[41] S.D. Collet, *op. cit.*, pp. 431 and 449.
[42] As cited in B. Majumdar, *op. cit.*, p. 36.
[43] *Ibid.*, p. 37.

(*iii*) ascertaining the views of 'gentlemen of intelligence and respectability'.[44] Only these classes seemed to him to be able to exert any influence on the government in those times.

Both through his writings and through his activities, Rammohun Roy supported the movement for a free press in India. When press censorship was relaxed by Lord Hastings in 1819, Rammohun founded three journals: *The Brahmanical Magazine* (1821); the Bengali weekly, *Samvad Kaumudi* (1821); and the Persian weekly, *Mirat-ul-Akbar* (1822). John Adams, who succeeded Lord Hastings as Governor-General, reimposed press censorship in March 1823. Against this a petition was made to the Supreme Court by Rammohun Roy, Dwarkanath Tagore and several others. When the petition was rejected by the Court, Rammohun submitted an appeal to the King-in-Council which too was rejected. The British colonial case against a free press in India was that India's was a colonial administration and not a representative constitutional government and that there was no effective public opinion in India. Rammohun argued that a free press will help to generate such a public opinion. He also maintained that precisely because India was a colony, it stood in greater need of a free press if a revolutionary overthrow of the rulers was to be avoided. In his famous appeal to the King-in-Council, he wrote:

[M]en in power hostile to the Liberty of the Press, which is a disagreeable check upon their conduct, when unable to discover any real evil arising from its existence, have attempted to make the world imagine that it might, in some possible contingency, afford the means of combination against the Government, but not to mention that extraordinary emergencies would warrant measures which in ordinary times are totally unjustifiable . . . . Your Majesty is well aware that a Free Press has never yet caused a revolution in any part of the world, because, while men can easily represent their grievances arising from the conduct of the local authorities to the supreme Government, and thus get them redressed, the grounds of discontent that excite revolution are removed; whereas, where no freedom of the press existed, and grievances consequently remained unrepresented and unredressed, innumerable revolutions have taken place in all parts of the globe, or if prevented by the armed force of the Government, the people continued ready for insurrection.[45]

Rammohun Roy and His Critics

We have already seen in the foregoing that in his life-time, Rammohun Roy was criticised by Radhakanta Deb, Henry Derozio and the *Bengal Hurkaru*. Let us turn now to some very recent critical appreciations of Rammohun's contribution.

---

[44] *Ibid.*, p. 34.   [45] As cited in V.P. Varma, *op. cit.*, p. 22.

To some of his interpreters, it has been disappointing that even though he favoured the freedom struggles in other countries, he welcomed the British imperialist domination of India as an act of divine providence. According to Asok Sen, Rammohun Roy's ideals of modernity and his determination to lead his land away from medieval decay has some basic weaknesses as they were 'largely locked up in a sense of identity with the forces of empire'.[46] Rammohun and the other members of the new middle class were thus participants in making India a colonial political economy under Britain. Sen finds 'most untenable' Rammohun's views 'about the benefits of expanding British trade, about the identity of his country's interests with the liberal stances of the British industrial revolution, or even about the prospects of his reformed Permanent Settlement.'[47] Sen concludes his excellent study by noting that these basic weaknesses in Rammohun Roy's thought were the tragic inevitabilities of his circumstances in history which he had no opportunity to choose.

Similarly, Sumit Sarkar points out that the process of modernisation pioneered by Rammohun Roy was a transition from pre-capitalist society in the direction 'not of full-blooded bourgeois modernity, but of a weak and distorted caricature of the same which was all that colonial subjection permitted.'[48] 'The ideology and role of Rammohun Roy's group,' writes Rajat Ray, 'marked it out quite clearly as a *comprador* group' in the development of sub-imperialist capitalism in India.[49] They failed to see that colonisation undermined the process of industrial accumulation in India and that through unproductive operations, the new middle classes were exploiting the productive labour of the peasants. Despite these shortcomings of his thought, Rammohun Roy is praised by Rajat Ray for 'the striking modernity of his philosophical premises and social vision, the concrete achievements of his fruitful career in Calcutta that led to the emergence of a modern urban culture containing the seeds of future Indian nationalism.'[50]

Asok Sen, Sumit Sarkar and Rajat Ray are indeed correct in pointing out that Rammohun Roy did not grasp or anticipate the evils of the imperialist penetration of India. In his writings, there were no expressions of patriotic or nationalist sentiments. Such sentiments would have been highly premature in his historical circumstances. His preoccupations were different. He regarded British rule as a *fait accompli* and sought to 'reform' it to the advantage of the subject peoples, who, he said, should enjoy the same civil liberties which the colonising peoples enjoyed at

[46] Asok Sen in V.C. Joshi, *op. cit.*, p. 111.
[47] *Ibid.*, p. 128.
[48] Sumit Sarkar, 'Rammohun Roy and the Break with the Past,' in V.C. Joshi, ed., *op. cit.*, p. 63.
[49] Rajat Ray in V.C. Joshi, *op. cit.*, p. 17.
[50] *Ibid.*, p. 20.

home. This was indeed a very courageous and progressive stance. He regarded the capitalist-industrial economy, which was then being introduced into India, as superior to the old feudal economy. The contradictions which the capitalist system has acquired over the years were hardly visible in Rammohun Roy's historical context. He regarded that compared to the old feudal economy, capitalism and its ideology of liberalism were truly progressive and emancipatory changes.[51] It was tragic that the capitalist-industrial economy and the liberal ideology were introduced in India in a distorted manner under imperialist auspices.

Rammohun Roy *was* concerned to mitigate that tragedy. While he welcomed British rule, he entertained a vision, howsoever faint it was, of a post-imperialist world order. This vision is ignored, it seems to me, by Asok Sen and Sumit Sarkar. Also while highlighting the economic aspects of both colonialised Bengal and Rammohun Roy's thought, they seem to underestimate his important contribution to the formation of a transnational culture. It is perhaps from an inadequate appreciation of the role of such a culture that Barun De writes that 'Rammohun's political and economic ideas merit veneration only by those who worship the history of India's liberalism.'[52]

Toward a Synthesis of Cultures

Rammohun Roy's appreciation of 'England's work in India' was centred on his grasp of the scope it held for the extension of the liberal revolution to the Indian society. His support of British rule was not due solely or mainly to the economic or career benefits it brought to him and to the other members of his new middle class. No doubt he shared in, and appreciated, those benefits. Yet, his main hope from British rule, which he accepted as a *fait accompli*, was that it would be instrumental in extending liberalism's civil and political liberties to the Indian society. This is clearly indicated in some of the earlier citations as well as in the following passage:

> Many of those . . . who engage prosperously in commerce, and of those who are secured in the peaceful possession of their estates by the permanent settlement, and such as have sufficient intelligence to foresee the probability of future improvement which present itself

[51] It is interesting to note that some two decades after Rammohun Roy's death, Karl Marx wrote that British imperialism played a regenerative role in India. For an interesting comparison of Rammohun Roy and Karl Marx's views on this, see Subrata Mukherjee, 'Political Ideas of Rammohun Roy,' *Democratic World* (New Delhi), 9 September 1984, pp. 10–11. See also T. Chattopadhyay, *op. cit.*

[52] Barun De, 'A Biographical Perspective on the Political and Economic Ideas of Rommohun Roy,' in V.C. Joshi, ed., *op. cit.*, p. 147.

under the British rulers, are not only reconciled to it, but really views it as a blessing to the country. But I have no hesitation in stating, with reference to the general feeling of the more intelligent part of the Native community, that the only course of the policy which can ensure their attachment to any form of government would be that of making them eligible to gradual promotion, according to their respective abilities and merits, to situations of trust and responsibility in the state.[53]

In the extension of the liberal revolution of the Indian society, Rammohun saw an opportunity for reforming and reordering the imperialist world system. While he did not deny or resist the political and economic integration of India into the British imperialist system, he strove to reform that system. Both the colonised and colonising societies, he said, must be reformed in their religions, cultures, politics and economy. The norms or values of such reforms, he said, were not the monopoly of either the colonising, modern West or the colonised, traditional Eastern countries such as India. For the reform of the then emerging world system, he felt, a new humanist culture had to be synthesised. Accordingly, he worked toward a synthesis of the world-affirming rationalist-deistic strands of Islamic thought, the liberal and scientific attitudes of modern Western thought and the spiritual and communitarian values of Advaita-Vedanta.

Rammohun Roy believed that the system of sovereign states is not permanent but historically contingent on developments in such areas as property-systems, linguistics and religion. This he indicated in his *Tuhfat-ul Muwahhiddin* in the following words:

> Although it cannot be denied that the social instinct in man demands that every individual of this species should have permanent regulations for the (different) stages of life and for living together, but social laws depend on an understanding of each other's meaning (or ideas) and on certain rules which separate the property of one from that of another, and provide for the removal of the pain which one gives to another. Making these the basis, the inhabitants of all the countries, distant islands and lofty mountains have according to their progress and intellectuality, formed words indicative of the meaning and origin of faiths on which at present stand the governments of the world.[54]

It was Rammohun Roy's declared objective to help remove some of the bases of the barriers imposed by the 'present governments' against the fulfilment of the species-wide 'social instinct in man'. He saw orthodox

[53] As cited in B. Majumdar, *op. cit.*, p. 26.
[54] *The English Works of Raja Rammohun Roy*, p. 947.

religions as one important type of such barriers. Hence he wrote: 'May God render religion destructive of differences and dislike between man and man, and conducive to the peace and union of mankind.'[55] Rammohun Roy also maintained that national sovereignty had to be transcended in solving the problems of the people. In a letter to the French Foreign Minister, he made the following proposal for a Congress of Nations:

> But on general grounds, I beg to observe that it appears to me the ends of constitutional government might be better attained by submitting every matter of political difference between two countries to a Congress composed of an equal number from the Parliament of each; the decision of the majority to be acquiesced in by both nations and the chairman to be chosen by each nation alternately, for one year, and the place of the meeting to be one year within the limits of one country and the next within those of the other; such as Dover and Calais for England and France.
>   By such a Congress all matters of difference, whether political or commercial, affecting the natives of any two civilised countries with constitutional government might be settled amicably and justly to the satisfaction of both and profound peace and friendly feelings might be preserved between them from generation to generation.[56]

Rammohun Roy's focus, however, was not on any organisational blue-print for a re-structured world order. His preoccupation rather was with synthesising a transnational, humanist culture. He appreciated the liberal, scientific, world-affirming attitude of modern Western thought. But he critiqued its foundation in the conflictual cosmology of the Judeo-Christian tradition of thought which justifies the violence done unto one being or person in atonement for the sins of another. He appreciated the spiritual (inner self and self-purification) and communitarian values of Advaita-Vedanta. But he disapproved of its world-denying and self-denying assumptions. By such a critique of cultures and religions, he undermined the cultural arrogance of orthodox Brahmans, Christian missionaries and Macaulayan educationists. Thus, he, as noted by Brajendranath Seal, paved the way for 'a synthesis between Eastern and Western social values and postulates against the common background of universal humanity.' In other words, he pointed the way 'to the solution of the larger problem of international culture and civilisation in human history, and became a precursor . . . a prophet of the coming Humanity.'[57] Hailing Rammohun Roy as the herald of a world society, Rabindranath Tagore writes:

[55] As cited in B. Majumdar, *op. cit.*, p. 49.
[56] As cited in D.H. Bishop, *op. cit.*, pp. 23–24.
[57] B. Seal, *Rammohun, The Universal Man* (Calcutta: Sadharan Brahmo Samaj, 1933), p. 1.

Rammohun was the only person in his time . . . to realise completely the significance of the modern age. He knew that the ideal of human civilisation does not lie in isolation of independence, but in the brotherhood of inter-dependence of individuals as well as nations. His attempt was to establish our peoples on the full consciousness of their own cultural personality, to make them comprehend the reality of all that was unique . . . in their civilisations in the spirit of sympathetic cooperation.[58]

[58]   As in note 1 above.

4

B.R. PUROHIT

The Social and Political Ideas of Swami Dayananda Saraswati

In the early history of the social and religious development of modern India, Swami Dayananda Saraswati (1824–83) occupies a significant place. At the beginning of the nineteenth century he was the chief architect of Indian socio-religious reform movements. The Swami was the Indian Luther inasmuch as he tried to liberate Hindu society from the bondage of dead customs, orthodoxy, superstition and idolatry. He fought against the prevailing caste system and suggested a new pattern of social order.

In a society wherein a myriad of religions and gods were worshipped, Dayananda propounded the concept of monotheism. Above all, he founded the Arya Samaj as the vehicle of his ideas and as a forum to unite Hindus for the sake of reformation. In the formative stage of the Indian Renaissance his ideas were of considerable import, leaving behind an indelible imprint on social thought and action.

Moolshanker—the original name of Dayananda—was born at Tankara in Morvi state (Gujarat) in 1824. His father was anxious to groom Moolshanker as a religious man. With this end in view he educated him on the subject of Hindu scriptures. Thus, in his early days he studied Sanskrit and the *Vedas*. However, as biographers of Moolshanker describe, two incidents changed the course of his life. One of them occurred during his night-long vigil in the temple of Lord Shiva when he saw a mouse running over the idol of Lord Shiva. Thereupon he told his father, 'I feel it impossible to reconcile the idea of an omnipotent, living God with this idol which allows mice to run upon its body, and thus suffers its image to be polluted without the slightest protest.' This incident turned him into a crusader to fight against the practice of idolatry.

The second incident was the sudden death of his sister. His resolve now was to win emancipation (*moksha*),[1] emancipation from the bondage of flesh and transmigration. Everything in this world, he thought, was ephemeral and hence the need to attain *moksha*. In 1846, he ran away from home in order to escape the tentacles of a married life. For nearly fifteen years Dayananda remained a homeless wanderer in search of a preceptor ('guru') who could impart true knowledge to him. During his days of wandering he became a *sannyasi* at Chanoda Kanyali and adopted the name of Dayananda Saraswati.[2] While looking for a preceptor, he

---

[1] *Moksha* is the liberation of the spirit from the cycle of transmigration.

[2] A *sannyasi* is one who renounces worldly things and yet serves society with a sense of detachment, in search of eternal truth.

met Swami Virjananda, a very learned *sannyasi* at Mathura. Dayananda accepted the blind swami as his *guru* and studied under him for two and a half years. When Dayananda left, the preceptor said, 'Yes, you have acquired knowledge, go and disseminate it. Dispel the darkness of ignorance which prevails. Wage war against falsehood which has taken hold of the minds of your misguided brethern. They quarrel about castes, creeds and know not the *Vedas*. Give them the message of the Vedic religion. I want this pledge. Give it if you are keen to pay my *dakshina*.'[3] This was the pledge that remained Dayananda's guiding-star for the rest of his life. All his future activities were directed towards the goal set by the preceptor.

Dayananda was also a prolific writer of books, commentaries and pamphlets. Some of his important publications are *Sandhya, Bhagavata-Khandanam, Advaitamat-Khandanam, Vedabhasya, Aryoddheshya Ratnamala, Bhratinivarna, Sanskarvidhi, Rigvedadibhashyabhumica, Vyavaharabhanu, Vedangaprakash* and *Satyarth Prakash*. Of these, *Satyarth Prakash* is his *magnum opus*. While other booklets and pamphlets deal with some particular aspect of his ideas—social, religious, educational or metaphysical—*Satyarth Prakash* is the first complete statement of his ideas covering a wide range of subjects.

In order to understand the ideas of Swami Dayananda, we should have an idea of the condition of Indian society to which he addressed himself. At the beginning of the nineteenth century Hindu society suffered from the ills of decadence and disunity. Superstition thrived under the cloak of religion. Caste and sub-castes kept the society fragmented, sapping its vitality to live as an organic unity. Thus, the forces that Swami Dayananda confronted were:

(a) the host of learned and unlearned Brahmans, justifying caste distinctions and backed by the forces of ignorance, superstition, prejudice, custom and conservatism;

(b) the organised forces of Christianity which had moral, political, intellectual and financial support;

(c) the analytic tendencies of modern science, which denied God, revelation and religion and substituted materialism;

(d) the ever-active propaganda of Islam;

(e) the collapse of the Hindu system of thought; and,

(f) the pessimism, apathy, fatalism and inertia which had been engendered by centuries of political and intellectual decline.[4]

---

[3] Har Bilas Sarda, ed., *Dayananda Commemoration Volume*, Ajmer, 1944. *Dakshina* is the debt of gratitude that a disciple owes to his preceptor.

[4] Lajput Rai, *A History of the Arya Samaj* (Orient Longman: 1967), p. 105.

It is against this background that we should study the social, religious, educational and political ideas of Swami Dayananda. A characteristic feature of Hindu society under study has been the intertwining of social and religious aspects. To work for social reform was at the same time to work for religious reform and *vice versa*. This was the case with Raja Rammohun Roy as much as with Dayananda Saraswati. The socio-religious movements of nineteenth century India represented this characteristic feature. Swami Dayananda's ideas were also cast in this mould.

Religious Ideas

The seventh chapter of the *Satyarth Prakash* deals with the problem of God, the unity of God, the proof of his existence, his attributes and his relation to the soul. Similarly, the final chapter of the book (which deals with Jainism) discusses in detail the existence and nature of God. The prevalent view about God (as propounded by various religious sects and Hindu mythology) was that God had various forms, emerging in various divine incarnations (*avataras*); there were, thus, as many gods as there were religions, mythologies or devotees.

Dayananda was opposed to this kind of polytheism. To him there was only one God; all the gods of the Hindu pantheon had no existence. Thereby he discarded the whole mythological superstructure of Hinduism and propounded that 'there is one God only. He alone is to be worshipped; and He must be worshipped spiritually, not by images.' His concept of God was of the *Upanishadic* description, the personification of *satchitananda* meaning that it is his nature to be the fullness of being, all intelligence and blissful. God is all-pervasive, omniscient, formless, unborn, infinite, almighty, just and merciful. This concept of God, as we shall see later, was adopted by the Arya Samaj in its constitution.

Opposed to the agnosticism of European philosophers, Dayananda had faith in a God who was knowable, could be felt and perceived in a transcendental vision. Dayananda's God is not an attributeless *nirgun brahman* but is the repository of noble attributes. Dayananda, the moralist, therefore, prescribed that the way to the attainment of moral life was the contemplation and worship of the divine attributes of God. His philosophy of God, at the metaphysical level, was a reassertion of the principles of the *Vedas*. The social upshot of such ideas was to forge unity for a social system which was divided by considerations of sects. The *puranas* had added much irrational chaff around Hindu scriptures. Dayananda was motivated to purify religion and consolidate Hindu society. His was the pioneering attempt to unite the Hindus under the banner of a unified religion and persuade them to get over the superficial distinctions that kept their society divided.

As a natural corollary to such ideas, we find Dayananda refuting the doctrine of *avataras* (divine incarnations). He condemned idolatry and the practice of animal sacrifices offered to God. At the same time he attacked, as a protestant Hindu reformer, the host of Brahmans who were clinging to superficial, meaningless religious rites. Hindu priesthood, claiming its right to sacerdotal authority merely by the right to birth, was his target of reform. He felt convinced that if Hindu society was to be reformed, it must be liberated from the unholy chains of an ignorant priesthood. Like Martin Luther, Dayananda also argued that there was no need for an intermediary between God and his devotees. Even the *Vedas* did not sanction this intermediate priestly class. Such an attack on idolatry and priesthood placed Swami Dayananda in the front rank of socio-religious reformers of Indian Renaissance in the nineteenth century.

The *Vedas* occupy a central position in the philosophy of Swami Dayananda. They are the main source of his thought and it was his mission to propagate the Vedic principles with a view to establishing a social order cast in the mould of such ideals. Aurobindo Ghosh writes in this respect:

> Dayananda accepted the *Veda* as his rock of firm foundation, he took it for his guiding view of life, his rule of inner existence, his inspiration for external work, but he regarded it as even more, the word of eternal truth on which man's knowledge of God and his relations with the Divine Being, and with his fellows can be rightly and securely founded.[5]

According to Dayananda the *Vedas* are of Divine origin. They are the wisdom of God, revealed, and universal, i.e., meant for all mankind. The *Vedas* are infallible and a sure way to human happiness. In his own words '. . . God has given us the way to happiness in the Vedas, . . . as the great Vedic age clearly demonstrates. Why have we Aryans changed so much? . . . . By going against the *Vedas*. The way to recapture that ancient glory is to act in acccordance with the *Vedas*.'[6] In his commentary on the *Vedas*, he held that as the *Vedas* were of a divine nature, they could not possibly contain anything that went against reason or morality. Another significant belief of Dayananda is that the *Vedas* are the repository of scientific truth. He was so committed to these 'sacred books' that he believed that the four *Vedas* by themselves contained the total and infallible revelation of the wisdom of God and scientific truth which no other religious books contained. Under the caption, 'My Beliefs and Disbeliefs,' Dayananda writes about the four *Vedas*:

> The four *Vedas*, the repository of knowledge and religious truth, are the word of God. I regard them infallible and of prime authority. They

[5] Aurobindo Ghosh, 'Dayananda and the Veda,' quoted by Lajput Rai, *op. cit.*, p. 71.
[6] *Rishi Dayananda Saraswati ke Patra aur Vigyapan* (Y-Mimansak: Amritsar, 1955).

are authority in themselves and do not depend upon other books for their authoritativeness. Just as the sun or a lamp is self-luminous as well as the light-giver of the earth so are the four *Vedas*.[7]

His claim continues:

God's knowledge is infallible and, therefore, the teachings of God's book should also be equally infallible . . . . There is nothing in them which might be contradictory to the laws of nature or invalid according to the laws of logic. The Bible and the Qoran do not stand this test and are not, therefore, God's books.[8]

To the question of whether the *Vedas* are eternal, his characteristic reply was, 'Eternal. God being eternal, his knowledge is also eternal. The *rishis* have composed books on grammar, philosophy, prosody, etc., after having read the *Vedas*. The *Vedas* are the books of God. All persons should act according to their injunctions.'[9]

On the strength of these beliefs Dayananda gave to the Aryas the clarion call of 'Back to the Vedas'. That course would unburden Hindu society of the dead-weight of dogmas, of the legacy of the *puranas*, and reunite the quarrelling sects of Hindu society. Thus his slogan was inspired by the ideals of national unity and kindling of national pride and consciousness. 'Back to the Vedas' was also a call for social-relgious reform. His desire to reestablish the superiority of Vedic religion was at bottom a plea for socio-religious reconstruction. By redefining Vedic religion, the Swami provided a formidable weapon in the armoury of defenceless Hinduism so that Hindu society could stand on its feet with confidence against other religions.

A far-reaching consequence of this plea was that it made Hindu society self-conscious and engendered therein a temper of racial and national superiority. 'When the sublimity of *Vedic* truths was revealed to the Hindus a new spirit began to pulsate in them. They felt that they could stand and stand boldly, they could feel proud of their past and hope for the future.' In the slogan, 'Back to the Vedas,' we find the seeds of Hindu revivalism. The Arya Samaj became the harbinger of the revivalist movement in modern India. In the years that followed, the revivalist spirit came down to organisations like the Hindu Maha Sabha and the RSS which made the 'revival of the past' the corner-stone of their ideological structures. Believing that the *Vedas* contained the totality of knowledge (whether it was spiritual, moral, political, social or even scientific) he reminded the Indians that they should recapture the Vedic Golden Age

[7] *Satyarth Prakash*, p. 489.
[8] *Ibid.*, p. 284.
[9] *Ibid.*, pp. 287–88. *Rishis* are sages.

by going back to the *Vedas*. It is perceptible that such ideas have the ingredients of Hindu nationalism, as well as of the nationalist spirit.

Dayananda's commentary on Vedic literature has a reformist dimension also. In his earlier phase of public life he did not permit the study of the *Vedas* to the Shudras, the low caste people. However, in the final years of his life he accepted that all persons, irrespective of caste status, had access to the sacred books. Thus he brought the *Vedas* out of the sanctuary of Brahmanic dominance and opened them to all Hindus. This step alone entitles him to be called the Luther of modern India. Thereafter, the Vedic scriptures did not remain the exclusive preserve of the Brahman caste. Thus Swami Dayananda Saraswati pulled down the walls of Brahmanic superiority, consequently heralding a social revolution. This was also the path followed by Mahatma Gandhi in the second decade of the twentieth century.

Social Philosophy

The Caste System

Dayananda's social philosophy was guided by reformist ideals. He found the Indian social system was based on caste. Hence, social reform meant that the caste system had to be reformed. Dayananda's approach to the problem of caste was a cautious one. He stood for the removal of various evils that had crept into the system. Yet he found in the caste system, as it existed in the past, a social institution which performed some useful functions. In its pure form it was a system founded on the division of labour: each caste, Brahman, Ksatriya, Vaisya and Shudra, performed its appointed functions. In the Vedic period there was no caste by birth. The *Vedas* recognised the division of their occuptaions and qualifications. But in its present form, argued Dayananda, the caste system had degenerated, leaving birth as the sole criterion of caste. It has kept society artificially divided, becoming at the same time a device of the privileged for the protection of their exalted position in society.

Rather than birth as the basis of caste, Dayananda suggested *guna* (character), *karma* (action) and *swabhav* (nature) as criteria. The caste of a person was to be determined by his character, by the actions he performed in society and by his nature.

> Those born Brahmans who undertake good actions are Brahmans and those low-born also whose merits, profession and temperament are of higher kind are of higher varnas. Similarly high born persons doing low things should be reckoned in the low varna . . . . It means that a man or a woman should belong to that varna for which he or she is fit.[10]

[10] *Ibid.*, p. 128.

Such ideas establish that Dayananda was a votary of intercaste mobility who rejected the birth-right to Brahmanism. He writes: 'The upper caste will always bear in mind that if their children would remain ignorant, they would have to go down to the level of Sudras . . . . Moreover, the lower castes will have incentive to climb up to the higher classes.'[11] Illustrating this principle, he said that a *chandal* (a low born) had every right to become a Brahman if his character (*gun*) and action (*karma*) justified it. Dayananda's theory of caste and social organisation is aptly described by a Christian missionary, Hoernle:

This (caste) the reformer (Dayananda) considers only as a political institution made by the rulers for the common good of society, and not a natural or religious distinction. It is not a natural distinction, for the four castes were not created by God as a distinct species of men; but all men are of equal nature, of the same species, and brothers. It is not a religious institution . . . . The castes are simply different professions or guilds, established by the state to guard against confusion and mutual interference, and for the better accomplishment of the different works. Each class was made up into a guild and furnished with its rights and privileges and made hereditary. But, as the whole classification is a creation of the state, any Sudra, who is deserving of the promotion, can be made by the state a Vaishya or Ksatriya, or *Brahman*, if he qualifies himself for the work of the respectiv class. Likewise, any *Brahman*, who deserves the degradation, can l : made by the state a Sudra. In fact, any Brahman, who is disqualified for his work, becomes at once a Sudra *de jure*, and a Sudra, who qualifies for it, becomes at once a Brahman *de jure*; though neither can become so *de facto* also either by his own will or the will of others, as long as the state does not make him so.[12]

To conclude, Dayananda viewed caste as a mode of social organisation. He disassociated caste from birth and religion and thus secularised the concept of caste. This step went a long way in dethroning the hereditary high castes and in elevating the social status of the oppressed and the Untouchables. Dayananda thus opened the flood gates for a social revolution in Hindu society. It is interesting to note that Mahatma Gandhi also took a similar stand about the upliftment of the depressed and untouchable classes.

Untouchability

Dayananda denounced untouchability as inhuman and tried to prove that it was contrary to the dictates of Vedic religion. Untouchability was not

[11] *Ibid.*, p. 134.   [12] Quoted by Lajput Rai, *op. cit.*, pp. 35–36.

divinely ordained. It was the result of bad environment, association and training and the resulting deterioration of character. This evil practice originated with the ostracism of such persons who violated established social customs and morality. It was, therefore, a matter of cleanliness, character-training and improvement in environment. Accordingly, any Sudra who was clean in body and mind had the right to be a *dwija*, twice-born. Here, again, we find Swami Dayananda as a forerunner of social reformers like Mahatma Gandhi who devoted his whole life to the service of the Untouchables. Mahatma Gandhi recognised the services rendered by Dayananda in this respect: 'Among the many rich legacies that Swami Dayananda has left to us, his unequivocal pronouncement against untouchability is undoubtedly one.'[13]

Marriage Reforms

Dayananda was opposed to the evil practices of child-marriage and enforced widowhood. These social evils, he said, had no sanction in the *Vedas*. To combat the practice of child-marriage he recommended that the marriageable age for women should be between sixteen and twenty-four years, and for men between twenty-four and forty-eight years. Marriages were of three types—inferior, medium and superior. Inferior marriages were those between women of sixteen and men of twenty-four years of age. Medium marriages were those between women of eighteen to twenty and men of twenty-five to forty years of age. Superior marriages were those between women of twenty-four and men of forty-eight years. The Swami's scheme of eugenics purports to have a healthy society and the eradication of the evil practice of child-marriage.

Dayananda pointed out the pitiable lot of child widows in Hindu society which prohibited remarriage on the authority of the scriptures. Dayananda had a deep concern for the sorry state of widows and hence recommended the institution of *niyoga*, a temporary union of widows and widowers; and, if this was not possible, he forcefully recommended widow-remarriage. In one of his lectures at Poona he said: 'Looking to today's blind adherence to false tradition one has to admit that widow-remarriage is altogether better than that.'

Education

Dayananda's way of looking at life was holistic. It was in this framework that he viewed morals, rituals, religion, social customs and education. If society was to be revitalised, every organic part of it had to be revitalised. This is how he recognised the significance of education and hence

---

[13] Mahatma Gandhi in *Dayananda Commemoration Volume: A Tribute*.

propounded his own concept of it. Chapter 3 of the *Satyarth Prakash* contains a comprehensive scheme of education.

Dayananda had the utmost faith in the power of education as an instrument for moulding individual character. He believed that the main objective of a sound system of education was the character formation of individuals of society: its aim was not to create ill-fed, aimless or half-starved individuals. A sound educational system should be based upon moral and religious foundations. Like Plato, he recommended compulsory education of children by the state. 'It was the duty of the king to arrange that girls and boys both should practise *brahmacharya* (celibacy) and receive education. The recalcitrant parents should be penalised. Nobody should be allowed, under state rules, to keep his daughter or son at home after the age of eight years.'[14] Education dispels ignorance, instils enlightenment among individuals and thereby helps the work of social reform and regeneration. To him, education was the key to Indian awakening.

Dayananda gave details even of the curriculum. He was for grammar, philosophy, the *Vedas* and the sciences. Later, he included medicine, music and art in his scheme of education.

He advocated education for all the four classes of men and women for the sake of 'prosperity of Aryavarta'. When each class, receiving proper education, discharged its appointed social task, 'prosperity and happiness would return to Aryavarta and benefit the whole world.'[15]

To realise such ideals of education, educational institutions like the Dayananda Anglo-Vedic (DAV) colleges and Gurukuls were established later on throughout the country by the Arya Samajists.

Political Ideas

If for his social and religious beliefs Dayananda looked to the *Vedas*, he sought inspiration from the *Manusmriti* for his political ideas. For his ideas on statecraft, Manu may be described as the teacher of Swami Dayananda. On the whole, the political ideas of Dayananda contain the essence of both the *Vedas* and the *Manusmriti*. Though his ideas were not in keeping with the political realities of the century in which he lived, there is certainly a deep concern in them for justice, for a righteous socio-political order and for the welfare of the people.

Dayananda places faith in kingship, the ideal kind of which existed in ancient India. The king should be an ideal *Ksatriya* whose primary duty was to protect the world and *dharma*. Kingship for him was divine as God created kingship and kingly power, *danda* for the sake of truth, justice and *dharma*. The king is subject to moral laws. He should be assisted by a

[14] *Satyartha Prakash*, p. 114.
[15] *Ibid.*, p. 59.

sabha, a council of wise men, and a cabinet of eight persons (including the prime minister, the chief of the army and the chief justice). The king is removable by the cabinet in case he neglects his duties. The whole army of officials is appointed by the cabinet for the management of various departments of administration. Thus, Dayananda's model king is an enlightened ruler, restrained by moral and natural laws. The king is the custodian of the commonweal. As the improvement of the state depends on the wealth, health and prosperity of its people, the king, like the paternal chief, should make his subjects happy like his own children. Likewise, the subjects should treat the king and the officials as their parents. According to him:

> The subjects are the kings of the king and the king is only their protector. There can be no ruler without the ruled and no ruled without the ruler. They should be independent in their own spheres and interdependent in common affairs. The absence of good government is sure to lead to chaos, quarrel and total destruction.

The main function of the ruler is the protection of his people. 'The king, in whose kingdom robbers rob and kill the subjects even before the eyes of the government officials, should be supposed to be dead along with his officials.' Rulers must be held accountable and responsible to the people and can be removed for corruption and incompetence.

Administration of justice occupies the central place in Dayananda's scheme. He considered equality before the law most significant. Justice is no respecter of persons and no person is above the law. He suggested even more severe punishments for higher officials found guilty of a crime. Dayananda was a votary of the rule of law. Law is the real head, the real ruler, and the administrator of justice. Law alone is religion. He who enforces law should be unprejudiced and learned. Law should be definite and unshaky because shakiness of law would destroy the country. Violation of law should invite deterrent punishment like branding, amputation of some limb, death by burning or by being eaten by dogs.

The institutional framework of Dayananda's state included three Councils of State—Education, Religion and Administration. The three bodies checked and balanced each other. About the working of these bodies he writes:

> It means that no single individual should be invested with absolute power. The king, who is the president of the Assembly, and the Assembly itself should be interdependent on each other. Both should be controlled by the people, who in their turn should be governed by the Assembly. When people become wicked and unjust, they are absolutely ruined. Let a nation, therefore, elect the most learned men,

as members of the Religious Assembly, the most devout men as members of the Educational Assembly, and men of the most praiseworthy character as member of the Political Assembly; and let that great man in it, who possesses the most excellent qualities, is highly accomplished and bears most honourable character, be made the Head or President of the Political Assembly. Let the three Assemblies harmoniously work together and make good laws, and let all abide by these laws. Let them all be of one mind in affairs that promote happiness of all. All men should subordinate themselves to the laws that are calculated to promote general well-being; they should be free in matters relating to individual well-being.[16]

Dayananda's state, in a nut-shell, is not a theocracy but a welfare state with wide-ranging obligations. Dr. Jordens writes in this respect: 'It [the state] should provide universal education and protect the *dharma*; it should be responsible for social welfare, providing support for widows and orphans, and pensions for state servants; and it should root out the evil practices of child-marriage and polygamy.'[17]

Dayananda's theory of statecraft went down to the level of village administration. He writes in the *Satyarth Prakash*:

Let him, therefore, have an administrative office in the midst of two, three, five and a hundred villages, wherein he should keep the required number of officials to carry on governmental business. Let him appoint an official at the head of one village, a second one over ten such villages, a fifth one over a thousand such villages. Let the administrator of one village daily apprise the administrator of ten villages privately of all crimes committed within his jurisdiction and the administrators of ten submit his report to the administrator of twenty . . . .

Certainly vague, but this passage portrays the network of communication and administration at the local level.

Patriotism

What underlies Dayananda's thought and activities is his uncompromising patriotism. With direct reference to the British Raj in India he condemned slavery and the rule of foreign government over other people. Political slavery, he believed, was a national curse. For India, his ideal was self-government, *swaraj*. In the concluding part of the *Satyarth Prakash* he writes: 'Say what you will, the indigenous native rule is by far the

[16] *Ibid.*, pp. 162–63.
[17] J.T.F. Jordens, *Dayananda Saraswati, His life and Ideas* (Delhi: Oxford University Press, 1978), p. 264.

best. A foreign government, perfectly free from religious prejudices, impartial towards all the natives and the foreigners, kind, beneficient and just to natives like their parents though it may be, can never make the people perfectly happy.' He was pained to see India in political bondage and even more pained to see Indians disunited. It was only when brothers fought among themselves that an outside entity posed as an arbiter. 'Mutual feud ruined the *Kauravas*, the *Pandvas* and the *Yadavas* in the past. The same fatal disease is still clinging to us . . . . May God through his mercy rid us of this dreadful disease.' Permeated by such feelings of patriotism, he made the rulers of many of the princely states his disciples and advised them to translate into reality his programme of socio-religious regeneration. Long before Lokmanya Tilak propounded his theory of *swaraj*, here was a patriotic *sannyasi* sowing the seeds of Indian nationalism and Indian *swaraj*.

The Arya Samaj

Dayananda was an amalgam of a thinker and a reformer, a theoretician and an activist. He was not content with the enunciation of social, religious and political principles but was keen to see them embodied in the warp and woof of an organisation. With this aim he founded the Arya Samaj in Bombay in 1875 with twenty-eight principles to guide it. Such principles were reformulated in 1877 at Lahore as the 'Ten Principles of the Arya Samaj'. Without going into the other detailed aspects of the organisation it would be in order to briefly mention the 'Ten Principles of the Arya Samaj,' as these principles are the gist of Dayananda's social, moral and religious ideas:

1. God is the primary cause of all true knowledge, and of everything known by its name.
2. God is All-Truth, All-Knowledge, All-Beatitude, Incorporeal, Almighty, Just, Merciful, Unbegotten, Infinite, Unchangeable, without a beginning, Incomparable, the Support and the Lord of All, All-Pervading, Omniscient, Imperishable, Immortal, Exempt from Fear, Eternal, Holy and the Cause of the Universe. To him alone worship is due.
3. The *Vedas* are the books of true knowledge, and it is the paramount duty of every Arya to read or hear them, to teach and preach them to others.
4. An Arya should always be ready to accept truth and to renounce untruth.
5. All actions must conform to virtue, i.e., they should be performed after a thorough consideration of right and wrong.
6. The primary object of the Samaj is to benefit the whole world,

namely, by improving the physical, spiritual and social conditions of mankind.

7. All ought to be treated with love, justice and with due regard to their merits.

8. Ignorance must be dispelled and knowledge diffused.

9. No one should be content with his own good alone, but every one should regard his/her prosperity as included in that of others.

10. In matters which affect the general social well-being of our race, no one should allow his or her individuality to interfere with the general good, but in strictly personal affairs everyone may act with freedom.

Conclusion

Swami Dayananda Saraswati was one of the makers of modern India. All his writings, speeches and activities are a veritable proof of his earnestness for social and religious reform. He was inspired by the ideals of social justice, social integration, religious revival and national unity, strength and emancipation. He reformed Hinduism and raised a banner of revolt and protest against the divisive forces and cumbersome customs of Hindu society. His scheme of national education based on the sounder foundations of moral values, his vehement attack on caste divisions, his enthusiasm for bringing back the 'out-castes' and the Untouchables into the Hindu fold, his advocacy of equal treatment and enlightenment of women-folk, and his full-throated eulogy of the Golden Age of the Vedic values testify to the fact that he was a radical reformer of modern India. He was one of the most ardent prophets of social reconstruction. The reforms undertaken or proposed by him laid the foundations of constructive social-political consciousness in nineteenth century India. His ideas brought home the lesson that the religion of India as well as the sovereignty of India ought to belong to the Indian people.

An unnoticed aspect of Dayananda's thought is his humanism. His whole philosophy revolves around the reformation of the individual. He has deep concern for man, for a rich moral and material life on this earth. It is in this context that we have to see his vexatious details about an ideal family life, prosperous economy, education, abolition of poverty, justice and the just ordering of wealth. His variety of welfare state is a means to human happiness. This humanism should not be blurred by Dayananda's other dogmatic pronouncements.

Despite the meritorious services rendered by Swami Dayananda in the social and religious fields, he could not escape the limitations of his own logic. The centre of his thought and action was Hindu society alone. When he looked at Islam or Christianity, it was to establish the superiority of the 'Aryas'. The cultural and religious diversities of Indian national life demanded an ideology and a programme which could inspire and bring together divergent religious communities. Instead, his ideas paved the way for the emergence of Hindu revivalism and Hindu nationalism. His theory of 'Back to the Vedas' created a revivalist spirit in the country and his Arya Samaj became the church-militant of Hindu society. Thus Dayananda became the forerunner of the revivalist forces of twentieth century India. These drawbacks in his throught, as Jordens has pointed out correctly, 'are but the contrasting shadows that accentuate the basic greatness of a man who made himself into one of the giant figures of nineteenth century India.'[18]

[18] *Ibid.*, p. 295.

5

PARTHA CHATTERJEE

Culture and Power in the Thought of Bankimchandra*

Bankimchandra Chattopadhyay (the anglicised variant of the surname is
'Chatterji'), 1838–94, was one of the first graduates of the University of
Calcutta. He worked in the provincial civil and judicial services of the
Government of Bengal. Bankim had a meteoric rise to literary fame with
his first published novel in Bengali—*Durgeśnandinī* (1864). He wrote ten
more novels, three volumes of short fiction, three volumes of humour and
satire, four treatises on social philosophy and religion and a collection of
essays. Many of these books were serialised earlier in his journal
Baṅgadarśan, which occupies a unique place in the history of Bengali
literature as a periodical which established entirely new standards of
scholarship, aesthetic taste and stylistic brilliance in the discussion of
literary and social subjects.

Bankim's own thought is often seen as having undergone a major
transformation in the course of his early and late literary careers. His
early writings reveal his acceptance of the most radical currents of contemporary European thought. Strongly rationalist and firmly committed
to the methods of 'science,' he thought of himself as a positivist and was
strongly influenced by Comte, John Stuart Mill, and later Herbert
Spencer. He was also sympathetic to the radical egalitarian ideas of
Rousseau and Proudhon. In his later works, however, there are clear
signs of how deeply he was caught in the intractable problems of reconciling
post-Englightenment European rationality with the patriotic urge to
assert the cultural and intellectual identity of a colonised people. In his
late life, he is much more of a 'conservative,' fiercely arguing for a revived
and purified Hindu religion as the true *dharma* of modern man. It is this
contradictoriness, its presuppositions, and the possibilities of movement
inherent in it, which will be the subject of this essay. Specifically, we look
at the ways in which his thought relates culture to power in the particular
context of a colonial country.

I

Let us begin with the question of power. Why has India been a subject
nation for such a long time? Bankim first considers one obvious answer to
this question: Because Indians lack physical strength and courage; because,

---

* This is an abridged version of a chapter from the forthcoming book, *Nationalist
Thought and the Colonial World*.

as the Europeans always allege, the 'Hindoos' are 'effeminate'. Yet, this answer is obviously false, because although the Hindus are notorious for their negligence towards the writing of their own history, the accounts left behind by chroniclers accompanying the victorious Greek and Muslim armies speak of the bravery and strength of the Hindus. Even as recently as the last four decades, the English had taken a beating from the Marathas and the Sikhs. The question is not, therefore, of the lack of strength or valour. There are two great reasons for India being a subject nation. The first is that Indians lack a natural desire for liberty. Some Indians probably nurse a vague feeling that independence is better than subjection, but never has this feeling become a compelling desire. Never have the majority of Indians fought for their liberty.

> For more than three thousand years, Aryans have fought against Aryans, or Aryans against non-Aryans, or non-Aryans against non-Aryans—Magadh has fought Kanauj, Kanauj has fought Delhi, Delhi has fought Lahore, Hindus have battled against Pathans, Pathans against Mughals, Mughals against the English—all of these people have fought against one another and continually stoked the fires of war in this country. But all of these were battles among kings; the bulk of Hindu society has never fought for or against anyone. Hindu kings or the rulers of Hindustan have been repeatedly conquered by alien people, but it cannot be said that the bulk of Hindu society has ever been vanquished in battle, because the bulk of Hindu society has never gone to war.[1]

And this led directly to the second great reason for the subjection of India: the lack of solidarity in Hindu society. National solidarity is crucially dependent on two kinds of attitudes. One is the conviction that what is good for every Hindu is good for me; that my opinions, my beliefs, my actions must be combined and made consistent with those of every other Hindu. The other attitude is a single-minded devotion to the interests of my nation, if necessary even at the cost of the interests of other nations. It is true that such an attitude leads to a lot of misery and bitter warfare, as the history of Europe clearly shows. But such are the realities of national feeling and the love of liberty. Hindus have always lacked this feeling and today, with diverse nationalities living in this country, separated by habitat, language, race and religion, national solidarity is completely absent.

However, argues Bankim, it is because of our contacts with the English that we have discovered for the first time the true basis of liberty and national solidarity. We know that the reason for our subjection does not

---

[1] *Baṅkima Racanāvalī*, Vol. 2 (Calcutta: Sahitya Samsad, 1965), p. 239. All subsequent references to Bankim's writings are from this volume.

lie in our lack of physical strength. We have seen in the examples of Shivaji and Ranjit Singh what can be achieved by the spirit of fraternity and united action. If only Hindus became desirous of liberty, if they could convince themselves of the value of liberty, they could achieve it.

Thus, Bankim's explanation of the subjection of India is not in terms of material or physical strength. It is an explanation in terms of *culture*. More specifically, it is an explanation which proceeds from a premise of cultural difference: an essential difference from all those attributes which make the European culturally equipped for power and for progress. Consequently, India, and the people of India, are defined as the 'Other' of the European. Sometimes it is the Bengali, sometimes the Hindu; sometimes Bankim is talking of the *bhāratavarṣīya*, the inhabitants of India. There is no attempt here to define the boundaries of the Indian nation *from within*. This definition of the Bengali, the Hindu or the Indian as the 'Other,' the 'subject,' is then extrapolated backwards into the historical past. In talking about the subjection of India, Bankim encapsulates into his conception of the cultural failure of the Indian people to face up to the realities of power, a whole series of conquests dating from the first Muslim invasions of India and culminating in the establishment of British rule. To Bankim, India has been a subject nation for seven centuries.

II

The crucial cultural attribute which, according to Bankim, stands out as the major reason for India's subjection is the Hindu attitude towards power. In a long essay, 'Sāṅkhya Philosophy,'[2] he argues that the central philosophical foundation of the overwhelming part of religious beliefs in India, including Buddhism, lies in the philosophy of Sāṅkhya. And the chief characteristic of the philosophy is its emphasis on *vairāgya*.

The present state of the Hindus is a product of this excessive other-worldliness. The lack of devotion to work, which foreigners point out as our chief characteristic, is only a manifestation of this quality. Our second most important characteristic—fatalism—is yet another form of this other-worldliness derived from the Sāṅkhya. It is because of this other-worldliness and fatalism that in spite of the immense physical prowess of the Indians, this land of the Aryans had come under Muslim rule. And it is for the same reason that India remains a subject country till this day. It is for the same reason again that social progress in this country slowed down a long time ago and finally stopped completely.[3]

[2] *Ibid.*, pp. 221–34.
[3] *Ibid.*, p. 222.

It is not as though the Sānkhya philosophers did not recognise the need for gaining a knowledge of the world. But the goal of knowledge was salvation.

> 'Knowledge is power': that is the slogan of Western civilisation. 'Knowledge is salvation' is the slogan of Hindu civilisation. The two peoples set out on the same road bound for two different goals. The Westerners have found power. Have we found salvation? There is no doubt that the results of our journeys have been dissimilar.
>
> Europeans are devotees of power. That is the key to their advancement. We are negligent towards power: that is the key to our downfall. Europeans pursue a goal which they must reach in this world: they are victorious on earth. We pursue a goal which lies in the world beyond, which is why we have failed to win on earth. Whether we will win in the life beyond is a question on which there are differences of opinion.[4]

It will be noticed here that Bankim's critique of the state of religious beliefs in India during its period of subjection, and perhaps also the period of decline beginning a few centuries before its actual subjection, is founded on a specific conception of the relation between culture and power. Certain cultural values are more advantageous than others in the real-political world of power relationships. Those which are advantageous imply a certain rational evaluation of the importance of power in material life, and indeed of the material bases of power in society, and attempt to sustain and extend those bases. Other cultures do not make such a rational evaluation and are consequently thrown into subjection. The critique of Indian culture is here, in every way, a 'rationalist' critique, and so is the critique of Sānkhya philosophy.

The argument is further clarified in another article. Here Bankim considers the allegation that the Bengalis are a weak people. Discussing several possible reasons as to why this should be so—the fertility of the land, the hot and humid climate, the food habits, customs such as child marriage, etc.—Bankim does not find adequate scientific grounds for believing that these establish sufficient conditions for the continued physical weakness of a people. But whether or not these reasons are adequate, they can only point to the lack of physical strength of a people. Yet, physical strength is not the same thing as force or power. Power, or the lack of it, is a social phenomenon. Power results from the application on physical strength of four elements, viz., enterprise, solidarity, courage and perseverance. The Bengalis as a people have always lacked these elements, which is why they are a powerless people. But these are cultural attributes; they can be acquired.

---

4 *Ibid.*, p. 226.

If ever (*i*) the Bengalis acquire a compelling desire for some national good, (*ii*) if this desire becomes compelling in every Bengali heart, (*iii*) if this compulsion becomes so great that people are prepared to stake their lives for it, and (*iv*) if this desire becomes permanent, then the Bengalis would certainly become a powerful people.[5]

The theoretical position implied in Bankim's discussion (and this is a position which recurs in much of his writing) involves, then, the following line of reasoning: (*a*) force or power is the basis of the state; (*b*) the liberty or subjection of a nation is ultimately a question of force or power; (*c*) but power is not something that is determined by material (environmental or technological) conditions; (*d*) power can be acquired by the cultivation of appropriate national-cultural values.

Let us stop for a moment and fix the location of this argument within our frame of reference.[6] The entire mode of reasoning in Bankim involves an attempt to 'objectify'; the project is to achieve positive knowledge. The 'subject' is a scientific consciousness, distanced from the 'object' which is the Indian, the Bengali, the Hindu (it does not matter which, because all of them are defined in terms of the contraposition between the Eastern and the Western). The material is the archive—historical documents, literary texts, archaeological finds—and the archivist (Oh, how helpless he feels about this, but there is nothing he can do about it!), the Orientalist scholar—William Jones, H.H. Wilson, Thomas Colebrooke, Albrecht Weber, Friedrich Max Müller, and all the rest of them. Of course, he often quarrels with their interpretations—these Europeans do not really have a good enough knowledge of India—but when he does, it is always as another scientist with a superior command over the facts (or else, he is alleging that the Englishman might have special interests for misrepresenting the facts); he never questions the 'objectivity' of the facts themselves or that they could in fact be 'objectively' represented. And the procedures for objective representation are laid down in the Great Science of Society of which the three greatest architects are Auguste Comte, John Stuart Mill and Herbert Spencer.

III

Indeed, Bankim's method, concepts and modes of reasoning are completely contained within the forms of post-Enlightenment scientific thought. One major characteristic of this thought is its celebration of the principle of historicity as the essential procedure for acquiring 'objective' knowledge.

[5] *Ibid.*, p. 213.
[6] My overall analytical framework is described in greater detail in the forthcoming book, *Nationalist Thought and the Colonial World*. For a recent biography of Bankim see Sisir Kumar Das. *The Artist in Chains: The Life of Bankim Chandra Chatterjee* (Delhi: New Statesman, 1984).

The study of social institutions or beliefs, for instance, had to consist of a description of their own internal histories—of their origins and processes of evolution—just as the study of non-human or inanimate beings became the field of natural history. History, indeed, was seen as reflecting on its surface the scientific representation of the objective and changing world of being.

To Bankim this was axiomatic. In his mind, for instance, the self-awareness of a people consisted of the knowledge of its own history. One might indeed say that to him a nation existed in its history. Thus, his distress at what he saw as the ignorance of the Hindus of their own history, indeed their apathy towards it, and his anger at the 'falsifications' of Hindu history at the hands of foreign (including Muslim) historians, are hardly surprising. And his repeated exhortations to the Indian people for urgent efforts to 'discover' their true histories are entirely in keeping with this 'scientific' mode of thought.

When he attempted, for instance, to set down in one of his last books, *Kṛṣṇacaritra*, a full statement of his ethical philosophy in the form of an appreciation of the character of Krishna, the first task he set for himself was to establish the historicity of the character. He accepted, of course, that Sanskrit literary texts consisted of an abundance of myths and legends, but this did not mean that they were entirely useless as historical sources. The accounts of Livy and Herodotus or Ferishta contained much that was patently mythical; yet they were still regarded as useful sources of history. The fact was, of course, that the texts on the life of Krishna as handed down to the present day contained numerous additions, abridgements and recensions on the 'original,' carried out by unknown and unidentifiable editors over a period of many hundreds of years. The first task, therefore, was to select and brush aside these later alterations and reach the 'original historical account' of the life of Krishna.

To do this Bankim devised several criteria, all of them strictly scientific and rational. Some of these criteria were formal and textual, having to do with continuity, stylistic consistency, uniformity of conception, and so on. But more important were the substantive criteria, because according to him, the formation of these texts as they now existed consisted of an original core of historical truth overlaid by subsequent layers of 'legends, fables and fantastic imaginings'. What is truly historical in a book such as the *Mahābhārata* must lie in its *original* text; the myths and fables were merely the dross of time. Therefore, if one followed the strict criterion of refusing to accept all 'unreal, impossible and supernatural events,' it would become possible to extract the rationally acceptable historical core of the *Mahābhārata*.

It is also significant that when Bankim quarrels with the Orientalists about their assessment of the quality of the sources of Indian history and the way these should be used, he does so from a thoroughly rationalist position. From that position, he accuses his adversaries of an ethnocentric bias and racial prejudices which, when they were not plain ignorant, deflected them from a strictly rational examination of the evidence. Albrecht Weber, for instance, had argued that the *Mahābhārata* could not have existed in the fourth century B.C. because Megasthenes did not mention it in his accounts. This, Bankim says, is 'deliberate fraud' on the part of Weber, because Weber knew perfectly well that only fragments of the original accounts of Megasthenes had survived, and in any case it was sheer prejudice to place such overwhelming reliance on Megasthenes' evidence merely because he was European. 'Many Hindus have travelled to Germany and have returned to write books about that country. We have not come across the name of Mr Weber in any of their accounts. Shall we conclude then that Mr Weber does not exist?'[7]

But what Bankim identifies here as an incorrect or incomplete application of the principles of rational scientific investigation, he can explain only as a case of racial prejudice.

It is impossible for one whose ancestors were only the other day barbarians roaming the forests of Germany to accept the reality of India's glorious past. Consequently, he is ever keen to prove that civilisation in India is only a recent phenomenon.[8]

These pundits of Europe and America . . . attempt to construct historical theories out of ancient Sanskrit texts, but they cannot accept that the subject and powerless people of India were ever civilised, or that this civilisation dates from very ancient times.[9]

It does not, however, occur to Bankim that such distortions might actually be a much more fundamental and systematic feature of the content of many of the theories which made up the natural sciences of society, even in those aspects not directly related to the subject of Indian civilisation. His critique of Orientalist scholarship remains at the level of technical criteria, showing how *a priori* prejudices could vitiate a truly objective enquiry. It does not extend to questioning the cognitive or explanatory status of the framework of concepts and theoretical relations which defined the science of society. Here he accepted entirely the fundamental methodological assumptions, the primary concepts and the general theoretical orientation of nineteenth century positivist sociology and utilitarian political economy. He wholly shared the Enlightenment belief in the perfectibility of man and agreed with the positivist view of looking at the history of social institutions as evolving from less developed and imperfect forms to more developed and perfect ones. 'In worldly matters

---

[7] *Bankima Racanāvalī*, p. 413.
[8] *Ibid.*
[9] *Ibid.*, p. 410.

I **accept** the teachings of science in demonstrating that the world is evolving gradually from an incomplete and undeveloped state towards a complete and developed form.'[10]

He accepted, for instance, that free trade was a more developed form of economic organisation than anything that had existed previously, including protectionism, because it represented a rational scheme of division of labour and was beneficial to all parties involved in economic exchange. Trade between Britain and India, he thought, had led to an expansion of agricultural activity in India.

> What we buy from England we pay for by exporting agricultural commodities, such as rice, silk, cotton, jute, indigo, etc. It goes without saying that as trade expands, the demand for such agricultural commodities will also increase by the same proportion. As a result, agriculture will expand in this country. Ever since the establishment of British rule, the trade of this country has increased, leading to a demand for more exportable agricultural products and hence to an expansion of agriculture.[11]

But had this not also meant a destruction of indigenous manufacturing, as many people in Bengal were already alleging? Perhaps, is Bankim's reply, but this did not necessarily mean that Indians were becoming less prosperous. If it was becoming difficult for Indian weavers to compete with imported textiles, the logical course to adopt would be for them to shift to those activities (e.g., rice-cultivation), which were expanding as a result of this trade.

The real reason why weavers were not seizing the opportunities opened up by expanded agricultural activities was cultural: the inertia of backward and outmoded social customs.

> People in our country are reluctant to give up their hereditary trades. This is unfortunate for our weavers, but it does not mean a loss of wealth for the country. The import of foreign cloth results in a corresponding increase in agricultural incomes—this is inevitable. What happens is merely that this income goes not to the weaver but to somebody else. The misery of the weaver does not indicate a loss of national wealth.[12]

Thus, Bankim's devotion to what he regarded as the fundamental principles of a rational science of economics makes it impossible for him to arrive at a critique of the political economy of colonial rule, even when

[10] *Ibid.*, p. 434.
[11] *Ibid.*, p. 289.
[12] *Ibid.*

the evidence from which such a critique may have proceeded was, in a sense, perfectly visible to him. He could not, for instance, formulate a problem in which the axiomatic equality of all exchange relations may have been called into question, in spite of the fact that late in his life he admitted that substantial wealth was probably being transferred to Britain in the form of payments to colonial administrators for which India was getting nothing in return. He was aware of the fact of deindustrialisation, but did not possess, and could not construct for himself, a conceptual apparatus by which this could be interpreted in any way other than free trade, increasing specialisation and division of labour, and hence inevitable progress and prosperity. It is indeed ironic that his infinitely less sophisticated, and obviously prejudiced, antagonists in the journal *Samājadarpaṇa*, who thought that Bengal was being impoverished by the trade policies of the colonial government, were, in a quite unreflective perceptual sense, correct.

On agrarian matters, again, Bankim's keen and sympathetic perception of the poverty of the majority of Bengal's peasantry is made sensible to him only after it is filtered through the conceptual grid of nineteenth century political economy. It is the Permanent Settlement which he thinks is to blame, but only because it was made with a class of unproductive landlords rather than with the tenants. It was a land settlement which could only have worked if the landlords were kind and sympathetic to their tenants, but this of course was an unrealistic expectation. What had happened to the Bengal peasantry was only the result of the greed and rapacity of a certain section of landlords, instances of which he catalogued at great length in his essay 'The Bengal Peasantry' and later incorporated into his book *Sāmya* (Equality). It was idle, and perhaps impolitic, he thought, to now attempt to reverse the Permanent Settlement. The only course open was for the landlords to mend their ways. 'If this is not done,' he wrote, 'there is no hope for the prosperity of Bengal.'[13] This is all he could suggest as a remedy for the poverty of Bengal's peasants.

Besides the rapacity of landlords who sought to skim off by force every available pice out of a submissive and helpless peasantry, the other great reason for the misery of the peasants was—and this again is part and parcel of Malthusian political economy—'the increase in population'.[14]

Reasoning from within his rational world of thought, made up of received concepts and objective criteria of validation, there was no way in which Bankim could arrive at anything other than a positive assessment of the overall social effects of British rule in India. Comparing the colonial order in India with a historical reconstruction of the Brahmanical

[13] *Ibid.*, p. 298.
[14] *Ibid.*, p. 301.

order, he had to admit that British rule had established a fairer and more impersonal legal and judicial system, greater access—at least in principle—for the lower castes to positions of power and status, and had made available the means for Indians to acquire the benefits of Western science and literature. All this had regenerated the conditions for social progress. The position of the upper classes may have declined somewhat because of the loss of liberty, but as far as the lower classes were concerned—well, 'for one who is oppressed, it makes no difference whether the oppressor is one's compatriot or whether he is foreign'.[15] If anything, the position of the lower classes in India had improved sightly under British rule.

> Some may become displeased with me and ask, 'Are you then saying that liberty or subjection makes no difference? Why then does every nation on earth fight for its liberty?' To these critics we can only reply, 'We are not engaged in settling that question. We are a subject people, and will remain that way for a long time to come: let us not get involved in fruitless debate. All that we set out to discuss was whether ancient Indians were in general better off because of their liberty than the people of modern India. We have concluded that the condition of the upper classes such as Brahmans and Kshatriyas has declined, but that of Sudras or ordinary people has improved.'[16]

IV

Bankim indeed undertakes the same classificatory project as the Orientalist, and arrives at precisely the same typologies under which the Oriental (the Hindu, the Bengali) is stamped with an essentialist character signifying in every aspect his difference from modern Western man.

What Bankim does not accept, however, is the immutability of this character. There is, he argues, a subjectivity that can *will* a transformation of this culturally determined character. This is the National Will, which can be summoned into existence by the nation acting collectively.

But how? How are these national-cultural values to be cultivated? One way is to imitate those who have demonstrated their capacities as powerful and freedom-loving nations. A perennial problem this has been in all nationalist thinking: How does one accept what is valuable in another's culture without losing one's own cultural identity? Rajnarayan Bose, in a public address entitled 'Then and Now' (1874), had castigated the newly educated classes of Bengal for ther fondness for English manners and life-style. This was only one—a somewhat colourless and self-righteous sermon—in a whole series of attacks on overt Westernisation which was in the nineteenth century the staple of social satire in the popular literature

[15] *Ibid.*, p. 244.
[16] *Ibid.*, p. 245.

and the visual and performing arts of Bengal. But Bankim's answer to the question is curiously half-hearted and ambiguous. 'Is all imitation bad?' he asks, in an uncharacteristically gentle rejoinder to Rajnarayan's speech.

> That cannot be. One cannot learn except by imitation. Just as children learn to speak by imitating the speech of adults, to act by imitating the actions of adults, so do uncivilised and uneducated people learn by imitating the ways of the civilised and the educated. Thus it is reasonable and rational that Bengalis should imitate the English.[17]

Of course, mere imitation can never produce excellence. That is the product of genius. But imitation is always the first step in learning. It is true that there have been nations such as the Greeks who have become civilised on their own, but that is a matter of protracted evolution. It is much quicker to learn from others who are more advanced.

> Such imitation is but natural, and its consequences can be most beneficial. There are many who are angry at our imitating English habits in food and dress; what would they say of the English imitating the French in their food and dress? Are the English any less imitative than Bengalis? At least we imitate the rulers of our nation; who do the English imitate?[18]

But almost as soon as Bankim has made this characteristic thrust of logic, he feels compelled to backtrack. 'Of course, we agree that it may not be entirely desirable for the Bengalis to be as imitative as they now are.'[19]

We can see Bankim's predicament here. He accepts that the reasons for India's subjection, and those for her backwardness, are to be found in her culture. He accepts that there exist historically demonstrated models embodying superior cultural values. His project is to initiate 'progress' by transforming the backward culture of his nation. But does this not necessarily imply losing the essential character of his culture which, within the thematic of nationalism, is defined in opposition to Western culture? Bankim does not have an answer.

There did, however, exist an answer, and Bankim was to find it in the later years of his life. This is the answer which he spent many pages in explaining in his last books, and it still remains an enduring element in nationalist thought.

It is an answer that can be found within the thematic and problematic of nationalist thought. It does no violence to its theoretical framework where the thematic of Orientalism is dominant, while it still provides a

[17] *Ibid.*, p. 201.
[18] *Ibid.*, p. 203.
[19] *Ibid.*

specific subjectivity to the East in which it is active, autonomous and undominated.

The superiority of the West was in the materiality of its culture. The West had achieved progress, prosperity and freedom because it had placed Reason at the heart of its culture. The distinctive culture of the West was its science, its technology and its love of progress. But culture did not consist only of the material aspect of life. There was the spiritual aspect too, and here the European Enlightenment had little to contribute. In the spiritual aspect of culture, the East was superior—and hence, undominated.

This answer did not conflict in any way with the fundamental classificatory scheme of Orientalist thought. All it did was to assert a cultural domain of superiority for the East and, in time, to tie this assertion with the national struggle against Western political domination.

Let me show how Bankim formulated this answer. In 1884 he wrote a long tract entitled *The Theory of Religion* in the form of a dialogue between a teacher and his pupil, in which he set out his concept of *anuśīlana* or practice. *Anuśīlana*, he said, was a 'system of culture,' more complete and more perfect than the Western concept of culture as propounded by Comte or, more recently, by Matthew Arnold. The Western concept was fundamentally agnostic, and hence incomplete.[20] *Anuśīlana* was based on the concept of *bhakti* which, in turn, implied the unity of knowledge and duty. There were three kinds of knowledge— knowledge of the world, of the self and of God. Knowledge of the world consisted of mathematics, astronomy, physics and chemistry, and these one would have to learn from the West. Knowledge of the self meant biology and sociology, and these too one would have to learn from the West. Finally, knowledge of God, and in this field the Hindu *śāstra* contained the greatest human achievements—the Upaniṣad, the *darśana*, the Purāṇa, the *itihāsa*, but principally the *Gītā*.[21]

But mere knowledge would not create *bhakti*; for that, knowledge would have to be united with duty. Duty meant the performance of acts without the expectation of reward. To eat is a duty; so is the defence of one's country. But these acts had to be performed because they should be preformed, not because they might produce beneficial results.[22] This non-possessive, non-utilitarian concept of duty was the core of *dharma* or religion.

> *Teacher*:   The day the European industries and sciences are united with Indian *dharma*, man will be god . . . .
>
> *Pupil*:   Will such a day ever come in the life of man?

[20] *Ibid.*, p. 585.
[21] *Ibid.*, p. 630.
[22] *Ibid.*, pp. 628–29.

Teacher: It will if you Indians are prepared to act. It is in your hands. If you will it, you can become master and leader of the whole world. If you do not aspire to it, then all my words are in vain.[23]

In fact, that day was not far off. '*Teacher*: Soon you will see that with the spread of the doctrine of pure *bhakti*, the Hindus will gain new life and become powerful like the English at the time of Cromwell or the Arabs under Muhammad.'[24]

Here then was a cultural ideal which retained what was thought to be distinctively Indian, while subsuming what was valuable in the culture of the West. The aim was to produce the complete and perfect man—learned, wise, agile, religious and refined—a better man than the merely efficient and prosperous Westerner.

But once again, the striking fact here is not so much the distinction between the material and the spiritual spheres of culture. What is remarkable is that this distinction should be defended on the most thoroughly rationalist grounds afforded by nineteenth century European philosophy. There are two planks on which Bankim builds his defence. One was the *rationalist critique of Christianity* which Bankim uses to demolish the claims of European religion as a suitable moral philosophy of man living in a modern scientific age and, by implication, to expose the irrationality of reformist attempts to 'Christianise' in some form or other the popular religious practices and beliefs in Indian society. The second referred to the contemporary philosophical debates in Europe about the finite limits of empirical science which Bankim employs to demonstrate the rational validity of a suitable philosophy of spirit and then to turn this argument around to show the much greater accordance of a purified Hindu philosophy of spirit with the rational scientific temper of the modern age. Bankim advances some strikingly ingenious arguments on both these points, and it is worth looking into some of them in detail in order to appreciate the subtle and immensely complex interplay between the thematic and the problematic in some of the philosophically most sophisticated variants of nationalist thought.

Bankim spelled out one part of the argument in an essay which was originally entitled 'Mill, Darwin and Hindu Religion' when it was first published in 1875 in *Baṅgadarśana* and later changed to 'What Science Has to Say About the [Hindu] Trinity' when it was reprinted in his collected essays. Here Bankim considers the common Hindu conception of Brahmā, Viṣṇu and Maheśvara—Creator, Preserver and Destroyer—as the three distinct forms of the Divine, and asks how far this conception accords with the findings of modern scientific investigations. For a start,

[23] *Ibid.*, p. 633.
[24] *Ibid.*, p. 647.

he takes the three posthumously published essays of J.S. Mill on religion[25] in which Mill assesses the validity of the 'intelligent creator' argument for the existence of an omnipotent, omniscient and all-merciful God. Mill argues that if the evidence for the existence of the omniscient creator lies in the massive intricacy of the skills involved in the act of creation, then the obvious imperfections of the products of creation—susceptibility to injury and pain, mortality, decay—would seem to militate against the creator's omniscience.

Of course, it could be argued that it is not a lack of omniscience, but rather certain limits to his powers which result in these imperfections in God's creation. Here, Mill advanced two explanations, both of which he held in different periods of his life. The first is the argument that God was not a creator, but only a constructor, working on material which was already in existence, and it was the imperfection of those materials which have resulted in the imperfections in the final products of creation. This, therefore, saves both the omniscient and the omnipotent qualities of God, but reduces him from the role of creator to that of a mere constructor. The other argument is that there is another power distinct from God which acts as an impediment to his actions, and it is as an effect of this antagonistic power that imperfections appear in the acts of creation. Mill's arguments, therefore, raise considerable doubts about the existence of an omniscient and omnipotent creator; moreover, they indicate the existence of two distinct forces—one, the preserver, and the other, the destroyer.

But what about the creator? Here Bankim brings in the results of Darwin's researches on evolution. Darwin had shown that the powers underlying creation cannot ensure survival; many more creatures are born in nature than are able to survive. Hence, a principle of natural selection had to operate in order to ensure that those who were the fittest would survive. This scientific principle could be interpreted to imply the existence of two distinct forces in nature—one, the creator, and the other, the preserver. It could, of course, be objected that this was not the implication at all. There was no need to think of the creator and the preserver as distinct entities. The principle of natural selection could easily be interpreted as the consequence of the acts of a destructive force which impeded the acts of the creator who was at the same time the preserver. But this argument is fallacious, because it requires one to believe in an omniscient creator-preserver who creates much more than he knows can be preserved. It is much more logical to conceive of a creator whose sole intention is to create, a preserver whose sole intention is to preserve, and a destroyer who seeks to destroy what has been created.

[25] J.S. Mill, *Nature, The Utility of Religion and Theism* (London: Watts, 1904).

Having advanced this argument, Bankim then establishes very clearly what he thinks its cognitive status is in relation to an empiricist epistemology. In the first place, he says, this argument does not prove the existence of God. It was, therefore, open to one to believe in God in the absence of an empirical proof either in favour or against his existence. If one did believe in God, however, the question would arise of the nature or form of the Divine. It is as a reply to this question that the argument establishes the logical accordance of the Hindu conception of the Trinity with the findings of modern science. Second, the argument does not assert that the founders of the Hindu religion had these scientific considerations in mind when they conceived of the Trinity. Third, although the argument establishes a natural basis for the religious belief in the Trinity, it does not purport to be a scientific proof of the existence of the Trinity, nor does it justify a belief in their existence in tangible physical forms. What the argument does imply, however, is the following:

> . . . it is true that there is no scientific proof of the existence of the Trinity. But it must be admitted that in comparison with Christianity, the religion followed by those great practitioners of science, the European peoples, the Hindu worship of the Trinity is far more natural and in accordance with scientific theories. The worship of the Trinity may not be founded in science, but it is not in opposition to it. On the other hand, Mill's arguments have shown conclusively that the Christian belief in an omnipotent, omniscient and all-merciful God is entirely contrary to scientific principles. The Hindu philosophies of *karma* or *māyā* are far more consistent with science.
>
> Science is showing at every step that there exists everywhere in this universe an infinite, inconceivable and inscrutable power—it is the cause of all being, the inner spirit of the external world. Far be it for us to deny the existence of this great force; on the contrary, we humbly pay our respects to it.[26]

The second argument which Bankim uses to defend a rational philosophy of spirit is based on the notion of finite limits to positive knowledge. He develops this argument in the course of his commentary on the *Gītā*. Science, he says, admits of two sorts of proof: one, direct sense-perception, and two, inference based on sense-perception. Neither is sufficient to prove the existence of the soul. Hence, empirical science is incapable of constructing a true philosophy of spirit.

> It cannot, because it is beyond the powers of science. One can only go as far as one is able. The diver tied by a rope to his boat can only search the bottom of the sea as far as his rope will permit him; it is beyond his

---

[26] *Bankima Racanāvalī*, p. 280.

powers to gather all the treasures which the sea holds. Science is tied to its epistemic leash; how can it find a philosophy of spirit which lies beyond its range of proof? Where science cannot reach, it has no privilege: it can consider itself beholden by resting on the lowest steps of that stairway which leads up to the higher reaches. To look for scientific proof where it cannot apply is a fundamentally mistaken search.[27]

Scientists could object here and say that since only empirical proof provides a valid basis of knowledge, all we can say about the existence of the soul is that we neither know that it exists nor that it doesn't. Only a thoroughly agnostic position would be consistent with science.

To this, Bankim says, there can be two answers. One is provided in Indian philosophy which admits two other kinds of proof, namely, analogy and revelation. Analogy, we know now from the findings of science, is a very uncertain basis of knowledge and can lead to numerous errors. Revelation, if one accepts it as a valid basis of knowledge, can eliminate all uncertainty since, unlike human perception or inference, God can never be wrong. However, revelation can only be accepted by the believer; a scientist can hardly be expected to admit it as a method of proof. The second answer, however, has been given in German philosophy. Kant has argued that besides phenomenal knowledge arising out of sense-perception or inference based on perception, there is also a transcendental knowledge based on concepts which are true in themselves. Of course, Kant's philosophy is not universally accepted.

> However, I am obliged to state here what I, in accordance with my own knowledge and beliefs, consider true. I firmly believe that if all one's mental faculties are suitably developed, the knowledge of this philosophy of spirit becomes transcendentally true . . .
>
> I have engaged in this extended discussion because many use the findings of a limited and imperfect science to ridicule the philosophy of spirit. They ought to know that the philosophy of spirit is beyond the limits of Western science, not opposed to it.[28]

V

The contrast with Christianity also brings out another crucial aspect of Bankim's philosophical system: the centrality of a rational philosophy of *power* within an entire moral project of national regeneration. In *Kṛṣṇacaritra*, Bankim discusses the rival claims of Buddha, Christ and Krishna as ideal characters. It is true, he says, that Krishna's life does not

---

[27] *Ibid.*, pp. 699–700.
[28] *Ibid.*, p. 701.

show the same concern for redeeming the fallen as do the lives of Jesus or Gautama. But the latter were men whose sole occupation was the preaching of religion—a most noble occupation, and Gautama and Jesus both revealed themselves in that occupation as great human beings. But their lives could hardly serve as complete ideals for all men, because the truly ideal character must retain its ideal quality for all men of all occupations.

> The true fulfilment of human life consists of the fullest and most consistent development of all human faculties. He whose life shows this full and consistent development is the ideal man. We cannot see it in Christ; we can in Sri Krishna. If the Roman Emperor had appointed Jesus to govern the Jews, would he have succeeded? No, because the requisite faculties were not developed in him . . . . Again, suppose the Jews had risen in revolt against Roman oppression and elected Jesus to lead them in their war of independence, what would Jesus have done? He had neither the strength nor the desire for battle. He would have said, 'Render unto Caesar what is due to Caesar,' and walked away. Krishna too had little taste for war. But war was often justified in religion. In cases of just war, Krishna would agree to engage in it. When he engaged in war, he was invincible . . . Krishna is the true ideal for man. The Hindu ideal is superior to the Christian ideal . . . .
>
> Krishna himself was householder, diplomat, warrior, law-giver, saint and preacher; as such, he represents a complete human ideal for all these kinds of people . . . . We cannot appreciate the comprehensiveness of the Hindu ideal by reducing it to the imperfect standards of the Buddhist or Christian ideals of mercy and renunciation.[29]

What, in fact, had happened in Europe was a complete divorce between its religion and its political practice. Europe's religion idealises the humble, peace-loving and merciful renunciator. Yet its politics is the battlefield of violent forces wholly dedicated to the amoral pursuit of worldly goods. A similar fall had occurred in Indian society too, from the supreme ideal represented by the Krishna of the *Mahābhārata* to the Krishna celebrated in popular cults and festivities. What was needed, above all, for a national regeneration in India was the reestablishment of a harmonious unity of religion and politics, harmony between a comprehensive ethical ideal and the practice of power.

Bankim then brings up what he thinks is the central problem in the field of law and politics: the establishment of a criterion based on a judicious combination of force and mercy. The two are opposed in their consequences. A show of mercy to all offenders would ultimately lead to the

²⁹ *Ibid.*, pp. 516–17.

destruction of social life. On the other hand, a society based entirely on force would reduce human life to a state of unmitigated bestiality. Modern and civilised Europe had hardly succeeded in finding the right balance between the two. The politics of modern Europe had overwhelmed its religion, which is why mercy had disappeared from European life and force reigned supreme in every sphere. In the Udyogaparva of the *Mahābhārata*, however, Krishna raises precisely this question: the right combination of force and mercy. Faced with the dilemma, the strong prefer a solution based on force and the weak appeal for mercy. But what is the answer for one who is both powerful and compassionate? That would be the ideal answer, and Krishna provides it in the Udyogaparva.

Bankim's interpretation of these passages in the *Mahābhārata* strongly emphasises a concept of duty which embodies what he regards as a rational as well as an ethical philosophy of power. One element here is the notion of moral right.

> I will not desire a paradise given to the pursuit of immoral pleasures. But at the same time, I will not relinquish to the swindler a single grain of what is morally due to me. If I do so, I may not harm myself too much, but I will be guilty of the sin of adopting a path that will bring ruin upon society.[30]

Another element consists of the notions of rightful self-defence and just war. 'It is moral to wage war in defence of myself and of others. To shy away from doing so is grave immorality. We, the people of Bengal, are bearing the consequences of our immorality of seven hundred years.'[31] But self-defence and just war are totally opposed to the European conceptions of conquest and glory. 'Apart from the bloodthirsty demons who pursue glory, anyone else will realise that there is only a small difference between *glorie* and theft: the conqueror is a great robber, others are petty theives.'[32] In any case, moral philosophers would agree in principle that it is ethically right to defend oneself against small as well as big thieves. 'The English name for self-defence against petty theft is Justice, while defence against the great robber is called Patriotism. The Indian name for both is *dharma*.'[33]

The third element is the concept of *ahimsā* or non-violence, but it is a concept entirely in keeping with the ideas of moral right, self-defence and just war. *Ahimsā* does not enjoin one to abhor violence at all times and under all circumstances. It is impossible to conduct even the ordinary acts of human living without in some form or other doing violence to other

[30] *Ibid.*, p. 529.
[31] *Ibid.*, p. 495.
[32] *Ibid.*, p. 533.
[33] *Ibid.*, p 534.

creatures. With every drink of water we gulp down a million microscopic germs; every step we take, we trample under our feet a thousand little creatures. If it is said that these are unintended acts of violence, then many other instances can be given where conscious violence is the only protection to life. When a tiger prepares to spring upon me, I must pull the trigger as quickly as possible because if I do not destroy it, it will destroy me. There are situations where violence is moral. The main consideration here is the following: '. . . the supreme moral duty is to refrain from violence except when it is demanded by *dharma*. To use violence to prevent one who does violence is not immoral; on the contrary, it is the highest moral duty.'[34]

However, the duty of non-violence (i.e., refraining from violence except when morally justified) is a higher duty than considerations such as honesty or truth. That is to say, there are situations where it is moral to utter falsehood in order to avoid unjustified violence. Bankim is particularly harsh here on Westernised moralists who pretend that there can be nothing more precious than honesty and who regard any compromise with that principle a licence for chicanery and deviousness. In the first place, Bankim says, nowhere in the public life of Europe is honesty given that kind of privilege: the entire corpus of Western jurisprudence shows, for instance, that a murderer is treated as a much greater offender than a liar. Second, such adulation, whether hypocritical or merely sentimental, of honesty and plain-speaking is precisely the results of the divorce between religious ideals and political practice which is the hallmark of European civilisation today. 'If there is any moralist who says, "kill if need be, but do not lie," then we say to him, "Keep your religion to yourself. Let India remain unacquainted with such a hellish religion." '[35]

The fourth important element in the concept of duty is the principle of control over the senses. Bankim is very careful here to distinguish this principle from both asceticism and puritanism. The philosophy of *dharma* is not an ascetic philosophy. It does not advocate the renunciation of sensual pleasure. It is a worldly philosophy which makes it a duty to achieve control over the senses. On the other hand, unlike puritanism, it does not set up a moral ideal as a result of which human life is constantly torn by an unnatural, and irreconcilable, opposition between sensual pleasure and spiritual salvation. Puritanism is opposed to sensual pleasure; the *dharma* of the *Gītā* advocates neither desire nor abhorrence: '. . . no room for hypocrisy here'.[36]

Bankim's concept of *dharma* attempts to reconcile a philosophy of spirit with a rational doctrine of power. In the process, the interplay between the thematic and the problematic of nationalist thought results

---

[34] *Ibid.*, p. 562.
[35] *Ibid.*, p. 563.
[36] *Ibid.*, p. 744.

in a curious transposition of the supposed relation between a puritan ethic and the rationalisation of social life in the modern age. Bankim's nationalism leads him to the claim that a purified and regenerated Hindu ideal is far superior as a rational philosophy of life than anything that Western religion or philosophy has to offer.

VI

We have in Bankim a reversal of the Orientalist problematic, but within the same general thematic. It is only in this sense that nationalist thought is opposed to imperialist (Orientalist) thought. Bankim then seeks a specific subjectivity for the nation, but within an essentialist typology of cultures in which this specificity can never be truly historical. Within the domain of thought thus defined, however, it seems a valid answer. The West has a superior culture, but only partially; spiritually, the East is superior. What is needed, now, is the cultivation of a cultural ideal in which the industries and the sciences of the West can be learnt and emulated while retaining the spiritual greatness of Eastern culture. This is the national-cultural project.

An élitism now becomes inescapable. Because the act of cultural synthesis can, in fact, be performed only by a supremely cultivated and refined intellect. It is a project of national-cultural regeneration in which the intelligentsia leads and the nation follows. The national-cultural ideal of the complete and perfect man was to be aspired for and approximated by practice, that is, *anuśīlana*. And it was not likely that large masses of people would reach this perfection. Bankim states this quite clearly: 'I do not entertain much hope at this time that the ordinary Hindu would understand the religion of *anuśīlana*.' But, 'a national character is built out of the national religion . . . . I do expect that if intellectuals accept this religion, a national character will finally be built.'[37]

Bankim's doctrine of power, in fact, drew him towards a singularly élitist project for a new national politics. Compared to the various forms of nationalist political movements in twentieth century India, Bankim's ideas were, of course, much less clearly specified in organisational terms. There was little in them from which one could derive anything by way of a nationalist political programme. But in accordance with the fundamental unity in his conception of power between a doctrine of force and the need for an organic moral authority incorporated into a national religion or culture, he became an unsparing opponent of the principal form of élite-nationalist politics of his times, namely, social reform through the medium of the legislative institutions of the colonial state. It is not as though he disagreed with the reformers' critique of various Hindu customs and practices; in fact, he seldom did. But he vehemently

[37] *Ibid.*, p. 651.

questioned both the mode of reasoning employed by the reformers and their means for achieving the reform. Relentlessly, he poured scorn and ridicule on their attempts, on the one hand, to persuade British administrators to legislate on social questions by appealing to enlightened reason and rationality, and on the other, to neutralise conservative opinion by a highly selective interpretation of Hindu scriptures in order to show that the reforms were sanctioned by the *śāstra*. This he thought hypocritical, because it implied a wholly opportunistic ambivalence with regard to the moral foundations of reform—rationality for some, scriptural infallibility for others.

Moreover, and somewhat paradoxically in the context of his general sympathy for utilitarian social theory, he had little faith in the efficacy of legislation to bring about a genuine reform of social institutions. Reform, in order to succeed, must flow from a new moral consensus in society. To the extent that this new morality was an inevitable consequence of changes in the basic economic and social conditions of living in the modern age, a new pattern of beliefs and practices would emerge on its own, and reform by legislation would become redundant. This was, for instance, Bankim's reading of the issue of polygamy. It was clear, he thought, that polygamy, to the extent that it was ever common in Hindu society, was rapidly on the decline. This decline had come about without state legislation or injunctions by religious leaders. Given the changes in social conditions, its ultimate disappearance was inevitable. Consequently, he thought there was little difference between the efforts of reformers like Vidyasagar and those of Don Quixote.[38]

More fundamentally, however, Bankim's conception of power, unlike the reformers' faith in the general accordance of British rule of law with the universal principles of reason and rationality, could hardly allow him to disregard the great and unbridgeable gulf which separated the colonial state from the rest of Indian society. The colonial state was founded on a superiority of force; its *raison d'être* lay in the maintenance and extension of British imperial power. In the process, many of the fundamental elements of the conditions of social life in India were undergoing rapid change. But the original superiority of force was the product of a superior culture which shaped and directed the British national project in the world. To match and overcome that superiority, Indian society would have to undergo a similar transformation. And the key to that transformation must lie in a regeneration of national culture embodying, in fact, an unrivalled combination of material and spiritual values. To Bankim, therefore, the remedy for cultural backwardness was not reform, but a total regeneration of national culture, or as he preferred to call it, the national religion. Indeed, mere reform negates the nationalist

[38] *Ibid.*, p. 315.

problematic itself, for it assumes that the Oriental (the Indian, the Hindu) is non-autonomous, passive, historically non-active, indeed for that very reason ahistorical, and therefore ever in need to be acted upon by others. Bankim's doctrine of power, as we have seen, is premised on a reversal of this historical relationship.

This autonomous subjectivity of the nation, now, would have to be provided by a new national religion. Its elements were all there. If religion, as Comte defined it, '. . . in itself expresses the state of perfect unity which is the distinctive mark of man's existence both as an individual and in society, when all the constituent parts of his nature, moral and physical, are made habitually to converge towards one common purpose,' then Bankim's burden was to show that 'Hinduism is the greatest of all religions'.[39] All that was necessary was to 'sweep it clean of the dross that had accumulated over the centuries,'[40] to interpret its tenets in the light of contemporary social conditions. And to do this one would need to set up a new moral ideal to be accepted and followed by the intellectual leaders of society. Their practice of the national religion would lead to the establishment of the new national character.

> The national religion can bring under its fold and shape the lives even of those who understand nothing of religion. Few people ever understand the subtle intricacies of religious thought. Most merely accept and initiate the example set by those who do understand. That is how the national character is determined.[41]

The crucial medium here, according to Bankim, was education. At times, of course, he made the most exaggerated and hollow claims on its behalf, as for instance in the conclusion of his book on *Equality* in which he called it 'the means to eliminate all social evils,' including foreign economic exploitation, the poverty of the peasantry and the oppression of women.[42] But elsewhere, he is more specific. At one level, Bankim is concerned with élite education—the advancement of rational learning among those who would be the cultural and intellectual leaders of society, the new synthesisers of the best of the West and the best of the East. But he was not particularly impressed by the 'filtration' theory of education.

> The argument is that it is only necessary for the upper classes to be educated; there is no need for a separate system of instruction for the lower classes. . . . The porousness of the newly educated class will guarantee that the ignorant masses will soon be soaked with knowledge! . . . We do not, however, have much faith that this will happen.[43]

[39] *Ibid.*, p. 676.
[41] *Ibid.*, p. 651.
[43] *Ibid.*, p. 282.
[40] *Ibid.*, p. 668.
[42] *Ibid.*, pp. 405–6.

It was necessary, Bankim thought, for the intellectual leadership to engage in a much more conscious programme of national education. A first step in this programme was to make available the results of modern learning in the Indian vernaculars. In his own case, it could certainly be said that his entire literary career was devoted to this single pursuit. But even more than these formal channels, Bankim was concerned with reviving the many cultural institutions of popular instruction which had long existed in India but which were rapidly dying out because of the exclusive concern of the upper classes with English education.

It is not true that in our country there was always this lack of means of popular instruction. How in that case did Śākyasiṃha teach the Buddhist religion to all of India? Just think of it; even our modern philosophers find it excruciatingly difficult to unravel the complex arguments of Buddhist philosophy! Max Müller did not understand it at all . . . . Yet Śākyasiṃha and his disciples taught this . . . immensely difficult doctrine to one and all . . . . And then Śaṅkarācārya demolished this firmly established, world-conquering, egalitarian religion and taught all of India the Śaiva faith. How, if there were no means of popular instruction? Much more recently, Caitanya converted all of Orissa to the Vaiṣṇava religion. No means of popular instruction? But in our day, from Rammohun Roy to the latest hordes of college students, three and a half generations have been peddling Brahmoism, and yet the people do not accept their teachings. Before there used to be means of popular instruction; they do not exist any more.[44]

In the case of Bengal, Bankim was particularly impressed by the historical example of the Vaiṣṇava cultural efflorescence of the fourteenth and fifteenth centuries. In contrast to his consistently derisive reference to the efforts of the nineteenth century intelligentsia for religious and social reform, Bankim unhesitatingly located the 'renaissance' in Bengali culture in that earlier period of Bengal's history.

How long has Europe been civilised? In the fifteenth century—only four hundred years ago—Europe was more uncivilised than we were. One event brought civilisation to Europe. Suddenly Europe rediscovered the long-forgotten culture of the Greeks.... Petrarch, Luther, Galileo, Bacon: suddenly there seemed to be no end to Europe's good fortune. But there was a similar age in our history as well. The rise of Caitanya in Nabadwip followed by Rūpa, Sanātana and countless other poets and theologians; Raghunātha Śiromaṇi, Gadādhara, Jagadīśa in philosophy; in law, Raghunandana and his

---

[44] *Ibid.*, p. 377.

followers. And then there was a new wave of Bengali poetry: Vidyāpati and Caṇḍīdāsa came before Caitanya, but the poetry which followed him is unparalleled in the whole world. Where did all this come from? How did our Renaissance happen? Where did our nation get this sudden enlightenment? . . . Why did this light go out? Perhaps it was because of the advent of Mughal rule—the land revenue settlement of the Hindu Raja Todar Mal. Gather the evidence and find out all of these things.[45]

This was, in fact, a major part of Bankim's project for a national history of Bengal. The hallmark of the 'renaissance' was its popular character. And this would have to be the character of the new national-cultural revival as well. It called for a very specific relationship between the intellectual leaders of society and the rest of the nation. The intellectual-moral leadership of the nation was based not on an élitism of birth or caste or privilege or wealth, but of excellence. The leaders were leaders because through *anuśīlana*, they had attained an exemplary unity of knowledge and duty. Their relationship with the masses must, therefore, be one of sympathy on the one side and deference on the other. 'The English have a good name for it: Subordination . . . . Not fear, but respect.'[46]

VII

This élitism of the intelligentsia, rooted in the vision of a radical regeneration of national culture, did not find any viable political means to actualise itself in Bankim's time—the heyday of colonial rule. Instead, the vision became a dream, a utopian political community in which the nation was the Mother, once resplendent in wealth and beauty, now in tatters. Relentlessly, she exhorts a small band of her sons, those of them who are brave and enlightened, to vanquish the enemy and win back her honour. Imprisoned within the rationalist framework of his theoretical discourse and powerless to reject its dominating implications, Bankim lived out his dream of liberation in his later novels. In form, *Ānandamaṭha* (1884), *Devī Caudhurāṇī* (1884) and *Sītārāma* (1888) are historical romances, but they are suffused with a utopianism which, by the power of the particular religious semiotic in which it was expressed, had a deep emotional influence on the new intelligentsia. It is not surprising that in the history of political movements in India, Bankim's direct disciples were the 'revolutionary terrorists,' the small groups of armed activists drawn from the Hindu middle classes, wedded to secret underground organisation and planned assassination.

But there was a more general implication of Bankim's formulation of

[45] *Ibid.*, p. 339.
[46] *Ibid.*, p. 619.

the national project which was shared much more widely. The divergence between the *modern* and the *national* was not really resolved in Bankim in any historically specific way, because the specificity of the modern and the specificity of the national remained distinct and opposed. Theoretically, the two could be synthesised in the ideal of the complete man, the true intellectual, but it was hardly possible to devise programmatic steps to achieve that ideal in the realm of politics. It remained an unresolved contradiction in all nationalist thinking. Yet the contradiction itself served as the basis for divergent political programmes within the nationalist movement. An emphasis on the modern meant arguing for a period of tutelage until the leaders of the country and its material bases had been sufficiently 'modernised'. For a long time this meant a continuation of colonial rule, a sharing of power between colonial officials and a modernised élite, and an emphasis on state action to reform traditional institutions and bring into being modern ones. It also meant, and indeed still means, a continued period of 'collaboration' with the West. Usually a political programme of this sort has been associated with liberal, constitutionalist and pro-Western circles. On the other hand, a more uncompromising position on the question of colonial rule has meant an ideological emphasis on what is distinctly national, i.e., culturally distinct from the Western and the modern. This is seen to be characteristic of revivalist or fundamentalist cultural movements, usually of a religious-communal nature. Both possibilities are inherent in ^ankim's unresolved problem.

6

RAJENDRA VORA

Two Strands of Indian Liberalism: The Ideas of Ranade and Phule

In India, colonialism generated new classes. Along with the rise of the commercial bourgeoisie there arose a new middle class or intelligentsia which was a product of the colonial educational system. This educated middle class was composed of members of the traditional elite or high castes—the Bhadralok in Bengal, the Brahmans in Madras and the Brahmans and the Prabhus in Bombay Presidency. Liberalism as a doctrine and programme was developed by this social class in Indian society, mainly during the nineteenth and early twentieth centuries. Raja Ram Mohan Roy (1772–1833), Dadabhai Naoroji (1825–1917), Surendranath Banerji (1848–1925), Pherojshah Mehta (1845–1915), Gopal Krishna Gokhale (1866–1915), Gopal Ganesh Agarkar (1856–95) and a number of other prominent thinkers tried to present a liberal critique of Indian society and colonial state and to provide a set of liberal ideas for the transformation of Indian society and polity. But none of them succeeded in providing a comprehensive philosophical framework of Indian liberalism. With Raja Ram Mohan Roy it was just the beginning of what has been called the Indian renaissance or the period of Enlightenment when systematic thought could not have been developed. Dadabhai's contribution was restricted to economics. Pherojshah Mehta was mainly an activist and never devoted himself to serious philosophic enquiry. Surendranath Banerji was known for his political ideas. G.K. Gokhale was a direct disciple of M.G. Ranade and tried to more or less follow his guru. G.G. Agarkar attempted to apply Herbert Spencer's evolutionary doctrine to Indian society. More than any one of these thinkers, it was M.G. Ranade (1842–1901) who presented in a fairly systematic manner a model of Indian liberalism in the second half of the nineteenth century.

Born in a Brahman family of Maharashtra, Ranade became one of the outstanding students of Bombay University. He began his career as a teacher in the University but later joined the British judiciary and rose up to the position of Judge at the Bombay High Court in 1893. His service in the government as a judge did not restrain him from involvement in social and political reform.[1] A strong believer in all-round reform, he was associated with a number of social, religious, educational, political and economic institutions of Poona and Bombay, either as a founder or as a leading member. His association with the Prarthana Samaj (Prayer

[1] For a biography of Ranade, see Richard P. Tucker, *Ranade and the Roots of Indian Nationlism* (Bombay: Popular Prakashan, 1977).

Society), Social Conference, Poona Sarvajanik Sabha (Political Organisation from Poona), Indian National Congress and Industrial Conference was very close and significant. Besides being a government servant and a leader of social and political reform movements, Ranade was one of the most sophisticated thinkers of nineteenth century India. In fact, he provided a philosophical foundation to the Indian liberal movement. He could do this because he was well grounded in Indian and European philosophy and had a historical and comparative understanding of socio-economic and political developments in India and the world at large. In his writings, Ranade has attempted to solve the conflict between the actions of the state and liberty of the individual.

II
The Role of the State

The focal point of Ranade's argument about the state is his critique of the *laissez-faire* doctrine which assigned a minimal role to the state. In place of it he advocates an alternative principle which assigns a positive role to the state especially in economic matters. His advocacy of state intervention is based on his reading of the Indian economy and society. He felt that India's economic problem was two-fold, namely, (a) phenomenal poverty, and (b) dependence on agriculture and that its solution lay in (a) industrialisation and (b) commercialisation of agriculture. The country; in his opinion, was in a transitional stage. It was passing from semi-feudal and patriarchal conditions into a commercial order, from laws of customs to the rule of competition. It was going to enter a stage of capitalist economy having freedom of contract and growing activity of commerce and manufactures. In fact, Ranade believed that unless the Indian economy followed the capitalist road of development her fundamental economic problem would not be solved.[2]

In the agricultural sector, for instance, he argued that the institution of private property would help to solve the problem of poverty without disrupting the established relations in a major way. In this context, he cited the progress achieved by French, German and Russian agriculture in the nineteenth century due to the establishment of peasant proprietorship.[3] The magic of property and free institutions were responsible for the wonderful change in French agriculture. The Prussian state encouraged the growth of absolute property both in the landlord class and in the peasantry. It removed the hurdles which prevented the individual from

---

[2] *EIE*, pp. 66, 325 (see *Abbreviations Used in References* at the end of article). See also N.V. Sovani, 'Ranade's Model of the Indian Economy,' *Artha Vidhyena*, Vol. 4 (1962), pp. 12–13; V.S. Minocha, 'Ranade on the Agrarian Problem,' *Indian Economic and Social History Review*, Vol. 2 (Oct. 1965), p. 359; and Tucker, *op. cit.*, p. 147.

[3] *EIE*, pp. 254–56, 276. See also Tucker, *op. cit.*, pp. 147–48.

attaining the degree of well-being which he was able to achieve by his own efforts and capacity. In Russia, the emancipation of the serfs had led to material and commercial prosperity. Ranade wanted similar principles to be followed while enacting the laws regulating land relations in India. Indian agriculture (on which the national prosperity depended) was controlled by the 'thriftless and poverty-stricken peasantry'. 'One found a dead level of small farmers all over the land.'[4] In place of the existing type of land relations, Ranade wanted a mixed constitution where there would be two classes, the petty peasantry having full proprietary rights and the class of capitalist farmers and landlords enjoying complete owner-ship of huge lands. Ranade thought that agriculture in India needed 'the leading and the light of propertied men'. Therefore, he defended the rights of the landlords of Bengal which were being limited by the Bengal Tenancy Bill of 1883, though he also wanted to confer full proprietary rights on the ryots. He believed that, according to the law of providence, the property in land or other goods must pass from the hands of ignorant, improvident and poor persons to the class having intelligence, foresight and the habit of abstinence. Comparing the Brahmans and the Banias with the 'military and cultivating classes,' Ranade predicted that property would go into the hands of the former because of their superior habits and education.[5]

In fact, an average Indian was the very negation of the economic man. His position in life was determined by his family and caste. Self-interest was not the principal motivation of the majority of the people. They lacked any desire for free competition. The strong belief in the concepts of *karma* and fate defeated the spirit and capacity of enterprise among them. Therefore, both capital and labour were immobile and unenter-prising.[6] In such conditions of backward economy, Ranade knew that capitalism would not develop and deliver the goods without aid and encouragement from the state. He realised that the economic conditions of India were so different from those of England that the theories of economics (such as the *laissez-faire* doctrine) which originated in England would not be useful to solve Indian economic problems. After all, no principle of economic science holds good universally and for all stages of civilisation. He distinguished between political economy as a hypothetical, *a priori* science and applied political economy. He pointed out that economic theories applicable to the peculiar conditions of backward societies like India were altogether different from those developed in England. He found that the conditions in the Indian economy were in

---

[4] *EIE*, pp. 284–87. See also Bipan Chandra, *The Rise and Growth of Economic Nationalism in India* (New Delhi: Peoples Publishing House, 1966), pp. 286–88 and 489–90.

[5] *EIE*, p. 326.

[6] *EIE*, pp. 9–10, 43 and 89. See also B.N. Ganguli, *Indian Economic Thought: Nineteenth Century Perspectives* (New Delhi: Tata Mcgraw-Hill Publishing Co Ltd, 1977).

many respects similar to those in Germany, Italy, France and America and hence the study of continental economy had more practical bearing for Indians than the textbooks of English political economy. The state in these countries was increasingly recognised as the 'national organ' for taking care of the 'national need' in all the fields in which individual efforts were not likely to be effective and economic. Theorists of this trend from Germany, France, Italy and America influenced Ranade's views on intervention by the state in backward countries. In England, J.S. Mill represented a similar viewpoint. Ranade fully concurred with Mill when he advocated state aid to encourage and nurture the spirit of individual effort and the state's guidance and direction to voluntary enterprise as far as possible in the form of education so as to alleviate the helplessness of individuals.[7]

The state in India had already enlarged its functions to include the working of iron and coal mines, and support to cotton, tobacco, tea and coffee plantations and railway companies. But these attempts, according to Ranade, were not sufficient compared to the needs of the economy.[8] The Indian economy required aid and encouragement from the enlightened state not only in liberal and technical education, railway and canal communications, or post and telegraphs but also in pioneering new enterprises and industries. The state could encourage the growth of new industries by subsidising such industries in their initial stage or starting such industries under the aegis of the state itself. The state could also regulate the cooperative efforts, help to form deposit and finance banks and provide loans at low interest to the industries. He agreed that finding capital for industries was not the function of the state according to the classical economic theory. But, at the same time, he indicated that the government was already providing capital for railways, canals or tea and coffee plantations. Secondly, cheap capital was an important need of India's economy. The savings of the people were very negligible and these savings were invested either in government stock or post office accounts. The people had not developed the skill of forming joint stock companies. Owing to these conditions, the capital available for investment at low interest had become 'national want' which could not be adequately met by private efforts. In this connection, Ranade found the experiment made by the Netherlands government (to improve the economic condition of its colony of Java through supplementing private efforts both in agriculture and industry) worth imitating.[9] The colonial rulers of India, Ranade felt, should follow this pattern and discard the non-interventionist policy.

Non-intervention should be discarded in foreign trade as well because the industries of the backward economy of India were not able to stand

[7] *EIE*, pp. 89–90.
[8] *EIE*, pp. 165–79, 189–93.
[9] *EIE*, pp. 91–92.

the competition of British industries. Here, again, Ranade cited examples of France and Germany where the state did not follow the orthodox English doctrine of free trade. The upcoming and new industries of India, according to Ranade, required a protection from the state in the form of differential tariffs on the lines of these countries. But at the same time he realised that it was futile to expect colonial rule to go in for the protection of industries in its colony.[10]

In this manner, Ranade provided a kind of rationalisation to the early phase of Indian capitalism. Though he belonged to the new middle class which was a product of the Western educational system and not of economic changes, he could be looked upon as an ideological spokesman of capitalism. He sincerely believed in state-supported capitalism as a solution to India's economic problems. Ranade was theorising in the early phase of Indian capitalism. Therefore, his ideas on economic liberalism could be seen as having 'scientific character' rather than ideological colour on the lines of Adam Smith's and Ricardo's ideas in the early capitalist phase of Europe.

Ranade advocated state action, not only for supplementing and supporting private enterprise or protecting indigenous industry from foreign competition but also for protecting the weaker sections of the society. He upheld the attempts to protect the poor tenants by ensuring fixity of tenure and the fixing of rent because he thought that agricultural workers and tenants were unable to organise effectively for their own protection. Similarly, he supported the fixing of rates of interest for loans taken by the unorganised, indebted peasants from money-lenders. He held that when the parties were not equally matched in intelligence and resources, the freedom-of-contract theory cannot claim to be upholding equality and freedom. 'The distribution of produce among the needy many and the powerful few has to be arranged in a spirit of equity and fair play.'[11] These views appeared in Ranade's celebrated essay entitled 'Indian Political Economy' which was one of his last essays on economic problems (written during the years 1891 to 1893). It seems that by this time he had come to accept the idea that the state had to intervene to protect the interests of the weaker groups of the society within the framework of capitalism.

On similar lines, he advocated state action to implement social reforms especially about the marriage and family system of high caste Hindus. He refuted objections to legal intervention in regulating the age of marriage and argued that even though widows and children do not complain about the injustices they suffer, the state should come forward to redress them effectively.[12] According to him, the state should intervene to minimise

---

[10] *EIE*, pp. 24–25, and 189. See also *VV*, pp. 19–63.
[11] *EIE*, p. 31. See also *VV*, pp. 57–58.
[12] *MW*, pp. 103, 137, 172–73, 192.

social evils if individuals or groups cannot check them adequately, speedily or effectively. He, however, saw the limits of state action for social reforms. Social reforms, he maintained, are valuable if they become the 'work of the people,' and not merely an 'act of the state'. The people must work for themselves to reform their social institutions. 'The agencies from outside' (such as the state) are not a substitute for individual efforts. The inner self of the individual, his thoughts and ideas determine his outward actions. The inner selves of the individuals have to be changed if real reform is desired. A change in outward forms and institutions alone will not bring out real reforms. Nothing great or good can be achieved unless the conscience is stirred up; outside agencies can only touch the surface.

III
Freedom and Equality

Ranade's views on the limits of state action are embedded in his theory of individual freedom, which, in turn, is based on his theistic metaphysics. He maintained that our notions of the individual and social well-being depend upon the answers we give to the questions: What is ultimate reality? What is the relation between man and the Infinite? According to him, the problem of existence determines the problems of morals, legislation and government.[13]

Ranade's mataphysical position was influenced by the theistic philosophy of A.C. Fraser. Fraser's lectures on theism in 1894–95 at the University of Edinburgh were interpreted from an Indian perspective by Ranade in a talk on Indian theism in 1896.[14] His views were also influenced by Joseph Butler's ideas. Butler's 'The Analogy of Religion' was one of the text-books on moral philosophy in the University of Bombay in Ranade's student days. He reviewed Butler's *Method of Ethics* in 1892, justifying his ideas on religion and morality.[15] Though Ranade was influenced by European theistic ideas, his metaphysics was deeply rooted in Hindu tradition. It goes as far back as the Upanishadic doctrines on the nature of the Infinite to locate the roots of theism. In Ramanuja's *visistadvaita* (modified non-dualism), he finds the beginnings of a higher concept of theism.[16] The Vaishnava sects (which believed in *visistadvaita*) also furnished instances of Indian theistic doctrines to Ranade. The Bhagwat

[13] *RSR*, p. 5.
[14] See A.C. Fraser, *Philosophy of Theism*, Being the Gifford Lectures, University of Edinburgh in 1894–95 (Edinburgh: William Black Wood and Sons, 1895).
[15] For Butler's influence on Ranade, see Mathew Lederle, *Philosophical Trends in Modern Maharashtra* (Bombay: Popular Prakashan, 1976), p. 93.
[16] For details about Ramanuja's philosophy see P. Nagaraja Rao, *Fundamentals of Indian Philosophy* (New Delhi: India Book Company, 1976), pp. 133–46. For Ramanuja's impact on Ranade see *RSR*, pp. 6 and 12.

Dharma, which was an offshoot of Ramanuja's Bhakti Yoga, provided him with a system of Indian theism. Ranade's article on 'Hindu Protestantism' was an attempt to interpret the Bhakti movement of Maharashtra in the light of the doctrine of theism which he had adopted. The movement of religious reform under the banner of the Prarthana Samaj was interpreted by Ranade as a continuation of the theistic movement of the saints.

In the light of the doctrine of theism, Ranade argues that one should not exaggerate any one of the three postulates of existence—(*i*) the 'I' or ego, (*ii*) the non-I or non-ego, and (*iii*) existence of the Infinite. He rejects mysticism because it exaggerates the first postulate—the ego or powers of man. He criticises the materialism of Europe and that of Sankhya and the atomistic system of India on the ground that they over-emphasise the second postulate of existence—the non-ego or material forces. Similarly, he also rejects German idealism as well as the *advaita* philosophy of Sankara because they believe that the supreme spirit, the third postulate, alone exists. At the same time, Ranade does not accept the agnostic view that the problems of existence and ultimate reality are insoluble because of want of logical proof. On the contrary, he believes that it is sufficient to have strong moral convictions about these matters of existence.

In this manner Ranade rejects mysticism, materialism, idealism and agnosticism and follows the framework developed by European and Indian theism.[17] The three-fold postulates of existence (according to Ranade's theistic argument) are distinct and at the same time harmonised together. They are not like disjointed parts of a mechanical whole. They are one, and at the same time many. Nature and man have definite relations of subordination to the Infinite. The Infinite rules over them and harmonises them. God is immanent in everything in the universe. God's immanence in nature is seen in the order and the purpose which animates nature. God is the cause of all natural changes. In this way, nature is supernatural in character. Similarly, man has also a super-human element in him and that element distinguishes him from other animals. The distinguishing feature of man is his self-conscious reason and his free will which makes him responsible for his actions. Free will is not present in brutes. Man has, on the other hand, a delegated freedom to choose between right and wrong, and good and evil. Man's relations with God are manifested by this sense of conscience in him. The spirit immanent in the universe manifests his presence in man through this faculty of conscience. Conscience is man's human nature in its fully developed stage and is the divine voice in man's heart.

This distinguishing nature of man provides bases for all law, government, morals, manners, social and family relations, literary and scientific

[17] *MW*, pp. 68, 116, 193–94. See also *RSR*, pp. 21, 103, 259, 265–68 and 278.

culture as well as religion and worship. According to Ranade, the freedom of conscience is the real freedom and the rights of conscience are paramount over all other considerations of mere political and social expediency. Man should not submit himself to any outward force or the authority of customs, religious scriptures, usages, traditions or great personalities but should submit to the voice of his inner conscience. Men must rise to the dignity of self-control by making their conscience and their reason the supreme guide of their conduct. Men are the children of God. It is the voice of God which men are bound to listen to. Ranade points out that because of neglect and dependence on outside help, men have benumbed their faculty of conscience within them. In place of this kind of dependence and helplessness, individuals should nurture a true freedom based upon conscience. Ranade agrees that we should have regard for wise men and great personalities but this regard for them should not come between us and God—'the Divine principle enthroned in the heart of every one of us.' We must cultivate a sense of self-respect or rather respect for God in us. It is true that human authority, prophets and revelations should be respected but, again, the reverence for them should not come in the way of 'the dictates of conscience' or 'Divine Command' in us. The same is true about the customs and conventions of society. Ranade observes that under the influence of customs and traditions, men usually do injustice to 'human nature' and to the sense of right and wrong and thereby limit the development of their higher life.

But the freedom of man is not unlimited. Delegated freedom is to be properly exercised. Man is responsible to exercise his freedom, with a deep sense of duty. His conscience comes to his help in this context. The faculty of conscience accuses him when he goes wrong and gives him satisfaction when he performs his duty. This kind of feeling is the connecting link between man's soul and God. Ranade seeks a change from a society based on the constraints of custom to a society based on freedom. But this freedom is the freedom of the individual's higher powers and not of his weaker nature. The freedom of higher powers implies a deep sense of duty and responsibility. Therefore, men must seek and realise the dignity of self-control instead of outside control. The freedom of action is a great force but Ranade thinks that this freedom is limited by the fact that it should not encroach upon the equal freedom of others or harm the social morality.

Man's freedom is also restrained greatly by his family background, early education and the environment in which he is brought up. The duties and limits of action are fixed for most of the people by the circumstances over which they have no control. But Ranade thinks that there is still a large margin left for freedom of action. This margin should be used in a responsible manner without doing any harm to morality.

This means that the freedom of action is to be used in such a way that it in no way imposes restraints on the equally free rights of other people in the society. Ranade has followed the theistic doctrine while arguing that all men and women are equally the children of God. In God's sight all men occupy only one level. God is the common father and, therefore, all men are brothers. The common divine element which is present in all men provides, according to Ranade's theism, a basis of union and a common bond of love and help.

His criticism of the caste system and justification of Bhagwat Dharma or the Bhakti movement is based on his belief in these doctrines. According to him, the saints asserted the dignity of the human soul quite independently of the accidents of birth and social rank. They elevated the conception of man's spiritual nature and tried to lessen the degree of caste intolerance. They rejected the idea that the Brahmans are the creations of God and that other castes should serve and worship them. In spite of their low origin, the low castes were free to attain salvation through faith and love. He preferred the Bhagwat Dharma or Bhakti Marg to the Yogamarg and Jnana-marg because the latter two systems do not allow any rights to Sudras. The Jnana-marg is meant for a selected few while the Yogamarg is difficult for ordinary men.[18] Compared to these two, the Bhagwat Dharma is simpler and is open to all castes. The members of the Mahar, barber, cobbler, butcher and other low castes could become saints. In this way, the movement of the saints raised the Sudra classes to a higher spiritual and social status almost equal to that of the Brahmans.

Ranade has thrown light on this particular aspect of the movement of the saints because he was of the opinion that the caste factor is the main blot on the Indian social system. The caste system had developed discriminations and distances in social life (e.g., in matters of food and marriage) and had fostered a feeling of pride in belonging to the smallest community. In place of such a tendency of isolation and exclusiveness, Ranade wanted Indians to cultivate 'the spirit of fraternity or elastic expansiveness' and to recognise the essential equality between man and man.

Ranade has also emphasised the equality between man and woman. He surveyed the history of female rights in India and pointed out that in the ancient period, especially during Vedic times, women used to take an equal part in religious rites and the deliberations of the state. The Aryan institution of marriage recognised female liberty and the dignity of womanhood. Among the Ksatriyas, a woman was free to choose her husband through the Swayamvara form of marriage; and, among Brahmans, women devoted to study and contemplation were free to remain unmarried without losing any of their importance.[19] In the Middle Ages, these Vedic institutions were abandoned. New usages, which developed

[18] For his views on equality, see *DV*, pp. 8–10, 25. See also *MW*, pp. 170, 193, 236, and *RSK*, pp. 270–74.

[19] For Ranade's views on equality between man and woman see *RSR*, pp. 29–30. See also *MW*, pp. 72–75.

during this period, limited female liberty and lowered the dignity of woman in the society. Ranade argued that the status and dignity of women should be reestablished by reforming the marriage and family system and by allowing them to avail of the benefits of education.

Thus Ranade felt that Indian society should undergo a transformation so that the liberty of the individual is enlarged, social equality is established and the status of women is improved.

IV
Organic Conception of Society

The transformation was to be brought about in all spheres of the society. Ranade believed that society is an organism which develops as a whole and that its parts are interdependent. He followed the evolutionary thesis of Herbert Spencer, who had constructed an analogical connection between society and a biological organism while formulating his theory of social evolution. Ranade, like Spencer, held that there are several similarities between the society and a living organism or human body. The interdependence among the parts is the most significant of them. In the case of the human body, one cannot develop the chest without developing the other organs or one cannot starve oneself and desire to have good muscles and elastic nerves. Ranade observed that one cannot separate the fragrance from the beauty of the rose; if one does it one would destroy both. This interdependence is to be found in the society on exactly similar lines. In the case of the social organism, one cannot separate the various activities except for convenience and that too provisionally. It is not possible to make progress in one aspect and neglect the other aspects of society. The change in accordance with the values of liberalism was to be sought, therefore, in all the fields of society. 'You cannot be liberal by halves' was Ranade's dictum.[20] He argued that one cannot be liberal in politics and conservative in respect of religion or the social system. The heart and the head must go together.

Ranade emphasised the need for social and religious reform while the extremist nationalist school emphasised political reform. Ranade's writings in this context were mainly addressed to the followers of this school whose philosopher was Lokmanya Tilak (1856–1920). But at the same time, it must be mentioned that Ranade nowhere gave priority to social reform. He believed in the mutual natural dependence of the social, political and economic spheres of society. Nowhere did he condemn the political aspirations of the people. He thought that politics represented an important department of human activity and that without the rights and duties of citizenship no one would feel the full dignity of human

[20] N.R. Phatak, *Nyayamurti Mahadeo Govind Ranade Yanche Charitra* (Biography of Ranade in Marathi) (Bombay: Phatak N.R., 1924), p. 531.

existence. The Indian National Congress (which strove for political reform) and the Social Conference (which strove for social reform) were regarded by Ranade as two sisters who should go hand-in-hand if they wanted to make real progress. Ranade insisted that people cannot have good social institutions when they do not enjoy political liberties. They are not fit to exercise their political rights unless their social institutions are based on reason and justice. Similarly, if their social system is imperfect they are unable to achieve real economic progress. If their religious institutions are degenerate, they cannot succeed in the social, political and economic fields. No question is purely political or economic. It is a mistake to suppose that there are separate departments in the composite nature of humanity. Therefore, liberation was to be sought not in one sort of activity or one sphere of social action but in all aspects of social life. There was, in Ranade's opinion, a need for developing the whole social being and renovating the whole human existence.[21] Unless Indians reform their social institutions like the family, it was, according to Ranade, hopeless to fight for political freedom. Even if people succeeded in achieving political freedom it would be impossible to preserve it without establishing the liberty of the individual in the social sphere and extending equal rights to women in society; the social and political spheres of the society are dependent on each other and they change simultaneously.

The transformation of the society as a whole was to be achieved gradually and slowly. This belief in gradualness was a second important feature of Ranade's liberalism. Here, too, he agreed with Spencer's analysis of social evolution, according to which growth is always structural, organic and slow. Ranade maintained that change towards the liberal society and polity was to be achieved step-by-step over a long period of time. The process of social growth is always slow and it would be so if you want real and sure growth. Some people desire to shorten the period of change but Ranade argued that this kind of temptation should be resisted by social and political reforms. He rejected the method of rebellion and preferred the moderate method of attempting each day to take the next step in 'the order of natural growth' and doing the work which lies nearest to the hand of the reformer in a spirit of compromise and fairness.[22] The moderate methods included legislation, executive action, public preaching, popular enlightenment and enforcing reforms by means of penalties by the state. But the last one (namely, the coercive method) was to be used only after the other methods were tried. In fact, Ranade believed that appealing to the conscience of the people, to their sense of right and wrong, sinful and virtuous, was the best method of reform.

[21] For Spencer's influence on Ranade's organic conception of society, see *MW*, pp. 113, 123–25, 230–32; and *RSR*, pp. 149–52.

[22] See *MW*, pp. 90, 117–18, 191; and Phatak, *op. cit.*, p. 587.

Ranade also favoured what he called the 'method of tradition'.[23] By this he meant the method of basing reforms on the old Hindu religious texts and tradition. He believed that a reformer does not write on a clean slate. His task is to complete the half-written sentence. The reformers of the nineteenth century were only carrying out the work left unfinished by the earlier generations. Ranade was proud of the rich inheritance of Indian society and never entertained the idea of breaking from the past. He thought that he and his generation of reformers were parts of one continuous stream of life. He agreed that the Hindu community was conservative but pointed out that conservatism was its real strength. He thought that a nation which changes its way of life and social institutions all too easily does not find a lasting place in the history of mankind. Though the Indian nation is conservative, it has absorbed new ideas and practices gradually. Ranade wanted to see a similar kind of slow change in the traditional Indian social institutions in the light of the new liberal principles of the nineteenth century. He pointed out that Indian society had changed in history without the shock of revolution or sudden conversion. The old order of society had changed over a period of time with the slow process of assimilation of new ideas. He favoured such a gradual transformation on the basis of the liberal values of liberty and equality.

He justified the method of tradition on the ground that it would not make the orthodox sections of society more reactionary. By basing new reforms on ancient religious texts or tradition, the reformers can present the changes as palatable to the conservative sections of the Hindu community. It must also be noted that Ranade was himself a strong believer in tradition and always tried to establish a link between contemporary liberal reforms and the ancient tradition of the Hindu community. As seen earlier, he attempted to present the Indian variant of theism by linking the Prarthana Samaj to the movement of the saints and to Ramanuja's philosophy. Similarly, he advocated equality between the sexes and reforms in the marriage system by reminding the Hindus that their women-folk used to enjoy equal status in Vedic times. He claimed that he was not imitating any foreign model but was attempting to restore the freedom and dignity of the ancient period. His justification of the new social reforms on the basis of ancient tradition cannot be interpreted as mere revivalism. There is no simple revivalism in social evolution. The dead past cannot be revived except by reforming the 'old materials into new organised being'. Accordingly, Ranade thought that a reformation of India's inherited tradition was the task for Indian liberals.

Ranade felt that Indians were not yet ready for full-fledged representative institutions. He was, therefore, very cautious about introducing representation even at the local government level. He felt that the Indians

[23] *MW*, pp. 90, 111–13, 118, 125–27, 132, 158.

should acquire enough experience before making experiments in representative government. The Indian nation, he maintained, was going through a period of political apprenticeship and unless the people received sufficient training in administration and representation, even partial self-rule would be unwise and worthless. He, therefore, advocated gradual progress towards representative and responsible government in India.

V

The Role of the Elite

The third and probably the most important feature of Ranade's liberalism was its elitism. He thought that only the elites were capable of providing direction and control over the complex process of India's transition from feudalism to liberalism. He believed that in all backward countries like India '. . . there is always only a minority of people who monopolise all the elements of strength. They are socially and religiously in the front ranks, they possess intelligence, wealth, thrifty habits, knowledge and power of combination . . . .'[24] Such a minority, because of its exceptional qualities, can play an influential part in all the spheres of society. Ranade's elite group was composed of Brahmans, Banias, zamindars and the educated middle class. These sections of the contemporary Indian society possessed qualities like intelligence, wealth, unity and initiative while the masses were 'unlettered, improvident, ignorant, disunited, thriftless and poor in means.' The masses, on their own, were not capable of understanding the significance of the principles of liberalism or of participating in the liberal movement.

Ranade held that 'power must gravitate where there is intelligence and wealth'. His scheme of introducing representation to Indians from the local to the provincial level contained provisions for giving political power to the rich and educated classes. At the municipal level, the elected seats were to be divided in the ratio of two to one between the property-holders and the 'intelligent class'. To the District Committee, one representative was to be elected from every taluka by those who pay Rs 100 as tax. Due representation was also to be given to the inamdars as they were an intelligent and influential class. Moreover, they were the natural leaders of their local communities. The educated class represented the intelligence of the district and it 'had special aptitude and an anxious desire to make a proper and intelligent use of the right of election'.[25] This class, according to Ranade, was to get two seats in the District Committee. At the provincial level, the non-official members were to be elected not

[24] M.G. Ranade, 'The Agrarian Problem and its Solution,' *Quarterly Journal of Poona Sarvajanik Sabha*, Vol. 2, No. 1 (1879–80), p. 18.

[25] See M.G. Ranade, 'Administrative Reforms in the Bombay Presidency,' *Quarterly Journal of the Poona Sarvajanik Sabha*, Vol. 4 (April 1882), pp. 1–56.

by the people directly but by the members of the Municipal and the District Committees. Such a body, Ranade admitted, would be 'far from democratic in its character and results,' but would nevertheless provide adequate representation to the people. The masses, he believed, were yet incapable of electing worthy men as their representatives. He held that full-fledged democracy could not be suddenly transplanted into Indian soil;[26] it required training and education for generations to come.

Ranade's views on representation indicate that he had assigned an important political role to the educated class. He thought that the educated classes were 'the brains and the destined leaders of the people'. Against the conservative forces which were at work in India, the educated minority 'represented the soul of Indian liberalism'. He thought that the educated class was unconsciously supported by the masses. In one of his essays, he described the special duties of young educated men towards their country and people.[27] Those who had taken higher education, and had achieved competence equal to those of the Englishmen, should be given equal opportunity in the civil service. He suggested that one-third to one-fourth of the appointments should be reserved for educated Indians.[28]

As Ranade believed that the educated class was to be the agent of change, he expressed his deep concern over the status of higher education. Defending state support for higher education, he argued that those who take advantage of it come from the middle or 'rather the hereditary literacy and mercantile classes' who are supposed to lead the work of regeneration in this country. Unless new ideas were communicated to them through higher education, the country could not hope for great progress. It was, therefore, in the interest of the state itself to provide sound and useful education to the 'elite of the rising generation'. Besides, the majority of students in high schools and colleges belonged to the poor middle classes who needed the help of the government.[29] The masses, on the other hand, were extremely poor and did not care for education. They wanted food and employment and not education.

Those who aspired for higher education and for positions in the civil service and in the legislative councils came predominantly from the Brahman caste.[30] Ranade wanted the Brahmans to play a leading role in the contemporary efforts for the all-round progress of the country. He pointed out that it had been the Brahman's privilege to be poor and ambitious. This privilege had helped the society before and must be cherished now. In his address to the Industrial Conference, Ranade

[26] M.G. Ranade, 'The Agrarian Problem and its Solution,' p. 19.

[27] Phatak, *op. cit.*, p. 63.

[28] G.N. Singh, *Landmarks in Indian Constitutional and National Development*, Vol. 1, 1600–1919 (Delhi: Atmaram and Sons, 1950), p. 50.

[29] See *MW*, pp. 266–74 and 277–93.

[30] *MW*, pp. 304–14.

explained the necessity of the industrialisation of the Indian economy and said, 'I can only appeal to the fact that it has been the Brahman's hereditary privilege to formulate the Nation's wants and suggest remedies.'[31]

Along with the Brahmans and the other educated middle class, Ranade included the zamindars and the *vatandars* in his category of elite. In his scheme of extending self-rule in India, he wanted special representation to be given to this class. He maintained that the vatani zamindars played a beneficial role.[32] In his essay, 'Chiefs of Indian States in Maharashtra,' he pointed out that the rich *vatandars* of Maharashtra spent their time lazily and their money in conspicuous consumption. They did not utilise the opportunity of learning from the government teachers specially appointed for their education. The zamindars of Bengal, on the contrary, took to higher education, went abroad and rubbed shoulders with the Englishmen and served their people.[33] Ranade exhorted the rich classes of Maharashtra to go to the cities like Bombay where they would receive a good education and come to know how the outside world was progressing. They would thereby be able to face the challenge of the new era and assume the leading role which they had been playing traditionally. Ranade also believed that agriculture, which was the principal and dominant sector of the Indian economy, needed 'the leading and the light of propertied men' for its development.

Ranade's justification of the aristocratic classes was similar to the conservatism of Edmund Burke, while his elitism was comparable to that of J.S. Mill. Mill had said that it was the privilege of the intellectual elite to see the 'futurity of the species'. Their knowledge was, according to him, the key to progress. The well-educated men were the wisest and best men and should, therefore, be elected to office at all levels. Mill sought to reconcile democracy and rule by the educated elite. He sought to undermine the influence of landed interests on politics. He considered aristocracy as the sole cause of bad government in England.[34] In India, Ranade recognised that the landlords were the natural and traditional leaders of the people and that their importance should not be undermined. He tried to combine the interests of his own educated class with those of the aristocratic class. He suggested that some posts in the civil service should be reserved for the members of the aristocratic families of sardars.[35]

[31] *EIE*, p. 194.
[32] Phatak, *op. cit.*, p. 245.
[33] *Ibid.*, pp. 63–65.
[34] Joseph Hamburger, *Intellectuals in Politics: John Stuart Mill and Philosophical Radicals* (New Haven: Yale University Press, 1966), pp. 63 and 86. See also Carole Pateman, *Participation and Democratic Theory* (Cambridge: Cambridge University Press, 1970), p. 31.
[35] Tucker, *op. cit.*, pp. 163–64.

With some variations of detail and emphasis, Ranade's ideas were shared by the other Indian liberals, namely, Gokhale, Mehta, Banerji and Naoroji. They all advocated the reform of Indian social institutions along liberal lines, economic development through industrialisation, and the extension of liberal-representative political institutions. The transition to liberal society and polity was to be brought about in all the spheres of society under the leadership of the elite by using moderate methods.

VI
Mahatma Phule

A liberal thinker who did not belong to the Ranade school or believe in Ranade's framework was Mahatma Phule (1827–90). He came from a low caste, mali (gardener) family and was educated in a Mission school.[36] The strategy of the capitalist path of development and the high caste politics of the Ranade school could not appeal to him. He opposed the elitism of the Ranade school and put forward an alternative liberal framework for the liberation of the sudras and atisudras, i.e., the low and downtrodden castes.

In his philosophical outlook, Phule was influenced by the revolutionary liberalism of Thomas Paine. Phule's book, *Sarvajanik Satyadharma Pustak*, restated the liberal principles contained in Paine's *Rights of Man*. Phule stated that all men and women are born free and equally capable of enjoying rights. The creator has made men and omen possessed of equal human rights and no man or group of men : ould suppress other men. The creator has bestowed upon all men and women equal religious and political liberties. They should, therefore, have equality before law and equality of opportunity for entry into the civil service or municipal administration.[37]

When Phule looked at the position of the sudras and atisudras in the light of these principles of liberalism, he found that these social groups were slaves for generations. They were deprived of human liberty. This slavery was sustained by Brahmanical rules. The Brahmans, according to Phule, cunningly devised mythologies, established an intolerable caste system and formulated cruel and inhuman laws. He exposed the falsehood and selfish motives behind the Hindu mythology and the cunningness of the codes of conduct propagated by the Brahmans in their own interest. For centuries the masses were kept in chains. The sudras and atisudras, according to Phule, experienced greater hardships and oppression than the slaves in America.

[36] For a biography, see Dhananjay Keer, *Mahatma Jotirao Phule* (Bombay: Popular Prakashan, 1964).

[37] For Phule's principles of liberalism and his criticism of Brahman domination, see Dananjay Keer and S.G. Malshe, eds., *Mahatma Phule Samagra Vangmaya* (Bombay: Maharashtra Rajya Sahitya and Sanskriti Mandal, 1969).

Phule observed that what little improvement had occurred in the contemporary position of the masses was due to British rule. While Ranade wanted larger state support to higher education, Phule blamed the British government for diverting large funds to higher education at the cost of the education of the masses. Phule argued that it was an injustice to neglect the education of the masses as a greater portion of the revenue came from the peasantry. He wanted to re-orient the whole educational system for the upliftment of the masses. He realised that, due to their education, the Brahmans were able to capture the administration from the top to the bottom. He suggested that the Brahmans should be appointed in government services in proportion of their number and that due share should be given to the other castes. The sudras should be educated to qualify themselves for positions in government.

Phule criticised the various organisations established by the liberals of the Ranade school. The Prarthana Samaj, he said, was used by the Brahmans to confuse the sudras and atisudras. He pointed out that though the 'Sarvajanik Sabha' was claimed to be a public organisation, it was, in fact, monopolised by the Brahmans; he did not find in it any Kunbi, Mali, Dhangar, Koli or Bhil. The Sabha demanded more seats for the Hindus but the word Hindu was misleading because only Brahmans reaped the advantage. The same was true of the Indian National Congress. He hoped that no sudra would join the Congress because the Brahmans would deceive the sudras at any moment. He exhorted the lower castes to acquire education and political unity.

While Ranade was proud of the Hindu tradition, Phule wanted to break with it. He criticised Hindu religion, its mythology and sacred books like the *Smritis* and the *Vedas*. He maintained that the history of Hinduism was the history of Brahman domination over the sudras. The Protestant Hindu saints, whose role Ranade had eulogised, were also criticised by Phule for their limited pro-Brahman vision. He wanted to substitute Hinduism with 'Sarvajanik Ishwar Pranit Satya'.

British rule, Phule believed, was meant by the Creator to rescue the sudras from slavery. Owing to English education, true knowledge was being imparted to the ignorant sudras and thereby they were becoming conscious of their rights and had begun to think of complete freedom from the cruel system of slavery. Phule wanted the sudras to exploit the golden opportunity given by British rule to get themselves emancipated from Brahman domination.

Phule's views on the economy were also different from those of Ranade. The former's views were guided by concerns for the peasants and the masses. He thought that they were being exploited by the Brahman elite and feudal rulers. He concentrated on the problems of agriculture while the elitist liberals had favoured industrialisation.[38] In this way, Phule's liberalism was radical, while that of the Ranade school was moderate and elitist.

Abbreviations Used in References

RSR   M.B. Kolaskar, ed., *Religious and Social Reform, A Collection of Essays and Speeches by Mahadeva Govind Ranade* (Bombay: Gopal Narayan and Co., 1902).

MW   *Miscellaneous Writings of the Late Hon'ble Mr. Justice M.G. Ranade* (Bombay: The Manoranjan Press, 1915).

EIE   *Essays on Indian Economics* (Madras: Natesan, 1906), 2nd edition.

DV   *Dharmapar Vyakhyanen* (Religious Discourses by Ranade) (Bombay: Nirnayasagar Press, 1902).

VV   N.V. Sovani, ed., *Vyaparasam bandhi Vyakhyanen* (Lectures on Trade and Commerce by Ranade) (Poona: Gokhale Institute of Politics and Economics, 1963).

---

[38] Gail Omvedt, *Cultural Revolt in a Colonial Society: The Non-Brahman Movement in Western India: 1873 to 1930* (Bombay: Scientific Socialist Education Trust, 1976), p. 118.

7

N.R. INAMDAR

The Political Ideas of Lokmanya Tilak

Tilak's political ideas were formulated during his political career as a national leader of India's freedom movement during 1885–1920. So, to understand the character of his political thought it is necessary to briefly review his political career and to trace the influences upon it.

Bal Gangadhar Tilak, popularly called *Lokmanya* (respected by the people), was born in a middle class Chitpavan Brahman family in Ratnagiri district on 23 July 1856 (a year before the sepoy mutiny or the war of independence). From his teacher-father he inherited his love for Sanskrit, which gave him a deep respect for the ancient religion and traditions of the country and its people. As the Maratha rule was the last viable native regime in India to be extinguished by the British, he was roused to thinking about India's national independence. He resolved to devote his life to the cause of education, which he felt was the best way of serving the people. After graduating from Deccan College, Poona, in 1876, he, along with some co-patriots, started his public career by launching New English School, Poona, an English-language weekly, *Mahratta*, and a Marathi weekly, *Kesari*. His editorship of these journals made Tilak deeply involved in the social and political affairs of Maharashtra and Western India. In *Kesari*, he developed his unique style of communicating ideas, which was both forceful and homely, and full of allusions to Sanskrit, regional lore and history.

During the nineties, Tilak participated actively in the annual conferences of the Indian National Congress. At the 1891 annual conference, he moved the resolution on the Arms Act, which demanded changes in the gun prohibition regulations and called for more Indian participation in the military. He was regarded as the most dashing and popular leader in Maharashtra politics. His first significant political move was to relegate the issue of social reform to the background in favour of political reform for which he led agitations against the British rulers. In order to make the Congress concentrate on political reforms (rather than on social reforms), in 1895, he succeeded in separating the annual meetings of the Social Conference and the Indian National Congress, which used to meet consecutively at the same venue and with several common delegates. Tilak used his journals to both learn from the masses and educate and mobilise them for public action against the negligent, unresponsive or exploitative nature of British rule. Among the issues that were singled out by Tilak were Commissioner Crawford's corrupt administration, the iniquitous system of land revenue, the British policy of divide and rule and the

British partisanship towards the Muslims. In 1895, Tilak wrested control of the Sarvajanik Sabha (All People's Conference) from the moderates led by Gokhale and Ranade and used it to organise agitations by the middle classes, artisans and peasants. The political situation was aggravated by the famines of 1896–97 and the 1897 plague in Poona. During this period, Tilak (who was then an elected member of the Bombay Legislative Council) campaigned against the collection of land tax. Largely as a result of Tilak's efforts, the Ganapati and Shivaji festivals were revived and celebrated on a large scale to mobilise the people. These festivals, Tilak maintained, helped to generate a sense of pride in Indian traditions as well as to promote inter-caste unity among the people.

Failing to implicate Tilak in the murders of two British officers, Rand and Ayerst, the British government arrested him in July 1897 on the charge of causing disaffection among the people against the government through his writings in *Kesari* and through other public activities. He was sentenced by Justice Strachey to eighteen months' rigorous imprisonment. There was widespread popular resentment against this outrageous punishment given to Tilak on such flimsy grounds. He was hailed as a great national leader. The charge of sedition by the alien rulers was regarded as a badge of honour by the people. Commenting on Tilak's imprisonment, a British newspaper wrote: 'We feel confident that Justice Strachey's interpretation of the law would not be tolerated in England and if not speedily overruled may produce grave mischief in India.'

From 1898 to 1908, Tilak was at the peak of his political career as a national leader. He (along with Lala Lajpat Rai of Punjab and Bipin Chandra Pal of Bengal) constituted the national leadership triad, which was referred to as 'Lal, Bal, Pal'. Bal, (i.e., Bal Gangadhar Tilak) popularised a four-fold programme of action for the annulment of the partition of Bengal, namely, *swaraj* (self-government), *swadeshi* (resort to the use of Indian goods), *bahishkar* (boycott of foreign goods) and *rashtriya shikshan* (national education). In his whirlwind tour of the country, he came to be identified with his famous slogan, '*Swaraj* is my birthright and I will have it.' But Tilak's campaign to have the Congress resort to passive resistance led to the split of the Congress. Both he and his extremist followers broke away from the moderates. In the wake of the terrorist acts of the Bengal revolutionaries, Tilak was charged with sedition and convicted in July 1908 for a fine of Rs 1,000 and transportation for six years. This was the finest moment in the saga of Tilak's sacrifice. After hearing the jury's verdict, Tilak declared in the court:

All I wish to say is that in spite of the verdict of the jury, I maintain that I am innocent. There are higher powers that rule the destiny of things and it may be the will of Providence that the cause which I represent may prosper more by my suffering than by remaining free.

During his six years' captivity in the Mandalay prison, Tilak wrote *Gitarahasya*, a commentary on the *Bhagavad Gita*. In it he analysed the teachings of the *Gita*, comparing it with other Indian and Western schools of thought. He also exhorted the people to lead an activist, humanist life and to follow *karmayoga*, i.e., the way of work or the performance of duties in a spirit of selflessness. In 1914, when Britain declared war on Germany, the extremists (led by Tilak) closed ranks with the moderates. In 1916, he started a Home Rule League, along the lines of the Irish Home Rule Movement, in order to further the cause of India's self-rule. He also played a leading role in bringing about the 1916 Lucknow Pact between the Congress and the Muslim League.

In 1918–19, Tilak spent thirteen months in England contesting a court case against Valentine Chirol, a British Journalist, who had sought to defame him in his writings. Tilak used this opportunity to advance the cause of Indian self-rule. To that end, he established cordial contacts with the British Labour Party. He also gave evidence on behalf of the Indian Home Rule League before the Joint Select Committee of the Parliament on the Reforms Bill. He was denied a passport to visit France to lead a delegation to the Paris Peace Conference, but he sent a memorandum to its president, arguing that a self-governing India can be a fortress of liberty in Asia.

During Tilak's absence from India, Gandhi had emerged as the leader of the people, now seething with discontent against the Jallianwala Bagh massacre and the repressions in the Punjab. At the 1919 Amritsar Congress, Tilak was able to get a resolution adopted in favour of responsive cooperation with the government in regard to the new Reforms Act. He also supported Gandhi's non-cooperation movement to undermine the powers of the British bureaucracy. Tilak was also an early advocate of the *swadeshi* movement against Britain's economic domination. His death on 1 August 1920 closed an era in Indian national movement.

II
Swarajya

Tilak believed that Hindu philosophy was superior to other philosophies and religions. '[O]ur Gita religion,' he wrote, 'is a permanent, undauntable religion and the Blessed Lord has not felt the necessity for Hindus to rely on any other book, or religion.' According to Vedanta philosophy, reality is ultimately non-dualistic and man's final goal is to become one with the *Paramatman*, the Absolute Self. The *Bhagavad Gita* teaches that man can and must achieve this self-fulfilment through *karmayoga*, i.e., through a life dedicated to the performance of one's duties in this world, in a self-less or disinterested manner, for *loksamgraha* (well-being of all). This *karmayoga* ethic, Tilak asserted, is superior to materialistic or hedonistic ethics. The latter justifies a model of politics centred on the pursuit of self-interest. The former entails a conception of spiritualised politics.

Tilak divided hedonistic philosophers into three categories, viz., (*i*) the advocates of self-interest; (*ii*) the advocates of enlightened self-interest; and (*iii*) the proponents of the compatibility of self-interest with common interests. He had the least esteem for the first category, which included Charvaka, Jabali (of the *Ramayana*) and Kanikaniti (of the *Mahabharata*). In their view, spirit is the product of matter, into which the former is dissolved at the time of death. Accordingly, these philosophers maintained that one's own material pleasures ought to be the objective of one's morality. Tilak rejected such an ethical position, which, he pointed out, militates against social harmony and spiritual salvation. The second category of hedonists included Hobbes and Helvetius, according to whom it was in one's own interest to pay heed to the interests of others as society is an interacting whole. This position was counted by Samuel Butler, who maintained that altruism, generosity, kindness, gratitude, courtesy, friendliness, and so on; were natural human impulses. Tilak's sympathies lay with Butler's position. Regarding the third category of hedonists, Tilak felt that in cases of conflict between self-interest and common interests, the former tended to prevail over the latter. Moreover, all these three strands of hedonism, Tilak felt, advocated a materialistic ethic.

Tilak was also opposed to the utilitarian ethics as formulated in Bentham's principle of the greatest happiness of the greatest number. Some of its difficulties, as pointed out by Tilak, were: How is 'greatest' happiness to be determined? Is the quantity of happiness to be preferred to its quality or *vice versa*? In cases of conflict over the empirical determination of the principle, whose opinion is to prevail? In place of the utilitarian formula, Tilak favoured the Good of All principle contained in the *Vedas* and the *Bhagwad Gita*. In bringing society to the latter principle, he assigned a special role to spiritual leaders or *yogis*. He maintained that the dichotomy between the interests of the self and those of others had to be overcome by subordinating the former to the latter. This, he believed, can be done by inculcating in the individual the virtues of kindness, prudence, foresight, bravery, fortitude, forebearance, self-control, etc. Bodily pleasures, he pointed out, are fleeting, while spiritual happiness is superior and lasting. In other words, inner happiness is superior to external happiness. Hence, according to him, a person's conduct is to be evaluated not merely on the basis of its outward effects but also on the basis of the inner motives and feelings. Like Kant, Tilak gave importance to reason. According to him, one whose reason is absolute and pure cannot sin. Pure reason and equanimity to all beings make one's conduct morally good

He emphasised the spiritual freedom of the individual, basing it on the Vedanta philosophy of non-dualism. In his *Gitarahasya*, he wrote:

Freedom was the soul of the Home Rule Movement. The divine instinct of freedom never aged . . . . Freedom is the very life of the individual soul which Vedanta declares to be not separate from God but identical with him. This freedom was a principle that could never perish.

In keeping with the political thought of the *Vedas*, the *Ramayana*, the *Mahabharata*, Kautilya's *Arthashastra, Shukraniti* and *Kamandaka Nitisara*, Tilak asserted that it was the duty of the king to promote the welfare of the people. After tracing the term *swarajyam* (self-rule) to the *Vedas*, he pointed out that since the people have the essence of God in them, they have the right to remove oppressive rulers. He, in other words, believed in the divine right of the people to hold their rulers accountable to themselves.

Tilak recognised four connotations of the term *swarajya*. First, it means that the ruler and the people are of the same country, religion or race. Second, it refers to a well-governed state or a system of rule of law. Third, it means a government promoting the well-being of the people. The fourth connotation, for which Tilak had his strongest preference, was that of a government elected by and responsible to the people. Tilak supported the right of the people to participate in the government of their country. He endorsed the slogan which Dadabhai Naoroji had given at the Calcutta Congress of 1906, namely that the thirst for self-government (*swarajya*) cannot be assuaged by good government (*surajya*). According to Tilak, a democratic government, by its very nature, is bound to promote the people's welfare. He opined that the ideal of democratic polity would be better served if political science were to be re-designated *rajanitishastra* (theory of political morality). He maintained that as Indians were suffering from the harmful effects of British rule and had become aware of the advantages of democracy, the time was ripe for Indian nationalism and *swarajya*.

Swarajya, for Tilak, had not only a political connotation (i.e., Home Rule) but also a moral/spiritual connotation (i.e., self-control and inner freedom). He described *swarajya* in the following words:

It is a life centred in self and dependent upon self. There is *swarajya* in this world as well as in the world hereafter. The Rishis who laid down the law of duty betook themselves to forests, because the people were already enjoying *swarajya* or people's domination which was ad- ministered and defended in the first instance by the Kshtriya kings. It is my conviction, it is my thesis, that *swarajya* in the life to come cannot be the reward of a people who have not enjoyed it in this world.

At the Lucknow Congress of 1916, Tilak raised the now-famous slogan *'Swarajya* is the birthright of Indians.' In the same year, he and Annie Besant started Home Rule League.

III
Nationalism

Tilak's conception of Indian nationalism was an amalgam of diverse strands of thought: pride in the legacy of ancient India; appreciation of the role of British rule in bringing about the political and administrative unification of the country; appreciation of Western learning and science; recognition of economic exploitation by foreign rulers; and the recognition of the need to form a national political movement of the people across the barriers of race, caste, religion and sex. Tilak thought of nationalism as operating at two levels—the regional and the national. He believed that a regional historical hero or a regional religious symbol could concretise the national sentiment in the people. As he matured as a national leader, the country-wide strand of his idea of Indian nationalism engulfed and assimilated the regional strand. Although he remained a devout Hindu and gave priority to the political self-rule movement over social reform movement, the impact of Western education on him was impressive. From it he derived his commitment to the liberal values of constitutional government, rule of law, indiviudual freedom, freedom of the press, scientific progress, and freedom of political expression and organisation. His advocacy of national freedom and self-rule within the British Empire was also the result of his Western education.

When the 1892 Indian Councils Act was passed providing for the indirect election of representatives from local bodies and economic associations, Tilak praised it as a gain from British rule. He regarded the arousal of political consciousness among the people as the most important consequence of British rule. He foresaw that *swarajya* would be the inevitable consequence of such a development. According to him, the other gains from British rule were political and legal order, administrative stability, infrastructural facilities for agriculture, trade, commerce and mining and educational institutions. He placed very high value on the freedom of the press, which he used effectively to arouse the people's national sentiments. He recognised the difference between Maratha rule and British rule as the difference between a traditional legal system and a modern, written, codified legal system. On the occasion of the death of Queen Victoria in 1901, Tilak noted that peace, impartial rule and progress were the beneficial aspects of her long rule. However, during the partition of Bengal (1903–8), he revised his assessment of the nature and consequences of foreign rule. He attacked British rule as unconstitutional and detrimental to the basic political rights of the Indians. Earlier, in 1892, he had gone to the extent of admiring the generosity, farsightedness and wisdom of the British electorate in returning Dadabhai Naoroji to the House of Commons from Central Finsbury. Tilak retained his admiration of Britain's contribution to constitutional government and parliamentary democracy, liberal values and freedom, and the field of science and technology. He stood for the application of the principle of rationality and scientific, logical reasoning to the political and economic spheres, but not to the socio-religious sphere.

Thus, Tilak's conception of nationalism was a combination of the Vedanta ideal of the spiritual unity of mankind and the Western notions of nationalism as propounded by Mazzini, Burke, Mill and Wilson. He was alive to and influenced by the development of nationalism in the world at large. In it, four phases may be distinguished. In the first phase (namely, the classical phase), nationalism in Britain and France was associated with historical continuity, linguistic, racial and religious unity and the unity of political aspiration. In the second phase, ushered in by the French Revolution, national sovereignty was identified with popular sovereignty. In the wake of the French Revolution, several nation-states emerged in Europe from out of the bewildering variety of peoples with diverse languages and traditions. In this phase, the unity of political aspiration came to be regarded as the overriding feature of nationalism. Renan, Fichte and Herder were some of the proponents of this view. In the fourth phase (i.e., at the close of World War I), the political map of Eastern Europe and West Asia underwent a metamorphosis in the wake of Wilson's famous principle of national self-determination.

To Tilak, a feeling of oneness among the people and pride in their country's heritage were the vital forces of nationalism. He believed that nationalism can be developed by fostering among the people the feeling that they have common interests to be pursued and realised through united political action. This idealistic and romantic conception of nationalism did inspire and unite the de-spirited and divided people of India. Tilak referred to Akbar and Shivaji as illustrious rulers who forged national unity across regional, religious and caste barriers.

The bases of nationalism, Tilak knew, were both objective and subjective. Such objective factors as common language, territory and religion contribute to the psychological or subjective feeling of oneness among a people. These subjective, psychological feelings are indeed of fundamental importance for nationalism. Tilak believed that nationalism can be promoted and strengthened if the peoples' psychological bonds are given symbolic expressions of an objective, visible or concrete type, namely, flags, insignia and the celebration of social and religious festivals. Accordingly, Tilak revived the Ganapati festival and used it as a means to foster the unity of Brahmans and non-Brahmans. Similarly, he also played a leading role in organising Shivaji festivals. In addition to the celebration of these festivals, Tilak also used social movements and political agitations as a means to foster the feeling of nationalism in the people. For instance, during the 1877 famine in Poona, he organised no-land tax campaigns.

Tilak maintained that neither the British Empire nor the world as a whole could be the proper national unit in which India could be a part. He found the British Empire to be comprised of diverse, antagonistic peoples (namely, the British rulers, the exploited Indians, the Malayans, the Malayan islanders, the white Australians, etc.). Moreover, the policy of discrimination pursued by the British government against other peoples within the Empire (such as the Irish or the Indians) disproved any claim that empire-building was also nation-building. Similarly, the world as a whole was too abstract and amorphous an entity. Sharing the romanticism and idealism of Fichte, Herder and Renan, Tilak believed that India can forge ahead as an independent nation.

He looked upon the different linguistic communities of India as sub-nationalities. He believed that the unity that language provides to the people of a region had to be strengthened. But more than any language it was Hinduism which, according to him, was the uniting force of the whole of India. He appreciated the fact that the Hindu epics, the *Ramayana* and the *Mahabharata*, had forged unity of thought and conduct among the Hindus from the Himalayas to Kanyakumari. Tilak pointed out that although different monarchs ruled over different parts of India, there existed a sort of 'Hindu Rashtra' in the sense that there was a religious unity among the Hindus from Kashmir to Cape Comorin and from Puri to Dwarka. He, however, maintained that historical legacies and linguistic and religious unity were insufficient bases of nationalism. The more important components of nationalism, according to him, were the political mobilisation of the people under a national movement and a nationalist economic ideology.

Tilak concentrated not only on the cultural or religious bases of information but also on the economic basis of it. He shared the econonic ideas of the moderate nationalists like Ranade, Naoroji, R.C. Dutt and Gokhale. But, unlike them, he maintained that economic issues had to be exploited to rouse the people's political consciousness and strengthen the freedom struggle. To this end, he wrote several articles in his vernacular journal, *Kesari*, on such issues as land revenues, land tenure systems, the destruction of arts and crafts, the wasteful government expenditure on wars and the conspicuous living of the British officials.

He endorsed Dadabhai Naoroji's famous 'drain theory' of British rule in India. He gave a favourable picture of the erstwhile native regimes of India, contrasted with exploitative rule of the imperialists. He, thereby, made out a case for replacing foreign rule by Home Rule. While sharing Ranade's concern for the industrialisation of India, Tilak opposed the former's defence of British rule for its role in industrial investment and the development of transport, communications and trade. Tilak also shared R.C. Dutt's anxiety over the deteriorating rural situation evident in recurring famines and the growing indebtedness of the farmers. He advocated a greater role of the state in agricultural development. But while Dutt was a moderate in his political outlook, Tilak was an extremist. He had a romantic view of village self-sufficiency, and strove to mobilise the peasants, artisans, craftsmen and urban dwellers into the freedom struggle.

IV
Passive Resistance

Tilak opposed the standpoint of the moderates that social reform was a necessary antecedent to political freedom. To him, the securing of political rights from the British rulers was of primary importance. Moreover, he feared that any emphasis on social reform would lead to social schisms and to greater bureaucratic interference by the colonial administration. He also believed that the caste system, about which so much was talked about, was actually a functional division of labour, contributing to social harmony. He subscribed to the organic theory of society and maintained that social customs, conventions and traditions had to be preserved for the sake of social unity.

Tilak's conservatism and political extremism led to a rift between him and his followers, on the one hand, and the moderates led by Gokhale and Ranade, on the other. The moderates insisted that Indians should not resort to any unconstitutional or illegal political actions such as the boycott of foreign goods, law-courts and educational institutions and the non-payment of land revenue to the British government. Tilak maintained that such methods of political action cannot be called unconstitutional as the country was not governed according to any constitution. He averred that the 1958 Proclamation of Queen Victoria could not be regarded as a constitutional document for India as it had not been legalised by any Act of the British Parliament. Moreover, even some British politicians (like Curzon) had regarded the Proclamation as 'unpractical' and 'illegal'.

Tilak challenged the moderates to persuade the Secretary of State for India to implement the Proclamation. He argued that even a liberal Secretary of State, like Lord Morley, would not act as a liberal on matters pertaining to the Indian colony. The differences between the liberals and the conservatives, he showed, were confined to Britain's domestic issues. On matters pertaining to the colonies, they would all act alike on the advice of the colonial civil servants, most of whom were conservative and imperialistic. Even the British working class, Tilak realised, would not favour the granting of self-government to India and the other colonies. Tilak's thought, which was counter to Marx's view on the identity of anti-imperialist interests between the working classes of the metropolis and the colonies, was later shared by the Indian non-communist socialists.

During the peasant struggles against the famine conditions of 1896–97 and during his trial in the following year, Tilak had professed his loyalty to the laws and regulations of the colonial government. What he then opposed were the maladministration by the governmental bureaucracy and their failure to give any famine relief. During the passive resistance of 1905–8 against the partition of Bengal, however, Tilak condemned colonial laws as unjust and oppressive. He, like T.H. Green, justified direct political action against bad laws. Tilak, however, not only theorised about the right to resist bad laws but also practised it. He, along with Aurobindo, led the passive resistance programme of *swadesi*, boycott and national education. This resistance was the precursor of Gandhi's non-cooperation and civil disobedience movements. In fact, in *Young India*, dated 23 July 1921, Gandhi wrote:

> Of all the men of modern times, he captivated most the imagination of his people. He breathed into us the spirit of *swaraj*. No one perhaps realised the evil of the existing system of government as Mr. Tilak did. And in all humility I claim to deliver his message to the country as truly as the best of his disciples. But I am conscious that my method is not Mr. Tilak's method.

On 2 January 1907, in his celebrated speech on 'Tenets of the New Party,' Tilak stated the goal of the extremists as follows:

> The point is to have the entire control in our hands. I want to have the key of my house, and not merely one stranger turned out of it. Self-government is our goal; we want a control over our administrative machinery. We do not want to become clerks. . . . At present we are clerks and willing instruments of our own oppression in the hands of an alien government.

Tilak went on to formulate the method of passive resistance in the following words:

> What the New Party wants you to do is to realise the fact that your future rests entirely in your own hands. If you mean to be free you can be free; if you do not mean to be free, you will fall and be for ever fallen. So many of you need not like arms; but if you have not the power of active resistance, have you not the power of self-denial and self-abstinence in such a way as not to assist this foreign government to rule over you? This is boycott and this is what is meant when we say, boycott is a political weapon. We shall not give them assistance to

collect revenue and keep peace. We shall not assist them in fighting beyond the frontiers or outside India with Indian blood and money. We shall not assist them in carrying on the administration of justice. We shall have our own courts, and when the time comes we shall not pay taxes. Can you do that by your united efforts? If you can, you are free from tomorrow.

After his release from prison in 1914, Tilak insisted that he was not for any sedition against the British Empire. He, in fact, was for the continuation of India's links with the British Empire, which he argued, should be transformed into a commonwealth of nations. India's defence and foreign affairs were to continue to be the concern of the Imperial government, while the domestic government of the country was to be democratised. In support of his advocacy of Home Rule or self-government, Tilak pointed out that empires have disintegrated, not because of delegation of power and authority to lower units, but because of the oppressive and wasteful rule from the 'centre'.

During the war, the colonies fought on the side of their imperial rulers. This, Tilak hoped, was a sufficient basis for a better understanding between the metropolis and the colonies. The latter, he proclaimed, deserve self-government or Home Rule. Naturally, he endorsed President Woodrow Wilson's famous principle of national self-determination. Tilak challenged the claim of the British rulers that Indians were too immature for the transfer of power to them. He believed that Indians had already gained political maturity. If they had not done so, he argued, the blame lay with the British rulers, and not with the Indians.

Doubting the efficacy of the moderate methods of petitions and appeals, Tilak urged the people to resort to direct political action. He believed that political methods and political concepts have different meanings in different socio-historical and political contexts. He maintained that what is 'constitutional' and 'legal' to the imperialist rulers and their supporters may really be unjust and immoral, not merely from the viewpoint of the people of the colonies but also from a broader humanistic standpoint. Governmental regulations and laws, he averred, should be evaluated not simply in terms of constitutionality or legality but in terms of justice and morality as well. The people, he believed, have the right and the duty to resist unjust immoral laws.

Bibliography

Biographies

Bal Gangadhar Tilak (Madras, G.A. Natesan, and Co., 1918).
BAPAT, S.V., *Reminiscences and Recollections of Lokmanya Tilak* (in Marathi), Vols. 1–3 (Poona, Author, 1924–28).

JOG, N.G., *Lokmanya B.G. Tilak* (New Delhi, Government of India, Publications Division, 1970).

KARANDIKAR, S.L., *Lokamanya Bal Gangadhar Tilak* (Poona, Author, 1957).

KARMARKAR, D.P., *Bal Gangadhar Tilak: A Study* (Bombay, Popular Book Depot, 1956).

PARVATE, T.V., *Bal Gangadhar Tilak* (Ahmedabad, Navjivan, 1958).

PRADHAN, G.P., and A.K. BHAGWAT, *Lokmanya Tilak: A Biography* (Bombay, Jaico, 1959).

RAM, GOPAL, *Lokmanya Tilak: A Biography* (Bombay, Asia, 1956).

TAMHANKAR, D.V., *Lokmanya Tilak: Father of Indian Unrest and Maker of Modern India* (London, John Murray, 1956).

Works of B.G. Tilak

The Artic Home in the Vedas (Poona, Kesari, 1903).

Bhagavadgitarahasya Athava Karmaryogashastra (in Marathi) (Pune, Lokmanya Tilak Mandir, 10th edition, 1955).

Lokmanya Tilakanche Kesaritil Lekha, Vols. 1–4 (in Marathi) (Pune, Kesari, 1922–30).

Samagra Lokmanya Tilak, Vols. 1–7, Collection of Marathi and English Writings and Speeches (Pune, Kesari, 1974–76).

Works on Tilak

CASHMAN, R.I., *Myth of Lokmanya Tilak and Mass Politics in Maharashtra* (Berkeley, University of California Press, 1975).

GOLDBERG and REISNER, *Tilak and the Struggle for Indian Freedom* (New Delhi, People's Publishing House, 1966).

Government of Bombay, *Source Material for History of the Freedom Movement in India*, Vol. 2 (1885–1920) Parts I–II.

INAMDAR, N.R. (ed), *Political Thought and Leadership of Lokmanya Tilak* (New Delhi, Concept, 1983).

MAJUMDAR, R.C., *History of the Freedom Movement in India*, Vol. 1, 1962–63 (Calcutta, K.L. Mukhopadhyaya, 2nd editition, 1971).

SHAY, T.L., *Legacy of the Lokmanya: Political Philosophy of Bal Gangadhar Tilak* (London, Oxford University Press, 1956).

SITARAMAYYA, P., *History of the Indian National Congress*, Vol. 1, 1885–1935, Part II (Bombay, Padma, 1946).

VARMA, V.P., *Life and Philosophy of Lokmanya Tilak* (Agra, Lakshmi Narain Agarwal, 1978).

8

The Ideology of Hindu Nationalism

I

In the last decade of the nineteenth century, the limitations of the politics of moderation vis-a-vis the British Empire became apparent to sections of the politically-conscious middle classes all over India. Contradictions between foreign imperialism and nationalist aspirations began surfacing in various forms and at various levels. The demands for equal benefits, equal opportunities as the 'loyal citizens of the Empire,' first mumbled feebly, developed into a crescendo towards the end of the century. The British administrators could not grant these demands without rendering their domination of India meaningless. Since imperialist interests could not be sacrificed, Indian interests had to be suppressed or ignored. The British administrators devised political and economic policies to undermine the economic position and the emerging unity of the members of the educated middle classes (who formed the backbone of the nationalist movement). This they did first by declaring the Congress a 'seditious organisation' and thereby frightening away a sizable section of the middle classes from its ranks. Their next step was the introduction of discriminatory measures in those provinces which were politically alive and where the middle classes were prosperous—Bengal, Punjab and Bombay. The hardest measure was reserved for the Bengali Hindus—namely, the partition of Bengal in 1905.

Alienation of the middle classes would have proved detrimental to the Empire. Therefore, new alliances were formed with those groups whose vested interests could be made directly dependent on the goodwill of the government. This would keep them amenable to its designs and make the manipulation of Indian politics easy. Besides enlisting the support of the feudal elements, the British gave special favours to the Muslim community. This was justified on the ground that the Muslims lagged behind the Hindus in social advancement. Thus, ignoring the economic backwardness of the masses in general, the British rulers became extremely solicitous of, and concerned with, the relative backwardness of particular communities and castes. A policy of special favours and facilities was conceived to remove the existing social disparities and help selected backward sections to rise up to the level of the upper caste Hindus. In this manner, a climate of social tension was created between communities and castes which the nationalist politicians could not transform (except, for very brief spells, into one of cordiality and cooperation). Before the century closed, the psychological and material background for the birth and growth of communal and sectional movements had been prepared. It required no politician of great imagination or stature to give these an organised shape.

The serious threat to their economic position posed by the Bengal partition forced the exponents of Hindu nationalism to descend from lofty spiritual heights and plant their feet firmly on the solid ground of politics. They had to redefine their priorities and drastically alter their ideology to shed some of its exclusiveness. The indifference towards the Muslims had now become injurious to the Hindu interests. They had to be acknowledged as a significant factor in Indian politics whose ambitions and feelings had to be accommodated in spelling out the concept of Hindu nationhood. The responsibility of giving new orientation to Hindu nationalism was undertaken by Aurobindo Ghose, who drew inspiration from Vevekananda's theory of India's cultural or religious superiority over the West.

Aurobindo agreed with Vivekananda that spirituality constituted the bedrock of Indian culture and that the 'function of India is to supply the world with a perennial source of light and renovation.' But this supreme task India could not fulfil, he added, 'while overshadowed by foreign power and foreign civilisation.' To put the cart of spiritualism before the horse of freedom betrayed a lack of wisdom. The separation between politics and spirituality was unacceptable to him He pointed out: 'It cannot be for a moment contended that we can ag; n be spiritually great without being politically dominant . . . . No human scheme of spiritual amelioration can be effective without the liberal and public spirited activity as a free citizen.'[1]

The frustration of the middle class Hindus, which had found refuge in the illusion of spiritual greatness and had produced a number of English-speaking monks, could not be sustained any more. Rejection of politics now indicated a deliberate flight from reality. Aurobindo said:

One who is of the opinion that Hindu philosophy had enjoined such maudlin hatred for matter, must have studied it very badly . . . . (W)hoever distinguished himself by a sojourn in Europe and America . . . is supposed to be competent to make any pronouncement on Hindu philosophy and religion. If political superiority is a question of minor importance, why do these people shun their own country and try to make some noise amongst people whose politically advantageous position fills them with some pride as the conqueror of the conquerors?[2]

[1] *Bande Mataram*, 2 August 1907.
[2] *Ibid.*, 9 November 1907.

Aurobindo exposed the reality behind the illusion and emphasised the significance of politics as a means of national regeneration. But he failed to rise above the constraints of his class. His synthesis of religion with politics and the use of religion as the vehicle of mass mobilisation was not due solely to his spiritual proclivities or the supposed, ingrained religious tendencies of the Indian masses. Stress on the religious bond had also the effect of blinding the masses to the social and economic chasm that separated them from the *bhadralok* and eliciting their full support for a movement that was launched largely to protect the interests of middle class Hindus. Awareness of the dangers posed by the social disparities is indicated in Aurobindo's plan of national reconstruction spelled out in *Bhawani Mandir*: One of the several tasks entrusted to the monks was 'to approach the zamindars, landholders and rich men generally, and endeavour (*i*) to promote sympathy between zamindars, landholders and rich peasants and heal all discords; (*ii*) to create a single and living religious spirit and common passion for one great ideal between all castes; (*iii*) to turn the minds of rich men to works of public beneficence and charity.'[3]

Muslim aloofness and the communal riots during the Swadeshi agitation culminated in the formation of the All India Muslim League. Muslims had now become a new force in Indian politics, which could not be countered by an open display of contempt or withdrawal into the shell of Hindu spirituality. The Bengali Hindu nationalists recognised the presence of this force, but failed to assess correctly the depth of its strength. In this, they were misled by their cultural arrogance and a false sense of security based on numerical strength and economic prosperity. Aurobindo, however, welcomed the formation of the Muslim League and wrote:

We do not fear Mohammedan opposition so long as it is the honest Swadeshi article and not manufactured in Shillong or Simla. We welcome it as a sign of life and aspiration . . . . In that faith we are ready, when the time comes for us to meet in the political field, to exchange with the Musalman, just as he chooses, the firm clasp of the brother or the resolute grip of the wrestler . . . . (India's new nationalism) is not afraid of Pan-Islamism or any signs of the growth of a special Mohammedan self-consciousness, but rather welcomes them.[4]

In the face of Muslim self-assertion, the goal of making India an exclusive nation of Hindus went beyond the realm of practical politics. A significant modification was, therefore, introduced by Aurobindo to make it relevant and realistic. In the place of Hindu nation, he put forth the idea of an Indian nationalism that was to be 'largely Hindu in its spirit

³ *Karmayogi*, 6 November 1909.
⁴ *Bande Mataram*, 17 December 1907.

and traditions'. Reacting sharply to the emergence of the Hindu Sabha in Pubjab, he wrote:

. . . We do not understand Hindu nationalism as a possibility under modern conditions. Hindu nationalism had a meaning in the times of Shivaji and Ramdas, when the object of national revival was to over-throw a Mahomedan domination which, once tending to Indian unity and toleration, had become oppressive and disruptive . . . . But under modern conditions India can exist only as a whole . . . . What geo-graphical base can a Hindu nationality possess? . . . Our ideal . . . is an Indian nationalism, largely Hindu in its spirit and traditions, because the Hindu made the land and the people and persists, by the greatness of his past, his civilisation and his culture and his invincible virility, in holding it, but wide enough also to include the Moslem and his culture and traditions and absorb them into itself.[5]

With the introduction of the Reforms Act of 1909, the momentary militancy of the middle class Hindus relapsed into complacent inactivity. Spirituality and religion, which had kept them obsessed for decades, receded into the background. Aurobindo's warning against the dangerous provisions of the Act fell on deaf ears:

Unless the Hindus have strength of mind to boycott a system which erects a distinction insulting as well as injurious to the community, this measure, while giving us not an atom of self-government, will be a potent engine for dividing the nation into two hostile interests and barring the way towards the unity of India.[6]

Aurobindo Ghose, Bipin Chandra Pal and other exponents of Hindu nationalism who became champions of regional aspirations during the Swadeshi movement, leap-frogged subsequently into internationalism or political exile. But when the material interests of the *bhadralok* were in grave danger, they reverted to their original position. In the 1940s, when the demand for the creation of Pakistan was under discussion, advocates of Hindu solidarity who had claimed sway over the whole of India as its original inhabitants, talked in terms of an independent sovereign state of Bengal and suddenly discovered the trinity of ties—blood, language and culture—with the Muslims of Bengal.

The British policy of protection and privileges to check the emergence of national solidarity amongst the Indians proved most successful in Punjab. Through various discriminatory measures (e.g., the Punjab Land Alienation Act of 1901 and the Canal Colonies Act of 1907) they

[5] *Shri Aurobindo*, Vol. 2 (Pondicherry, 1972), pp. 1–62.
[6] *Karmayogi*, 10 February 1910.

were able to divide the Punjabis on communal and caste lines.[7] The apparently innocent administrative reforms were, in fact, meant to reduce the importance of the urban middle classes (an overwhelming majority of whom were Hindus). Among the Hindu trading castes, money-lenders, officials, businessmen and professionals, the Land Alienation Act created a deep feeling of insecurity. All found their investments in land checked and lawyers suffered a serious diminution in their income due to a precipitate decline in litigation. To these were added the definite possibility of loss of government jobs, a significant portion of which would in future be reserved for the Muslims on a preferential basis.

Not unexpectedly, Punjabi Hindus found themselves in an unhappy position and were anxious to recover their lost ground and check the further erosion of their privileges. It was clear to them that their sectional interests could not directly be saved and furthered by a national organisation like the Congress. Being small in number and having, besides the Muslims, the Sikhs too as claimants to the protection and privileges extended by the government, they could not exploit regional sentiments for the realisation of their objectives as was possible for the Bengali Hindus. They did not grope in the dark for long. The formation of the All India Muslim League showed them the way which they could also tread to save and promote their interests without either assistance from the Congress or conflict with the authorities. Modelled on the Muslim League, the Punjab Hindu Sabha was founded in 1907. It was specifically aimed at being 'ardent and watchful in safeguarding the interests of the entire Hindu community.'[8]

The ideology of the Hindu nation, as conceived by the Punjabi Hindus, was fundamentally different from the one developed by their co-religionists in Bengal. The latter did not regard Hindu nationalism and Indian nationalism as two distinct entities and treated both as identical phenomena. Owing to their greater social advancement and numerical strength, the Hindus in Bengal could confidently hope to absorb or assimilate the non-Hindu elements and direct the national movement mainly on Hindu lines. Muslim separatism did not generate in Aurobindo or Bipin Chandra Pal any feeling of insecurity or of impending disaster. They happily greeted it as a sign of political maturity among the Muslims that would help, rather than hamper, the fulfilment of the national ambitions of the Hindus.

This was not the case with the Punjabi Hindus. They were outnumbered by their Muslim rivals. The latter were also not illiterate, poor and docile like the Muslim peasants of Bengal. It was, therefore, not possible for the Punjabi Hindus to entertain the fond dream of assimilating or absorbing the non-Hindus or of equating Indian nationalism with Hindu nationalism.

---

[7] P.H.M. Van den Dungen, *The Punjab Tradition* (London: Allen and Unwin, 1972).
[8] *The Punjabi*, 7 January 1907.

Even the Hinduisation ,of the Congress could not serve their purpose because 'that would mean not a mere change in name but a change in ideas,' argued Lala (later Sir) Shadi Lal, a founder-member of the Punjab Hindu Sabha.

> The difference, therefore, is not merely a difference of form . . . but a difference in root principle . . . . A person who believes in Indian ideal would subordinate the Hindu interests as of secondary importance; and this has actually happened in the conduct of the Congress leaders . . . . Whereas those who believe in the Hindu ideal must subordinate the Indian as of secondary significance and lend their support to it only so far as the ideal does not militate against the real Hindu interests.[9]

The difference between the two ideologies was not limited to their political aspect. In their cultural aspiration, content and orientation also they differed radically from each other. The Hindu cultural world of Punjab was not disturbed by the phoney war-cry between Western and Hindu culture, or more accurately, it did not witness the collision between the forces of traditionalism and modernism as had happened in Bengal. The Brahmanic culture, which everywhere had been the source of a distinct *weltanschauung*, had disappeared from the soil of Punjab long ago. The vacuum thus created by its disappearance had been filled by the culture of the new ruling class, the Muslims. Hence, there were no traditions to conserve whose life-span covered centuries and formed the ideological justification for the survival of certain distinct groups. In short, the Punjabi Hindu culture was not a true regional variation of the all-India Brahmanic culture; it was vaguely Hindu but mainly Islamic in content. The problem before the Punjabi Hindus, therefore, was how to de-Islamise themselves and evolve a distinct Hindu cultural identity. In other words, the question before them was not of devising ways and means of integrating the non-Hindu elements within the framework of the Hindu nation, but Hinduising themselves for establishing their claims as bonafide members of the larger Hindu community of the country.

Explaining his new-found love for Hinduism, Lala Lajpat Rai recorded in his autobiography:

> I never learnt Sanskrit and did not even know the alphabet of Hindu . . . . The whole of my boyhood was taken up by the study of Urdu, Persian and Arabic . . . . (But) when I came to Lahore, Islam lost its charm for me. The company I had in Lahore made my mind turn away from Islam, and, what is more important, I became attached to Hinduism and Hindus. This attachment was not so much theological or religious, it was nationalistic.[10]

---

[9] Lala Lalchand, *Self-Abnegation in Politics*, 2nd edition (Lahore: 1938), pp. 119–200.
[10] V.C. Joshi, *Lala Lajpat Rai: Autobiographical Writings* (Delhi: 1965), p. 77.

The Hindu nationalism of Lala Shadi Lal, Lala Hardayal or Lala Lajpat Rai was not arrogant and self-assertive. It stemmed from the deeply felt insecurity of the urban Hindu middle class and was sustained throughout by their class interest. In communal solidarity on an all-India basis, they sought a counter-weight to the imbalance of their position in Punjab. Addressing the Hindu Conference at Bombay, Lala Lajpat Rai impressed on his co-religionists that communal solidarity had become essential for the security of their political future because the Muslims

> insisted on communal representation all along the political line and also on organising their separate communal entity in India. This is bound to come about if the other communities refuse to organise themselves; their refusal or neglect to do so means acquiescence in a condition of things which must sooner or later end in their merging in or subordinating to the other community. Organisation means power and prestige. Those who neglect to organise must give way to the organised. If the Hindu community does not wish to commit political harakiri, they must move every nerve to be communally efficient and united. To divide itself into religious sections, with separate political ambitions, is the greatest folly of which a community can be guilty.[11]

Thus, a situation had arisen when, due to the government policy, the political status and economic power of the upper caste Hindus had become dependent on the numerical strength of their community. Neither could the Sudras be kept in isolation and under subordination nor could the non-Hindu groups be assimilated indirectly through the gradual process of Sanskritisation as had happened in the past. The Hindu leaders now had to adopt such means that would prevent the outflow from their community and facilitate instant conversion and direct recruitment to the Hindu fold. The programme of Shuddhi (purification), originally conceived by Swami Dayanand to create an opportunity for the Sudras to rise above their inherited social status, was turned into an instrument of proselytisation by the Punjabi Hindus for political purpose to safeguard their vested interests. By making Shuddhi a legitimate means of acquiring access to the Hindu community as well as to the Brahmanic culture, they transformed the very character of Hindu religion. With the transformation disappeared the indifference towards the lower orders of the Hindu society as well as towards non-Hindu groups. Religious assimilation inspired by political needs met with vehement opposition from the Muslims and became one of the major factors responsible for communal riots in Punjab.

Fusion of fear psychosis with middle class Hindu ambitions is best exemplified in the famous statement of Lala Hardyal, a renowned revolutionary of Punjab, when he declared:

[11] *The Tribune*, 1 December 1925.

The future of the Hindu race, of Hindustan and of the Punjab rests on these four pillars: 1. Hindu Sangathan, 2. Hindu Raj, 3. Shuddhi of the Muslims, and 4. Shuddhi of Afghanistan and the frontiers. So long as the Hindu nation does not accomplish these four things, the safety of the Hindu race will be impossible . . . . The Muslims and Christians are far removed from the confines of Hinduism, for their religions are alien and they love Persian, Arabic and European institutions. Thus, just as one removed foreign matter from the eye, Shuddhi must be made of these two religions.[12]

Although the Punjabi leaders occasionally raised the slogan of Hindu Raj, in their heart of hearts they were convinced that it was a Utopian dream. They, therefore, did not wish the slogan to be taken at its face value by their followers: 'If there are among you,' Lajpat Rai warned the Punjabi Hindus, 'who will dream of Hindu Raj in this country; who think they can crush the Mussalmans and the supreme power in this land . . . they are fools, or to be more accurate, they are insane, and their insanity will ruin their Hinduism along with their country.' The lasting cure to this insanity, which was looming large in the political horizon of India, was communal segregation on an all-India basis. Endorsing Maulana Hasrat Mohani's scheme of smaller states containing compact Hindu and Muslim populations, Lajpat Rai produced his own solution of the problem:

If communal representation with separate electorate is to be the rule, then Maulana Hasrat's scheme . . . seems to be the only workable proposition. Under the scheme the Muslims will have four Muslim States: 1. The Pathan province and the North-West Frontier; 2. Western Punjab; 3. Sindh; and 4. Eastern Bengal. If there are compact Muslim communities in any other part of India, sufficiently large to form a province, they should be similarly constituted. But it should be distinctly understood that it is not a united India. It means a clear partition of India into a Muslim and a non-Muslim India.[13]

The Punjabi leaders did not use Hindu spirituality or religion as a cover for their vested interests. Nor did they pretend that the Hindu antipathy towards the Muslims was merely a mental phenomenon, an attitude, born out of ignorance of Islamic culture and the existing social distance between the members of the two communities. Hence, they did not regard a mere change of heart or remoulding of mind as the antidote to the conflict which was economic in character. Lajpat Rai was frank enough to acknowledge that:

[12] V.C. Joshi, *Lala Lajpat Rai, Writings and Speeches*, Vol. 2 (Delhi: 1966), p. 221.
[13] *Ibid.*, p. 213.

it is a question of bread and butter and refuses to be solved whether by resolution or by Fatwas, and it is certain that as long as government services and the profession of law continue to be the mainstay of our educated countrymen, the antagonism between the Hindus and Mohammedans, which is economic in its basis, will not cease. It is a fight for loaves and fishes. It begins with educated men and then filters downwards by a natural process to the masses.[14]

When material bonds were shattered, cultural ties could not stop the generation of animosity and hostility in the social relationship of the two communities. The Punjabi Hindu leaders endorsed the division of available power and privileges between the Hindus and the Muslims through territorial reorganisation. By destroying the source of political rivalry, they argued, they would be able to end social tension and revive the dead feeling of cordiality again. In other words, the re-solution of social tension was in political settlement with the Muslims and not in the cultural or religious rejuvenation of the Hindus—a programme strongly advocated by the Bengalis.

Thus, before an ideology of Hindu domination of the sub-continent was conceived, the Hindu nationalists had come out with two diametrically opposed solutions: one involved territorial integration and the other fragmentation of provinces into culturally compact units. While the Bengalis (whose material interests were rooted in land and government service) endeavoured hard to retain the integrity of their province, the money-lenders, traders, lawyers and contractors of Punjab were eager for partition. It was this political reality which they had transformed into an ideology of Hindu Raj. However, the Hindu Raj they were striving for, in terms of territory, did not extend beyond the frontiers of Bengal or Punjab. Hindu domination of India was a Utopia, the domination of the Punjab was their real aim. The Hindus being in a majority, their domination over India in a political sense and under a democratic form of government was inevitable. But the Hindus of Bengal and Punjab were not satisfied with such domination. They wanted the advantages and privileges of the majority where the Muslims definitely outnumbered them.

After the Reforms Act of 1919 and the non-cooperation movement, the Indian struggle for freedom entered a new phase. Alongside, the area encompassed by the communal triangle also got widened. The regional issues lost their former significancè. Further, realisation of regional aspirations now became dependent on the realisation of national goals. These had, therefore, to be coalesced with the mainstream of the national struggle in an effective manner. The decision to dethrone the British and achieve 'purna Swarajya' brought the vital question of the pattern of power distribution at the centre to the fore. For obtaining maximum

[14] *Ibid.*, p. 146.

share, the Muslims began to claim themselves as a separate nationality. The communal confrontation was now no more a mere confrontation between a minority and a majority but between two distinct nationalities. The ball was set rolling in the thirties by Sir Mohammed Iqbal, Chaudhari Rahmat Ali and others, who evolved a well-thought-out ideology of Muslim nationalism based on religion and culture. In such a situation the All-India Hindu Mahasabha (which in spite of its all-India pretensions had remained confined to the Hindus of Punjab, Bengal and U.P.) was compelled to elevate itself to the all-India level in the true sense of the term and evolve an ideology that could run parallel to the ideology of the Muslim League and the Congress.

II
V.D. Savarkar

As spokesman of the majority interests, V.D. Savarkar formulated an ideology which could demolish the claims of national parity made by the Muslims, negate the territorial concept of nationhood propagated by the Congress, blunt the edge of the demands made by the Depressed Classes, and prevent further atomisation of the Hindu community. For achieving this objective, Savarkar synthesised the territorial concept of nationalism upheld by the Congress with the cultural concept of nationalism popularised by the Muslim League. This synthesis was not a matter of choice but was necessitated by political compulsion. Without this synthesis, the Hindu nationalists could not hope to realise their objectives. A major portion of Savarkar's ideology, therefore, shows a legitimate preoccupation with two main questions: What is a Hindu? What is Hinduism?

Savarkar regarded the question 'Who is a Hindu?' as the main source of misunderstanding and confusion. According to him, the right way of posing the question is: 'What is a Hindu?' Hindus are neither the followers of a particular religion nor are they the inhabitants of a particular region. The Hindus are a nation united not only by 'the bonds of the love they bear to a common motherland but also by the bonds of common blood.'[15]

Hinduism means the 'ism' of the Hindus, and as the word Hindu has been derived from the word 'Sindu'—meaning primarily all the people who reside in the land that extends from 'Sindhu to Sindhu'—Hinduism, must, therefore, necessarily mean the religion or religions that are peculiar and native to this land and the people living in this land. Instead of this, the term Hinduism is mistakenly applied, according to Savarkar, to that system of religion which the majority of the Hindus follow. This identification of Hinduism with the religion of the majority results in the unjustifiable expulsion of unorthodox Hindu communities from its fold.

---

[15] V.D. Savarkar, *Hindutva* (Bombay: Veer Savarkar Prakashan, 5th edition, 1969), pp. 85–86.

'And .thus we find,' Savarkar pionted out, 'that while millions of our Sikhs, Jains, Lingayats, several Samajis and others would deeply resent to be told that they—whose fathers up to the tenth generation had the blood of Hindus in their veins—had suddenly ceased to be Hindus . . .'[16] Hindu dharma of all 'shades and schools, lives and grows and has its being in the atmosphere of Hindu culture, and the dharma of a Hindu being so completely identified with the land of the Hindus, this land to him is not only a *Pitrbhu* but a *Punyabhu*, not only a fatherland but a holyland too.'[17] This is why the Hindu converts to Christianity and Islam who share with Hindus a common culture and a common fatherland 'are not and cannot be recognised as Hindus'. 'For though Hindusthan to them is fatherland . . . it is not to them a holyland too. Their holyland is far off in Arabia or Palestine . . . . Their love is divided.'[18] If these converts to alien religions wish to be counted as Hindus 'they must recognise this country both as their fatherland and their holyland.' But as long as 'they are not so minded thus, so long they cannot be recognised as Hindus.'[19]

Through his broad definition of the term Hindu and Hinduism, Savarkar tried to halt the process of political fragmentation of the Hindus and prevent the Sikhs and Depressed Classes from forging a common front with the Muslims. He did not object to the Sikhs seeking separate representation. His only regret was 'that the claim should not have been backed up by . . . untenable and suicidal plea of being non-Hindus. Sikhs, to guard their own interests, could have pressed for and succeeded in securing special and communal representation on the ground of being an important minority.'[20] He warned them: 'Your interests are indissolubly bound with the interests of your other Hindu brethren. Whenever in the future as in the past a foreigner raises a sword against the Hindu civilisation it is sure to strike you as deadly as any other Hindu community.'[21]

As pointed out earlier, Savarkar did not totally reject the territorial concept of nationhood; he merely modified it. He asserted that in the formation of nations, religious, racial, cultural and historical affinities count immensely more than their territorial unity. There was no distinction or conflict between the national and communal aspirations of the Hindus.

A Hindu patriot worth the name cannot but be an Indian patriot as well. To the Hindus, Hindustan being their fatherland and holyland, the love they bear to Hindustan is boundless. What is called nationalism can be defined as in fact the national communalism of the majority

[16] *Ibid.*, pp. 105–7.
[17] *Ibid.*, pp. 115–17.
[18] *Ibid.*, p. 113.
[19] *Ibid.*, p. 115.
[20] *Ibid.*, p. 126.
[21] *Ibid.*, p. 127.

community . . . . Thus, in Hindustan it is the Hindus, professing Hindu religion and being in overwhelming majority, that constitutes the national community and create and formulate the nationalism of the nation. It is so in every country of the world . . . . The minorities while maintaining their separate religions and civilisations cooperate with the majority communities and merge themselves in the common life and administration of these countries.[22]

The Hindus cannot take this country as jointly owned by those who either come running away from their countries and sought protection here or those descendants of ex-Hindus, who for the greed of power and money or of fear, renounced their glorious faith and became converts, or those who are the descendants of those barbarous invaders who spoiled our very sacred land, demolished our sacred temples . . . the country cannot belong to them; if they are to live here, they must live here taking for granted Hindustan as the land of the Hindus, of no one else.[23]

Thus, in Savarkar's political scheme, partnership in power was available to the minority groups on the criterion of presence or absence of 'Hindutva' in their religio-cultural roots. Partnership was denied only to those minorities whose holyland lay outside the confines of India (namely, the Muslims, Jews, and Christians). It was assumed that they cannot be genuine patriots. Their love for India remains divided and subordinated to their love for their holyland. The Muslims are a case in point. 'Their love towards India as their motherland is but a handmaid to their love for their holyland outside India . . .'

On behalf of the Hindus, Savarkar made it plain to the minorities:

We shall ever guarantee protection to the religion, culture and language of the minorities for themselves, but we shall no longer tolerate any aggression on their part on the equal liberty of the Hindus to guard their religion, culture and language as well. If non-Hindu minorities are to be protected, then surely the Hindu majority also must be protected against any aggressive minority in India.[24]

The Hindus were ready to accept the cooperation of the minorities for the creation of a united India, provided it was based on an equitable, not equal, footing. They were 'ever ready to grant equal rights and representation to all minor communities in India in legislatures, in services, civil and political life in proportion to their population and merit,' but

[22] *Hindu Mahasabha Records* (New Delhi: Nehru Memorial Museum and Library).

[23] Inder Prakash, *Where We Differ: The Congress and the Hindu Mahasabha* (New Delhi: 1942), p. 66.

[24] V.D. Savarkar, *Hindu Rashtra Darshan* (Collected Speeches) (Bombay: 1949), p. 26.

would reject outright any demand for preferential treatment. Referring to the safeguards sought by the Muslims, Savarkar pointed out that it was meant 'to brand the forehead of Hinduism and other non-Hindu sections in Hindustan with a stamp of self-humiliation and Moslem domination'.[25] To grant the preposterous Muslim claims would mean endowing them

> with the right of exercising a political veto on the legitimate rights and privileges of the majority and call it Swarajya. The Hindus do not want a change of masters, are not going to . . . fight and die only to replace an Edward by an Aurangzeb simply because the latter happens to be born within the Indian borders, but they want henceforth to be masters themselves in their own house, in their own land.[26]

Despite chauvinistic elements in Savarkar's ideology, it cannot be termed Fascist nor can he be put in the category of the Hitlers and Mussolinis. The right of minorities to co-exist with the Hindus was never denied. The attack was directed against those privileges which gave the minorities more political strength than warranted by their numbers. That is why, except for a few vague and confused suggestions, Savarkar's ideology contained no elaborate plan to develop the future India on the lines which would make the full expression of the so-called national spirit of the Hindus possible. He wanted the government of independent India to be purely Indian in which all citizens were to be treated 'according to their individual worth, irrespective of their religious or racial percentage in the general population.'

Savarkar's political philosophy was born out of frustration and rested on resentment which certain sections of the Hindus felt due to the fact that they enjoyed neither the privileges of the minority in the Muslim majority areas nor did they enjoy the advantages of the majority in the areas where they outnumbered the Muslims. They were afraid that the same pattern would be repeated at the Centre. Defiance of secular nationalism was the defence of Hindu vested interests which had no option left but to protect them against the extreme demands of the Muslims. Various compromises entered into by the Congress with the Muslim League were not an encouraging sign for a happy future for the Hindus. The fight against the unreasonable demands of the Muslims, therefore, also became a fight against the Congress which was dubbed 'un-national' and 'pro-Muslim'.

The most noticeable feature of Savarkar's ideology is that while it gave the Hindus exclusive proprietary right over the entire Indian sub-continent, it did not demand the expulsion of the English. At the practical level, the Hindu Raj of his vision became synonymous with the

[25] *Ibid.*, p. 21.
[26] *Ibid.*, p. 104.

Hindu monopoly of jobs available to the Indians under the British government. Subordination of Muslims was desired but the superordination of foreign rulers was never questioned. He did not ask the Hindus to fight for freedom. He urged them to cooperate with the government. He rationalised his position as 'responsive cooperation'.

Savarkar's ideology failed to realise its political goal because it lacked the strength that comes from mass support. His uni-dimensional approach to politics—protection of Hindu interests against Muslim encroachment—had no relevance for the Hindu masses. In the majority of cases, their immediate tormentor and exploiter was a Hindu zamindar, money-lender or an officer of the British government. Ties oi common culture (which did not prevent oppression) could not be used for winning the cooperation of the oppressed. 'Hindu' was not an abstract concept but a living reality which had several forms—caste, class and region. Savarkar's ideology did not take off because it did not recognise this reality in a meaningful manner.

III
M.S. Golwalkar

The debacle of Hindu nationalism in 1947 did not destroy the faith of its adherents in the righteousness of their cause. For success in the future, they made some additions and alterations in the ideology of their predecessors in order to make it suitable to the new environment that had emerged after independence. M.S. Golwalkar and his organisation, the RSS, played an important role in this.

Golwalkar did not formulate any new ideology. He merely reshaped the ideals propagated by his predecessors in a new pattern. Lack of originality at the level of the ought was, however, well compensated by the novelty of technique that he developed to translate his ideals into practice. Briefly put, the aims of this new version of Hindu ideology are: (i) to convert the secular state of India into a Hindu state for the full growth of Indian personality; (ii) to re-occupy those parts which once belonged to the Hindu nation; and (iii) to infuse a sense of solidarity amongst the Hindus through a process of purification and revival of their culture.

The idea of exclusive Hindu domination at the regional or national level (which the middle class votaries of Hindu nationalism had pursued for nearly three decades) lost its relevance after independence. Democracy, which guarantees the rule of the majority assured the Hindus a predominant position in the political affairs of the new nation. The partition of the country in August 1947 made the Hindu nationalists feel humiliated and the presence of the Muslims filled them with resentment. However, these psychological factors were not strong enough to sustain a political ideology. A wider objective was required that could appear meaningful to a large section of the Hindus.

But Hindu nationalism did emerge from this ideological impasse through the new orientation given by Golwalkar and the RSS. Making a significant departure from Savarkar, he shifted the emphasis from state to society and declared Hinduisation or Indianisation of the entire Indian society in all its aspects as the ultimate objective of his movement. Transformation of Indian society on these lines, he argued, was necessary to create an invincible united Hindu nation and to cure the internal maladies of disunity and discontinuity which had been the root causes of the political ruin of the Hindus for the last several centuries.[27] The past record of the Hindus shows that the basic ills of their society stemmed from the perversion and neglect of their commonly shared cultural values. Hence, to preserve stability and ensure future glory, the Hindu nation must return to its perennial source of strength—the values of its *dharma*.[28] Indianisation was the only way that could enable the Hindu nation to rediscover its inner being. It demanded total rejection of all elements of non-Indian origin, on the one hand, and a revival of ancient culture, on the other.

A careful survey of the targets of Golwalkar's attack and the values of Indian culture emphasised by him would reveal the full dimension of the philosophy of reactionary conservatism that he wished to inject into the country's body politic. His philosophy of Hindu nationalism aimed at countering those progressive forces whose slow but steady hammering was causing a serious dent in the hierarchical structure of the Hindu society and eroding the social base which supports the privileges of the upper caste Hindus.

Golwalkar was vehemently critical of the Constitution of free India because its ideals and principles are not derived from indigenous sources.[29] The concept of territorial nationalism was also an anathema to him. In his view, substitution of the natural living nationalism (as mirrored in the cultural unity of the Hindus) by an 'un-natural, unscientific and lifeless hybrid-concept of territorial nationalism' had produced forces of 'corruption, disintegration and dissipation' in our national life.[30]

Golwalkar repeated each one of Savarkar's arguments to establish the exclusive claims of the Hindus but left him one step behind by denying political and cultural rights to all the non-Hindu inhabitants of this ancient land. They could obtain these rights only by discarding their distinct religious identities. He made his terms explicit:

[27] M.S. Golwalkar, *Bunch of Thoughts* (Bangalore: Vikram Prakashan, 1966), pp. 39, 215–16, 218, 228, 332–33.

[28] Shri Guruji, *Samagrah Darshan* (Nagpur: Bharatiya Vichar Sodhna, 1975), Vol. 3, p. 54; Vol. 6, pp. 90–91; Golwalkar, *op. cit.*, pp. 10, 39, 215, 218.

[29] Shri Guruji, *op. cit.*, Vol. 3, p. 41; Golwalkar, *op. cit.*, pp. 56, 227.

[30] Golwalkar, *op. cit.*, pp. 142, 156.

The non-Hindu peoples in Hindustan must either adopt the Hindu culture and language, must learn to respect and hold in reverence Hindu religion, must entertain no idea but that of the glorification of the Hindu race and culture . . . or may stay in the country wholly subordinated to the Hindu nation, claiming nothing deserving no privileges, far less any preferential treatment—not even citizen's rights.[31]

In Golwalkar's opinion, the attempt to recast Hindu society in the mould of other 'isms' at the cost of ancient ideals and traditions was detrimental to the nation and had resulted in the introduction of such un-Indian slogans in the country as 'socialism,' 'socialistic pattern of society,' etc.[32] This large scale borrowing from foreign sources had made Indians rootless. For reversing this process Golwalkar said:

We should shake ourselves free from the mental shackles of foreign isms, foreign ways and fleeting fashions of modern life. There can be no greater national humiliation than to be a mere carbon copy of others. The Hindus should avoid such pitfalls, rekindle in themselves the consciousness that they have of their positive foundations, thereby strike their own roots deep into the solid rock of their national ideals and ambition, history and heritage.[33]

Golwalkar did not want India's new society to be built on the ideals of socialism because 'socialism is not the product of this soil, it is not in our blood and tradition . . . . Adoption of such a doctrine is degrading for the honour of the Hindu nation.'[34] Its acceptance shows 'sheer bankruptcy'.[35]

Equality as an ideal did not receive Golwalkar's approval. He indirectly endorsed the inequalities and disparities of the iniquitous system by claiming that they were in perfect accord with the law of nature.

Equality is acceptable only on the plane of Supreme Spirit. But on the physical plane the same spirit manifests itself in a wondrous variety of diversities and disparities. This disparity is an indivisible part of nature and we have to live with it. Our efforts should be only to keep it within limits and take away the sting born of disparity . . . . [T]he wise sages of India, who mastered the knowledge of the world of Nature as of Man, never talked of equality but laid stress on harmony of disparate elements.[36]

[31] M.S. Golwalkar, *We or Our Nationhood Defined* (Nagpur: Bharat Prakashan, 1939), pp. 55, 56.
[32] Shri Guruji, *op. cit.*, Vol. 6, pp. 104–5, 107; Golwalkar, *op. cit.*, p. 227.
[33] Golwalkar, *op. cit.*, p. 32.   [34] *Ibid.*, p. 228.
[35] *Ibid.*, pp. 193, 225; Shri Guruji, *op. cit.*, Vol. 7, pp. 130–31.
[36] Golwalkar, *op. cit.*, p. 18.

Golwalkar was vehemently opposed to the clamour for 'rights' as they would contribute to the disunity among the Hindus and as they were alien to their thought. He advised the Hindus to replace the assertion of rights by the selfless performance of duties.[37] Social harmony would automatically prevail in society when the only consciousness that people would have would be of their duties.

> The spirit of cooperation that is the soul of society can hardly survive in a climate of consciousness of egocentric rights. This is why we are finding conflicts among the various component parts in our national life today, whether it is between teacher and the taught or labour and the industrialist. It is only by an assimilation of our cultural vision that the true spirit of cooperation and consciousness of duty can be revived in national life.[38]

Voluntary surrender of rights and acceptance of duties, according to Golwalkar, promotes cooperation and 'takes away the sting of disparity'.

Golwalkar's determination to preserve the unique character of the Hindu nation as well as social harmony amongst its members made him a staunch supporter of the *varna vyavastha* (caste system) in its pristine form. He maintained that there was nothing wrong in caste being based on birth, since the *varna* of one's birth is the consequence of one's past *karma*. Members of the lower *varna*, however, were consoled by citing a verse from the *Gita* which tells that the individual, who does his assigned duties in life in a spirit of selfless service, only worships God through such performance. Untouchability was the only aspect of the caste system which received his unmitigated condemnation because it was a later-day perversion and was against the spirit of the original scheme.[39]

Every plan of national reconstruction, even if it is restricted to the sphere of culture, carries in its womb some definite political goals. Golwalkar's professed disdain for politics is, therefore, nothing but a posture which had been adopted by many twentieth century political saints to obscure the underlying political orientation of their religious or cultural philosophy. In fact, the whole inspiration behind his plan for cultural revival was political.

However, Golwalkar differed from other Hindu politicians on two counts. One, he did not make direct seizure of political power an avowed goal of his movement. Two, he did not differentiate between organisation and ideology—the RSS is an organised form of an ideology. By doing so he was able to introduce a new method in Indian politics—the method of remote control. It incorporates the basic features of the ancient Brahmanic

---

[37] *Ibid.*, p. 27.
[38] *Ibid.*, pp. 107–9; Shri Guruji, *op. cit.*, Vol. 7, pp. 142–43, 150–51.
[39] Shri Guruji, *op. cit.*, Vol. 3, p. 43.

model which was immensely successful in casting the entire society in a single mould through the application of *dharma*, the universal code of values and conduct.[40] The responsibility of keeping society on the right path, on the path of *dharma*, rested on the virtuous men who were above the 'mundane temptations of self and power'.

But this Brahmanic model of remote control could not be used as a counterpoise against the established pattern of politics without the revival of a universal code of values and conduct and proper men who could exercise *dharmasatta*. Golwalker, therefore, devoted himself exclusively to the development of techniques which could produce and organise selfless men for propagating and enforcing universal values to preserve the integrity and harmony of the Hindu nation.

This gigantic 'mental revolution'—'panacea for all the ills of the nation'—was to be 'brought about by taking individual after individual and moulding him into an organised national life.' Moulding means 'awakening a passionate devotion to the motherland, a feeling of fraternity, a sense of sharing in national work, a deeply felt reverence for the nation's ideals, discipline, heroism, manliness and other notable virtues.'[41]

The techniques to imprint these permanent *sanskaras* consisted of 'three factors: first, constant mediation of the ideal that is to be framed into a *sanskara*; secondly, constant company of persons devoted to the same ideal; and finally, engaging the body in activities congenial to that ideal.'[42] This was done at a definite time, in the morning, evening or at night. In the language of the RSS this technique i called *shakha*. Daily participation in the *shakha* teaches

> the individual to behave in a spirit of oneness with the rest of his brothers in society and fall in line with the organised and disciplined way of life adjusting himself to the varied outlook of other minds. The persons assembling there learn to obey a single command . . . . More important than the discipline of the body is the discipline of the mind. They learn to direct their emotions and impluses towards the great national cause.[43]

The individual trained in this fashion, although called a *swayamsevak* (volunteer), was expected to be a 'missionary with a national vision'. These missionaries of the Hindu nation would remain 'aloof from the lures and tentacles of political power,' but would be 'alert and powerful enough' to check any deviation from or violation of the universal code by the state or individual.[44]

[40] Golwalkar, *op. cit.*, pp. 65, 71, 332.
[41] *Ibid.*, pp. 34, 39, 40, 41, 333.
[42] *Ibid.*, p. 350.
[43] *Ibid.*, p. 352.
[44] *Ibid.*, pp. 70, 73, 356; Shri Guruji, *op. cit.*, Vol. 5, p. 11.

Golwalkar had no aversion to the use of force for bringing about the necessary transformation of society.

> Today (there are people) who do not care for human goodness due to headiness of power, and greed of wealth and sex; no purpose would be served by telling or explaining our principles to such most impudent people. The use of force may be needed to make them follow our principles . . . sometimes there is need to pull ears also. But who will pull ears? He who has both explicit and internal capacity. He alone, who has good qualities can influence people, can control them due to his self realisation.[45]

The RSS is not merely a cultural or political organisation; it is the microcosm of the society which Golwalkar intended to create in India—'A perfectly organised state of . . . society wherein each individual has been moulded into a model of ideal Hindu manhood and made into a living limb of the corporate personality of society.'[46]

Once the indoctrination of the entire society was accomplished through the propagation of the ancient values after their denationalised features have been completely obliterated, the question as to who controlled the society or what goal the state should pursue would become totally irrelevant. Thus 'political power shall only reflect the radiance of culture, integrity and power of the organised society . . . just as the moon reflects the radiance of the sun.'[47] In other words, Golwalkar did not believe in altering the character of the state in order to alter the character of the society. He aspired to cast the society in a new mould so that the basic difference between the state and society—between Hindu state and Hindu nation—would disappear altogether.

In sum, the thesis of a duel between the spiritual culture of India and the material culture of the West (which was emphasised by Vivekananda to unify the fragmented Hindu society and to proclaim its superior status in the world community) was substantially modified by Aurobindo. For the latter, the scaffolding of political power and physical strength were urgently required to save Hindu spirituality from its impending collapse. The challenge to the Hindu nation that came from the Muslims diminished the significance of the duel between spirituality and materialism from the twenties onwards.

Savarkar had to go beyond spirituality to the roots of Indian history to prove that the Hindus were the original inhabitants of this land and were a nation in the modern sense of the term. He battled for two decades to resist the increasing encroachment on the Hindu rights by the minorities.

[45] Shri Guruji, *op. cit.*, Vol. 6, pp. 19, 178.
[46] Golwalkar, *op. cit.*, p. 61.
[47] *Ibid.*, p. 74.

This narrowed the dimensions of Hindu nationalism and virtually made it a one-point political programme—realisation of the superior claims of the Hindus vis-a-vis the minorities. The strategies forged by Savarkar and his one-point programme lost their significance after independence. The challenges which the upper caste, privileged sections of the Hindus had to face now were related to the entire multidimensional structure of their society.

Golwalkar's new strategy was to meet the challenges of the radically changed situation. Although he borrowed much of his ideology from Vivekananda's ideas, he also leaned occasionally on Dayanand, Aurobindo and Savarkar. The *swayamsevak* of the RSS represents the latest and perfected version of the ashram-trained missionary-monks idealised by Bankim, Aurobindo and Vivekananda.

From this analytical survey of the ideology of Hindu nationalism, it becomes apparent that throughout its history (from Bankim to Golwalkar) it has remained wedded to the philosophy of social conservatism and overt or covert antagonism towards the minorities. In a society where the Hindus constitute the dominant community and where the Muslims are a sizable minority, the fusion of social conservatism with religious exclusiveness has made the ideology of Hindu nationalism a formidable force. Frequent demands of the minorities for special rights and privileges confer a legitimacy on similar Hindu demands and keep their resentment alive. If the political failure of Hindu nationalism shows its limitation, its survival is reflective of its strength.

9

MOIN SHAKIR

Dynamics of Muslim Political Thought

Muslim political thinking in the nineteenth and twentieth centuries constitutes a part and parcel of what is called Indian political thought. A dogmatic emphasis on the distinction between Muslim and non-Muslim thinking is, therefore, not only misleading but fraught with dangerous implications. The Muslim or Islamic form or content does not make it distinctive and unique. In fact, the similarities in the form and content of Hindu and Muslim ideas are striking. Muslim political thought exhibits the same reformist, liberal, extremist, radical, secular or even Marxist trends that are found in the political thinking of other communities or social groups. The Muslims encountered challenges and threats which were also faced by the non-Muslims.

The question may be asked: Why does this kind of classification persist? One answer may be that the British rulers recognised the Indian people in terms of their ethnic, religious or cultural identities. The British were also interested in emphasising the sub-groups, castes and sub-castes in every community. It should also be noted that the logic of the imperialist model of growth reinforced such distinctions. The economic and social effects, generated by the British Raj, promoted communal groupings. However, I will elaborate this point later.

Another important element was the nature of the national movement. After the advent of the British Raj, the beneficiaries of the new educational and economic policies were the exploiting classes of pre-British India. The new arrangement could also be described in terms of caste and communal identities. The new dominant groups, the supporters and the opponents of the British Raj, attempted to establish a society after the European model, which was capitalist in character. They wanted to establish bourgeois hegemony in the intellectual, social and organisational spheres.

All these groups and leaders, however, did not follow the same political strategy, nor did they adopt a common political idiom. In the changing context, the strategy and the idiom were either liberal or socialist, conservative or radical. For the achievement of their objective, the leaders of the national movement wanted all the other communities to toe the line. The drawbacks here were the colonial interests, the peculiar situation of the Muslim communities in different regions, separate electorates, the support structure of electoral politics and the elitist character of the political leadership. All these determined the national movement's approach to the so-called communal problems in the country. The history of the national movement shows that this approach has always been inadequate and incapable of resolving the communal deadlock. In other words, the communal factor acted as an important political force, implying the perpetuation of communal identity and communal politics.

Muslim political thought may be analysed in terms of the Muslim response to colonialism and its effects or in terms of the desire of the Muslims to develop and consolidate their position in the emerging polity. The presence of the British Raj was indeed *the* determining factor of Muslim political thought.

The British, as the most powerful capitalist country, colonised India and integrated it into the world capitalist system. An account of the impact of British rule is, therefore, essential in order to comprehend the ethos of Muslim thought. It is true that the British were 'the unconscious tool of history' in causing a social revolution in India wherein the 'ancient world' was lost and the 'new' one was to emerge. It is claimed that the British made an outstanding contribution in making India modern, industrial, democratic and secular. They made the Indians familiar with a superior civilisation, modern science and technology. They established civilised government, provided a rule of law, stability, peace, and so on. They laid the foundations of popular, responsible and responsive government, in which the voice of every citizen could be heard. Therefore, it was the duty of every Indian to extend support and to be loyal to this government which was a 'gift of God' to their country. If social customs came in the way, they should be changed; cultural difficulties, if any, should be overcome; religious postulates should be reinterpreted; politics should accommodate this and aim at achieving the objective of creating unity between the ruler and the ruled. The entire liberal thought, of which the great spokesmen were Sir Syed Ahmed Khan, Abdul Latif, Ameer Ali, etc., revolved around these problems and issues. Undoubtedly the British rulers encouraged this line of thinking and supported the liberals in their efforts.

This assessment of the nature of British rule and the call to support alien rule were opposed by the leaders who mobilised the peasantry throughout the nineteenth century. The crucial question, then, is: What changes did the Britisn rulers introduce in the field of agriculture? And what effects did these produce on the different strata of rural society? The pre-British Indian agrarian structure was a class-divided set-up, in which the agricultural surplus, extracted in the form of revenue, was distributed among a large number of nobles, soldiers, bureaucrats, servants and retainers.[1]

The colonial rulers introduced a number of changes in the existing

---

[1] Tapan Raychoudhri, 'The Agrarian System of Mughal India,' *Enquiry*, Spring 1965, pp. 118–20; see also Irfan Habib, *Agrarian System of Mughal India* (Bombay: Asia Publishing House, 1963).

agrarian structure. New agrarian relations and a new class structure were the result of these changes. There occurred the growth of tenancy and a hierarchy of intermediaries between the state and the actual cultivators on a scale unprecedented in Indian history. Vast populations consisted of the landless, tenants-at-will, sharecroppers and petty peasant proprietors.[2] Thus the social basis of agriculture became regressive. The new forms of surplus extraction and utilisation (*a*) did not provide incentives or opportunities to any class or stratum to make modern improvements in agriculture, and (*b*) led to the siphoning off of resources from agriculture.[3] Consequently there was a stagnation in output, decline in productivity, fall in per capita availability of food and the increasing impoverishment of the cultivator.

It may be mentioned here that the British, who supported the landlords, were not interested in developing any national capitalist-industrial formation in India. They did not transform the whole socio-economic structure along capitalist lines. In the second half of the nineteenth century, the British policy underwent a certain change. They developed the transport system, set up private industries on the principle of free trade and established several units for processing raw materials for export. Heavy industries, which did not conflict with colonial interests, were also set up. The steady growth of industries helped the Indian bourgeoisie to become politically and economically strong. This new class did exercise a considerable influence on the national movement in the 1920s.

The purpose of the foregoing account is to show that Muslim political thought must be appreciated against the background of the colonial policies and the development of the national movement in the last quarter of the nineteenth century and in the first half of the twentieth century. One aspect of the situation needs to be highlighted. The effects of British rule varied from region to region and the national movement, when it got the support of the inhabitants of small towns in different states, produced unanticipated social tensions and economic conflicts. The different communities were variously affected by colonial economic and administrative measures. This aspect is extremely important for analysing the variations in political thinking and political action. In addition to this, there is a commonly-held notion that the communities in India are well-knit and homogeneous groups, which have a common culture and common interests. This is an incorrect understanding and it underlies the theory of one community, one leader, one language and one political organisation. In fact, all the communities are divided in terms of religious beliefs, language, culture, region or class. The description of political ideas should not ignore their social and economic foundation. After all, ideas

---

[2] Bipan Chandra, *Nationalism and Colonialism in Modern India* (New Delhi: Orient Longman, 1979), pp. 328–29.

[3] *Ibid.*, p. 329.

are the abstractions of certain interests and relationships in a given time and space. It is wrong to attribute these ideas uniformly to the entire community.

Let us take the case of the Muslim community. They roughly constituted, during the period under study, one-fifth of the total population. They were unevenly divided in different parts of the country. In 1921, they formed 6.71 per cent of the total population of Madras; in Bombay 19.74; Bengal 54.00; United Provinces 14.28; Punjab 55.33; Bihar and Orissa, Central Provinces and Berar 4.05; Assam 28.96; and North West Frontier Province 91.62. Within the community, different sects (like the Shias, Sunnis, Bohras, Khojas, Memons, etc.) existed. More often than not, their political interests and ambitions were at variance. It is also wrong to presume that the entire Muslim community was educationally backward. The rate of literacy varied from region to region. They were certainly backward, educationally, in Bengal but were quite advanced in Bombay Presidency and in the United Provinces. Their social customs and belief patterns were not common throughout the country. The Muslims belonging to the aristocratic families complained about the rural Bengali Muslims that 'nearly all of them have Hindu names; their manners and customs are those of the Hindus; they celebrate the Pujas'.[4] The point to be stressed here is that the differences between the elites and the masses were real. In Bengal the political interests and political problems of the Urdu-speaking elite and the Bengali-speaking masses did conflict. In the United Provinces 'the men of property and influence' and the 'gentlemen of progressive tendencies' represented different class interests. The Hindu and Muslim zamindars more often than not were one against the Hindu and Muslim peasants.

As stated earlier, the economic and administrative measures adopted by the colonial rulers generated dissimilar effects in different regions. The upper classes of the Muslim community in Bengal were adversely affected by the Permanent Settlement of Land Revenue (1793), the Resumption Proceedings (1828–46) and the removal in 1837 of Persian as the official language. These measures had a telling effect on the growth of higher education and the recruitment of Muslims in government services. They destroyed 'the economic basis of Muslim educational institutions, which were almost entirely maintained by revenue-free grants.'[5] By the end of the nineteenth century, most of the land in Bengal was owned by the Hindus. In Eastern Bengal where the Muslims were most numerous, this was particularly evident. In Bogra district (where Muslims formed 80 per cent of the population) there were only 5 Muslim zamindars. In

---

[4] Rafiuddin Ahmed, *The Bengal Muslims 1871–1906—A Quest for Identity* (Delhi: OUP, 1981), p. 7.
[5] Mushirul Hasan, *Nationalism and Communal Politics in India* (New Delhi: Manohar, 1979), p. 13.

Bakargunj district, Muslims were 64.8 per cent of the population but owned less than 10 per cent of the estates and paid less than 9 per cent of the total land revenue.[6]

Unlike in Bengal, the situation of the Muslim upper classes in UP and Punjab was radically different. In UP they continued to be 'advanced, prosperous and influential. This was due, in part, to the fact that the British introduced fewer drastic changes in the administrative machinery of northern India . . . . Recruitment was . . . on account of family background and tried loyalty to the Raj.'[7] Moreover, all those who tried to put down the 'Mutiny' were rewarded. The irrigation scheme helped them to further improve their economic position. Likewise, 'the Taluqdars of Oudh were brought forward as the "natural leaders of the people" and as the bulwarks of the Raj. In 1859 they received Sanads which conferred on them full proprietary rights, titles, possession of their Taluqas.'[8]

The response of the lower classes of the Muslim community to colonialism and colonial changes was not like the reaction of the upper classes. Also, the political thinking of the lower classes and that of the upper classes followed conflicting patterns. The lower classes were compelled to adhere to the old (i.e., pre-British) religio-political thinking and social institutions. They were aware of the fact of political decline but attempted to explain it in terms of their religious ideology and way of life. They accounted for their degeneration in terms of a deviation from the 'purity' of their doctrine. Hence the need for a reform movement to go back to Islam. They had to oppose everything that the colonial ruler had brought with them in their world—modern education, a new economy, new morality, etc. Their political goal was to drive the British out of the country. The colonial rule had brought for them impoverishment, and had taken away everything which was worthwhile for them. But the upper classes, even if they happened to be losers in consequence of the colonial policies, did not join hands with the aspirations of the lower classes. The reasons were many: absence of any contact with the lower classes, perception of cultural values and historical identity, great desire to have a share in jobs and the political imperatives to find out the ways and means to strike a compromise with the ruling powers.

Against this background, the Wahabi and the Faraizi movements should be appreciated. The Wahabis were described as 'communists and red republicans' in politics. Their objective was to free themselves both from the political tyranny of the British and from the Muslim oppressors as well as from the economic exploitation of the vested interests. The Wahabi government, under Bakht Khan, had 'abolished duty on such

---

[6] Anil Seal, *The Emergence of Indian Nationalism: Competition and Collaboration in the Later Nineteenth Century* (Cambridge: Cambridge University Press, 1968), p. 300.

[7] Mushirul Hasan, *op. cit.*, p. 16.

[8] *Ibid.*, p. 17.

articles of common consumption as salt and sugar, penalised hoarding
and offered five bighas of rent-free land in perpetuity to the families of
those soldiers who happened to die in the fight against the British.[9] They
constituted a 'persistently belligerent class' and a 'source of permanent
danger to the empire.' The Wahabis believed that both the Hindus and
Muslims should forge unity and fight against the British. It is also not an
accident that there was 'a close link between the rural districts of Bengal
and the jihad camps in the frontier.'[10] They had set up compact organisations in the rural areas. People marched regularly from Bengal to the
frontier and actively participated in the holy war. Those who could not
join the jihad were urged 'to resist passively and refrain from all intercourse with the *Kafir* rulers.'[11]

The Faraizis had suspended their congregation *Jummah* (Friday prayers)
and *Id* indicating that Bengal had become *dar-ul-Harb* suggesting an
inevitable antagonism with the alien rulers. Every Faraizi family in the
Bogra district contributed a handful of rice daily for religious purposes
which was regularly collected by the local head of the community.[12] The
objective was the promotion of jihad.

The Wahabis and the Faraizis promised economic benefits to the poor
peasantry. They preached the expropriation of the landlords without
compensation and proclaimed that 'no man has a right to levy taxes on
God's earth.'[13] The Wahabis and the Faraizis were considered 'dangerous'
not only by the British but also by the Hindu and Muslim landlords. In
order to counter their activities, the landlords created a new class of
'prosperous ryots' to whom land was distributed on fixed rent. This
measure was acclaimed by the government as 'the best conservative force
and the best security for peace and observance for law.'[14]

The support structure of the Wahabi and the Faraizi movement, as
R. Ahmed has pointed out, rested on the cultivating and labouring
classes. As Rev. J. Long has noted, 'the sons of tailors, butchers, hide-
merchants, petty traders (and) shop-keepers' also joined them in large
numbers.

In a sense, the Faraizi movement was more directly concerned with the
aspirations of the poor and the oppressed. Although some of its
members were engaged in small business dealings in rice, jute, hides
and tobacco, almost all the rest came from the very lowest strata of the

[9] K.M. Ashraf, in P.C. Joshi, ed., *Rebellion 1857* (Delhi: People's Publishing House,
1957), p. 88. See also Moin Shakir, *Khilafat to Partition* (New Delhi: Kalamkar Prakashan,
1970), pp. 13–16.
[10] Rafiuddin Ahmed, *op. cit.*, p. 42.
[11] *Ibid.*, p. 43.
[12] *Ibid.*, p. 43.
[13] *Ibid.*, p. 44.
[14] *Ibid.*, p. 45.

society, e.g., Jolahas, Kulus and the like. This was precisely the reason why the founder of the movement, Haji Shariatullah, came to be derided by its opponents as the *Pir* of the Jolahas. The Faraizi principle of equality induced many from these lower occupational groups to discard their 'caste' affiliations and join the movement.[15]

The anti-imperialist ingredient of Muslim political thought was continued in the second half of the nineteenth century and in the first half of the twentieth century. The Ulema (scholars of religion) provided the ideology and political strategy to this anti-British school of thought. The Deoband school or the Khilafat agitation were the great landmarks of this movement. The Deoband school was founded by Mohammed Qasim Nanatvi in the early 1860s. He did not oppose modern science but believed that greater emphasis should be on Islam and traditional learning. In agreement with the leaders of the movement of the 'mujahdeen,' he held that the extending of support to the British rule amounted to accepting slavery, which was contrary to the spirit of Islam.[16]

After the establishment of the Indian National Congress, the Ulema have been its consistent supporters. Some members of the Ulema have been in the forefront of formulating an anti-imperialist strategy with the active support of some foreign powers. Here, the case of the Silk Letters Conspiracy may be cited in which Maulana Mahmoodal Hasan and Ubaidullah Sindhi of Deoband were involved. The Ulema had succeeded in getting support and help against the British from the Turkish War Minister, Anwar Pasha. The following message was given to the tribal people of the Frontier:

> The Muslims of Asia, Africa and Europe, equipped with all sorts of weapons, have started a Jihad in the path of God. Thanks to Him who is omnipotent and Eternal, the Turkish army and the Mujahedeen have succeeded in subduing the enemies of Islam. Therefore, O Muslims, attack the tyrannical Christian regime which has kept you enslaved for years. Devote all your efforts with determination to kill the enemy, expressing your hatred and enemity towards it.[17]

[15] *Ibid.*, p. 46.

[16] Shah Abdul Aziz's *Fatwa* of 1803 had carried the same message:

In this city (Delhi) the Imamal Musalmin wields no authority. The real power rests with the Christian Officer. There is no check on them, and the promulgation of the commands of Kafir means that in the administration of Justice, in matters of Law and Order, in the domain of trade, finance and collection of revenue—everywhere the infidels are in power. Yes, there are certain Islamic rituals, e.g., Friday and Id prayers, Azan and Cow-slaughter with which they brook no interference, but the very root of all these rituals is of no value to them. They demolished Mosques without the least hesitation and no Muslim or any Zimmi can enter into the city or its suburbs except with their permission . . . . From here (Delhi) to Calcutta the Christians are in complete control.'

[17] See Moin Shakir, *Secularisation of Muslim Behaviour* (Calcutta: Minerva Associates, 1973), pp. 53–54. The letters urging rebellion against the British were wrapped in a piece of silk cloth. Hence it came to be known as the Silk Letters Conspiracy.

Apart from anti-imperialism, the Ulema also supported the principle of unity of the people irrespective of their religious beliefs. They upheld the principles of the protection of religious and political rights, moral and social reform and active participation of the people in the freedom struggle. They also propounded the notion of composite nationalism, in which religion is not given a determining position. They never believed that religion makes any community a nation. For them the territorial consideration is of much greater importance. The Ulema never sided with the supporters of the ideology of Pakistan. Some of these Ulema, after the Russian Revolution of 1917, believed that there is no difference between Islam and communism, which aims at the establishment of a just society. In the early 1920s, the Ulema were active in propagating the ideas of communism and in establishing a communist party.[18]

II

Pro-imperialist thought found expression in the writings of Sir Syed's Aligarh movement. It was based on the 'emancipatory,' 'democratic' and 'progressive' characterisation of the British rule. The Aligarh movement was essentially reformist in matters of religion and social customs. Its objective was to show that Islam does not conflict with progress and reason. A good government should have nothing to do with religion, and genuine religion is not concerned with worldly affairs. Religion lays down certain principles but they are ethical in character. The people should not rise in revolt against the ruler even if he is tyrannical, because, as Islam teaches, he is responsible to God.

Sir Syed noted that the Western notion of democracy and nationalism cannot operate in a country like India. The reasons given by Sir Syed are quite interesting as well as instructive. In one of his speeches, in 1883, he said:

In a country like India, where caste distinctions still flourish, where there is no fusion of the various races, where religious distinctions are still violent, where education in its modern sense has not made an equal or proportionate progress among all sections of population, I am convinced that introduction of the principle of election, pure and simple, for the representation of various interests on the local boards and the district councils should be attended with evils of greater significance than purely economic considerations. So long as differences of race and creed, and the distinctions of caste form an important element in the socio-political life of India, and influence her inhabitants in matters connected with administration and welfare of the country at large, the system of election cannot safely be adopted. The larger

[18] See Moin Shakir, *op. cit.*, 1970, pp. 47–63. See also Moin Shakir, 'Remembering Hasrat Mohani,' *Mainstream*, Annual Number, 1981.

community would totally overide the interests of the smaller community and the ignorant public would hold government responsible for introducing measures which might make the difference of race and creed more violent than ever.[19]

Elaborating his view of the Indian National Congress, he said:

The aims and objects of the Indian National Congress are based upon an ignorance of history and present day realities; they do not take into consideration that India is inhabited by different nationalities: they presuppose that the Muslims, Marathas, the Brahmins, the Kshatriyas, the Banias, the Sunars, the Sikhs, the Bengalee, the Madrasis, and the Peshwaries all be treated exactly alike and all of them belong to the same culture. The Congress conducted itself on the complacent assumption that all Indians profess the same religion, speak the same language, have the same way of life, that their attitude to history is similar and is based upon the same historical traditions. For the successful running of democratic government, it is essential that the majority should have the ability to govern not only themselves but also unwilling minorities.[20]

He, therefore, concluded that the Congress was harmful to the Hindus as well to the Muslims.

The reformist activities of Sir Syed were confined to the liberal reinterpretation of the Islamic doctrine and the popularisation of the rational approach towards social, cultural and educational problems.[21]

Here he could be compared with Raja Rammohan Roy. But unlike the Hindu social reform movement, his movement did not register any significant success. For analysing its weakness or failure, the nature of the two religions—Hinduism and Islam—should be considered. Hinduism is characterised by the absence of rigidity in matters of faith. In this sense, Islam is different. In the process of interpretation and adaptation, Hinduism was constantly reviewed and its base was broadened. It bore its time-honoured name without precluding change, enrichment and adaptation. But the fundamental tenets of Islam have, on the contrary, a

---

[19] Quoted in Reginald Coupland, *India, A Restatement* (London: Oxford University Press, 1945), p. 93.

[20] W. Theodore de Bary, ed., *Sources of Indian Tradition* (Oxford: Oxford University Press, 1958), p. 747.

[21] The aims and the objectives of the M.A.O. College which Sir Syed established were: (*i*) to provide a centre of Western learning for the *Muslims of the higher classes*, so they might recover the ground lost as a result of the opposition of the Ulema to Western education; (*ii*) to show the British rulers that Islam was not antipathetic to the West in culture, religion and social relations; (*iii*) to promote loyalty towards the rulers and solicit their favours; and (*iv*) to teach the Muslims that Islam was not a stereo-typed static religion but a progressive and liberal religion in consonance with reason and the laws of nature.

rigidity which would not brook any such liberties of interpretation as Hinduism allowed. The Hindus could reject any scripture (right from the *Vedas* to the *Gita*) or any doctrine which no Muslim could ever do. He might offer any interpretation of any aspect of the faith but he dare not reject it. The Hindu intellectuals could launch movements for religious reform and start various organisations for the purpose, while the efforts in the Muslim community remained confined to individuals as there was no possibility of creating powerful organisations.

Liberal thought represented the aspirations and the interests of the upper classes of the Muslim community. Their considerations were to support the British government and to have a share in the spoils. They expected that by supporting the government they would get concessions and favourable treatment. They were not concerned with the problems of the lower classes of the community; communal representation, separate electorates or even a separate homeland were not to deliver the goods to the lower sections of the society!

III

The liberals interpreted Islam in a way that was to serve their interests. One of the supporters of Sir Syed went to the extent of saying that the fundamental purpose of the Shariat and of the English laws was not different, as both provide security. There was no question of opposing the British rule on religious grounds.[22] The liberals did not conceal their hatred and hostility towards the lower classes. In one of the public meetings at Lucknow, Sir Syed said:

You will see that it is one of the necessary conditions of sitting at the same table with the Viceroy, that the person concerned should have a high social status in the country. Will the members of noble families in our country like it that a person of lower class or lower status, even if he has taken the B.A. or M.A. degree and possesses the necessary ability, should govern them and dispose of their wealth, property and honour? Never . . . . Not one of them will like it. The seat of the counsellor of the Government is a place of honour. Government cannot give it to anybody except a man of high social status. Neither can the Viceroy address him as 'my colleague' or 'my honourable colleague' nor can be invited to royal levees which are attended by dukes, earls and other men of high rank. So Government can never be blamed if it nominates men of noble families . . . .

In India, the people of higher social classes would not like a man of low birth, whose origin is known to them, to have authority over their life and property.[23]

[22] Nazir Ahmed, *Al Huquq wa al Faraiz* (Delhi, 1906), p. 131.
[23] See S. Abid Husain, *The Destiny of Indian Muslims* (Bombay: Asia, 1965), pp. 36–37.

Sir Syed appears to have been more concerned with protecting the interests of the aristocracy rather than propounding the Islamic notion of equality.

If the differences between the upper and lower classes were so deep, how could one explain the unity and consensus between them as was demonstrated in the Pakistan movement? In other words, what made the Muslims support the two-nation theory? Or why did Jinnah become the undisputed leader of the community? The reasons are many. The anti-imperialist tradition, in one way or the other, emphasised the validity of Islam as an ideology and the necessity of Islamising unorthodox beliefs and customs. The imperialist school always considered the interaction between progressive religion and liberal politics as important. It is not an accident that the language and idiom of politics, in the early twentieth century, became more and more Islamised. Not that politics or political thinking was becoming medieval or backward-looking. Abdul Kalam Azad, Mohamed Ali, Abdul Ala Maudoodi or Mohammed Iqbal were concerned with the strains and stresses of the contemporary situation. What Marx wrote about tradition may be applied here to Islamisation in India. He wrote:

> The tradition of all dead generations weighs like a nightmare on the brain of the living. And just when they seem engaged in revolutionising themselves and things, in creating something that had never yet existed, precisely in such periods of revolutionary crisis they anxiously conjure up the spirits of the past to their services and borrow from them names, battle cries and costumes in order to present the new scene of world history in this time-honoured disguise and this borrowed language . . . . a beginner who has learnt a new language always translates it back into his mother tongue but he has assimilated the spirit of the new language and can freely express himself in it only when he finds his way in it without recalling the old and forgets his native tongue in the use of the new.[24]

The process of Islamisation was strengthened by the upward mobility of the underprivileged. R. Ahmed has noted that in rural Bengal

> the craze for identity as reflected in the census figures was closely related to the social aspirations of the underprivileged, as an indicator of social change, as also of the popular urge to acquire an identity that was "Muslim" and not "Bengali". Ashrafisation would confer a double benefit—social status as well as Islamic identity.[25]

[24] Karl Marx, 'Eighteenth Brumaire of Napolean Bonaparte,' in *Selected Works*, Vol. 1 (Moscow: Progress Publishers, 1962), p. 247.

[25] Rafiuddin Ahmed, *op. cit.*, p. 116. Ashrafisation was the Muslim equivalent of Sanskritisation.

Similar developments were taking place in other regions also. Such aspirations and political assertions on the part of the underprivileged Sunnis created the Shia-Sunni problem in UP. These sections' access to education (which was inevitable in view of the colonial economy, with the rising prosperity of jute-growing areas in Bengal) also accelerated Islamising tendencies. Rejection of the typical local customs, the urge to learn Urdu, and preference for 'Muslim' culture are the elements of the same process.

Islamisation effectively influenced the political process. It bridged the gulf between the elite and the lower classes. Real economic differences became unimportant. There appeared a kind of unity at the surface of the community. The principal contradiction and antagonism with imperialism remained but the initiative and decision-making power was transferred to the leaders belonging to the middle and upper classes of the community. Linguistic and regional differences were forgotten. Hinduism was conceived as a threat and the Hindus were regarded as enemies. 'Historical' and 'spiritual' differences between the two communities were emphasised. The Hindus and Muslims were described as 'inconsistent elements in India'. The burden of the argument was that not separate electorates but a separate homeland should be created for the Muslim community.

> The Muslims cannot divorce their religion from the politics. In Islam religious and political beliefs are not separated from each other. Religion and politics are inseparably associated in the minds and thoughts of all Muslims . . . . Their religion includes their politics and their politics are a part of their religion. The mosque not only constitutes a place of their worship but also the Assembly Hall . . . . They are born into a system . . . . Hence Hindu-Muslim unity or nationalism, signifying homogeneity between them in all non-religious matters, is unimaginable. The Islamic polity in which religion and politics are inseparably united requires perfect isolation for its development. The idea of a common state with heterogeneous membership is alien to Islam and can never be fruitful.[26]

This was Jinnah's two-nation theory. These politics did not benefit the lower classes but ensured the hegemony of the upper classes who kept the exploitative economic structure intact.

There is another aspect of this phenomenon. It is the ideological and social character of the national movement. The leadership of the national movement has been the monopoly of middle and upper class Indians. It aimed at forging the unity of the middle and upper classes belonging to all the communities. The developments within the Muslim community

---

[26] 'A Punjabi,' *Confederacy of India* (Lahore, 1932), pp. 88–89.

certainly obstructed such a unity, as the process of emergence of the classes was uneven and slow compared to that of the Hindu community. The national movement in its early phase was not at all favourably disposed towards the staunch anti-imperialist activities of the lower classes. The upper classes and their leaders were out to appease the British so that they could reach a compromise with the rulers. They also entertained certain apprehensions about the working of democracy and nationalism which they feared would render them ineffective.

The national movement, therefore, attracted only a few of the highly educated and some members of the business community who were alienated from the socio-religious and political process among the Muslims in different parts of the country. In order to win over the middle and the upper classes, 'protection' and 'safeguards' were provided by the rulers to these interests; consequently, the leaders of these classes seldom referred to the religious, cultural and social rights of the community.[27] In this regard, the *liberal, extremist and Gandhian* strategies were the same. Even the Khilafat was a popular movement but not a peoples' movement.[28] The approach of the national movement towards the communal problem was to solve it 'through a scheme or pact between the leaders without bringing in or educating the people at all. The latter were seen as unfit to discuss or decide such an important matter.'[29] In matters of communal riots, no mass political or ideological struggle was waged against the organisers of the riots and the outlook which enabled them to flourish.[30] The constraints of electoral politics led the national movement leaders away from the masses and close to the middle and upper classes.[31] Separate electorates also strengthened this approach.[32]

It has been argued that the national movement was dominated by the

[27] Bipan Chandra, *op. cit.*, p. 253. In 1888, at Allahabad, the Congress passed a resolution stating 'no subject shall be passed for discussion by the subjects committee or allowed to be discussed at any Congress by the President, thereof, to the introduction of which the Hindu or Mohamedan delegates as a body object, unanimously or near-unanimously.'

[28] *Ibid.*, p. 255.

[29] *Ibid.*, p. 256. Bipan Chandra says:

In fact all the serious Congress efforts at bringing about Hindu-Muslim unity were in the nature of negotiations among the top leaders of the Hindu, Muslim and Sikh communalism and the Congress. Quite often, the Congress assumed the role of an intermediary between the different communal leaders instead of acting as the advance-guard and active organiser of the forces of secular nationalism.

[30] *Ibid.*, p. 257.

[31] In the Provincial Assemblies' election of 1937, the Muslim League won 108 out of 482 seats. On the 73,19,445 Muslim voters, only 3,21,722 voted for the League candidates.

[32] When the Muslim communalists agreed to have joint electorates—in 1927 (Nehru Committee discussions), in 1931 (Second Round Table Conference) and in 1932 (All Parties Unity Conference)—the Congress leaders refused to clinch the issue because of the pressure of Hindu communal opinion.

middle and the upper classes and always protected the interests of the zamindars and the Indian capitalists.[33] The peasants were advised 'to abide by the terms of their agreements with the zamindars, whether such an agreement is written or inferred from custom.'[34] In 1930, the famous Eleven Demands, which, in the words of Gandhiji, constituted 'the substance of independence,' included restoration of the exchange rate of 1s. 4d., a protective tariff against foreign cloth and the reservation of coastal trade for Indian shipping.[35] Thus the Indian bourgeoisie

> did not see a mass movement as a threat to its interest so long as it was confined within limits that did not threaten its hegemony over social development. And here it may be suggested that while the Moderates established bourgeois ideological hegemony over the intellegentsia, the political leadership of the Gandhian era established bourgeois ideological, political and organisational hegemony over the vast mass of peasants, workers, and lower middle classes.[36]

The ideology of the national movement and the functioning of the Congress promoted the Islamised and exclusive image of the Muslim middle and upper classes. In the forties, the Muslim League received not only the official patronage and support of the Muslim zamindars but also the backing of Muslim bourgeoisie. The Ispahanis, a Calcutta-based Muslim business family with all-India connectic s, helped Jinnah in asserting his control over Bengal Muslim polit..s by ousting Fazhul Haq.[37] The Muslim League papers, *Star of India* and *Dawn*, were financed by the Ispahanis and Adamjee. A Federation of Muslim Chambers of Commerce and Industry was started with Jinnah's blessings, and Muslim banks and an airline company were planned. The Muslim League promised 'the hedging off of a part of India from competition by the established Hindu business groups or professional classes so that the small Muslim business class could thrive and the nascent Muslim intelligentsia could find employment.'[38] In his letter of July 1942 to Mahadev Desai, G.D. Birla wrote, 'You know my views about Pakistan. I am in favour of separation, and I do not think it is impracticable or against the interests of Hindus or of India.'[39] Thus the character of the national movement, and of the Congress, the aspirations of the Muslim upper classes and the

---

[33] Moin Shakir, *Politics of Minorities* (New Delhi: Ajanta, 1980), Ch. 1.
[34] See Bipan Chandra, *op. cit.*, p. 167.
[35] *Ibid.*, p. 139.
[36] *Ibid.*, p. 136.
[37] Sumit Sarkar, 'Popular Movements and National Leadership, 1945–47,' *Economic and Political Weekly*, Annual Number, 1982, p. 679.
[38] *Ibid.*, p. 679.
[39] *Ibid.*

nature of Muslim League politics shaped the consensus of the Muslim masses and the *Ashrafs* of the community. The political thought of Mohammed Iqbal and Jinnah clearly reflected the basic characteristics of this emerging political situation. It not only highlighted the emerging crisis of identity but also proposed a strategy for resolving that crisis.

IV

A proper understanding of Muslim thought can be had by grasping the basic features of the political thought of Abul Kalam Azad and Abul Ala Maudoodi. The ideas of both these intellectuals have significant relevance not only in India but also in the Muslim world, where a good deal of politics and political thinking still revolve around the issues raised by these leaders.[40]

Azad was an outstanding Muslim intellectual of modern India. By training a fundamentalist,[41] Azad was secular and a democrat in politics. He rejected the Aligarh tradition of loyalism and attempted to provide an Islamic programme of unity and participation of the Muslim community in the national movement. This programme clearly revealed the influence of Jamaluddin Afghani and Shibli Numani. He surveyed Indian politics in terms of Islam. His view of Islam did not come into conflict with territorial nationalism, pan-Islamism or anti-imperialism. The annulment of the partition of Bengal, the Kanpur mosque incident, the Jalianwala Bagh tragedy, and the anti-Muslim foreign policy of the British rulers convinced Azad that an imperialist rule could not be democratic. Therefore, he decided to side with the Indian National Congress which was fighting for the political independence of the country.

The end of the Khilafat institution marked, for Azad, the end of the romantic phase of Muslim politics. It also revealed the futility of spiritual-ised politics and pan-Islamism as an instrument for the liberation of the

[40] For an interesting discussion of this point see M. Rodinson *Marxism and the Muslim World* (New Delhi: Orient Longman, 1980), pp. 15–17.

[41] Compare Aziz Ahmed, *Islamic Modernism in India and Pakistan* (London: OUP, 1967), pp. 184–85.

But in religious thought he (Azad) put the clock back undoing much of the work of the Aligarh modernists and Iqbal. Unlike them he was not interested in the problem of the reform of Muslim Law. He did not concern himself with the validity or historicity of *hadis*. On the question of Ijtehad his position was ambivalent, inclining more towards conservatism than modernism. In spite of his preoccupation with the quest for an idealised theocratic but modern state, Iqbal had placed man at the centre of the scheme of things, in charge of the dynamism of creativity and action, at the centre of the universe as God's viceregent on earth. Despite his eclecticism and humanism, Azad reasserted God's suzerainty as the provider, the benefactor, the judge, the guide, the beautiful; and left very little for his man to achieve except greater faith in God and an impeccable, balanced, and tolerant moral life.

country. It brought Azad closer to nationalism. He made it clear that the prophet of Islam proclaimed the truth of human brotherhood as soon as he delivered the message of monotheism and announced his prophethood. He cited the prayer of the Prophet: 'O God, I bear witness that all people are brothers to one another. Differences they might have created among themselves, but you have united them together with a single bond of humanity.'[42] Thus Islam fosters, Azad concluded, nationalism, avoiding communal and racial prejudices. Every Indian Muslim, therefore, is a member of the Indian nation and cannot, by virtue of a common bond of religion, separate himself from the larger Indian society and claim the status of separate nationhood. He is a part of the indivisible unity that is Indian nationality. In his Congress Presidential Address (1940), he said;

Eleven hundred years of common history have enriched India with our common achievements. Our languages, our poetry, our literature, our culture, our art, our dress, manners and customs, the innumerable happenings of our daily life, everything bears the stamp of our joint endeavour. There is indeed no aspect of our life which had escaped this stamp . . . this joint wealth is the heritage of our common nationality and we do not want to leave it and go back to the time when this joint life had not begun. If there are any Hindus amongst us who desire to bring back the Hindu life of a thousand years and more, they dream and such dreams are vain fantasies. So also if there are any Muslims who wish to revive their past civilisation and culture which they brought a thousand years ago from Iran and Cental Asia, they dream also and the sooner they wake up the better. These are unnatural fancies which cannot take root in the soil of reality. I am one of those who believe that revival may be necessary in religion but in social matters it is the denial of progress.[43]

Unlike many of his contemporaries, Azad insisted that Hindus and Muslims will have to think of their position and interest 'not as a Hindu or Musalman but as a peasant or zamindar, or a labourer or a capitalist, and so on . . . . It will be worth nothing unless it reflects equality of opportunity and economic freedom of all.'[44]

Azad viewed Islam as a liberating force which opposed slavery. Therefore, there should not be any conflict between democracy and Islam. The sovereignty of the prophet and the concept of Khilafat was in consonance with democratic equality. Khilafat literally means nothing more or less than representations. Under Khilafat, a nation's free will,

[42] G.N. Sarma and Moin Shakir, *Politics and Society* (Aurangabad: Parimal Prakashan, 1976), pp. 352–53.
[43] A.K. Azad, *Congress Presidential Speeches* (edited by Shankar Ghose), (All India Congress Committee, 2nd edition, 1975), p. 362.
[44] Cf. A.B. Rajput, *Abul Kalam Azad* (Lahore, 1946), pp. 158–59.

unity, suffrage and election could operate.[45] The people have every right to rebel against a government founded on untruth and injustice. He declared that 'ours is essentially a democratic age and the spirit of equality, fraternity and liberty is sweeping over all the people of the world. The Asian countries must reconstruct their polity and the society in conformity with that society.'[46]

Azad's role in Indian politics and his political ideas are not usually subjected to objective and critical analysis. He is unjustly rejected, as the Muslim League leaders did, or wrongly accepted, as the anti-Muslim League leaders have been doing.[47] Azad's image as a great scholar of religion and religion-oriented politics would have served the interests of our upper classes of Muslims much more effectively than that of any other leader. His notion of nationalism and democracy and vision of society was in keeping with the bourgeois spirit. (It is not an accident that at the first available opportunity, in his first speech before the Constituent Assembly in Pakistan, Jinnah abandoned his two-nation theory and supported a secular polity.) But Azad's leadership was not accepted as the Muslim League politics of 'religion in danger' and a 'promise of Islamic state' stirred the Muslim masses. The upper classes were aware of the fact that Jinnah could succeed in creating a separate homeland. Besides, Azad's passionate attachment to the Congress made him unpopular in the eyes of the Muslim upper classes.

The Congress wrongly tried to project Azad as the Muslim leader. This strategy was bound to fail. Like other Congress leaders, Azad was for establishing the bourgeoisie hegemony in the country. On the question of labour and their demands, he unreservedly supported the interests of the government and the possessing classes. In 1946 (a year marked by militant strikes), he 'publicly welcomed the ration-cut' (a major labour grievance) as 'far-sighted' and declared that strikes were 'out of place today,' as the British were 'now acting as caretakers'.[48] The Congress condemned these strikes as 'hasty or ill-conceived stoppages' and 'growing lack of discipline and disregard of obligation on the part of the workers'.[49]

As against the liberal nationalism of Azad, Maoodi represented the fascist trend. His movement—the Jamaat e-Islami—may be viewed as the counterpart of the Ikhwan-al-Muslamin of Egypt. His concept of Islam, approach to the past and attitude to Indian politics are borrowed from Abu Musleh[50] and the earlier writings of Azad. For Maudoodi, Islam is a

[45] See Humayun Kabir, *Abul Kalam Azad* (Bombay: Asia, 1959), p. 44.

[46] A.K. Azad, *Speeches of Azad* (New Delhi: Government of India, Publications, 1950), p. 150.

[47] It should be noted that Azad's writings became quite popular in Pakistan. A number of editions of his books have appeared there after 1947.

[48] Sumit Sarkar, *op. cit.*, p. 682.   [49] *Ibid.*, p. 682.

[50] For details see G.N. Sarma and Moin Shakir, *op. cit.*, pp. 359–61, and also M. Shakir, *op. cit.*, 1970, Ch. 4.

religion which determines the relation between man and God as well as between man and man. No aspect of life is excluded from Islam and it is, therefore, a complete guide to life and conduct. He held that all Muslims belong to one and the same community (*Ummat*). All Islamic countries are like a single unit. Though dispersed and separated geographically, their common spiritual bond transcends barriers of space and unites them in a single spiritual homeland. The objective of the movement is the establishment of the rule of God on earth.

The greatest obstacles to Islam are the Western system and communism. The West constitutes a menace and an impediment to the spread of Islam. The West, by emphasising utilitarian morality and materialist welfare, seeks to make man independent of God and replace the sovereignty of God by the sovereignty of man. According to Maudoodi, the Western concept of nationalism is nothing but social selfishness. It divides mankind along race and territory and is nurtured on the sentiment of hostility and revenge. Similarly, democracy is unaccountable because it believes in the sovereignty of the people while Islam is wedded to the sovereignty of God. Besides, human intelligence is not equipped to make perfect laws. Hence, there is no need for elections or legislative assemblies. Popular franchise, to Maudoodi, is religiously prohibited (*Har'am*). It is the violation of the fundamental principle of unity and supremacy of God.

Maudoodi attacked the communist and socialist doctrine. According to him, Islam and communism are poles apart. Islam upholds the institution of private property and private ownership of the means of production. Islam recognises and maintains economic classes and never supports the abolition of the haves. Maudoodi did not agree with other interpretations of Islam which show that the spirit of Islamic doctrines is communistic.[51]

What are the implications of Maudoodi's interpretation of Islam and Islamic politics? The fight against the British was futile and those who were fighting against it are not on the 'right path' as expounded by Islam. They lack the righteousness of viewpoint. The objectives of the freedom movement were regarded as not only un-Islamic but anti-Islamic. The Indian National Congress was described as 'politically Indian, Ideologically Communist and culturally Western.' It represented the interests of Hindu nationalism. The achievement of independence, and the establishment of democratic government, would mean slavery for the minorities. It would not be self-government for them but a rule of the majority. Maudoodi's ideas are essentially anti-secular, anti-democratic and anti-communist. They serve the interests of a reactionary and anti-people government and constitute the ideology of the exploiting classes. Maudoodi does talk of Islamic socialism but his Islamic socialist is not different from Hitler's national socialist.

[51] For Maudoodi's political ideas, see his *Political Theory of Islam* (Pathankot: Jamate-Islami, 1939); *Nationalism and India* (New Delhi: Jamate-Islami, 1948, 3rd edition); and Khursheed Ahmed, ed., *Islamic Law and Constitution*. (Karachi: Jamate-Islami, 1955).

Muslim political thinking was thus a response to colonialism and to the national movement. Broadly speaking, there have been two dominant trends—anti-imperialist and pro-imperialist. The communal, secular or religious categories have been of secondary importance. The pro-imperialist trend represented the interests and aspirations of the middle and upper classes of the Muslim community. From Sir Syed to Iqbal and Jinnah and from Badruddin Tyabji to Abul Kalam Azad, the interests of the same class/classes are being represented. In the absence of their capacity to dominate, the anti-imperialists and the lower classes were bound to be ineffective. The same story gets repeated after independence, more as a tragedy and less as a farce, both in India and Pakistan.

10
ELEANOR ZELLIOT

The Social and Political Thought of B.R. Ambedkar

I

Dr *Bhimrao Ramji Ambedkar* (1891–1956) is known as the leader of India's Untouchables, as the 'modern Manu' for his work in piloting the Constitution of independent India through the Constituent Assembly, as well as, in Nehru's words, a symbol of revolt against all the oppressive features of Hindu society. His political life and thought spanned nearly forty years. During this time, he organised and politicised his own Mahar caste and a great many other Untouchable groups in urban areas; he founded three political parties; he served in the cabinets of both British India and independent India; and he wrote and spoke extensively on political problems and the political process.[1] Although Ambedkar's basic political beliefs in human equality, parliamentary democracy and legal redress for social wrongs were formed early in his life, his political philosophy in practical details was often shaped by the politics of social reform and by India's special brand of minority politics.

Since Ambedkar's political thought and action was also formed in relationship to his own caste status and the Maharashtrian world around him, it is necessary to note the events of his life in those special contexts. Ambedkar was born in Mhow (now Mahu) in Madhya Pradesh, the fourteenth child of a headmaster in the army normal school there. The Mahar caste (to which he belonged) held the traditional place of 'inferior village servants,' in British terminology, but several members of his family had left their poor villages in the Ratnagiri area south of Bombay to join the British army. Ambedkar's birth in 1891 coincided with two trends: the Mahars were beginning to organise in protest against British cancellation of their army recruitment and the increasing awareness of the problem of untouchability among Marathi-speaking Brahmans (such as the poet Keshavsut, the jurist and reformer Mahadeo Ranade, the

[1] See Owen M. Lynch, *The Politics of Untouchability* (New York: Columbia University Press, 1969); Barbara R. Joshi, *Democracy in Search of Equality* (Delhi: Hindustan Publishing Corporation, 1982), and Eleanor Zelliot, 'Learning the Use of Political Means: The Mahars of Maharashtra,' in Rajni Kothari, ed., *Caste in Indian Politics* (New Delhi: Allied Publishers, 1970) for specific studies of Ambedkar's influence; D.R. Jatava, *The Political Philosophy of B.R. Ambedkar* (Agra: Phoenix Publishing Agency, 1965), A.J. Rajasekhariah, *B.R. Ambedkar: The Politics of Emancipation* (Bombay: Sindhu Publications, 1971), and C. Bharill, *Social and Political Ideas of B.R. Ambedkar* (Jaipur: Aalekk Publishers, 1977) for studies of his political thought.

Sanskritist R.D. Bhandarkar and the reformer, Gopal Ganesh Agarkar). The Satyashodak (truth-seeking) movement of reform begun by Jotirao Phule, a non-Brahman, was at a low ebb at the time of Ambedkar's birth, but the movement for equality and for non-Brahman power, which he set in motion, inspired the Maharajas of Baroda and Kolhapur who helped Ambedkar get his extraordinary education.

Although Ambedkar experienced discrimination, he was never locked into the village pattern of traditional work and status. He grew up in an atmosphere of changing aspirations and incipient organisation among his own caste fellows, and in a caste which accounted for 10 per cent of the Marathi-speaking area. And although the intellectual elite of that area spoke for the removal of the disabilities of the Untouchables, they did not promote any action. Apart from the educational efforts of non-Brahman reformers—Phule in the nineteenth century and V.R. Shinde in the early twentieth—the reformers left the leadership of any movement for change up to the Untouchables themselves. The result of all these factors was to create an opportunity of unusual proportions for an Untouchable of Ambedkar's intelligence and character.

Ambedkar's family had moved to Bombay in his youth to enable their brightest child to attend good and fairly open schools. After graduating from Elphinstone College in 1913 (he was one of the first members of his caste to hold a degree), Ambedkar was sent by the Gaikwad of Baroda to Columbia University in New York, where he received a Ph.D. Chhatrapati Shahu Maharaj of Kolhapur provided Ambedkar aid which enabled him to get a D.Sc. from the University of London and to pass the bar from Grey's Inn. Ambedkar returned from his two trips to America and Europe finally in 1923, one of the best educated men in the province of Bombay. The influence of these years seems to have been the development of pragmatism and self-confidence, faith in education and a deep belief in flexible parliamentary democracy. Curiously enough, any sort of doctrinaire socialism left no mark on him, and he had no alliances with European political groups. He seems to have returned with the idea that India must evolve its own form of parliamentary democracy and its own cure for its problems of inequality.

Until 1935, Ambedkar's work took three directions: the most visibly successful was the awakening and organising of the Untouchables—through newspapers of their own, social and cultural institutes, and widely attended conferences, then called 'Depressed Classes' conferences. He also participated in every opportunity to petition the British government for political representation for Untouchables, and these opportunities were many: the Southborough Committee on Franchise, the Simon Commission to evaluate the reforms and the famous Round Table Conferences in London. Ambedkar also served in the Bombay Legislature to which his efforts had won token representation for the Untouchables.

The third direction his work took was that of encouraging education among the lower classes, first by exhortation and the founding of hostels so that they would have a place to stay while attending school, and eventually by establishing a still-growing network of colleges under the Peoples Education Society.

These years of activity reveal some changes in Ambedkar's political ideology, but more striking are the constant patterns. He believed that only Untouchables could lead Untouchables. He never joined or supported any caste Hindu-led group, although he invited high caste Hindus to serve on his institutes and in his activities. He firmly believed in Untouchable self-improvement, and constantly wrote and spoke against practices (such as, drinking and the eating of carrion beef) which were associated with low caste behaviour, with the corollary that the lower classes were capable of exemplary behaviour and self-respect. He was sure that honest and sufficient representation in governing bodies would enable the Depressed Classes to 'redress their grievances' via legal means. There is also a pattern during these years of attempts to claim equality within Hinduism: three temple satyagrahas, none of them successful, none of them supported by Gandhi or the Indian National Congress; efforts to join the popular Ganapati festivities in Bombay; at least one public donning of the sacred thread of the three upper varnas; multi-caste dinners in which sympathetic caste Hindus, chiefly from marginal higher castes, joined with Untouchables. It is clear that Untouchables felt deeply their inability to participate in the religious life around them; it also seems clear that Ambedkar never placed much trust in the ability of Hinduism to reform itself.

Two instances during the early years of Ambedkar's leadership seem to mark the turning points in his philosophy—the Mahad Conferences of 1927 and the battle with Gandhi over the Communal Award that was the outcome of the Round Table Conferences of 1930–32. However, both, analysed closely, are consistent with his pragmatic faith in parliamentary democracy and legal redress for Untouchable grievances. Both also, it must be said, illustrate the gift Ambedkar possessed for dealing with the psychological dimension of untouchability, the need to create pride and self-confidence. During the first Mahad Conference, Untouchables and some non-Brahmans met at a town south of Bombay in what began as a normal Conference of the Depressed Classes. A sudden impulse to test the Bole Resolution of the Bombay Legislative Assembly (which had declared all public places open to Untouchables) led the conferees to the town pond to drink water. They were met with open violence and retreated from Mahad, only to return to a second Conference later in 1927. Here, in a historic gesture, the classic Hindu law book which explicitly condoned the practice of untouchability, the *Manusmriti*, was burned in public. This was a telling gesture, and not even the fact that one of Ambedkar's renegade Brahman friends, G.N. Sahastrabuddhe, participated in the act kept it from shocking the Hindu community. In spite of this highly publicised act, however, Ambedkar pursued the matter of the right to water in Mahad in the courts, not in the streets, winning a legal victory years later.[2]

Mahad is seen as the real beginning of Ambedkar's leadership of the Untouchables; the Round Table Conference is seen as a recognition by all of that leadership. Ambedkar attended all three Conferences during 1930–32 as one of the two Untouchable delegates chosen by the British government. At the Second Conference, he came into direct conflict with Gandhi. Ambedkar's public position was not at variance with Gandhi's before the Conferences. In 1930, at a Depressed Classes Conference in Nagpur, he urged independence for India—the first Untouchable leader to urge the British to leave. His position on political rights for Untouchables, articulated most recently in testimony to the Simon Commission, urged joint electorates for both the Depressed Classes and the Muslims, but with adult suffrage and reserved seats, as well as some special attention to the education and employment of the Depressed Classes in government positions. In the midst of the clamour in London of every other minority for an election process in which they alone would elect their representatives, however, Ambedkar changed his position to one demanding separate electorates for Untouchables.

Gandhi opposed Ambedkar in London, but his most effective opposition came later in 1932, after the Communal Award of the British government granted separate electroates for the Depressed Classes. He 'fasted unto death' in his cell in the Yeravda Prison in Poona, protesting separate electorates as a device which would separate the Untouchables from Hindu society forever. As Gandhi weakened, Ambedkar capitulated, but only when some Hindu leaders gathered to pledge their help in the removal of untouchability, and the agreement that the Untouchables would have reserved seats in all elected bodies.[3]

The 'Poona Pact' set the pattern for reserved seats for Untouchables (soon to be called Scheduled Castes as they were enumerated on a schedule or list for the purpose of the elections) which still exists in Indian elected bodies. It also illustrated the basic difference in political philosophy and tactics between Gandhi and Ambedkar. Gandhi believed that only a change of heart on the part of caste Hindus would remove untouchability,

---

[2] The most complete account of Ambedkar's life is still Dhananjay Keer's *Dr. Ambedkar: Life and Mission* (Bombay: Popular Prakashan, 3rd edition, 1971), although W.N. Kuber's *B.R. Ambedkar* in the Builders of Modern India Series (New Delhi: Government of India, 1978) is a competent briefer summary of all the important incidents.

[3] An entire book on this episode by Pyarelal entitled *The Epic Fast* (Ahmedabad: Mohanlal Maganlal Bhatt, 1932), which tells the story from the Gandhian point of view, illustrates the dramatic impact of the Gandhi-Ambedkar clash.

but he also believed this was an imminent change. His further efforts for the Harijans (people of God), a name he coined after the Poona Pact, reflect this stress on the need for penance on the part of upper castes. Ambedkar, on the other hand, believed in legal redress of grievances and guarantees of rights, backed up by political power on the part of the aggrieved. Even though the Poona Pact guaranteed what Ambedkar most wanted—the political participction of the Depressed Classes—and even though it might be seen as a mighty advance over the one nominated member in the Bombay Legislative Assembly given the Depressed Classes just over ten years earlier, Ambedkar was to look back on the Poona Pact as the beginning of his bitter quarrel with Gandhi.[4]

II

The mid-thirties, however, found Ambedkar in a triumphant if obstinate mood. He cut off the seven years of temple entry satyagrahas with an announcement in 1935 that he 'would not die a Hindu,' and called a conference in 1936 to discuss conversion. There is no reason to think that Ambedkar was not sincere in his personal rejection of Hinduism. One can speculate, however, on the circumstances and timing of the announcements. Ambedkar's dramatic rejection of Hinduism took place at a conference of 10,000 Depressed Class people meeting at a site not far from Nasik, the scene of a five year bitter battle over the right to enter the famous Kalaram temple there. The 1936 Conference was well publicised, and Ambedkar began to receive requests to visit the Depressed Classes in the North and in Kerala. The announcement also came as a shock to the Gandhians and the Hindu leaders who had been pursuing their campaign of attempting to persuade temple committees to open their temples to the Depressed Classes. A pamphlet published by Ambedkar in 1936, *Annihilation of Caste*, which states the necessity to uproot the concept of the hereditary priesthood in order to make Hinduism more than a 'religion of rules' was as defiant a gesture as his own personal vow to leave Hinduism. It seems to me that the 1935–36 statements on religion reflect Ambedkar's growing sense of the commitment of his following, his need to shock the Hindu community out of complacency, and his understanding of the need of Untouchables to grasp their own future.

Startling as the religious announcements were, Ambedkar did no more than investigate various possible religions—Sikhism, Christianity and Islam among them. The religion he had been drawn to since boyhood, Buddhism, had no viable remnant left in India, and there was little understanding of it as a living religion, even among the elite. The choice

* Ambedkar's side of the Poona fast and a general polemic against the Gandhian and Congress position was published much later as *What Congress and Gandhi Have Done to the Untouchables* (Bombay: Thacker and Co., 1945).

was not at all clear, and Ambedkar simply moved along in the political world, shelving the religious aspects of the movement for two decades. The political efforts he made, however, represent a different world of opportunity from the pre-1935 era of Indian politics. The Government of India Act of 1935 set the stage for the election in 1937 of truly representative political bodies, and Ambedkar prepared his political campaign.

Ambedkar's first political party, the Independent Labour Party (undoubtedly a conscious tribute to the British Labour Party), was born in great optimism to fight the elections of 1937, the first elections in which the Untouchables, or Scheduled Castes, were to have a specific number of designated seats according to their strength in numbers. The first announcement of the party came in August 1936, two months after the conference called by Ambedkar declared that the Mahar caste was ready to leave Hinduism. The spirit of the two moves was much the same—independent, innovative, intolerant of paternalism, determined to build new structures outside the old ways, determined to make a mark on India.

The platform of that first party reveals much of Ambedkar's political ideology—socialist, centrist, committed to industrialisation and to education, with specific remedies for specific economic problems. It is worth looking at them closely. This essay has so far dealt only with Ambedkar's ambitions for the Untouchables; it should be made clear that from the start he had bold ideas about India's other problems.[5] The platform paid no attention to religion, and indeed the securing of reserved seats for Untouchables was dependent upon their being in the Hindu fold. But the party was not to serve the needs of Untouchables alone; its aim was 'mainly to advance the welfare of the labouring classes'. Its platform accepted 'the principle of state management and state ownership of industry wherever it may become necessary in the interests of the people.' The party would undertake to establish land mortgage banks, agriculturist producers' cooperative and marketing societies and to avoid fragmentation of land. Tenants under the oppressive khoti and talukdari land rent systems in Ratnagiri and Gujarat would be protected, and the *watan* system (which bound the Mahar to his plot of land in the village by virtue of his hereditary duties) would be amended. Industry would be promoted to drain off the excess population on the land and technical education stressed. Workers' rights were to be guaranteed, unemployment relieved by schemes of land settlement and public works, the tax system reformed

---

[5] All Ambedkar's dissertations for Columbia and London University were on financial matters, such as 'The Problem of the Rupee,' and in his testimony to such bodies as the Southborough Commission, the Simon Commission, the University Reforms Commission, he went into elaborate detail about all matters of franchise, electorates or education. This essay, however, is chiefly limited to his political thought as it applied to untouchability, since he is the only Untouchable leader included in India's roster of important political thinkers.

to relieve the poor. There would be free and compulsory primary education, and university education would be reorganised with teaching universities to remedy 'the curse of examination which has blasted the intelligence and effort of the student population.' The judiciary would be separated from the executive, a cardinal principle in all of Ambedkar's constitutional ideas.[6]

None of this ambitious program came to life, the Congress party which dominated the Bombay legislature being considerably less socialist minded. The Independent Labour Party had won eleven of the fifteen seats reserved for Scheduled Castes in the Bombay Province, which included portions of Gujarat, Sind and Karnataka as well as the western section of Maharashtra. The Congress won four reserved seats, including the one in the district in which the Mahad Conference of 1927 had taken place! And the high caste Hindu candidate for the general seat in that area, Surendranath G. Tipnis, one of Ambedkar's closest associates, also lost the election, but three other caste Hindus were returned on the Independent Labour Party ticket. Four seats in the Central Provinces and Berar were also won by Ambedkar's party. The party was second only to the Muslim League as an opposition party to the Indian National Congress in Bombay, and it functioned with vigour but little effect. Not even the protest against the use of Gandhi's term for Untouchables, Harijan, in a Local Board Act by the very people involved was heard. Extra-parliamentary action included a march by peasants in Bombay city in 1938 to protest the *khoti* system and a one day strike in the same year which protested the Industrial Disputes Bill, which Ambedkar called the 'Workers' Civil Liberties Suspension Act,' but which was nevertheless passed by the Congress-dominated legislature.

This detailed account of Ambedkar's first political venture is necessary to point out several factors. Most important, perhaps, is the fact that Ambedkar's electoral success was of absolutely no use in passing legislation as long as his party was a small and lonely minority in a legislature dominated by a majority party. Second was the knowledge that in the areas in which Untouchables' actions had been highly public, the Congress Untouchable would win the reserved seat over the Untouchable allied with Ambedkar. The record of the Congress in the 1937–39 legislatures also led Ambedkar to distrust its economic and social platform, and here Ambedkar's sense of Congress conservatism was probably not far different from that of Jawaharlal Nehru (who nevertheless could not be so openly scornful).

Ambedkar's further political efforts had to deal with matters such as the impotence of a minority, the unlikelihood of a 'trouble-making'

---

[6] *Times of India*, 15 August 1936. The *Times* full report on the party platform was printed as a publicity booklet by the Independent Labour Party.

Untouchable being elected by a caste-Hindu constituency, and a Congress far less committed to socialism than Gandhi's acknowledged heir, Nehru. He never found a solution to these problems. His attempts included the foundation of the Scheduled Castes Federation in 1942 (which was intended to unite Untouchables all over India) and to press for separate electorates once again. The Federation combined with socialists in some areas, but with such a lack of success that Ambedkar himself was defeated.[7] Ambedkar's third political party was a return to the universality of the Independent Labour Party. The Republican Party, a reflection of Ambedkar's admiration for Abraham Lincoln, was conceived in the year of Ambedkar's death, 1956, and was to unite all the dispossessed Untouchables, Scheduled Tribes, the working man and the poor, with all those yearning for a better India. This party, like the first one, was the product of a time when Ambedkar's mind was turning to religion, and here the connection is much closer than that of the Independent Labour Party with the rejection of Hinduism. The Buddhist conversion movement, set in motion two months before Ambedkar's death in 1956, was to offer a new way for all those dissatisfied with Hinduism to participate in a religion that was truly Indian, but cleansed of inequality, the hereditary priesthood, the faults, as Ambedkar saw them, of Hinduism.

Ambedkar's political contributions, however, encompass more than the winning of political representation and the establishing of political parties. He was as much, if not more, a statesman as a politician, and his work as statesman adds another dimension to his political biography. In 1942, Ambedkar was appointed Labour Member in the Viceroy's Executive Council, and he held this position until 1946. In this post, he was able to secure such benefits for Scheduled Castes as a Mahar batallion in the Indian army and overseas scholarships for Untouchable boys, but his main work was in the field of labour arbitration law, the condition of industry, and such far-reaching projects as the Damodar Dam. This four year period was Ambedkar's chief opportunity to work in the field of economics, a subject in which he was highly trained, and a close analysis of his actual effect on the Indian situation during these four years needs to be made. It is clear that here, once again, he concerned himself with the working man and the labour laws that affected both men and industry.

The years between 1942 and 1946 were also years in which Ambedkar

---

[7] Ambedkar was defeated in the elections of 1951–52 in the Bombay (North) constituency by his long-time Chambhar Congress opponent. The Scheduled Castes constitute 17 per cent of that district. He also contested the bye-election of 1954 in Bhandara, a district near Nagpur, running with a Socialist candidate, Ashok Mehta. Mehta won the general seat, Ambedkar lost the reserved seat. The Scheduled Castes Federation made a fairly significant showing in 1957 in the western area of Bombay province, as the battle for the linguistic state of Maharashtra took precedence over all other issues. The formation of the state in 1960 broke the unity of the samiti to which the SCF had belonged and the Republican party, which replaced it, was not able to find a similar over-riding issue.

was harshly critical of the Congress. Nevertheless, after he was elected to
the Constituent Assembly in 1946, Ambedkar was named as the nominee
for the cabinet post of Minister of Law. Shortly after independence was
achieved on 15 August 1947, Ambedkar became a member of Nehru's
first Cabinet and Chairman of the Drafting Committee of the Constituent
Assembly. Not only had Nehru, in the euphoria of the days of gaining
freedom and probably with Gandhi's urging, named one of his most bitter
critics to his Cabinet, but Ambedkar also fell under the sway of the dream
of a new united and progressive India, and abandoned many of his more
radical convictions as he steered the Constituent Assembly through the
process of agreeing on a Constitution. The proposed 'Constitution of the
United States of India' which Ambedkar had published in *States and
Minorities* in March 1947, just four months before his appointment to the
Cabinet, is a very different document from the actual draft Constitution
he ably defended before the Constituent Assembly in November 1948.
Gone was the provision for agriculture as a state industry, which
Ambedkar had regarded as the only solution to the problems of the
Scheduled Castes, the majority of whom were agricultural laborers
without land. Gone also were the provisions for separate electorates and
separate villages for Scheduled Castes, the first an obvious casualty of the
separation of Pakistan from India and the consequent dropping of all
separate electorates, the second perhaps a practical necessity more than a
renewal of faith in the ability of Hindus to change their village discrimination. Similar in both documents are anti-untouchability clauses, provision for a government officer to look after 'minority affairs,' representation of Scheduled Castes in legislatures and the governmental
services, and special government responsibility for the education of the
Scheduled Castes.[8] All these demands became part of independent India's
governmental policy.

The Constitution, of course, is a reflection of the thinking of Congress
leaders and Constitutional experts more than Ambedkar's personal
philosophy. His contributions to it, however, were far more than the
provisions for Scheduled Castes, but included a stress on centralised
government, which he felt not only a necessity for Indian democracy but a
guarantee of all minority rights, an insistence on a separate and unitary
judiciary, and a pledge to use the individual rather than the village or a
group as the unit of government. His great skill guiding the draft Constitution through the Constituent Assembly can be seen in the verbatim
reports of the Constituent Assembly *Debates*.[9]

    [8] *States and Minorities* has been reprinted in *Dr. Babasaheb Ambedkar: Writings and
Speeches*, Vol. 1. (Bombay: Education Department, Government of Maharashtra). Two
volumes of this series, which will eventually reprint all Ambedkar's available work, have
been edited by Vasant Moon and a Publication Committee of the Maharashtra government.
    [9] Ambedkar resigned from the Cabinet in 1951 in protest over the slowness of the
adoption of the Hindu Code Bill, India's non-aligned foreign policy (he favoured links with

III

This essay must deal, however, with Ambedkar's work as the Untouchable spokesman more than with his Constitutional work, and although the general pattern of Ambedkar's ideas can be gleaned from the chronological report of his actions, it is necessary to go beyond this to glimpse the philosophy, principles and beliefs which were behind his flexible and pragmatic program. Ambedkar's views on caste and the origins of untouchability are basic to his political philosophy. The first writing he published, a paper given in an anthropology seminar at Columbia University in 1916,[10] was on the origins of caste. His thesis in brief was that Brahmans as a priestly class 'enclosed themselves' into a caste, and through imitation and the process of being closed out, other classes became castes. He denied that a racial or colour basis was behind caste and near the end of the essay is the statement: 'In spite of the composite make-up of the Hindu population, there is a deep cultural unity.'

Ambedkar's theory about the origin of untouchability did not appear until 1948. In the years between 1916 and the publishing of *The Untouchables: Who Were They and Why They Became Untouchables* (1948), he held firmly to his belief that neither racial nor ethnic differences set Untouchables apart, and this in spite of the prevalence of the idea that the lowest of castes was pre-Aryan, brought into servitude as the Aryan culture swept through India in the second millennium before Christ. The earliest document of the modern Untouchable movement, the 1890 petition regarding army recruitment, was in the name of the Anarya Doshparihar Mandali, the non-Aryan group for the removal of wrongs, and the belief that the Mahars were pre-Aryan, once 'Lords of the Land,' can still be found in that community. The idea was prevalent among other Untouchable groups also. In the 1920s, organisations in the Punjab called themselves 'Ad-Dharm,' original religion (or pre-Aryan)[11] and the term 'Adi-Dravida' or original Dravidian was used extensively in the South. But at the time when this basis for separate recognition was popular, Ambedkar testified to the Simon Commission in 1928 that Untouchables derserved treatment as a distinct minority, separate from the Hindu community , only on the grounds that they suffered disabilities which no

---

the West), and the general treatment of Scheduled Castes. He then served in the Rajya Sabha and published some commentaries on political matters such as *Thoughts on Linguistic States* (1955) which advocated that several single-language states be carved out of large linguistic areas.

   [10] 'Castes in India: Their Mechanism, Genesis and Development', was subsequently published in the *Indian Antiquary*, Vol. 41 (May 1917), pp. 81–95.

   [11] See Mark Juergensmeyer, *Religion as Social Vision: The Movement Against Untouchability in 20th Century Punjab* (Berkeley: University of California, 1982).

other community suffered. Asked directly if Untouchables were pre-Aryan, he said simply, 'Well, I do not know. That is a view.'[12]

In his 1948 book, *The Untouchables*, Ambedkar specifically denied a racial, ethnic or occupational basis for the origin of untouchability, using anthropometric and ethnographic evidence. His conclusion was that Untouchables clung to the faith and practice of Buddhism in the early centuries of the Christian era, and were pushed aside in 'the struggle for supremacy between Buddhism and Brahmanism which has so completely moulded the history of India.'[13] Interestingly enough, the book itself is dedicated to the memory of three Untouchable saints in the Hindu *bhakti* tradition—Nandnar of Tamil Nadu, Ravidas of the Hindi-speaking area, and Chokhamela of Maharashtra—as if to re-assert Ambedkar's early view of the 'deep cultural unity' of India.

Ambedkar's theory of the Buddhist origin of the Untouchables has been accepted by some scholars, but denied by the majority. Nevertheless, it has been a very satisfactory theory for those who have become Buddhist. It allows the Untouchables a place of pride in India's past, a most important psychological factor. It gives them a rationale for their despised place that does not reflect upon 'past lives' or current behaviour. It rejects the idea of pollution, a very sensitive issue for the Untouchables. It gives them an alternative culture to Hinduism, which, according to him, denies equality and independence to the untouchables. From 1948 onwards, Ambedkar became personally more committed t Buddhism, visiting Buddhist countries and working on *The Buddł   and His Dhamma* (published the year after his death as the first publication of the college he had founded in Bombay in 1946 and named after the Buddha—Siddharth College). He appreciated the fact that morality, rather than God, occupies the central place in Buddhism. Buddhism, moreover, according to him, concentrates on 'man and righteousness between man and man' whereas other religions concentrate on 'problems of the soul and of worship'. Ambedkar's governmental work, however, and the matter of the important benefits which were to serve as 'compensatory discrimination'[14] for the Scheduled Castes and which would be forfeited by conversion, delayed a call for mass conversion until 1956.[15]

[12] Indian Statutory Commission, *Report* (Sir John Allsebrook Simon, Chairman). (London: H.M.S.O., 1930), Vol. 16. Selections from Memoranda and Oral Evidence, Part I, pp. 52–75.

[13] *The Untouchables: Who Were They and Why They Became Untouchables* (New Delhi: Amrit Publishing Co., 1948), p. 155.

[14] The phrase 'compensatory discrimination' was created by Marc Galanter, whose new tome, *Competing Equalities: Law and the Backward Classes in India* (Berkeley: University of California Press, 1984) is the definitive study on the subject.

[15] After the conversion, Republican Party pressure gained the benefits of government schemes for Scheduled Castes for Buddhist converts. See my 'Buddhism and Politics in Maharashtra,' in Donald E. Smith, ed., *South Asian Politics and Religion* (Princeton: Princeton University Press, 1966), for a study of the relationship of the conversion to politics.

In a sense, the conversion to Buddhism was Ambedkar's ultimate answer to the question of how to eradicate the practice of untouchability. He could not test the efficacy of the conversion, however, since he died within two months of the great event at Nagpur in October 1956. He may have been misled into thinking that not only the Untouchables but many from other castes would enter the Buddhist fold, since creative writers like Tagore, scholars like Dharmanand Kosambi and even Nehru himself had expressed admiration of or commitment to Buddhism.[16] Independent India's symbols of the lion pillar of Ashoka and the wheel of law were Buddhist; her neighbours were Buddhist and she was more aware of them as she took her place as a leader in Asia. But in any case, however hopeful Ambedkar was about a widespread turn to Buddhism, he had created over forty years a set of principles, standards and goals relating to the removal of untouchability, and these must be considered perhaps more basic than conversion to its eradication:

1. Untouchables must possess pride and self-respect, must disassociate themselves from the traditional bonds of Untouchable status. This meant refusing to do traditional Untouchable work such as dragging dead cattle out of the village, but also refraining from drinking and from the village vaudeville called *tamasha* (whose actors were chiefly Mahars). It meant a campaign to abolish *watan*, the system by which Mahars performed traditional work for the village with the perquisite of a piece of land of their own in return. This, of course, was a plan that cut at the Mahar's economic security as well as his bond to the village. Since the Mahars possessed little but *watan* land, it also meant, although Ambedkar did not articulate this, a move to the city if the village traditional links were to be broken.[17]

2. Untouchables must become educated, not only to literacy but to the highest level. Ambedkar said:

   Coming as I do from the lowest order of the Hindu society, I know what is the value of education. The problem of raising the lower order is deemed to be economic. This is a great mistake.

[16] See Eleanor Zelliot, 'The Indian Rediscovery of Buddhism, 1855–1956,' in A.K. Narain, ed., *Studies in Pali and Buddhism* (A homage volume to the memory of Bhikkhu Jagdish Kashyap), (Delhi: B.R. Publishing Corporation, 1979) for a study of the Indian interest in Buddhism.

[17] It will be noted that these examples are for the Mahar caste from which Ambedkar came. Although he generally spoke for all Untouchables, his examples of traditional work were usually from the caste he knew best. He also did not feel able, it seems likely, to ask Chambhars to give up their highly profitable work of shoe-making, which in any case was an occupation that fits well into the modern world. It would seem that his general principle was that any practice or any pattern of behavior which was degrading should be given up.

The problem of raising the lower order in India is not to feed them, to clothe them and to make them serve the higher classes as the ancient ideal of his country. The problem . . . is to remove from them that inferiority complex which has stunted their growth and made them slaves to others, to create in them the consciousness of the significance of their lives for themselves and for the country, of which they have been cruelly robbed by the existing social order. Nothing can achieve this purpose except the spread of higher education. This is in my opinion the panacea of our social troubles.[18]

3. Untouchables must be represented by their own representatives at all levels of government. As noted earlier, Ambedkar's plea until the Round Table Conferences of 1930–32 was for reserved seats in a general electorate, provided a universal adult franchise was in operation. This shifted to a demand for separate electorates in the context of other demands, and separate electorates were demanded again ten years later as independence neared and the frustration of operating in a Congress-dominated system was felt. The degree of separatism which Ambedkar spoke for seems to have been dependent upon the context of the demand. While he was always firm on the matter of Untouchable leadership for Untouchables, he was inconsistent on the degree and kinds of separatism. In terms of the general demand of Untouchables (both North and South) for separate villages, his occasional plea for separation seems fairly mild. A statement made during the debates over the Constitution seems to express his basic belief:

I know today we are divided politically, socially, economically. We are a group of warring camps and I may even go to the extent of confessing that I am probably one of the leaders of such a camp . . . . with all this, I am quite convinced . . . nothing in the world will prevent this country from becoming one. With all our castes and creeds, I have not the slightest hesitation that we shall in some form be a united people.[19]

Ambedkar's basic position seems to be that Untouchables must be seen as a minority, as a separate people, so long as they are treated

[18] Dr. Ambedkar or 1 September 1951, while welcoming Rajendra Prasad, President of India, to the foundation stone-laying of the Milind Mahavidyalaya at Aurangabad. Quoted in K.B. Talwatkar, 'People's Education Society: A Glorious Heritage,' *Siddharth College of Arts and Sciences Silver Jubilee Number*, 1973–74, pp. 77–83.

[19] Constituent Assembly *Debates*, 59; pp. 100–1, 13 December 1947. Quoted by Rajeev Dhavan in his unpublished manuscript, 'Fighting for Rights: A Study of B.R. Ambedkar' (1980).

as a separate people.[20] And as long as they have special needs, those needs must be represented in the government by the Untouchables themselves.[21]

4. The government must take responsibility for the welfare of all its people, creating special rights for those to whom society had denied education and occupational opportunities. A strong central government with a clear concern for the welfare of all its people was central to Ambedkar's views, and political representation was the key to the legal reforms that would determine the duties of the government. Corollary with this was legal redress for those discriminated against. When untouchability was legally abolished in the Constituent Assembly, the shout went up for Mahatma Gandhi's victory! But although Gandhi may have been the moral force behind the Act, it was Ambedkar who held the belief that law was essential for change. The Indian government's commitment to 'compensatory discrimination'[22] today is responsible for the most widespread network of benefits any modern government has created for its lower classes, and the practice of untouchability is subject to penal servitude.

5. All forms of caste must be abolished. The functions of the Brahmans as priests should be performed by trained persons from any caste, under state supervision.[23] The sense of Gandhi and some other

[20] The most striking plea for separatism came from the platform of the Scheduled Castes Federation in 1942, in which there was a call for the transfer of Scheduled Castes to separate villages, 'away from and independent of Hindu villages,' but the following sentences note the rationale for such separatism: 'The village system, now prevalent in India . . . is the parent of all the ills from which the Scheduled Castes are suffering for many centuries at the hands of the Hindus.' *Report of the Depressed Class Conferences* (Nagpur: G.T. Meshram, 1942). Ambedkar's inability to find a solution to discrimination and economic backwardness in the village (except for the socialisation of land) is a major lacunae in his philosophy, and his differing attitude towards, the village brought him, of course, in direct opposition to the Gandhian stress on the village as the centre of Indian life.

[21] Ambedkar's absolute refusal to work under anyone else's banner was inexplicable to many caste Hindu reformers, but the idea of indigenous leadership has become standard to all minority movements today. This is, of course, another issue that brought Ambedkar into conflict with Gandhi, who felt that he spoke for all Indians.

[22] See Marc Galanter, *op. cit.*, for the most complete review of the Government of India's policy. Lelah Dushkin, 'Scheduled Caste Politics,' J. Michael Mahar, ed., *The Untouchables in Contemporary Indias* (Tucson: University of Arizona Press, 1972), gives a brief but competent historical review of the development of the policy.

[23] Ambedkar's full program is detailed in *The Annihilation of Caste*, first published in 1936 and reprinted in *Dr. Babasaheb Ambedkar: Writings and Speeches, op. cit.*, Vol. 1. This is a very legalistic view of societal change; Ambedkar's more practical approach consisted of 'persuading, embarrassing, pressurising and, where possible, forcing the majority to change their attitudes.' Rajeev Dhavan, *op. cit.*

reformers that *varnashramadharma*, the four-fold division of society into priests, rulers and warriors, merchants and Shudras (with untouchability eliminated by the inclusion of Untouchables in the Shurdra fold), was anathema to Ambedkar, and a major cause of his rejection of Gandhi's program. Ambedkar was not optimistic about the swiftness of the disappearance of the caste system, both in terms of the broad varna categories and the smaller living units of endogamous groups called jatis. Ambedkar felt that caste had been created by man and could be dispensed with also by man.

It is not the purpose of this paper to analyse Ambedkar's success. For one thing, the current situation in India reveals that the very achievement of special rights for Untouchables has brought violent retaliation when those rights have been seen as too much privilege. But it is possible to conclude this essay with a note on Ambedkar's legacy. It is easy to point out the legal measures, the government commitment, the progress in education and in securing government jobs that are a result, at least in part, of his long battle. It is also easy to note the comparative failure of the political parties and the smashing success of the educational network he created. The Buddhist conversion movement has slowed in momentum, but is still very much alive.

Ambedkar's legacy is apparent also in the on-going creativity found in the Untouchable community. In Maharashtra (and to a lesser degree in Karnataka and Gujarat) *Dalit sahitya*, the literature of the oppressed, has become an important new intellectual contribution to Indian life. There is Dalit theatre, and the Dalit Panthers, a clear adaptation of the American Black Panthers' idea of militancy, arose in the eary 1970s to combat village violence. The very word *dalit* now used indicates a new attitude—the disabilities of Untouchables, or the ex-Untouchables now that untouchability is illegal, are caused by their oppressors, not by any inherent pollution within themselves. It may be that the self-respect and the pride that all this indicates, the educational level that a sizable minority have reached, and the still powerful image of the achievements and the commitment of Dr Ambedkar himself may yet result in some new political action. As in Ambedkar's day, new tactics and new organisations rise to deal with specific problems, but basically within the same perimeters of basic beliefs in human equality, parliamentary democracy, legal redress, government responsibility, an undefined Indian cultural unity and, above all, the power of education.

11

RADHARAMAN CHAKRABARTI

Tagore: Politics and Beyond

Writing about Tagore, one is invariably struck by the regularity with which the poet wrote and spoke about society and politics. He freely allowed the blissful domain of his literary creation to be invaded by issues that were not merely mundane but extremely disturbing. From 1875 through 1941, these issues kept coming back with amazing frequency.[1] And the great mind responded with total concern, not just the occasional flutter of a poet. Admittedly, somewhere there has to be some intermix between the realm of creative thinking and the objective world. But the fact that the intermix becomes compulsive with a poet of Tagore's stature is remarkable in itself. Indeed, he faced political and social realities quite deliberately, and independently of his literary urge. And he did so no less in action than in thought.

Tagore not only watched the politics of his time but also came quite close to it. His early association with the Hindu Mela (1875), Calcutta Sessions of the National Congress (1886, 1896 and 1906) and Bengal Provincial Congress in Natore (1897) and Pabna (1908) were preparatory to the prominent role he played in the countrywide agitation against the partition of Bengal (1900–5). For all that is sublime in his creation, he was never oblivious of the painful reality of living under the imperial yoke. He was a keen and critical observer of the struggle for freedom. His voice was distinct and loud, not merely in protest against the evils and excesses of alien rule but more so in admonition of the failings of his own countrymen. Eventually, as he came to place the misfortune of his country in the global perspective of imperialism, he had to speak out his political conviction with all the force at his command.

True, his ideas were never clouded by any theoretical pretension. They flowed spontaneously from and registered the profound disturbances occurring in his mind. He knew that politics was not his domain. Yet he felt that the problems facing mankind, both within and outside his country, were so ominous that passivity on his part would be unpardonable. This is why he invariably got involved in some of the great debates of his time—whether they concerned the boycott of Western goods and education, the pristine values of Indian culture, the follies of begging reforms of the British rule, the romantic extremism of young Indian revolutionaries, the hollowness of Western materialism, or the curse of aggressive nationalism in all its manifestations. The poet's passionate involvement in these

---

[1] See the chronological index of relevant writings of Tagore in Chinmohon Sehanobis, *Rabindranather Antarjatik Chinta* (Calcutta: Navana, 1983).

debates seems to suggest that somehow the trends of contemporary events did not quite square up with the broad world-outlook he consciously personified. And that is precisely where one should look for the ultimate philosophical basis of the various strands of his thought. To be sure, this calls for no excessive speculation nor much ingenious interpretation. This is because whatever Tagore had to say about politics he said it in no uncertain terms. There is, thus, little difficulty for the discerning commentator to identify the main thrust of Tagore's thought. His task is certainly made easier by the fact that most of Tagore's political writings are unusually clear and straightforward. Even for literary pieces, where politics is skilfully relegated to the background, reading between the lines is not as baffling as it is generally assumed. In this sense the political thinker in Tagore is surprisingly conspicuous and mercifully unpretending.

II

What compulsions were there that pushed the poet so frequently to the political arena? To begin with, they were directly connected with the historical predicament of his class. It was an age of transformation for the upper middle strata of the Indian society. On the one hand, they were engaged in reaping the full benefit of the colonial land dispensation; the permanent settlement guaranteed them leisure with wealth. On the other, they took advantage of Western education with an eye on the loaves and fishes of colonial administration. Some of them, of course, had been dismayed at the bitterness inherent in the master-slave relationship. They were steadily losing their earlier hopes about the possibility of a transplant of what they learned about Western liberalism in British India. It required no special genius to realise that the foreign rulers had little reason to be interested in the well-being of the subjects. Those who suspected this were mostly professional people; they did not dream of fighting for self-rule but only arrogated the privilege of initiating what was called constitutional agitation for reforms of the administrative system.

To put the record straight, the poet belonged to one of the leading and most affluent zamindar families of Bengal with many records of rewarding association with the British Raj. Yet, as a practitioner of zamindari, he did rise above the narrowness and cruelty so common to his genre.[2] He certainly never disowned his affiliation with the landowning class, though, at a fairly mature age, this made him feel genuinely apologetic and embarrassed. In a private correspondence to his son and daughter-in-law after his visit to the Soviet Union, he wrote:

[2] Sachindranath Adhikary, *Shilaidaha O Rabindranath* (Calcutta, 1974), esp. pp. 221–22; also Dhurjati Prosad Mukherjee, *Tagore: A Study* (Calcutta, 1972), p. 5.

I had long nourished a repugnance for that business of zamindar, now it has become more solid. This time in Russia I have seen with my own eyes the shape of things which I had dreamt of so long. That is why I feel so ashamed about the zamindari business . . . .

May we never again have to burden the poor tenants on the land for maintaining us in food and comforts.[3]

Zamindari was thus on his conscience; though it might not have been consequential in the formation of his political ideas except for one very important matter. This concerned the legitimacy or otherwise of the landed aristocracy to represent the interests of the people, and the occasion was a petition from a section of the Bengali zamindars, which was published in an English daily *Pioneer*, patently to impress upon the British government the advantages of patronising them instead of the professional people who had captured the Congress organisation. In two extremely stern and sarcastic papers. Rabindranath not only demolished the zamindars' claim to represent the interests of the people but demonstrated in unequivocal terms how the Bengal zamindars were nothing but parasites created by and therefore tied to the apron-strings of the colonial rulers.[4]

Equally vehement was his disapproval of the political mendicancy preached and practised by the so-called intelligentsia within the Congress. Narrow opportunism and utter slavishness characterised this group to such an extent that the poet would not be surprised if they traded the country's interests for their immediate gain.[5]

It was, therefore, a moral imperative for the poet to extricate himself and his poor countrymen from the political deception of the self-styled political leaders of his time. So great was his disappointment with them that even years later he would say:

In the beginning of our history of political agitation in India . . . there was a party known as the Indian Congress, it had no real programme. They had a few grievances for redress by the authorities. They wanted larger representation in the Council House and more freedom in the municipal Government. They wanted scraps of things, but they had no constructive ideal.[6]

The moderates in the Congress were, of course, challenged by a group of radicals and the poet had great sympathy and admiration for their leaders (such as, Balgangadhar Tilak, Aurobindo Ghosh and others). It was Tilak's activities that seem to have inspired him in shaping one of the

[3] *Letters from Russia* (tr. Dr Sasadhar Sinha) (Visva Bharati, 1960), pp. 156–57.
[4] 'Ultra Conservative' and 'Mukhujje banam Bandujje,' *Rachanavali*, Vol. 12.
[5] See his sarcastic article 'Townhall-er Tamasa' (Farce in the Townhall) and the poem 'Bangabhumir Prati' (To Motherland) in 'Kadi O Komal,' *Rachanavali*, Vol. 1, pp. 206–7.
[6] *Nationalism* (New York: Macmillan, 1917), p. 134.

oft-discussed characters, Dhananjoy Vairagi, in his play *Prayaschitta* (1909), one through whom he is believed to have communicated his own ideology of a popular confrontation against foreign misrule.[7]

In his repudiation of the moderate conservatives, the poet was not looking so much for an activist alternative as an immediate change of guards in favour of the young generation. He had great expectations from the youth, who alone could be called upon to rescue the country from its inertness. For, he was convinced that the principal weakness of the Indians lay in their social arrangement which offered little room for independent thinking, far less any initiative against the crippling effects of an authoritarian order. The plight of his people did not simply consist in appalling poverty but also in the absence of any real liberty, primarily in the social and eventually in the political sphere. By comparison, the people in the West have become 'a force to reckon with and not merely a figure in the census report. They no longer beg but demand; whereas the common people in our country neither know and therefore cannot make others realise that they form part of a powerful mass.'[8] In their condition, Europeans would behave differently. 'Any excessess would be resisted forthwith. Any inroads of the government into the freedom of the governed would pave the way to revolutionary upsurge—attempts of the church to enchain the free intellect of humanity would lead to religious upheaval.'[9] Such conditions alone enabled people to claim and enjoy their freedom, and they were lacking in India precisely because a servile mentality had deliberately been planted in their minds. It was time, the poet proclaimed, the youth took the reins of the society and put an end to the culture of dependence on the elders that had emasculated the masses.

Tagore was thus concerned about a two-fold evil against whom the power of the people was to be organised. There was, on the one hand, the age-old curse of social oppression, obscurantism and divisiveness which incapacitated the people to unite against the other evil, namely, foreign domination. Where the common people were yet to learn what dignity of man really meant, it was sheer self-deception to talk about political emancipation of the country through militant rhetoric and crafty resolutions. The poet's one unmistakable advice to the politicians was to bring about a change in the social psychology of the people before they could be properly asked to participate in the struggle for the country's freedom.

At the same time, the poet was wary of the hypnotic spell cast by terrorist extremism on the youth of Bengal. For all his belligerence

---

[7] This refutes the widely-held belief that the character is a virtual reflection of Gandhi. For an illuminating discussion on this point see Debipada Bhattacharya, 'Tilak and Tagore in the Light of the Character of Dhananjay Bairagi,' *Socialist Perspective*, Vol. 10, No. 3, pp. 141–52.

[8] 'Kalantar,' *Rachanavali*, Vol. 24, p. 264.

[9] 'Karmer Umedar,' *Rachanavali*, Vol. 12, p. 468.

towards imperialist rule, he could not approve of two things—namely, romantic adventurism and violence born of intolerance. For a section of the sentimental middle class youth these had great momentary attraction. But the poet was not sure if they were not drawn by it for the sake of mere sensationalism. What he deprecated was the practice of creating a mystique around patriotism so as to inebriate rather than inspire the adherents to the revolutionary order.[10] In adopting this attitude, he did not in the least underrate the sacrifice of the intrepid heroes of the terrorist movement. His works during this period abound in the passionate call to the youth to be the guiding spirit of the national awakening.[11] What he hated was all forms of self-deception in a sacred mission like this. He was, therefore, outspoken in his denunciation of the leadership of those who had the least concern for the plight of the multitude and whose life-style itself forfeited their claim to represent the common people.[12] For precisely the same reason, he did not want the precious youth of the country to be trapped by the politics of stray violence totally dissociated from the real needs of the people.

In other words, the poet wanted the revolt against alien rule to germinate from the grassroots of society. As for the leadership, his emphasis was on a genuine commitment to the people's cause and a scrupulous avoidance of all forms of irrational contrivance to get the people involved in the struggle. This is what made him differ so frequently and so sharply with Gandhi, notwithstanding the great expectations he had about his leadership. His mind revolted against the symbolic, sporadic and short-lived promise of self-sufficiency held out by the *charkha* movement. Neither could he appreciate the tendency of uncritical acquiescence demanded of the people in Gandhi's programme of non-cooperation. In an exceptionally brilliant political article, the poet regretted that the Mahatma's voice (which was supposed to have the divine power to awaken the people into the new age) should have been spent in merely calling upon them to weave their own cloth and burn all imported textiles.[13] He particularly feared that the Mahatma's charisma was compelling people to accept his words at their face value and engaged in an animated argument with Gandhi (at his Jorasanko residence on 6 September 1921) on the injurious effect on the public mind of using untruth (in this case the belief that Western textiles were impure) to sustain a political agitation. The poet was also indignant to find the Mahatma blaming the practice of untouchability for the devastating earthquake in Bihar. Most glaring of

[10] A fairly accurate reflection of Tagore's disparaging views on terrorism is found in his novels *Ghare Baire* and *Char Adhyaya*.

[11] For instance, *Vivechana O Avivechana*, 'Kalantar,' *op. cit.*, p. 260. Also, his celebrated poem 'Balaka,' *Rachanavali, ibid.*, p. 2.

[12] See his presidential address at the Pabna Provincial Conference.

[13] 'Satyer Awhan,' translated in *Modern Review*, October 1921.

all was the refusal by the Congress leadership to allow even a mention of the poet's surrender of knighthood in protest against the Jallianwala Bagh massacre (30 May 1919) at the Amritsar Congress (December 1919) where Gandhi simply moved a resolution condemning the agitated mood of the Panjabi community.[14]

Perhaps the most unhappy episode of the Tagore-Gandhi controversy was the poet's resolute opposition to the non-cooperation movement launched by Gandhi in the 1920s. He regarded the programme as entirely negative and whipping up blind national pride. His main apprehension was that the parochial anti-West tendencies within the national movement would augur ill for India's cooperation with the international community.[15]

The poet was just back from his lecture-tour of the West where he had made a strong plea against the doctrine of the nation-state and spoke highly of the Indian ideal of cooperation and coexistence among the races. He was also busy expanding the international connections of the *Santiniketan*. In fact, his concern was entirely different from the immediate compulsion of the national movement to mobilise mass discontent against British rule to a point where the rulers would be forced to come to terms. True, the non-cooperation movement was abdicated and betrayed just before it reached that culmination. Nonetheless, the reality of the people's readiness to revolt did not warrant the attitude the poet took at this time. His allegations about a possible exclusiveness being nurtured by the Indian leaders were ably refuted by both C.R. Das and Gandhi on the ground that short of the right of self-determination, no nation could ever think of a rightful place in the community of nations.[16]

III

The foregoing, rather brief, survey of Tagore's encounter with the cross-currents of the national movement would show for certain that all along he had been ploughing a lonely furrow. This is a significant aspect of Tagore as a political being and largely accounts for the uniqueness of his political thinking. Tagore was, perhaps, one of the very few among the modern thinkers of India who did not start and end by just assimilating Western ideas and moderating them to suit Indian conditions. His perceptions of what politics is and what it should be were inseparably linked with his reading of the social and political tradition of the country in particular, and the course of human civilisation in general. Hence his expectations of,

[14] See D.G. Tendulkar, *Mahatma*, Vol. 1, pp. 249–50. On the Jallianwala Bagh episode see Amal Home, *Purushottam Rabindranath*, pp. 72–75.
[15] Tagore-Andrews correspondence in *Letters to a Friend* (Visva Bharati), pp. 127–36.
[16] See Nepal Majumdar, *Bharater Jatiyata, Antarjatikata O Rabindranath*, pp. 181–83; Tendulkar, *op. cit.*, Vol. 2, pp. 61–65; also *Young India*, 13 October 1921 and 5 November 1925.

and admonitions to, the practitioners of politics at home appeared to be rather at odds with the immediate demands of the time. They were not to the liking of those actively leading the country's struggle against foreign domination. They were even liable to produce misgivings, to the effect that the poet's main concern lay not so much in an early end to alien rule as in an all-out programme to pave the way for social regeneration.

The poet certainly had a blue-print for the reconstruction of society, which will be taken up later in this paper. Yet it would be wrong, and perhaps uncharitable, to read any intention of compromise with foreign rule into his exchanges with those who were experimenting with all sorts of formulae for giving shape to the national struggle. After all, hesitations, prevarications and even compromise (often just short of a sell-out) were precisely what many prominent figures in the latter group could easily be accused of. Without entering into this rather irrelevant question, it is necessary to restate here that the poet's agony at the plight of his country-men was no less poignant than that of these leaders. More important still, he was never found wanting in his awareness of the nature of imperialism, not merely as it operated in India but all over the backward world.

Two successive trips to Europe in his early youth gave Tagore the first opportunity to size up the imperialist order right in its homeland. On the one hand, he detested the hollowness of the exhibitionist materialism which seemed to have overtaken the traditional culture of Europe. On the other, he intensely resented the arrogance of power which was all that characterised Europe's relations with her colonies. Alongside the large-hearted liberalism of some of the finest men in England, the poet saw a general lack of respect for other peoples' rights. The disgrace and dis-comfiture suffered by the Irish members of the British House of Commons was an eye-opener for him.[17] The perpetration of human indignity (both at home and abroad) by the colonial powers was what the poet hated most. For it shattered his earlier belief in the unifying and mutually beneficial effects of the West meeting the East. At the same time, he was appalled by the atrocities of the Western powers in China, the Congo, South Africa, Australia and America, and wanted his countrymen to realise the magnitude of the crime involved in using Indian soliders to protect British interests elsewhere.[18] The same system kept the colonies emaciated, disarmed and divided and made them easy prey for the political and economic rivalries of the imperialist powers.

To the poet, there was an intimate connection between imperialism and the outbreak of World War I. In a searching analysis of the roots of war he wrote:

[17] 'Europe Prabasir Patra,' *Rachanavali*, Vol. 10, pp. 253–57.
[18] *Cheene Maraner Byabsaya, Bharati* (Calcutta, 1881). 'China, India and Imperialism' in *Oriental Press*, New York, 30 April 1927; also 'Rajnitir Dwidha,' *Rachanavali*, Vol. 10, pp. 404–5; *Imperialism, ibid.*, p. 433.

Of late the world has come under the sway of the commercial interests. Trade today no longer means business pure and simple, it has got wedded to imperialism with the result that the sovereign and the subject no longer belong to the same land as it used to be in the traditional empires . . . . Being a late-comer in this grand feast of colonial expansion Germany stood little chance of satisfying her hunger and therefore would not hesitate to occupy whatever it could grab by force from others.[19]

In seeking the political origin of this all-out aggressiveness of the imperialist powers, Tagore was greatly disturbed by the spirit of Western nationalism. He thought this was what was causing so much antagonism in the world. In his words, 'The truth is that the spirit of conflict and conquest is at the origin and in the centre of the Western nationalism.'[20]

His verdict on *Nationalism in West* (1916–17), when stripped of its war-time emotion, does contain a series of thought-provoking observations on the nature of the Western state system itself. The nation-state, in his view, is no more than the 'political and economic union of a people . . . for a mechanical purpose' which consists in merely contributing to the strength of the political superstructure called state at the cost of society which provided its necessary basis. If the state had previously played a specialised and well-defined role of a power centre for self-preservation of the society, the modern state, 'trading upon the greed and fear of man . . . occupies more and more space in the society'.[21] This overwhelming encroachment of the state is, according to the poet, further assisted by the compulsions of industrialism, consumerism and, significantly enough, 'the interminable economic war [that] is waged between capital and labour' within the society to satisfy the greed of the wealthy and powerful.[22]

From this unholy union between the state and the dominant economic interests in the society, it was only a short step to engage in the conquest and exploitation of other races. The idea of the nation-state carries with it an irresistible exclusiveness which makes it easier to rationalise and internalise this aggressive design. Hence the poet calls the idea of the nation 'one of the most powerful anaesthetics that man has invented. Under its influence the whole people can carry out its systematic programme of the most virulent self-seeking without being in the least aware of its moral perversion—in fact, feeling dangerously resentful if it is pointed out.'[23]

Nationalism of this sort is a strange doctrine in that it proclaims a system in which only the few most powerful had the privilege to practise it

---

[19] 'The Roots of War,' 'Kalantar,' *Rachanavali*, Vol. 24, p. 271.
[20] *Nationalism*, p. 33.
[21] *Ibid.*, p. 20.
[22] *Ibid.*, p. 22.   [23] *Ibid.*, p. 57.

while the others either could not afford it or would, perforce, be excluded from that privilege, if they showed signs of coming up to it. The poet did discern that the nation was 'the greatest evil for the nation,' in that it militated against the emergence of new nations in the world. Otherwise, he rightly posed the question: 'Why is it that I saw in an English paper an expression of bitterness at Japan's boasting of her superiority of civilisation—the thing that the British, along with other nations, has been carrying on for ages without blushing?'[24]

Of course the poet was not holding any special brief for Japanese nationalism. His advice to the Japanese youth was 'never to follow the West in its acceptance of the organised selfishness of nationalism as a religion, never to gloat upon the feebleness of its neighbours.' While it was alright for Japan to assimilate Western technology and achieve her full industrial potential, she must guard herself against 'the motive force of Western nationalism as her own'.[25] And as his worst fears proved true in the wake of World War II, Tagore took the sternest possible stand towards Japan. It was fairly well known then that Japan had promised active cooperation to the Indian revolutionaries under the leadership of Rashbehari Bose. Concerned at the decision of the Indian national leaders to boycott Japanese merchandise as a protest against Japan's wanton aggression upon China, Bose cabled an earnest request to Tagore seeking his intervention 'to prevent Congress and Pandit Nehru's anti-Japanese activities for the sake of Indian interest and Indo-Japanese friendship.' Notwithstanding his genuine affection for Bose, Tagore wrote back:

> I know in making this appeal you counted on my great regard for the Japanese, for I along with the rest of Asia, did once admire (her), but Japan has not taken long to betray that rising hope . . . and has now become itself a worse menace to the defenceless peoples in the East.[26]

It appears that the poet was against the tenet of expediency preached by some political circles that the enemy of one's enemy could be counted as a potential friend. And, to the Japanese poet Noguchi, he not only conveyed his utter contempt for Japan's militarism but wished him and his people 'not success but remorse'.[27] It is, therefore, clear that the poet's denunciation of nationalism actually flowed from his conviction that sooner or later it was likely to be drawn into imperialist rivalry. Japan was a test case for the hypothesis.

[24] *Ibid.*, p. 53.
[25] *Ibid.*, pp. 52, 96.
[26] *Amrita Bazar Patrika*, Calcutta, 11 October 1937.
[27] 'Poet to Poet, Nanking and Santiniketan,' *cit.* Sehanobis, *op. cit.*, p. 102.

IV

At home, the views of Tagore about the pernicious effects of nationalism were not likely to be appreciated. Those who were fighting against imperialism were certainly not going to share the poet's fear that nationalism was the breeding ground of imperialism. Neither were they impressed by the poet's concern that the people would be isolated from the mainstream of international transactions if they were taught to hate the Westerners. In two successive sessions of the Congress (1921 and 1922) C.R. Das referred to the contradictions in the poet's thinking and pointed out that it was never contemplated that India would refuse to welcome the positive aspects of Western culture. His considered opinion was that true assimilation of other people's culture could not occur without achieving national independence. Else, what would happen would be nothing but slavish imitation, thereby completing the Englishman's conquest of India even in the cultural sphere. Das wanted Tagore not to confuse the ideal of nationalism seeking self-determination for an oppressed people with the selfish, aggressive nationalism of the West. A people might find its proper place in the family of nations only when it had achieved an identity, an independent status which alone could enable them to have a give-and-take relationship with others. If European nationalism had given birth to the monster of imperialism, it was incumbent upon the resurgent nationalism of the colonial people to repel it by all means.[28]

The claim of the colonial people to national self-determination cannot, of course, be gainsaid. Yet, to put the record straight, one feels that Tagore was not merely concerned about the dangers of national exclusiveness. He was also perturbed by the fact that Indian society, as it was, permitted little room for that unifying spirit called nationalism. He pointed out that the social distance between the ethnic components of Indian society was too formidable to provide an enduring basis for national unity. To quote:

> In India there is no common birthright. And when we talk of western nationality we forget that the nations there do not have that physical repulsion, one for the other, that we have between different castes. Have we an instance in the whole world where a people who are not allowed to mingle their blood shed their blood for one another except by coercion or for mercenary purposes?[29]

Exclusiveness was thus inherent in Indian society. It was further exacerbated by the growing menace of communalism and the politicians were

---

[28] See Aurobindo Poddar, *Rabindranath: Rajnitik Byaktitwa?* (Calcutta: Uchharan, 1982), pp. 237–39.

[29] *Nationalism*, p. 146.

out tó exploit it to the full. The short-sightedness of communal politics provided an open invitation to the policy of 'divide and rule' of the British.[30]

To overcome these internal barriers to the crystallisation of Indian unity, it was not enough to mobilise the people against foreign rule. On the contrary, it was, Tagore thought, imperative to work out a systematic and concrete programme of restructuring the social bases of authority. For, even if it was possible to capture political power, it would be, indeed, largely a liability for a society that did not provide the primary opportunities of cooperation and cohesion among its units. The conditions necessary for the assertion of individual dignity were also lamentably wanting. The remedial measures considered to be urgent in this situation were laid down by the poet in the form of a blue-print entitled *Swadeshi Samaj.*[31]

To sum up the salient points of his philosophy, there is first the significant distinction he used to draw between the sphere of the state and the spheres of society, a distinction which is not easy to gloss over. In the old Indian scheme of things, the state was concerned primarily with the problems of war and peace, administration of justice and enforcement of law. In matters of social and individual well-being, however, the responsibility rested mainly upon the decision-making agency of the society itself. In the context of foreign domination, this autonomous decision-making and decision-implementing power of the society was being increasingly negated. It was, indeed, absurd to expect the alien government to step into the welfare role of a whole society. And it would ruin the virtues of self-reliance of the people if the society tended all the time to wait for the government to accomplish its objectives. That would only increase the bondage of the country to the foreign power.

As society would take care of its problems, the people should be made increasingly aware of their common tradition and common destiny. One way of achieving a sense of collectivity among the people who were divided in more than one respect was, according to the poet, to revive the old institution of community festivals and spread it far and wide.

For a rallying point necessary to hold together the diverse social forces seeking unity, the poet would prefer the election to the position of social patriarch (*samajpati*) of at least one Hindu and one Muslim leader to whom the rest of the people would owe unflinching allegiance.

The institutional framework for achieving autonomous social decision-making would be provided by the village panchayats which still retained some of their old vitality. The panchayats would constitute the base of a four-tier organisation with *samitis* or councils at the district, provincial

---

[30] To a curious Russian peasant who wondered why the Hindus and Muslims quarrelled in India, the poet's instant explanation was that this lamentable practice was a side-effect of the political agitations in India. See also 'Raja Praja,' *Rachanavali*, Vol. 10, pp. 419–81.

[31] *Rachanavali*, Vol. 10, pp. 653–57; Vol. 12, pp. 748–49.

and national level. These could well provide a parallel authority structure, working in spite of the foreign government. In thus contemplating a 'state within the state' the poet is believed to have been inspired by the example of clandestine institutions devised by the Georgians and the Armenians in an attempt to by-pass and supplant the Czarist administration.

This brief account gives but an imperfect glimpse of the kind of society the poet had in mind for its members to qualify for an eventual political independence. The arrangement, patently, was all too transitional and left many a loophole that could easily prompt his critics to bring against him charges of being Utopian, anachronistic, personality-oriented and, above all, unusually naive about the reactions of the powers that be.[32]

However, it can be pointed out that the central concern of Tagore's scheme was to highlight the gulf that would inevitably appear between nationalism at the political level and community-consciousness at the social level, unless the latter was allowed to mature simultaneously with, if not ahead of, the former. If Tagore's disenchantment with nationalism in the West was due to its expansionist étatism, his anxieties about nationalism at home arose from the inadequate social base on which it was likely to rest. Theoretically, the positive virtue of nationalism is supposed to be its unifying effects that enable men to rise above petty loyalties and parochial interests. But nationalism, by itself, cannot act as a magic wand capable of conjuring away the numerous divisive forces which have already arrested the growth of cohe on in a society. Of course, one need not share the poet's ideas about t e specifics of a social awareness programme. But it is not without reason that one should ponder over the basic social contents of nationalism in a country if only to help shape its political dimension.

V

This leads us to a very interesting phase in Tagore's political thinking where he freely and wholeheartedly shed some of his constant reservations against the nation-state making inroads into the sphere of autonomous social decision-making.

The poet came across a completely different model where the state was not inimical to society; neither was national unity detrimental to ethnic diversity. This he saw for himself during his visit to the Soviet Union. His instant reaction to the first-ever socialist experiments was recorded in a bunch of letters and did not change much till he breathed his last.[33] In the *Crisis in Civilization* written three months before his death, he wrote,

[32] See Poddar, *op. cit.*, pp. 107–14.
[33] An English version of these letters (first published in *Modern Review*, June 1934) was instantly banned by the British government.

I have also been privileged to witness, while in Moscow, the unsparing energy with which Russia has tried to fight disease and illiteracy, and has succeeded in steadily liquidating ignorance and poverty . . . . Her civilisation is free from all invidious distinction between one class and another, between one sect and another . . . . One aspect of the Soviet administration which particularly pleased me was that it provided no scope for unseemly conflict of religious differences nor set one community against another by unbalanced distribution of political favours . . . . in the USSR I found a genuine attempt being made to harmonise the interests of the various nationalities that are scattered over its vast area.[34]

This amazing transformation of the Czarist imperialist order was certainly not achieved by mass prayers for a change of heart of the oppressors. The philosophy of the revolution was basically different and the poet was able to read its fundamental message. Worth quoting in this connection is this passage from one of Tagore's *Letters from Russia*:

Man has two sides—the individual and the social. One is unreal without the other . . . . when individualism turns into downright selfishness and runs foul of society, the topping off of 'Self' at one stroke from self-interest is the proposed remedy for all troubles . . . . the tremendous power that wealth gives to the rich today can never bring dignity or happiness to all. It produces insatiate greed at one end, acute envy at the other . . . . Competition rages between one class and another within the country and between one country and another. Bolshevism originates in this background of widespread suffering.[35]

Though this cannot be taken as a sufficient or precise summing up of the Bolshevik revolution, it nonetheless conveys Tagore's unequivocal appreciation of a great theory of social change. After all, there was nothing in the poet's immediate class interests that would make him an admirer of socialist revolution as such. He was also honestly critical of the lack of individual freedom under the Soviet scheme of uniform adherence to the doctrine of socialism. What turned him on so spontaneously was the concrete evidence in the Soviet Union of what man could achieve by dint of a revolutionary consciousness. Elsewhere, the poet had seen much organised assault on the dignity of man with little ever being done for the downtrodden. He aptly described them as the 'lampstand bearing the lamp of civilisation' only to be 'smeared with the trickling oil'. He had wielded his pen to echo their sighs and share their agony. However, prior to his visit to Russia he did not know which way human civilisation must be

[34] *Crisis in Civilization* (Visva Bharati, 1957).
[35] *Letters from Russia, op. cit.*, pp. 120–21.

steered if it was to avert self-annihilation. He was totally critical of the conventional path followed by the thinkers and practitioners of politics in his own country as well as in the West. His own ideas and prescriptions, though refreshingly different, did not have any great following outside his own circle. He felt that the political movements launched by the Indian leaders in single-minded pursuit of the goal of capture of power did not promise much for the downtrodden. In other words, the very social content of a nationalist upsurge was missing from the superficial agitations for formal political power.

At the same time, the world of nations was set on a collision course. The poet knew that capitalism, nationalism and imperialism got so greatly entangled with each other in the West that a global conflagration was inevitable. And he never believed that the restoration of peace and freedom could be entrusted to the 'cowardly guardians' of Western democracies. On the contrary he proclaimed, 'We cannot have peace until we deserve it by paying its full price, which is that the strong must cease to be greedy and the weak must learn to be bold.'[36]

Way back in 1914, the poet had observed that the current conflict of the colonial powers did not presage the last great battle of human civilisation. There lay ahead a larger war in which confrontation would take place between the haves and the have-nots. It was only after the conclusion of this historic struggle that peace could properly be said to have dawned on earth.[37] Three decades later, just before his death, the poet was even more certain that this last great ordeal would be hailed by the 'paeans of victory to the coming of Man'.[38]

VI

Man, or rather, the problem of his emancipation and self-realisation, was thus Tagore's central concern. Hence, in conventional wisdom, Tagore's political ideas are generally depicted as the off-spring of humanism and internationalism. One is, however, entitled to ask if that tells us much about the nature of his political thinking. For a poet of Tagore's sensitivity and sophistication, is it not expected that humanism and internationalism should permeate his writings? Even if he did not write much about politics, his basic frame of mind would continue to be characterised as that of a humanist and an internationalist. Politics apart, his intellectual association with men like Romain Rolland, H.G. Wells, G.B. Shaw, Anatole France and Albert Einstein indicated, more than any thing else, his profound urge to do his part in the common cause of humanity.

[36] Message to Brussells World Peace Conference (1936), *Modern Review*, October 1936.
[37] 'Kalantar,' *Rachanavali*, Vol. 24, p. 270.
[38] 'The Great One Comes,' *Crisis in Civilization, op. cit.*

What then is particularly distinctive about the political ideas of Tagore? A few things seem to be quite remarkable. One is the range and variety of issues to which the poet addressed himself. Whether it concerned the bona fides of self-styled representatives of the people or the futility of the *charkha* movement, the personality cult or obscurantism fostered by the Indian leaders, the hollowness of Western materialism or the perniciousness of oriental fatalism, the imbibing of Western culture or education through the mother-tongue, the wanton aggressiveness of the fascist powers or the compromising attitude of some 'cowardly guardians' of Western democracies, the poet simply could not keep himself aloof from the centre of controversy. His approach to politics was as uninhibited as his subtle sojourn into the nooks and crannies of the human mind though, of course, the latter was evidently far more penetrating than the former. Though politics was not his domain, one can easily discern a highly alert and openly responsive mind in Tagore regarding social and political questions.

Second, Tagore's political thinking was based on a value system that was all his own. He would give vent to his ideas, often knowing fully well that his path would not be traversed by any one else. His ideas were hardly liked by the contemporary politicians at home, moderates as well as extremists. He had a fierce debate with the Gandhians and inspired little confidence in the contemporary leftist circle, his *Letters from Russia* notwithstanding. This is not true only of his own countrymen. Even abroad he was misunderstood. In Japan, USA and even in the Soviet Union his addresses were not tailored simply to please his audience. Was it because he was swimming against the current of history? Or, to quote an American journalist's comment on his lectures on nationalism, 'utterly opposed to all modern conceptions'? The poet was certainly the last person to be carried away by the drift of events. He was used to taking the long view and placing things in the larger context of reason and well-being in human affairs. He would not mind ploughing a lonely furrow where his convictions were in harmony with the permanent and common interests of humanity. And he would certainly have no hesitation to correct himself when his views ran contrary to this value frame. His misguided emotion at his first encounter with Mussoiini and his subsequent stand against fascism are all too well known to be repeated here as an example.

Third, the poet was never inclined to think of politics exclusively in terms of the state, separated from the men within it. The state, in his view, was no better than a contrivance and must justify itself by the kind of service it renders to society. He felt that society had greater relevance than the state so far as the needs of the individual were concerned. Hence, he would insist that the state should not be allowed to usurp the functions of society. Was he then wedded to the liberal conception of a stand-by state with the minimum of functions? The poet evidently did not have any great admiration for a state that stifled individual initiative. At the same time, he would not approve of a state that exercised a lot of authority and yet did not fulfil its responsibility to the people. The kind of state he was looking for had little in common with the bourgeois state. It was perhaps modelled on the ancient Hindu polity conceived as a trust with defined welfare functions. I say 'perhaps' because the poet deeply resented the overbearing character of the later Hindu empire with its record of unrelenting crusade against the Buddhist minorities. Similarly, one cannot say with certainty that the author of *Letters from Russia* would opt for an out and out socialist state. For, in spite of his genuine appreciation of the Soviet experiment, he harboured considerable reservations about the relevance of 'class-hatred' and 'revengefulness' of the communists toward the vested interests. He even advised his Russian hosts 'to try to convert them by pity and love' so as to be 'great in your mind, great in your mercy'.[39]

There is thus a lot of ambivalence in Tagore's attitude towards the state as a political phenomenon. He wanted man to emerge in his best and fullest stature. He also wanted society and, on its behalf, the state to create the necessary conditions for this to happen. Yet he would not tell us how an old, detestable order could fade out of existence without there being the inevitability of class war in a divided society. His faith in the essential unity of mankind blocked his vision about the historic battle of the nationalism of the East against the imperialism of the West. So too his faith in the capacity of society to out-do the state leaves one completely in the dark as to what would happen to the warring classes in society, of whom the more powerful were already aligned with the state itself. The fact is that the poet came quite close to an understanding of the basic malady of human society, namely, exploitation of the many by the privileged few. But, instead of raising his finger against the very political machinery which was being used for this exploitation, he advised men to turn their face away from such a terrible institution. Tagore was thus drawn into questions that were essentially political. Yet he did not want to remain within the confines of politics. Politics was there because it could not be helped and the poet certainly would not try to avoid it. However, he would seldom feel satisfied with an entirely political solution of the questions that disturbed him. For that he would look far beyond politics. 'Not here but elsewhere' as he would inimitably say.

[39] *Letters from Russia, op. cit.*, p. 215.

12

KENNETH L. DEUTSCH

Sri Aurobindo and the Search for Political and Spiritual Perfection

> This erring race of human beings dreams of perfecting their
> environment by the machinery of government and society; but
> it is by the perfection of the soul within that the outer environ-
> ment can be perfected.
>
> Sri Aurobindo[1]

Sri Aurobindo Ghose, the great Indian nationalist, world visionary and
mystic, is one of the most profound prophets of a spiritually unified and
politically redeemed humanity that the twentieth century has produced.
For him, the quest for political and spiritual liberation rests on 'the hope
of the kingdom of heaven within us and the city of God upon earth'.[2]
Although Aurobindo is best known for the yogic aspects of his 'integral
philosophy,' it would be an error to separate his philosophy from his
political thought. According to him, the metaphysical and cosmic understanding cannot be divorced from the socio-political existence of humanity.
Before one can appreciate Aurobindo's understanding of the interrelation-
ship between cosmic consciousness and human social existence, one
should be aware of certain facts of his fascinating and complex career as a
militant Indian nationalist and great yogi.

The Life of Aurobindo Ghose

Sri Aurobindo Ghose's life (1872–1950) addresses both the political and
spiritual dimensions of human life. He was actively involved in the Indian
national struggle for freedom from British imperialism (1905–10) and

Acknowledgements: There have been a number of book length studies that were helpful in
the construction of this chapter including: D.P. Chattopadhyaya, *History, Society and
Polity: Integral Sociology of Sri Aurobindo* (New Delhi: Macmillan and Co., 1976), June
O'Connor, *The Quest for Political and Spiritual Liberation: A Study in the Thought of Sri
Aurobindo Ghose* (Rutherford, New Jersey: Associated University Presses, 1977) and
V.P. Varma, *The Political Philosophy of Sri Aurobindo* (New Delhi: Motilal Barnarsidass,
1976, second revised edition). I also wish to acknowledge the intellectual support and
encouragement of Professor V.R. Mehta, Professor A.P. Rana and Dr. Thomas Pantham
during my Fulbright Professorship in India.

[1] *Sri Aurobindo—Thoughts and Aphorisms* (Pondicherry: Sri Aurobindo Ashram,
1959), p. 55.

[2] Sri Aurobindo Ghose, *Sri Aurobindo Birth Centenary Library*, Volume 15 (Pondicherry:
Sri Aurobindo Ashram, 1972—referred to hereafter as BCL), p. 165.

became an internationally respected yogi during his contemplative existence at Pondicherry (1910–50). In addition, we discern within his life and thought a living dialogue between 'Eastern and Western' philosophy and civil society. Professor Robert McDermott correctly states that:

> The dual ideal of a total resurgence of India and the total transformation of man characterised the mature work of Aurobindo Ghose, the political revolutionary of Bengal (1905–10), and Sri Aurobindo, the mystical Yogi of Pondicherry (1910–50). This complementarity of politics and spirituality typifies Sri Aurobindo's ability to draw diverse strains into a rich and dynamic synthesis: as he combined politics and Yoga, he also combined Western and Indian values. The conditions for this synthesising ability were created by the highly diverse strains in his personal life.[3]

Let us now examine how his personal history contributed to his search for political and spiritual liberation.

Aurobindo Ghose was born into an influential family of Konnagar in West Bengal on 15 August 1872. His father was strongly committed to Western values, with scientific thought becoming almost a religious commitment to him. His children were sent to Western schools. He took Aurobindo to England when he was seven. Aurobindo was a truly outstanding student, eventually securing a senior classical scholarship at King's College, Cambridge, where he won all the prizes for Greek and Latin verse.

From 1893 to 1906, he was in the service of the Baroda state, first in the Revenue Department and then as Professor and Vice-Principal of the Baroda College. During this period, he studied Sanskrit, and Indian philosophy, culture and religion. He left Baroda in 1906 and went to Calcutta as Principal of the National College.

Aurobindo was clearly one of the most popular leaders of the Indian nationalist movement. He was much respected for his successful work as a political orator and journalist. His nationalism was not embittered or aggressive. For him the 'ideal of human unity' which is grounded on a spiritual basis must acknowledge that 'it is the Spirit alone that saves and only by becoming great and free in heart can we become politically great and free.' This ideal was to have an enobling effect upon his nationalism.

Aurobindo became convinced that it was unrealistic to expect the British administration in India to be concerned with the good of the Indian people. He considered the British administrators to be the sort of people with 'narrow hearts' and a 'commercial habit of mind' who were neither 'high-souled' nor 'sincere'. With this point of view in mind,

---

[3] Robert McDermott, 'Introduction to Aurobindo's *The Mind of Light* (New York: E.P. Dutton, 1971), p. 9.

Aurobindo set out to radicalize the policies and programs of the Bengal Congress. He advocated boycott of goods, schools and indeed of the whole imperial administration. *Swaraj* would demand service and self-sacrifice.

Aurobindo's activities eventually earned him the inveterate hostility of the British authorities. The Viceroy, Lord Minto, claimed that 'he is the most dangerous man we now have to reckon with.'[4] The year 1908 became a watershed year in Aurobindo's political career. Bengal in that year was a likely site for the growing Indian spirit of repression and even terror. These clashes became highly dramatized in the Alipore Bomb Conspiracy. Two youths engaged in an attempted assassination of the District Judge of Muzaffarpur, Mr. Kingford, on 30 April 1908. The bomb was misdirected and the plan failed. However, the government viewed this assassination attempt as a convenient opportunity for greater repression of the nationalists and anyone involved in revolutionary action. This included Aurobindo; he was arrested on 2 May 1910. During the investigation and his famous trial he spent a year in the Alipore jail.

While in jail, Aurobindo had a mystical experience which he considered extremely profound. For him, the experience was a realization of the personal-impersonal Divine which he would later claim to be 'more real, dynamic, intimately present to the consciousness' than he had previously comprehended. *Brahmatej* (i.e., moral power) seemed to him greater than *kshatratej* (i.e., the power of arms).

After his acquittal and release through lack of evidence, he abandoned his political career and became a yogi. Additional threats of incarceration in 1910 as well as the suggestion of an *adesh* (on inner command) made him leave Calcutta for the French territory of Pondicherry south of Madras. Here he founded an *ashram*, where he lived till his death on 5 December 1950. During those years, he practised yogic discipline and published a philosophical journal, *The Arya*, in which he serialized his famous works, namely, *The Ideal of Human Unity*, *The Life Divine* and *The Synthesis of Yoga*.

The Philosophical and Spiritual Foundations

The revolution Aurobindo pursued was a 'spiritual revolution'. His was a 'moral and spiritual' task. This task is grounded upon three basic concepts of his philosophy—*Sachchidananda* or the Supreme Reality, Supermind or the Truth Consciousness, and Evolution.

His interpretation of Vedantic doctrine centred on the notion that 'all this is Brahma'. The entire world—of our senses—was one in Brahma, the foundation of it. Brahma was the Idea behind humanity. Man, though born to the world of matter, has as his purpose to become the true embodiment of the Idea informing humanity. Man possesses in Mind the means for realizing communion with Brahma. If man's mind could control his senses, he would see Brahma directing the world of matter from behind Matter. Man's self-realization or spiritual perfection—the purpose of his being—consists in man's transcending the level of Matter to that of Mind. Communion with Brahma, the Mind behind all minds, can be realized only by such a transcendence.

Brahma as the very Idea of humanity means that each member of humanity equally shares its freedom and that each human is organically related to all the other humans. Bliss or delight refers to the Brahma— that Omnipresent Reality which is the basis of the universe—to its presence and to the purpose of its self-manifestation. As delight it manifests itself in order to share its delight. Delight or bliss answers the why of evolution.

The supermind is the fullest spiritual consciousness. To be in the realm of the supermind is to possess the divine all-knowing and all-powerful qualities. A link is necessary between the Absolute (Brahma) or Super-consciousness and the Mind (ordinary consciousness). Aurobindo gives the name 'Supermind' to this link. It alone contains the self-determining truth of the divine consciousness. To enter supramental awareness is to live consciously in the *Sachchidananda* (the Absolute, Bliss, Brahman). The human mind, which is capable of intellectual knowledge, deals 'with cognition and intelligence, with ideas, with mental or thought perceptions' integrating reality through abstractions rather than through the concrete vision and the spiritual contact sought by the yogi. The human mind participates in the supermind in a limited and diminished way. The human mind merely interprets the truth of universal existence for practical purposes; it is a fall from the supermind and its salvation lies in 'climbing back' to or evolving towards the supermind.

Aurobindo conceived the whole of reality as a process of spiritual evolution. Evolution is the means by which Consciousness liberates itself. This does not mean that *Sachchidananda* is incomplete. Rather, the teleological (or purposive) nature of evolution has to do with the world and man. Spiritual evolution for Aurobindo becomes a pressure from 'above' and an impulse from below which together permit a gradual unfolding of the Absolute. The pressure from above calls the lower forms to evolve out of their limitedness and break through to higher stages of consciousness. Evolution is possible because the Absolute is involved in inconscient matter. Evolution is purposive in the sense that it is the gradual expression of the Spirit's presence in all levels of being for the simple delight of sharing Itself.

Human beings alone are able to participate in evolution consciously. It is our task to reflectively create a psychic change in which the whole person is converted into a 'soul instrumentation' This is a spiritual liberation whereby even the lowest dimensions of life, body and sub-conscience are permeated by the descent and presence of a 'higher Light, Knowledge, Power, Force, Bliss, Purity' and that is the ascent into the Supermind. History is evolving towards this spiritual liberation. A new order of being and a new socio-political order is possible for those who radically open their life to the divine. Yoga is that discipline which aids one to bring about the spiritual and political transformation. There is then, for Aurobindo, an intimate connection between evolution, yoga, and social change.

It is important to note that Aurobindo is quite critical of the notion of the autonomous mind or rational faculty as the norm of life—a norm that is dominant in Western liberalism and philosophy. He specifically rejects the philosophy that views man as a discrete individual—a self-motivated system. Aurobindo was also particularly critical of utilitarianism and its political philosophy of the greatest happiness for the greatest number. This approach does not only betray the limited range of rationalism and technology, but also its helplessness in evolving to the level of spiritual and political evolution.

For Aurobindo, man is neither a simple reflection of matter nor a mere soul animal. Man is a spiritual and evolutionary being, and a necessary conscious force of the Spirit for its evolutionary and progressive manifestation in worldly existence. As we shall be exploring for the remainder of this essay, the individual and the collectivity is a field for the manifestation of the Absolute. The liberated individual is both the means for the realization of the Collective Will of Mankind and an instrument for the expression of the omnipotence of the Absolute. The chief purpose of civil society is the spiritual evolution of its members by providing *Swaraj* (political liberation) the necessary conditions of life and growth, and to express to the rest of mankind the Light, Power, Beauty, Harmony and Joy which are found in the Spirit. Spiritual and political liberation is to be found in a very specific kind of relationship between the individual and society. It is Aurobindo's insightful discussion of this relationship that makes his great contribution to world political thought and becomes the basis for his solution to the perennial question of how political freedom can be realized within the context of spiritual perfection.

Sri Aurobindo and Pierre Teilhard de Chardin

Sri Aurobindo's vision of evolution is closely related to the evolutionary theory of the great French Roman Catholic Jesuit, Pierre Teilhard de Chardin (1881–1955). For both Aurobindo and Chardin, the phenomenon of man discloses not a heap of stones held together by inter-fused elements of material energy, but the highest creative reaction in the universe, consisting, as it were, in a collective human consciousness and action in the process of development. Chardin's viewpoint—found in such works as *The Phenomenon of Man* (1940) and *Man's Place in Nature* (1949)—is never to look at man as a single 'ego' cut off from the whole of reality. Rather, Chardin looks at mankind in the context of the whole of the universe evolving upwards in the direction of spirit. Like Aurobindo, he looks at man from the viewpoint of totality. When one looks in the direction of totality or wholeness, he observes the one immense process: the evolving development of the universe. Here one vast phenomenon is taking place. The meaning of man lies within that phenomenon. The evolving universe is attaining its purpose in living forms of human self-consciousness.

As a phenomenon in the universe, the embodied unified living centres which we call man disclose the psychic current of energy hidden in the universe. In the world of man, the psychic factors of self-consciousness and freedom become the central phenomena. The human mass is weaving its way around the world, building a network of communication with shared thought and conversation. The world is being humanized. The phenomenon of evolution seems to have reached its climax in human consciousness as such, and the process appears irreversible. Chardin does not like to set up a clear division between spirit and matter in the universe. Man is embodied spirit, and God enters into creative union with the reality of his creation. Man can be viewed as the demand for and anticipation of the ultimate unification of everything. From his Christian viewpoint, Chardin considers Jesus Christ to be the Divine Word—or the immanent yet also transcendent creating and unifying principle of the universe.

Both Aurobindo and Chardin sense that the human struggle for the self-conscious experience of being a person with dignity is *communal* with the human goal of unity hidden in the future. God's creative, loving act gives rise to the multiplicity of creation with the attending gropings and pains. Yet, multiplicity gives rise to the loving self-consciousness found in man and his creative effort to bring the whole in communion. This means that there must be an organization of personal human energies into something greater than the human person, through a communal effort. Both Aurobindo and Chardin envision a contemporary morality of movement inclining man toward a creative relationship with the world, with his fellow men, and the pursuit of God.

It is because man is able and free to think and reflect that it becomes possible for him to create human society as such; and through the instrument of technology to create technological society. With technological society eventually embracing the whole world, there will be a greater compression of socialization whereby men will be forced to reflect and converse in a communal manner more profoundly. No matter how independent a person believes himself to be, he cannot escape the present historical situation which constrains him to think collectively. We now notice more lucidly that beyond the mechanization of our life with its forced compression, men have come closer together as conscious beings and are faced with the problems of the whole of mankind. For both Aurobindo and Chardin what is needed in modern society is not religionism, but true religion—being governed by the law of the Spirit.

Aurobindo Ghose on Freedom and the Nationalist Ethic (1905–10)

Sri Aurobindo's particular love of his motherland was not motivated by either sentimentalism or chauvinism. India was a spiritual entity as well as a geographic entity that could lead humanity to spiritual perfection. India during the Raj was enchained and therefore nationalism was a spiritual *sadhana* (a moral endeavor). As Aurobindo put it in one of his speeches, 'Nationalism is not a mere political programme, nationalism is a religion that has come from God.'

For Aurobindo the emancipation of India was essential for fulfilling her destiny as a spiritual guide to humanity; India must play a seminal role in the spiritual regeneration of humanity. *Swaraj* is the necessary condition in order for India to accomplish the work for which she is destined: 'The success of the national movement, both as a political and spiritual movement, is necessary for India and still more necessary for Europe. The whole world is interested in seeing that India becomes free so that India may become herself.'[5]

Swaraj cannot be fully realized by political independence alone, however, but in the resumption by India of her role as spiritual guide to mankind. *Swaraj* is the fulfilment of the ancient life of India under modern conditions, the return of the *satyayuga* of national greatness, the resumption by her of her great role of teacher and guide, self-liberation of the people for the final fulfilment of the Vedantic ideal in politics; this is the true *Swaraj* for India.[6]

Nationalism for Aurobindo is a religious activity. It is not a 'religion' in the sense of an inactive contemplative life, rather it is a 'religion' as an active type. The nationalist movement, though occasionally resembling a political movement, is really a religious movement 'and the weapons which it uses are the weapons of the spirit . . .' Its creed is a 'gospel of faith and hope,' 'a creed of faith, love, and knowledge'. It is a religious aspiration and a 'moral attitude'.

The political independence of India is a prerequisite for the spread of Vedantic realization to the entire world. But Aurobindo constantly

[5] BCL, *op. cit.*, p. 862.
[6] *Ibid.*, p. 902.

reminds us that political independence was only the immediate goal. *Swaraj* is also advocated for other reasons:

> . . . first, because Liberty is in itself a necessity of national life and therefore worth striving for its own sake; secondly, because liberty is the first indispensable condition of national development, intellectual, moral, industrial, political (we do not say that it is the only condition)—and, therefore, worth striving for for India's sake; thirdly, because in the next great stage of human progress it is not a national but a spiritual, moral and psychical advance that has to be made and for this a free Asia and in Asia a free India must take the lead, and, Liberty is therefore worth striving for for the world's sake.[7]

The realization of *Swaraj* in Aurobindo's fuller sense of the term must begin at the individual level. In 'The Morality of Boycott,' he makes a claim that it is to be expected that the nation may interfere with individual liberty:

> The whole of politics is an interference with personal liberty. Law is such an interference; protection is such an interference; the rule which makes the will of the majority prevail is such an interference. The right to prevent such a use of personal liberty as will injure the interest of the race is the fundamental law of society.[8]

In 'The Doctrine of Sacrifice' Aurobindo conceives of the necessity for individuals to sacrifice themselves for the interest of the nation. Only by way of sacrifice on the part of the individual, the family, and the class can occur 'the supreme object of building up the nation'. The nation was not a mere physical aggregate of those composing it. Rather, the nation was an abstracted group of individuals. As such, a nation was an organism like the individual itself, with a personality unique to itself. The fulfilment for the individual person could be achieved by means of identification with the national will. Aurobindo drew a fascinating simile between the nation and the *Virat Purush* (the Collective Being), by claiming that the nation was not to suppress the freedom of its subjects, yet it was the purpose of the individual to search for the true station of his life within the national organism.

The individual's quest for the true station of his life within the national organism may have 'to wade through blood and ruins' if the oppressors of one's nation are foolhardy enough to obstruct this quest. Those pursuing their spiritual perfection under these oppressive conditions might have to experience a variety of sufferings, but 'without such sufferings there

[7] *Ibid.*, p. 465.
[8] *Ibid.*, Vol. 1, p. 127.

could be no growth (spiritual)'. Man must pursue his spiritual perfection regardless of the likely political consequences vis-a-vis the oppressors. As a supporter of the *Swadeshi* movement, Aurobindo was the initiator of the Boycott and Passive Resistance strategies in defiance of the colonial authorities. *Swaraj* could be pursued without murdering the foreign agents of the British Raj.

This leads us to a very important segment of Aurobindo's early nationalist political thought, namely, the kind of resistance that is necessary to deal with national oppression. Since political liberty is the very life-breath of the nation, Aurobindo claims that any means must be taken to secure that life against those who wish to destroy or suppress it. Whether resistance be passive or aggressive is a question to be resolved on the basis of the pressures experienced. As Aurobindo puts it:

It is the nature of the pressure which determines the nature of the resistance . . . . Where the need for immediate liberty is urgent and it is a present question of national life or death on the instant, revolt is the only course. But where the oppression is legal and subtle in its methods and respects life, liberty and property and there is still breathing time, the circumstances demand that we should make the experiment of a method of resolute but peaceful resistance.[9]

In summary, Aurobindo's reflections during his activist career, from 1905–10, prompted him to recommend the specific strategies of (*a*) self-help and the prudentially appropriate resistance for the realization of political freedom, and (*b*) yogic discipline and concentration for the realization of individual and collective liberation.

Aurobindo and the Ideal of Human Unity (1910–50)

As we have previously indicated, it was during Aurobindo's incarcerations in British jails in connection with his nationalist resistance that he became aware of the need to develop a conception of *Swaraj* broader than the merely political or economic. In order to pursue a spiritual and political improvement of Indian society, he removed himself from the Indian political scene and developed the techniques of integral yoga that would realize his vision of the 'life divine'. During his Pondicherry years his socio-political thought became, as we shall see, fully integrated into his 'life divine' and a continuing concern of his life and philosophy.

The Goal of Society

For Aurobindo, science and technology have become the essential basis of social and political organization in the West. Those societies dominated

Ibid., p. 98.

by these principles only lead to the autonomy, isolation and loneliness of the individual where a sense of insignificance and helplessness eventually creates political resignation and powerlessness.

Our approach to society must emphasize goals (a teleology) and ideals and how the ideals can be realized. Given the fact that the purpose of society is to provide the conditions that are necessary to achieve human ideals, it follows that the ideals of society are to be derived from a correct understanding of the 'real' characteristics of human existence. As Aurobindo puts it:

> The object of all society should be, therefore, and must become, as man grows conscious of his real being, nature and destiny and not as now only a part of it, first to provide the conditions of life and growth by which Individual Men—not isolated men or a class or a privileged race, but all individual men according to their capacity—and the race through the growth of its individuals may travel towards this divine perfection. It must be [possible] secondly, as mankind generally more and more grows near to some figure of the Divine in life and more and more men arrive at it—for the cycles are many and each cycle has its own figure of the Divine in man—to express in the general life of mankind, the light, the power, the beauty, the harmony, the joy of the Self that has been attained and that pours itself out in a freer and nobler humanity.[10]

In twentieth century societies, men do not know where they are going; they have no goals. This ignorance of his 'real' or authentic existence can only be rectified when he is aware that his 'true being' does not rest on science or technology but rather can come only 'by living in the Spirit'. Aurobindo wishes to demonstrate how previous societies have failed to provide the conditions that will enable man to fully realize his deeper and more spiritual potentialities. Ideal society lacks the conflicts which characterize present human relationships on the mental level. Ideal society would abound in a freedom which permits and supports each individual to develop his spiritual potential without restraints. Because individuals would be transformed, '. . . a self aware spiritual unity of being and a spiritual conscious community and interchange of nature would be the deep and ample root of understanding.'[11]

In Aurobindo's ideal society, there would be no need for coercive legal instruments that impose good upon human beings. This ideal society will transcend the dichotomies of good and evil, this duality would, in effect, have disappeared! The basic principle of Aurobindo's political ethics

[10] Sri Aurobindo, *The Human Cycle* (Pondicherry: Sri Aurobindo Ashram, 1962), pp. 83–84.

[11] BCL, *op. cit.*, p. 1041.

(like Chardin's) is to provide conditions for the spiritual transformation of individuals and promote the evolutionary process which will produce the spiritualization of the race, the arrival of the 'ideal of human unity'. Before we can explore more fully the importance of this 'ideal' for Aurobindo's political philosophy, it is important to examine explicitly the evolution and typology of societies which provide us with important clues to the guiding principles and institutions of this ideal society.

Evolution and Types of Society

The evolution and dominant types of society—namely, symbolic, typal, conventional and rationalistic-individualistic—establish Aurobindo's basic critique of dominant social structures in the 'modern' world. To better understand the defects of modern society, Aurobindo analyzes earlier societies, for contemporary society grows out of elements of earlier types of society, which are primarily 'symbolic,' 'typal,' 'conventional and 'rationalistic-individualistic'.

Symbolic Society: Societies at their earliest stages are dominated by '. . . a strongly symbolic mentality that governs or at least pervades its thought, customs and institutions'.[12] Human relationships are grounded almost entirely in terms of religious symbols. Nothing can deviate from the symbol; everything must be made sacred—'everything in society is a sacrament, religious and sacrosanct . . . .'[13]

Typal Society: Typal society evolves from symbolic society when the psychological and moral ideals have primacy In typal society, 'religion becomes then a mystic sanction for ethical motive and discipline.'[14] When the moral ideals and motives of discipline of various classes (varnas) become dominant, we have society organized according to types (priests/intellectuals, warriors/administrators, producers, and laborers) each with their own notions of honor, rules and duties that provide the structural foundation of society.

Conventional Society: When the external or outward expression of societal types takes on more importance than the actual types and ideals themselves, then conventional society emerges out of typal society. Conventional society, according to Aurobindo, creates 'the tendency . . . to fix, to arrange, to formalize, to erect a system of rigid grades and hierarchies . . . to cast a stamp of finality [conventionality] on what seems to it the finished life of man.'[15] Conventions become eventually rigid and

[12] *The Human Cycle, op. cit.*, p. 3.
[13] *Ibid.*, p. 8.
[14] *Ibid.*, p. 9.   [15] *Ibid.*, p. 12.

lifeless. Eventually this imprisonment of the human spirit in conventional and rigid grades leads to a revolt. The revolt produces an individualistic and rationalistic society.

Rationalistic-Individualistic Society: People in a conventional society feel they are living a rigid, fixed life. They seek new basis for constituting society. As a result, they constantly question and deny the formalities of conventional society. Western civilization in the modern age is an excellent example of a culture that rejects the formal traditions of church and state in the European middle ages and substitutes autonomous reason, the scientific method and technology for those traditions. Eventually, every form of authority is to be questioned and physical sciences are to be the new standard of truth. Aurobindo puts the important point this way:

> The attempt to govern and organize human life by verifiable Science, by a law, a truth of things, an order and principles which all can observe and verify in their ground and fact and to which therefore all may freely and must rationally subscribe is the culminating movement of European civilization.[16]

For Aurobindo this rationalistic-individualistic society has made a great contribution to the notion that each person has an equal right to his own development. Reason has made a cont .bution in critiquing arbitrary discrimination against certain persons an ɩ classes that conventional society perpetuated. Yet Aurobindo is also quite dissatisfied with this form of modern European society. This society has emphasized the objective part of man—the lower aspects of human nature and rejects some deeper Truth, a Truth not amenable to the objective methods of the physical sciences. This emphasis on the lower or physical aspects of brute strength and power can lead to a barbarian mentality. The modern barbarian in this type of society is described by Aurobindo in the following way:

> His idea of civilization is comfort, his idea of morals social respectability, his idea of politics the encouragement of industry, the opening of markets, exploration and trade following the flag, his idea of religion at best a pietistic formalism or the satisfaction of certain vitalistic emotions. He values education for its utility in fitting a man for success in a competitive, or, it may be a socialized, industrial existence, science for the useful inventions and knowledge, the comforts, conveniences, machinery of production regulation, stimulus to production. The opulent plutocrat and the successful mammoth capitalist organizer or industry are the supermen of the commercial age and the true, if often occult [secret] rulers of its society.[17]

[16] *Ibid.*, p. 23.   [17] *Ibid.*, p. 104.

Aurobindo's characterization of the barbarian mentality of modern Western liberal-individualistic society clearly presages contemporary Western critics of 'possessive individualism' that is so deeply rooted in the West.[18]

A Perfect Society: The Dominance of the Law of the Community

This rationalistic current in modern Western civilization must be challenged by *subjectivism*—the recognition that 'the primal law and purpose of the individual life is to seek its own self-development. The development of the individual and the community must be based in an eternal truth, a 'self-manifestation of the cosmic Spirit'. The subjective view of life rejects the notion that life is to be technically managed, mechanized and manipulated. Life must concentrate on a need for a developing self-consciousness where *intuitional* processes of knowing allow the individual to be in touch with the self.

Growth in realizing one's divine destiny is not rooted in egoism or 'lonely salvation'. Rather, spiritual growth is intensely communal. For Aurobindo, the 'true goal' is in a 'Self, one in difference which related the good of each, on a footing of equality and not of strife and domination, to the good of the rest of the world.'[19] Community properly functions to help the individual and humanity to fulfil or complete the other. A community that imposes a sovereign claim on the individual is as perverse as an individual's decision to live egoistically. The individual must contribute to the well-being of the community. The community must satisfy the needs and aspirations of divergent individuals. Ultimately, the perennial tension between the individual and the community in politics is to be resolved by the following two principles: 'treat others as self' and 'help any other person in need'. Only with the realization of these two moral imperatives as the basis for the ideal of human unity will individual existence within the community be held sacred. The ideal human society will adopt, from symbolic society, the need to look beyond the immediately given to a deeper reality and to communicate this reality via symbols. From typal society, those ethical and psychological modes of life that reflect a deeper and more spiritual life are to be absorbed. From conventional society, those forms that can be imposed from within are to be viewed as valid. From the rationalistic-individualistic society can be taken the notion of the value of the individual without egoism and the notion that scientific reason must be subordinate to the life of the spirit. In effect, in the ideal human society it is the aims and ideals of man in his spiritual perfection that must determine socio-political structures. In an important

[18] See especially C.B. Macpherson, *The Political Theory of Possessive Individualism: Hobbes to Locke* (Oxford: Clarendon Press, 1962).

[19] BCL, *op. cit.*, Vol. 15, p. 47.

statement, Aurobindo summarizes the intimate holistic (or 'integral') relation between the 'law' of the individual, the community and humanity in his political vision:

> Thus the law for the individual is to perfect his individuality by free development from within, but to respect and to aid and be aided by the same free development in others. His law is to harmonize his life with the life of the social aggregate and to pour himself out as a force for growth and perfection on humanity. The law for the community or nation is equally to perfect its corporate existence by a free development from within, aiding and taking full advantage of that of the individual, but to respect and to aid and be aided by the same free development of other communities and nations. Its law is to harmonize its life with that of the human aggregate and to pour itself out as a force for growth and perfection on humanity. The law for humanity is to pursue its upward evolution towards the finding and expression of the Divine in the type of mankind, taking full advantage of the free development and gains of all individuals and nations and groupings of men, to work towards the day when mankind may be really and not only ideally one divine family, but even then, when it has succeeded in unifying itself, to respect, aid and be aided by the free growth and activity of its individuals and constituent aggregates.[20]

In an explicit political application of his vision, Aurobindo contends that there is an inherent relationship between liberty, equality and fraternity. When liberty is taken to the extreme, 'it arrives at competitive individualism' in liberal democratic societies. When equality is taken to its extreme, 'it arrives first at strife, then . . . constructs an artificial and machine-made society'[21] that is prevalent in socialist societies.

In the spiritualized polity, the fulfilment of the individual and the community can emerge only through a supramental (supermind) consciousness and power where the predominance of fraternity of brotherhood allows the union of the impulses for freedom and equality. Fraternity is grounded in the spirit and without it neither liberty nor equality can be actualized. Aurobindo expresses the soul-power of brotherhood by claiming that:

> . . . brotherhood is the real key to the triple gospel of the idea of humanity. The union of liberty and equality can only be achieved by the power of human brotherhood and it can be founded on nothing else. But brotherhood exists only in the soul and by the soul it can exist by nothing else.[22]

[20] *Ibid.*, pp. 63–64.
[21] *Ibid.*, p. 546.   [22] *Ideal of Human Unity, op. cit.*, pp. 546–47.

In effect, the primal law and purpose of the individual is to seek its own self-development within the context of a spiritualized polity based on the soul power of brotherhood that is grounded in a supramental realm of Divine consciousness. In such an 'integral society' there is an intimate concern to discover the Divine in a holistic appreciation for education, administration, protection and the productive economy.

A contemporary political philosopher, Professor V.R. Mehta, has been profoundly influenced by Aurobindo in formulating his notion of 'Integral Pluralism' as an alternative to liberalism and Marxism for India. As Professor Mehta puts it:

> Aurobindo was perhaps the first to emphasize the profound insight contained in the millenniums of Indian thought . . .; he was the first to relate all of them to the bi-polar world of the individual and the collective, and to define all subsidiary values as freedom and equality in terms of this holistic picture of society.[23]

Yet Mehta remains quite critical of Aurobindo's failure and the failure on his followers to explicate a strategy that can lead to the fulfilment of his vision. Mehta presents his criticism pointedly:

> It must be clearly stated the enunciation of the deeper elements of the Indian value system by Aurobindo remains confined to an esoteric circle, not only because it was couched in the most obscure language, but also because no attempt had been made to link it to any concrete plan of action or to the concrete issues raised by the fulfilment of human needs. He did not take into account the real determinants of the social situation which the historical process had created at this point of time, nor did he provide the precise action required to remove the poverty of the teeming millions, the gap between the proclaimed ideals and their practice.[24]

Toward a Critical Analysis of Aurobindo's and Chardin's Political Vision

Aurobindo's greatest contribution to political theory is the construction of a holistic vision of human evolution in the life of the Divine that attempts to reconcile matter and spirit, the individual and the community and liberty and equality in the context of compassion, love and aid toward the whole human community. It is a magnificent spiritual vision of politics which calls for self-surrender and infinite self-knowledge akin to the work

---

[23] V.R. Mehta. *Beyond Marxism: Towards an Alternative Perspective* (New Delhi: Manohar Pub., 1978), p. 78.
[24] *Ibid.*, p. 58.

of Teilhard de Chardin. In Aurobindo's integral vision there is an attempt at a grand synthesis of the partial truths of other positions. This synthesis, of course, emanates from the yogic experience. Ultimately his vision is based on what he had seen and is beyond conventional modes of political analysis. One can accept the Divine Reality intuitively as Aurobindo and Chardin see it, one can deny it completely on empirical scientific grounds or one can be intellectually drawn to its all-encompassing quality without fully accepting or rejecting it. Few can deny that they beckon us to go on a Utopian search for political and spiritual liberation that might serve as an alternative to the 'modern barbarian mentality' in 'Liberal Democracy' or the 'war of classes' found in 'Socialist Democracy'. This vision of totalism and communalism is worth the scrutiny of both Eastern and Western political thinkers during our age in which there is a compression of socialization due to the influences of technology.

There are, however, great pitfalls for those who wish to join Aurobindo's and Chardin's quest. Aurobindo's yogic surrender, as Professor Mehta has indicated in the foregoing, shows the proclivity to underplay specific socio-political obligations in the face of *specific* human needs and specific historical circumstances. How one can maintain high levels of political and spiritual sensitivity is a basic question that Sri Aurobindo's life and thought do not answer.

Chardin's work certainly provokes us to take seriously the notion that we are advancing towards a phase of collective and superior thought which is the critical point of socialization and co-thinking. Yet those who are not completely socialized are regarded as 'lower' forms of evolution. The future belongs to the 'human mass' not to individuals. Individual man's alienation and frustration are cries that find no echo for Chardin.

In conclusion, we can state that both Aurobindo and Chardin provide students of political thought with a vision that completely negates the notion of 'original sin' as inherent in the human condition. They both see the dawn of a new era towards the 'ultra human'—the finally awakened human intelligence and spirit which is at the threshold of a greater consciousness. Man's ordinary qualities are blown to cosmic proportions. Both Aurobindo and Chardin are political enthusiasts who see everywhere signs of incipient collectivization which make them supremely confident in the future. In the coming centuries we shall take enormous steps toward an 'enlarged consciousness'. Like all political enthusiasts in history, they exalt the individual's unique experiences in a 'collective will of Mankind' or a 'superhumanity' without the benefit of rational norms.

The Utopian impulses of Aurobindo and Chardin see a fabulous future which in reality can become a nightmare. Both these great visionaries ignore the essential freedom of the soul, the fact that socio-political change involves not only gain but loss as well and that human nature retains an aggressive dimension. The dreams and prophecies of Aurobindo and Chardin are not the products of purely arbitrary imagination. They both proceed from the two-fold supposition that man is a 'divine' entity of infinite power and possibilities, and that political paradise on earth alone is truly worthy of him. These *gnostic* (the view that man is perfectible and is able to discern that perfection) approaches to politics do not simply scale the heights of religious and political lyricism.[25] Rather, they are a perennial type of thinking, in both the East and West, which claims that the 'spirit' is sovereign as a source of knowledge and illumination. They claim that 'impure' elements will gradually be eliminated or become suffused with spirit. Aurobindo and Chardin betray a contempt for creation, for the world and for nature as they are. Original sin can truly be transcended. Universal purity is the task of man. For man possesses, in the depths of his psychic essence, the spark of knowledge when acting together which can provide human salvation. Only a coalescence of all individuals will create a restoration of original unity—a flawless whole. Man, in effect, recreates God by restoring his lost unity and perfection. God will only emerge with the establishment of a peaceful and harmonious *human* society.

We are told by Aurobindo and Chardin about the benevolence which the collectivity offers humanity. This type of collectivity can possibly bring a defiance of a transcendent God, pride unlimited, a yearning for enormous power and the assumption by this collectivity of 'divine attributes' with a view to manipulating and shaping mankind's fate. The Utopians' real political vice is their construction of thought experiments which dismantle *human* individuality through the dissolution of individual conscience and consciousness, and then to replace these with an abstract collectivity and coalesced consciousness. In a moment of madness, the Roman Emperor Caligula wished that mankind had only one head that he might more easily chop off with one decisive blow. Similarly, both Aurobindo and Chardin give intellectual support to those who wish to deal with one entity so as to simplify the political task of transforming indomitable human nature into a far more manageable phenomenon.

---

[25] The word gnostic (gnosis) means perfect knowledge of the cosmos.

13

SUDIPTA KAVIRAJ

The Heteronomous Radicalism of M.N. Roy

The Context of Nationalist Discourse

In order to explain the nature and significance of M.N. Roy's political thought, let me first try to reconstruct the context of the nationalist discourse in which he made his intervention.

By definition, all forms of nationalist thought grew out of the historical conflict with colonialism. Domination by European colonial powers not only denied political sovereignty to the non-European societies but also deprived them of intellectual resources of self-expression. The story of colonialism unfolds at two levels: a political level (on which a society loses control of its political destiny) and a level of culture (on which it gradually loses its 'voice,' a language of its own). Nationalist ideology sought to break out of these political and mental bondages of colonialism. But colonialism exerted such an overarching influence on the subject peoples that it was exceedingly difficult for them to be conscious or critical of all the constraints it imposed on them. Often the critiques that nationalist thought advanced were passionate but partial, and remained essentially fragmented. Each brand of nationalism named a feature of colonial social life, and turned that into its own special theatre of war. But the more complete its rejection of colonialism on that particular front, the less attentive it was about others.

Thus, culture of colonialism is a world of tragic paradoxes. It is a culture marked by a constantly renewed contradiction between its two fundamental characteristics from either of which it is unable to escape. These are the urge towards independence and the givenness of a heteronomous existence. Nowhere is this contradiction more explicit than in its political thought. Nationalist politics, except for minor aberrant trends, symbolize the urge for political emancipation; yet the language or alphabet which this politics employs to recognize and interpret its world, its acts, its history, and even the arguments it uses against the enemy are often taken from the colonizer.[1] Almost all solutions which can be worked out within the historical confines of this language and experience are tragic in this sense.

Acknowledgements: Some of the basic ideas in this interpretation occurred to me on reading Partha Chatterjee's analysis of the nationalism of Bankimchandra Chatterjee. I am indebted to him for allowing me to see his work before it was published. It should be apparent, however, that there are also some differences, partly because the individual thinker I have addressed had a very different structure of theoretical consciousness. I am of course solely responsible for any analytical indiscretions that may have occurred.

[1] Ashis Nandy, *The Intimate Enemy* (Delhi: Oxford University Press, 1983).

Nationalist thought was not a homogeneous body of political ideas, nor did it develop in a teleological succession of stages as often represented in the popular mythology of nationalism. Its internal structure is extremely complex because it contains critiques within critiques.[2] Nearly all forms of nationalist opinion agreed that in culture what was required was a fundamental critique of colonial conceptions of history, politics and society; but there were sharp, often irreconcilable, disagreements about what this critique would consist of—what arguments ought to be advanced to contest the claims of colonial ideology, and what, once that was discredited, should be substituted. Traditionally, the history of political ideas concentrated attention on ways in which each particular form of nationalism sought to articulate its opposition to imperialist ideology and practices or on the explicit differences between varying strands of nationalism.[3] It emphasized accordingly the opposition of extremism to constitutionalism, of radical terrorism against Gandhian non-violence, of socialist aspirations of the leftists to the ambiguous conservatism of the ordinary Congressman.

I do not wish to argue the irrelevance of these distinctions, but to show their limits. There could be other criteria or central questions through which the history of nationalist thought could also be interpreted; and the ordering of relations that these other criteria would yield might be startlingly different. Evidently, nationalist thought was internally divided. There was a sort of permanent competition among its various strands in being anti-colonial. Each trend accused others of making a break with colonialism that was insufficient, inconsistent, temporising or dishonest. In effect, they were criticizing each other for not carrying the struggle against colonialism to its limits, or not waging it on all possible fronts. The extremists criticized the moderates of being simple-minded prisoners of a liberal rhetoric that was clearly disingenuous, of having chimerical dreams of fighting colonialism with colonialism. Rationalists could and often did claim that if Indians were ever to free themselves, they must learn to master what were not merely European, but simply scientific, ideas. Ideas were simply right or wrong; they were devoid of nationality.

All forms of nationalism were critical of imperialist power; but being critical in a colonial culture is not a simple idea. Nationalist ideology gave rise to an intricate pattern of interpretations of the colonial experience, centred on the question: how did our society come to be colonized? For, in some ways, this was a precondition for answering the practical question of how it could possibly be freed of imperialist rule. Beyond a trite unity, nationalist thinking divided into two general intellectual responses of affirmation and negation. Both of these tended to get involved in contradictions eventually, contradictions that were far more significant

---

[2] See Partha Chatterjee's paper on Bankim Chatterjee in this volume.
[3] This would include most of the nationalist and academic interpretations.

than mere logical difficulties. Unlike logical errors, these could not be simply written correctly, but had to be lived through to their bitter end.

A first natural response to colonialism is one of affirmation of the nationalist's own culture. A colonized people, precisely because they are colonized, attempt to affirm the symbols of their identity. For this marks the political boundaries more sharply; this defines and discourages transgressions. Often, colonized societies go through periods of exaggerated cultural self-assertion after conquest, as if to tell their conquerors that they can take away their political sovereignty but not their cultural autonomy. After territory is lost to the invader, the internal spaces of the mind can still remain free. At the beginning, people could still view the historical fact of colonial conquest as a contingent one, a result of fortuitous incidents. This response denies any systematic superiority to the colonizer's technology or the principles of his social organization. As a corollary it is often believed that colonized people will be able to fight against their domination by drawing upon the resources of their own unreconstructed self, by reaching deeper into the resources of their own distinct civilization. To become like the European colonizers would then look like a civilizational betrayal.

Not surprisingly, an affirmative response to colonialism was fairly common in early British India. Programmes of the revolt of 1857 contained this explicitly; so did the intellectual activity of the early Hindu conservatives in Bengal, and in later times the political ideology of the terrorists. If colonial conquest was a result of a series of contingencies (as nationalist novels and dramas like to portray it), it followed that there was nothing fundamentally wrong with the indigenous social structure—the skills, institutions and distributive principles on which it was based. Determination to obstruct any form of change, to turn it into anything other than itself became part of a definition of autonomy. For this society to turn into something else, in particular to become something resembling the colonizer, would be a further victory of colonialism.

However, from the early days of colonialism a response of negation was also, curiously, fairly common. Colonialism destroyed the hermetic isolation of the Indian civilization, the compulsive viewing of its practices in its own terms simply because of the unavailability of any other criteria. In earlier cases of conquest, the social and intellectual principles of those other cultures were not sufficiently distinct to resist absorption into a reinterpreted whole. British conquest of India was altogether different. To those who wished to use this opportunity, it offered new external criteria to re-evaluate the social institutions of their society. Particularly in its more extreme forms, the responses of negation required acceptance of the presuppositions of European rationalists. Thus the first reformers were sometimes people who modelled their attitudes on the classical rationalism of the eighteenth century—an attitude which could be regarded, given different ways of seeing, as either radical or inauthentic. Historical events (especially the crucial ones of the experience of colonization) were not seen by these writers as contingencies, a string of happy accidents for Europeans, or simply the lower phases in a cyclical turnover of misfortunes. For even the hardest traditionalists, the phenomenon of colonization must have made a strictly logical belief in a cyclical history particularly difficult. Those who adopted a negative response, however, brought to their understanding of history a distinctly linear vision. It was importantly inadequate to simply say that societies were different, and equal in their difference, and accept an untroubled cultural relativism. Societies were different and unequal. They were unequal in power, because different principles of social organization yielded different degrees of technical effectivity. Different types of societies, this implied, could be ranked in a hierarchy of effectiveness, or what European ideologists more lyrically called 'rationality'. Historical transformation of societies were to be made sense of in terms of this vision. History was to be seen as progress; but a logical corollary of it, unfortunately, was to have to regard one's own as indefensible in rational terms. It was this that explained persistent British superiority—in military and organizational terms, and explained the British conquest of India—perhaps, as one nationalist observer called it, the greatest historical wonder of all times. This, therefore, required a more serious, structural explanation.

An explanation of this kind necessarily implied a shift in the structure of the explanation itself, turning the point of the critique to some extent inward, against practices and institutions of one's own society, instead of blaming the British. This will apportion the blame quite differently. Just as there were some unlovely aspects to a society which colonized others, there were some faults in a society which let itself be colonized. A great deal of early liberal thought in India exhibited this belief. Its acceptance of European presuppositions went from philosophical to political ones; as in the case of writers like Naoroji, it went to the extent of accepting the preconceptions of the ideology of British colonialism, and seeking to work out a critique within its narrow confines. For liberal constitutionalists, there was no contradiction between the two great critical themes—a critique of social practices and a critique of colonial dominance. One was a condition for the other. For the more traditional streams of nationalist consciousness the two critiques were in conflict.

If one saw colonization in this light, the preconditions of independence would appear very differently from the affirmative case. Colonization was not due to personal faults of character, lack of military skill or the simple ineptitude of rulers. The decisions they could, in principle, take would be over a possible range determined by the resources and practices of their own society. It was this social form of inferior effectiveness—in war, trade, scientific knowledge, inventive ingenuity, skills of economic and political organization—which had to be reformed. The question of the nature and destiny of capitalism was always at the heart of the colonial discourse; but obviously it was structured in a way quite different from the way it arose in European rationalism; it was rationalism in a distorted mirror. The dialectic of nationalist discourse continued into the twentieth century, and when the time came, communist theorists found themselves participants in it. They did not create the terms of the debate into the midst of which they arrived. These terms were, to a large extent, set for them by the previous course of events. Were there colonial presuppositions underlying all kinds of nationalist thought? Was a political opposition to colonialism the only or the most reliable criterion of authenticity? M.N. Roy's political thought is a particularly apt case for study to answer these questions, precisely because of the extremity and confidence of his political radicalism. He was one of India's first communist theorists, deeply self-conscious about his application of radical doctrine, entirely convinced that his position was simultaneously more radical and more correct than all the others. Yet, on closer inspection, his work shows some strange presuppositions existing, ones that he failed to bring to critical attention. He is an example of the tragedy of colonial nationalism, of how its greatest audacities are fraught with an insidious dependence. His opposition to British imperialism was uncompromising but the language in which he articulated this opposition could in some senses be called heteronomous; his most critical remarks about Indian history were often marked by a feeling of its inauthenticity. Roy was a living paradox. His heresies from the Marxism of the Comintern are usually given the greatest amount of critical attention. But it is perhaps this peculiar combination of political radicalism and philosophical heteronomy which explains the futility of his politics.[4] This may also show that underlying the obvious divide between his communist and humanist phases there was perhaps a substratum of philosophic continuity.

Roy's thought is ordinarily studied in the rather restrictive context of his relationship with the communists. To me it seems that the underlying complexity of Roy's attempted mix of nationalism and radicalism can be revealed only if it is set in a double context—the immediate one of communist theory on nationalist politics, itself part of the larger discourse of colonial culture. This double context can bring out both the astonishing daring of Roy's radicalism, and a tragic heteronomy within its historical consciousness.

[4] In contrast to other communist leaders, the biographical literature on Roy is quite large. One of the most detailed and adequate is John Patrick Haithcox, *Communism and Nationalism in India: M.N. Roy and Comintern Policy, 1920–39* (Princeton: Princeton University Press, 1971).

Roy's Political Career

Manabendra Nath Roy (1887–1954) was a most remarkable failure in the history of the Indian national movement. In personal terms, his failure appears inexplicable. He showed all the proverbial qualities of a successful political leader. Few other individuals of our nationalism had the ingredients of political success in such abundance. In few other cases was failure so complete. Political failure, of course, does not mean a fate of utter oblivion. It means simply a disproportionality between what the actor intended and what he eventually managed to do. Ordinary Congressmen had less imposing ambitions and moral standards of a less exalted kind. Although many of their biographies range from the unspectacular to the contemptible, in their own terms they were eminently more successful. Terrorists, by the symbolic violence of their acts of self-sacrifice, drew much more attention and a great deal of sympathy. Communists after Roy went through a history of indecision and occasional marginalization, but always fought back into political reckoning. Roy's political life, by contrast, was a classic of failure. As an individual, Roy had great qualities of intellect and character. In his width of reading and ability to polemicize, he was at least as good as Nehru. He lacked Nehru's literary ability; but was perhaps superior in organizing and presenting an argument economically. He had a remarkable sense of purpose and determination—though most of it was spent in support of forlorn causes. He had a tremendous ability to organize and inspire personal loyalty. Finally, his failure was not the inevitable but regrettable inability of a saint to handle the world of politics; he showed at various points the ability to rise above moral scruples which often distinguishes a successful political figure. But despite these personal qualities, Roy never became much more than a leader of a small political sect. The recurring interest in Roy's story must have something to do with this riddle.

M.N. Roy's original name was Narendranath Bhattacharya. He came from a Bengali Brahmin family, and apparently had quite an unremarkable childhood. He was attracted to nationalist terrorism as an adolescent, but did not rise to first-rate eminence among terrorists, although this set him on his political career. Piecing together information on his life is sometimes difficult, and of all the available sources his memoirs are not the most reliable. This is not because he distorted history to magnify his own role in it—the most excusable fault in autobiographers in any case. The problems arise more because he looks at history, and what happened to him, through a strongly coherent grid of concepts. Some people write autobiographies to share anecdotes, to put down interesting slander and give them permanence, to the lasting indignity of their personal enemies. Others write to avenge themselves on history. Much of Roy's reminiscences are written in the high moral tone of unreconciled failure.

His brief experience with the terrorists was crucial to his career. It was not an apprenticeship in making a revolution; but his terrorist days may have shaped some of his persistent dislikes. Roy rose to middling eminence in the terrorist ranks, to be entrusted with the task of meeting a German steamer off the coast of Bengal which was to carry arms to be used by the Indian revolutionaries against the British. The steamer did not arrive, and Roy made his way eventually to the United States, where he came into contact with socialist ideas, and married Evelyn Trent. He went to Mexico afterwards, where he participated in the formation of the Mexican Communist Party. Curiously, it was as a representative of the Mexican Communist Party that Roy went to Moscow to attend the second congress of the newly formed Communist International, an event which was to confer on him early celebrity. In Moscow, Roy offered his critical comments on Lenin's Draft Thesis on the National and Colonial Question. In 1927, Roy headed a delegation of the Communist International to China. Roy's mission was a failure and before long he was expelled from the Comintern. He returned to India in 1930 and was jailed for six years for his involvement in two earlier cases of communist conspiracy. From 1930 to 1940 he joined in the Indian National Congress, which he tried to radicalize. He advocated a twentieth century Jacobinism for India. Unable to influence the Congress leadership (especially Gandhi), Roy left the Congress and founded the Radical Democratic Party, which was to be a broad, united front of the workers, peasants and the petty bourgeoisie. As his party failed to make any dent in Indian politics, Roy dissolved the party in 1948 and founded a new movement for a radical or new humanism.

To discuss his political ideas is to be struck by another paradox. His significance in the Indian nationalist tradition is because of the particular combination he made of nationalism and Marxist theory. Indeed, in this respect he was a pioneer. But he himself moved decisively away from Marxism in his later years; this must have been because of intellectual conviction. This leads to an implicit difference between the way most interpreters evaluate his career and the way he must have seen it himself. If Roy had written the tracts he did in his later life without having been a communist earlier, it is doubtful if he would have received the same amount of political attention.

A systematic application of Marxist theory to the questions of Indian nationalist politics was rare before Roy's cryptic and ambitious 'An Indian Communist Manifesto' appeared in a relatively obscure Scottish labour journal.[5] Although several others (e.g., Nehru, Jaya Prakash Narayan and other communists) tried the same articulation of Marxist and nationalist ideas after him, probably with a greater sensitivity to the

[5] Roy, 'An Indian Communist Manifesto,' in G. Adhikary (ed.), *Documents of the History of the Communist Party of India* (hereafter *DHCPI*), Vol. 1 (Delhi: People's Publishing House, 1971), pp. 151–55.

inherent complexity of such an enterprise, Roy's attempt remained intellectually a most impressive one, though perhaps the most consistently wrong-headed in reading Indian social reality.

Roy's Debate with Lenin

The foundation congress of the Communist International was essentially concerned with the organizational set-up of the movement, and with formalizing its break with the socialists. It was in the second congress that the Comintern began to devote serious attention to the working out of a strategy for world revolution. In contrast to the socialists, the communists had always been sympathetic to colonial nationalist movements. In working out its international strategy, therefore, the Comintern had to address itself to very different political questions—the problem of a proletarian revolution in the European metropolitian states, and the distinct question of what attitude to take towards national movements against colonialism. A second factor contributed to the great attention given to the colonial question at the second congress. In 1919, the European states had just emerged from a great revolutionary wave. Most of the European states faced difficulties in the war crisis but, except in Russia and briefly in Hungary, no state actually fell to a successful revolution. Another revolutionary wave did not appear likely in the short run. However, the Leninist theory of imperialism taught that the international capitalist system had a total structure linking metropolitan countries with their colonial territories; and continued stability at both ends was necessary for the survival of the system. Conflict in the colonies, therefore, could be seen as an integral part of the crisis of the imperialist world system. A rupture of this system in the colonies could be equally vital in the breakdown of imperialism: the road to London lies via Peking.[6] The importance given to the colonial debate resulted directly from the structure of Leninist theory.

Applying Marxist theory to the colonies, however, was a far from unambiguous affair. Marxist theory assumed that decisions about what to do in politics depended on what kind of society it was, what its class structure was, and how these classes were likely to behave in political life. But the primary difficulty was, of course, that these societies were structured quite differently from European societies which had either undergone capitalist transformation, or were on the brink of it. As a result, there could be several ways of 'applying' Marxism to colonial societies, especially in regard to two crucial tasks: (*i*) the analysis of classes in colonial society, and (*ii*) the political strategy which followed from this. Analyzing the class structure of a society involved not a simple

[6] Lenin, 'Preliminary draft thesis on the national and colonial question,' *Selected Works*, Vol. 3 (Moscow: Progress Publishers, 1977), pp. 372–77.

transfer of the class analysis Marx had made of nineteenth century European states, but the application of his method to a society that was structured in a very different way. It was not the categories or the formulations that were to be common between the European analyses and the colonial analyses, but the method. Indeed, the method might require the application of quite different categories. The 'application problem,' was so intractable (though few people, like Lenin, saw it at the time) because of a common misjudgement about what Marxist theory of history offered. It was not merely a set of conclusions, but a set of resources from which conclusions could be drawn. What kind of conclusions would be appropriate to a particular case depended on which particular set of resources were considered appropriate for use.

One set of propositions which could plausibly invite application to a colony was what was called the theory of 'late capitalism,' or what Trotsky called 'the law of uneven and combined development'. Marx had shown, in his political writings, that the development of capitalism in Europe tended to slip from a revolution first way, to a more compromising second way. The bourgeoisie, like the German one (which arrived late on the scene, controlled relatively larger-sized industries and had an insecure social base), caught between two historical contradictions. The first was in front—their contradiction with feudal classes; but they were constantly kept in check by the contradiction with the rising proletariat behind. Bourgeois groups in these cases tended to arrive at compromises with feudal reaction. A classic presentation of this analysis could be found in Marx's 1849 article on the 'Bourgeoisie and the Counter-revolution'.[7] In communist debate, some theorists (like Roy initially and Trotsky later) applied this model to the colonial countries and the bourgeoisie there. Trotsky put it in a celebrated universal form: 'the further east you go, the more reactionary the bourgeoisie becomes'. In the theory of the Russian revolution, Lenin had applied Marx's model of late capitalism. Yet he did not stretch it to colonial countries. For Lenin it was inappropriate to apply the late-backward model to the colonies because, in moving from Russia to the colonies, one crossed a significant logical threshold. A colonial situation introduced a consideration—the contradiction between imperialism and the entire people, to use Mao's terms—which overrode all others. As Lenin's preliminary draft thesis to the congress asserted, the revolutions in the colonies were bourgeois in their socio-political character. The communists' task in the colonies was 'to assist bourgeois-democratic liberation movements in these countries,' but being careful to maintain the ideological distinctness of the radical communist position. The communists ought to, in Lenin's view, support nationalist movements;

[7] Marx, 'The Bourgeoisie and the Counter-revolution,' in Marx and Engels, *Articles from the Neue Rhenische Zeitung, 1848–49* (Moscow: Progress Publishers, 1972), pp. 177–202.

but they ought to see it not as a finished product but as an ongoing progress, something necessarily incomplete and something that could be influenced; they ought to try, therefore, to radicalize its content. The Comintern should enter into a 'temporary alliance' with bourgeois democracy in colonial countries, but should 'not merge with it'. The communists should follow a dual strategy which followed from the famous thesis of the dualism of the nature of the bourgeoisie.[8] As we shall see later, like many other apparently unambiguous propositions of Marxist political thought, dualism was not an entirely unequivocal idea; it could be, and indeed was, taken to mean different things by Lenin and Roy.

On the eve of the second congress of the Comintern, Lenin invited Roy to prepare a draft thesis on the colonial question, besides Lenin's own, as Lenin felt he was unfamiliar with the concrete political situation in the colonies. The perspective that Roy advanced in his draft theses was, however, in important respects different from Lenin's. Surely, Roy's theses too applied the conceptual apparatus of Marxist political economy, but his judgements on political questions were vastly different. In 1920, in the aftermath of the great disappointment with the European revolutionary wave, there was considerable plausibility to Roy's view that a crisis of the world capitalist structure should be expected from the side of the colonies, not from the metropolitan centres. This was reinforced by the emergence of the Kuo Min Tang in China and the outbreak of non-cooperation in India. If this was so, it was obviously vital for communists to arrive at a correct evaluation of these societies and their political possibilities.

But, methodologically, Roy's main difference with Lenin came in at this point. Lenin saw between countries like Russia and the colonies a difference in kind, Roy only a difference in degree. Roy thus felt justified, like Trotsky after him, in applying the logic of late capitalism to the colonies. So Roy's picture of the political economy of colonial India was markedly similar to Marx's depiction of Germany in the mid-nineteenth century. Compared to other colonies, the bourgeoisie in India was highly developed. If understood relatively, this judgement was certainly correct; but Roy crucially misjudged its corollaries. He overestimated the strength of the proletariat both in economic terms (i.e., in terms of its size, concentration in big industries) and politically (i.e., in terms of its political self-awareness, organization and political maturity). Owing to both these reasons—the relative weakness of the bourgeoisie and the relative strength of the working class—bourgeois political groups like the Congress seemed predestined to Roy to compromise with feudal and imperialist interests. Roy thus anticipated a deep-rooted structural tendency in political organizations of the bourgeoisie towards compromise and eventual surrender

---

[8] For a detailed historical discussion, see G. Adhikary (ed.), *DHCPI*, Vol. 1, pp. 155 ff.

to imperialism. Compromise meant to him, unlike to Lenin, not just a temporary prudential truce with the enemy before hostilities could be begun again on more favourable terms, but a fundamental reversal of position. It meant, to use a language often used in Comintern literature, a 'sell-out' to imperialism, a decisive, once-for-all acceptance of a subordinate position to imperialist bourgeoisie, collusion in colonial rule for better economic wages. The political implications of this understanding of colonial economies were equally significant. This meant that the bourgeoisie, and of course its political organizations, were predestined to 'betray' the national movement, exactly as the German bourgeoisie of Marx's times sided with the counter-revolution. Of course, the historic task of the national movement—achievement of political and economic freedom—would still be there. By the bourgeoise's default, it would have to be performed by other classes and their political organizations, especially the fictionally large proletariat and the radical petty bourgeoisie. Roy's expectations of how politics would go in the short term were determined by these theoretical premises. He foresaw a continuous process of radicalization in the national movement. Leading classes, like the bourgeoisie or the petty bourgeoisie (or their political organizations), would assume leadership for some time. Every change in leadership would polarize the movement and give it a higher political content. Each of these would be transcended eventually by the movement's growing militancy. Leading groups would be terrified by popular initiative and ˈrestrain the struggle and be cast in the capacious 'dustbin of history,' a m chanism much in use in Roy's historical machine. Only the communists were capable of leading national movements to final victory.

Accordingly, the coming history of nationalism was seen as a process of relentless polarization; at every stage, one of the earlier leading classes being winched out of the nationalist coalition. Thus, the coalition would become increasingly narrow in class terms, but homogeneous. The national revolution was to become, after the betrayal of the bourgeoisie, a dual revolution in a strict sense: a national revolution which would be able to realize its objectives only if it became indistinguishable from a socialist revolution; a national revolution led by a proletarian party.

Thus both views about the likely behaviour of the bourgeoisie could be plausibly called theories of 'dualism'. Both envisaged a duality in its historical role and political behaviour; but duality meant rather different things for them. Perhaps it was this convenient ambiguity in the term dualism which made a compromise so easy at the second congress.[9] When the behaviour of the bourgeoisie was authoritatively characterized as dualist, both sides could see this as a vindication of what it said or meant. But precisely, therefore, it is important to distinguish clearly the two

---

[9] For an account of the history of Indian nationalism in these terms, see Bipan Chandra, *Nationalism and Colonialism in Modern India* (Delhi: Orient Longman, 1979).

meanings of dualism; for the strategy of the communist movement in the colonies oscillated politically between these two ideas. Ironically, Roy's thesis was also adopted by the second congress of the Comintern as a supplementary thesis, though considerably toned down. Actually, in its logical tendencies, it was hardly a supplement; more an alternative way of viewing the coming history of the colonies.

Dualism for Lenin meant contradictory behaviour, because it was rooted in the contradictory position of the colonial bourgeoisie in the political economy of the colonies. The growth of capitalist enterprise depended, in legal and institutional terms, on the sufferance of the governing elite, but this was in a situation in which imperialism and nationalism fought out what Gramsci called a war of position. If the relation degenerated into a violent, possibly extra-legal, war of manoeuvre, the legal and juridical preconditions for the growth of the colonial bourgeoisie would no longer exist. The colonial bourgeoisie competed with the imperialist bourgeois class in terms of control over the colonial market, control over resources and liberalization of the legal regime which provided the juridical context for the economic activity of imperialist interests. As the indigenous bourgeoisie could not escape these conditions of its economic existence, it was likely, thought Lenin, that political organizations which would represent their interests would periodically press for an intensification of nationalist struggle; but once concessions were extracted, put brakes on militancy. Dualism, therefore, meant a patterned behaviour, which was not contradictory in the sense of being merely disorderly or without rational design. It indicated a deliberate strategic oscillation between a politics of confrontation and a politics of compromise.[10]

For Lenin, the structure of objective interests in which the bourgeoisie was placed precluded its being either consistently radical or consistently reactionary. Some modern historians have called this the politics of pressure—compromise—pressure, a fairly accurate anticipation of the way colonial bourgeoisies were, in fact, to behave. Roy's understanding of dualism was wholly different. For him, it meant an application of the model that Marx had applied to the European bourgeois classes. The historical career of the bourgeoisie will show a progressive phase, though marred by compromises; but it will eventually arrive at a final political crisis in which the bourgeoisie would betray the national movement. Dualism simply referred to the existence of these two stages in the political biography of the bourgeois class.

Some important implications followed from this view. The revolution he envisaged in the colonies was a combined revolution. Overthrow of colonial rule would be 'the first step towards a revolution in the colonies'. 'So to help overthrow the foreign rule in the colonies is not to endorse the

[10] *Comintern and the National and Colonial Questions* (hereafter *CNCQ*), (Delhi: CPI, 1970), p. 43.

nationalist aspirations of the native bourgeoisie, but to open the way to the smothered proletariat there.'[11] Roy clearly distinguished between the two trends in the nationalist movements, one led by the bourgeoisie tending to political compromise and reformism, and another—a social revolutionary trend—would strive for national independence at the same time, with an end of exploitation. This political judgement was based on some optimistic untruths, especially the claim that in the 1920s 'in most of the colonies there already existed organised revolutionary parties'.[12] This was not true of India, let alone other more backward colonial states. But, given this, proletarian hegemony was seen as a precondition for a successful fight for national freedom.

The Lenin-Roy debate ended in 1920, but these issues continued to concern the Comintern. At significant turns of events, these questions were opened anew and answered afresh. The verdict of the Congress went more Lenin's way, but the events of the next decade seemed to go in Roy's favour. By the mid-twenties, the non-cooperation movement was withdrawn, apparently vindicating Roy's belief that Gandhi had sung his 'swansong'. A few years later, communists were murdered in China by a Kuo Min Tang turning increasingly reactionary. Largely on this evidence, the sixth congress of the Comintern reversed its strategy, coming ironically close to the one Roy had advocated in 1920.[13] Though, in a final paradox, Roy was by then condemned as a right-wing renegade.

Despite early differences with Lenin, the Comintern admitted Roy's intellectual eminence, and he was entrusted with the leadership of the communist movement in India. But Roy's understanding had important consequences for the early political initiatives of Indian communism. A careful analysis of the history of its first decade shows that the policy actually followed by the communists in India was an unhelpful mean between Lenin's and Roy's. Averages often serve to combine the disadvantages of the two policies as often as their merits. The Indian communists arguably lost the possible advantage of following either of the two more consistent policies—consistent alliance or consistent opposition. Roy's leadership ensured that the relation between the nationalists and the communists in India began with a trail of quite avoidable bitterness.

However, more significantly, in the years he led the Indian communist movement from abroad, Roy tried to work out the lineaments of a

[11] *Ibid.*, p. 74
[12] *Theses of the Sixth Congress of the Comintern on the National and Colonial Questions, ibid.*
[13] This is not to deny that others too had tried to bring Marxism to the notice of the nationalist intelligentsia. But these attempts, like Har Dayal's, were very different from Roy's. These were mainly biographical accounts of Marx's intellectual life. Roy, by contrast, showed the usefulness of an application of Marx's theory to Indian history.

Marxist analysis of Indian society, the first of its kind.[14] At the second congress debates, his views were presented in a necessarily synoptic form—in a succession of large generalities which were supposed to apply to conditions in all colonies. When he applied these insights to the peculiar complexity of the Indian situation, both its strengths and weaknesses were to become more apparent. He was to develop a detailed theory of Indian political economy on two distinct theoretical levels, and it is worthwhile to follow his arguments on both. He provides two analyses of India—a long-term one which showed the formation and rhythms of capitalism, the slow crystallization of a social form. This provided the necessary background to an analysis of politics of the everyday, a withering commentary on the politics of Gandhian nationalism in the twenties.

The Long-term Analysis of Indian Society

The analysis of the long term was contained in Roy's main Marxist work, *India in Transition*, a remarkable accomplishment by any standard. Part of the writing (or probably the economic research) was done by one of his colleagues, Abani Mukherjee, a circumstance which Roy underplayed at the time. Later on, he did not hesitate to blame some of his over-estimations of proletarian politics on Mukherjee's apparently incompetent statistics. The judgements concerned, however, appear in retrospect to have been, to a significant extent, the results of statistical miscalculation rather than faults of method. Apart from its simple historical signficance as the first systematic exposition of a Marxist view of Indian history, *India in Transition* deployed Marxist concepts with considerable skill. Its significance has, in fact, to be measured against two standards. It used Marxist theory to offer a decisive and comprehensive critique of the presuppositions which governed nationalist thought, especially its assumption that Indian history and society were unique. Nationalists normally meant this not in the sense in which hermeneutic theorists would assert this about all societies, but in a simpler, more chauvinistic sense of exceptionalism of Indian history. Laws could explain the history of other nations, but not one's own. Roy's theoretical skills shone all the more in the surrounding poverty of theory in early Indian nationalism. His Marxism appeared in striking contrast to the lack of precision, logical

[14] Gandhi is an obvious exception to this. Despite appearances, his thinking on social issues was not marked by a lack of curiosity about the West, or an inability to make sense of it. What he offered was a critique of Western capitalism which has an internally highly complex character, and an affirmation of what he considered to be an authentic Indian social vision. What is required in a Marxist analysis of Gandhi is precisely a registration of the internal complexity of his thought. For instance, the usual criticism against his positions that they are not consistent is rebutted by the philosophical assertion that placing consistency as the highest intellectual value is only one possible ordering. There could be plausible orderings of other kinds.

consistency and theoretical vision of early nationalist thought.[15] Although Roy's Marxism has received severe strictures as to its methodology from later Indian Marxists, this critique conceals a certain historical inappropriateness; for Roy's context, against which he must be historically judged, was the nationalist discourse of the twenties, and not the considerably refined accents of nationalism and Marxism of decades later. A second context for Roy was, of course, the theoretical tradition of Marxism; and the same formulation applies there too. Against modern Marxist historiography, Roy's analysis must appear unidimensional and crude; but compared to the general run of discussions on colonial politics of the early Comintern period, it was not distinctly different. It shared the general strengths and weaknesses of that discourse.

The trouble with Roy's analysis of the long-term changes in Indian society was not its economic determinism, but the historical judgements which were made within its confines. Surely, he attempted to explain not only the long-term rhythms of social change, but also short-term fluctuations of politics by reference to alterations in the economic structure. Implicitly, it offered a critique of conventional historiography—'thanks to the painstaking researches of some modern historians, one can learn how many sacks of kishmish the great Aurangzeb consumed in his life,' but there was little documentation of the social history of the Indian people.[16] However, some of Roy's fundamental assumptions were extreme, even for his times. British colonialism brought the Indian economy, Roy argued, not only into contact with European capitalism, and what some, following Marx's remarks, would call a formal subsumption into the capitalist economic structure. In this form, this would mean that although capitalist forms did not transform the existing forms of production and the labour process, the economy as a whole was brought under controlling impulses of the international capitalist structure. Roy's position was more extreme: British colonialism meant to him an implantation of a capitalist economy in India. This was not an external or isolated judgement. On the contrary, his judgement that India was already a capitalist society formed the premise of all his critical judgements about Indian society and its political tendencies. This legitimized the application of Marx's model of class analysis to India without any adaptations. What he applied was Marx's analysis of classes in nineteenth century capitalist society in Europe. Class analysis was seen as a *method* which Marxists apply to all societies with necessary modification, which would imply that when a Maxist undertakes to analyze any society, he must ask, first, what was its economic structure, its form of production, which were its major social classes, and how they were likely to behave. Each of these questions was to be logically determined by the way the earlier question had been

[15] Roy, *India in Transition* (Bombay: Nachiketa, 1971), p. 17.
[16] *Ibid.*, p. 20.

answered. Roy, however, saw Marxist theory as a set of *conclusions* which were to be transferred to another society, if capitalism had historically emerged there. This was a simpler process of writing in Indian personae into a historical drama whose structure Marx had deciphered, and which always remained unchanged.

Thus, the classes Roy saw acting on the political stage in India in the twenties were exactly the same as those which occupied the European one in Marx's time. Four classes attracted Roy's attention—the bourgeoisie, the petty bourgeoisie, the peasantry and the proletariat. Roy's analysis of classes in Indian society is in marked contrast to Mao's famous depiction of the Chinese rural structure. While Mao applies a method, Roy applies a model. India, Roy declared, 'was not under the feudal system'.[17] Feudalism had been destroyed in a peaceful process by the emergence of an indigenous bourgeoisie and the gradual domination of the entire economy by British capital. It was noted that this form of capitalism showed some historical peculiarities—the existence of capitalist appropriation without a fully developed capitalist socio-economic structure. Indian society was marked by the existence of the following classes—the landed aristocracy, the bourgeoisie and intellectuals, the petty peasantry, and the working class (including the landless peasants). The bourgeoisie was, crucially, a product of colonialism; its development was not opposed to but dependent on colonial domination. Although there was brisk commercial activity before the arrival of colonialism in India, this did not produce an industrial bourgeoisie. Industrial capital emerged under British auspices. This was a crucial element in Roy's political analysis. Since the 1880s, the bourgeoisie gradually moved into lower forms of industrial enterprise, and thickets of legal restrictions favouring British capital naturally obstructed its growth. Nationalism of the Indian bourgeoisie is traced to this legal obstruction; and Roy was suitably derisive about early economic nationalists who tried to alter the laws of imperialism by petitions. The intensification of nationalist struggle under Gandhi's leadership is seen as a result of a deeper economic-juridical conflict with a stronger capitalist class. This picture was not wholly misleading, for later Marxist research has also set the political aspirations of the indigenous bourgeoisie in the context of its economic interests. Roy's distinctiveness lay in expecting a resolution of all political proclivities in the economic interests of a particular class—a fault surely, but one that he shared with Marxists of his generation. This, however, led to some false conclusions about the potential of the nationalist movement. The way he pictured the contradiction between the bourgeoisie and imperialism, it could never be irreconcilable. The colonial administration would accede to political pressures after some reluctance; correspondingly,

---

[17] *Ibid.*, p. 203. This is stated with greater assurance in *The Future of Indian Politics* (Calcutta: Minerva Associates, 1971), p. 65.

the capitalist class would be content with a satellite role, making it a permanent political compromise. After this, nationalism would have to find more radical forms of articulation through the leadership of the lower social classes. Two ideas were crucial in making Roy reach this conclusion: he saw the connection between economy and politics too narrowly and one-sidedly; he also saw the political organization of nationalism too narrowly, as a mere instrument of the capitalist class.

Assessment of Gandhi and Congress Nationalism

Given his theoretical frame, Roy's assessment of Gandhi could not have been favourable. But it is important to note that what Gandhi signified for Indian politics changed markedly over time. Because of methodological differences, seemingly identical characterizations often yielded contradictory implications in Lenin and Roy. This was true of their picture of nationalist movements too. To Lenin the colonial contradiction was primary, and therefore he sometimes went as far as to suggest that the bourgeoisie in the colonies were the historical inheritors of the traditions of the revolutionary bourgeoisie of the European enlightenment. For Roy, the historical role of the colonial bourgeoisie was clearly reactionary. 'The movement for national liberation is a struggle of the native middle class against the economic and political monopoly of the imperialist bourgeoisie.' Clearly, the nationalist movement was not a popular or mass movement in the sense in which Marxists use these terms. For there was no objective correspondence between the aims of the bourgeoisie and the historical aspirations of the entire nation. The ambitions of the bourgeoisie were centred on controlling the economy within the colonial regime, and not the attainment of national political sovereignty. As early as 1922, Roy thought he could see the signs of political accommodation between an increasingly assertive bourgeoisie and an increasingly conciliatory colonial administration. A mass movement could not result from a coincidence of interests of the capitalist class and other social strata. Nationalist ideology, which spoke necessarily in terms of the whole nation, therefore appeared to Roy as a simple deception—bringing pressures to bear on imperialists, and making popular forces fight the bourgeoisie's battle for it.

When the latter (the working class) will begin the struggle earnestly, it is expected to be more of a social nature than a political movement for national liberation. Since 1918, the Indian movement has entered this stage. It may still have an appearance of a national struggle involving the mass of the population, but fundamentally it is a social strife, the revolt of the exploited against the exploiting class, irrespective of nationality.[18]

[18] Roy, 'Present Events in India,' *DHCPI*, Vol. 1, p. 324.

Consistent with this, there are a series of subsidiary arguments in Roy, using the appearance-reality inversion, but all, unfortunately, used in wrong ways. Only apparently, is the contradiction between imperialism and the Indian bourgeoisie the predominant one; actually, it was one between the exploiting and exploited classes, 'irrespective of nationality'. What appeared to be a political conflict was essentially a class struggle, in an economic sense. In appearance, the stage of the nationalist movement represented by Tilak and Gandhi was a higher level of opposition to British colonialism than the earlier moderate phase. But the criterion of judgement should be socio-economic, not political. Who was more progressive than the others ought to be judged by their views on the socio-economic form, rather than simple opposition to imperialist rule. Despite appearances, the extremist phase represented a retrograde step in the history of nationalism. The extremists, in this sense, were more dangerous than the constitutionalists. Only apparently was Gandhi at the peak of his political career, in control of a vast nationalist upsurge; actually, the end of non-cooperation was 'Mr. Gandhi's swansong,' the beginning of the end of his era. Whatever the faults of Roy's political construction of the twenties, lack of consistency was not one of them.

Not surprisingly, despite their often erroneous short-run judgements, Roy's political writing shows a sense of history of great sophistication, not only in analytical or conceptual ways, but also in its sensitivity towards political change, though exaggerated determinism misdirected his search for causes. Roy has a clear realization that he has arrived at a crucial point of transition in Indian nationalism. The resources of moderate nationalism were exhausted, and the situation contained several contradictory possibilities of further advance. Several proposals for advance were historically offered: extremism was one of them, communist radicalism was another, but the most dramatic and potent alternative was proposed by Gandhi. Roy was, therefore, quite right in believing that Gandhism historically was his greatest enemy. But he believed, quite wrongly, that a critique of Gandhism could be provided by a simple extension of European rationalism.

Roy's assessments of Gandhi show a peculiar evolution—from a more complex appreciation to one increasingly simplistic and critical. In one of his first articles in *Imprecor*, he appreciated several characteristics of Gandhian ideology which were later to fade from his view. Through the non-cooperation movement, 'the agrarian movement, the proletarian movement and the nationalist movement are moving concertedly towards one object, national independence.' Congress was the 'acknowledged head' of the nationalist movement, an instance of political generosity which is rare in his later writings. Gandhi had tried 'to break the class insularity of (the Congress) and to make it truly representative of the national aspirations of all classes of Indians.' Roy considered non-cooperation 'much more dangerous than an armed uprising, which-can always be met face to face and put down.'[19] Even the *charkha*, a particular butt of Roy's derision in later years, was seen to have a practical symbolic value. Non-cooperation was indeed 'the only path' against the colonial government of repression. Roy was to move decisively away from this assessment in a short time. Historically, at the time Roy had only seen Gandhi's ability to launch a mass movement on an unprecedented scale, not his equal ability to contain it, when its objectives threatened to overshoot his. The phase of retreat must have convinced Roy that his earlier assessment of Gandhi was wrong.

Roy sought to extend his argument about nationalism in a manifesto to the Ahmedabad session of the Congress. 'Ours is not a mere political game,' he warned Congressmen, 'it is a great social struggle.' Congress had graduated in political consciousness; it had ceased to be a debating society for lawyers but it should not convert itself into an organ of merchants and manufacturers. If it did, 'the inevitable consequence of this failure will be the divorce of the Congress from the nation.' More categorically, 'if the Congress makes the mistake of becoming the political apparatus of the propertied class, it must forfeit the title to the leadership of the nation.'[20] Non-cooperation had already failed; the *charkha* 'has been relegated to its well-deserved place in the museum'; 'the spirit of the people cannot be raised by such impotent tactics, nor is the government terrorised.'[21] The working masses, Roy predicted, would eventually conquer in their mainly socio-economic struggle against exploitation irrespective of nationality.

It is not easy to explain this radical shift in the assessment of Gandhi and non-cooperation. From the only method of struggle, and one superior to even armed struggle, it had changed into an impotent tactic and a failure. In 1922, in *India in Transition*, his line had hardened: 'Gandhism is the acutest and most desperate manifestation of the forces of reaction trying to hold their own against the objectively revolutionary tendencies contained in the liberal bourgeois nationalism. The impending wane of Gandhism signifies the collapse of the reactionary forces and their total elimination from the political movement.'[22] In July 1924, an *Imprecor* article misread the temporary advantage the swarajists had gained over Gandhi to conclude that 'the defeat of orthodox Gandhism is complete and final; the swarajists have won the day and Mr. Gandhi, as leader of the Indian national struggle, has sung his swansong.'[23] Roy's theoretical apparatus led him to this conclusion; and his conviction in its correctness

[19] Roy, 'Manifesto to the 36th Indian National Congress,' *DHCPI*, Vol. 1, p. 346.
[20] *Ibid.*, p. 349.
[21] Roy, *India in Transition*, *DHCPI*, Vol. 1, pp. 394–95.
[22] 'Mr. Gandhi's Swansong,' *DHCPI*, Vol. 2, p. 411.
[23] Santi Devi, 'Mr. Gandhi—An Analysis,' *DHCPI*, Vol. 1, pp. 437–44, 450–59.

was so firm that he spent the rest of his political life, as a communist, looking for this illusory red line across the bourgeoisie's political career— a catastrophe after which it will conclusively betray the Indian nation.

The substance of the theoretical criticisms of Gandhism was given in an article by Santi Devi.[24] The most important political defect of Gandhism was its lack of an economic programme, rooted in 'the obstinate and futile desire to unite all the Indian people, landlords and peasants, capitalists and proletariat, moderates and extremists, in a common struggle for an undefined goal.' It was full of vacillations and inconsistencies lacking a 'steady driving power towards a given goal'. Gandhi's metaphysical politics became 'an unconscious tool of reaction'. The collapse of Gandhism was not because of the terror of the colonial government; it was due to the rising tide of popular revolt. Roy's understanding had arrived at one of its crucial points of analogy, a point at which the logic of European history took over from the concrete discussion of specific political facts of India, a point from which he diverged into one of his characteristic descriptions of

---

[24] One often comes across the charge that Indian Marxists have neglected to analyze Gandhi. This is simply false. Indeed, it would have been very odd if they did, because as rational political actors they could see after the 1920s that he was their main political obstacle. Considering how they could move forward or expand their political base meant calculating how Gandhi's appeal could be reduced. Accordingly, Indian Marxists came back repeatedly to attempted explanations of the phenomenon of Gandhi. These began with Dange's *Gandhi vs Lenin*, and Santi Devi's articles in the *Imprecor*, and have continued even today. Of these, the outstanding analysis is, of course, E.M.S. Namboodiripad's *Mahatma and the Ism*. But very often Marxists, while intending serious explanation, actually evaded the issue. Conclusive statements about the class characterizations of Gandhi's movement were, unfortunately, conflated with an explanation of its success. The two questions, however, are really distinct. Statements of class characterization answer the question: since the benefits issuing out of a political movement (in which all classes participated) are unevenly distributed, which classes gained disproportionate amount from the successes of Gandhian nationalism? But this is clearly distinct from the other question, which runs: what were the reasons for his success? Why did people from all, but particularly crucial classes (which did not benefit particularly from its consequences), contribute so heavily to its success? I think this was related to a persistent weakness in Indian Marxist historiography—its tendency to use only a set of external criteria of objective consequences for making judgements about either single or complex acts. This tendency (when unmodified by Lukacs's Hegelianism or Gramsci's interpretative concerns) made them so hostile to Gandhi's premises that the other necessary hermeneutic business of 'understanding' his politics remained unaccomplished. It is not surprising that it is authors like Namboodiripad, who had a critical cultural sensitivity, came much closer to an adequate analysis of Gandhi. To others with a more positivistic cast of mind, Gandhi remained an irritating riddle—to be treated as an exception, which was often a disingenuous way of hiding an explanatory impasse. Recently, several papers on Gandhi have tried to emphasize the non-rationalist premises of his thought; but to these interpreters 'non-rationalist' is not a term of abuse. Cf. three very different analyses in Thomas Pantham, 'Thinking With Mahatma Gandhi,' *Political Theory*, Vol. 11, No. 2, May 1983; Ashis Nandy, *The Intimate Enemy* (Delhi: Oxford University Press, 1983); and Partha Chatterjee, 'Gandhi as a Critic of Civil Society,' in Ranajit Guha, ed., *Subaltern Studies*, Vol. 3 (Delhi: Oxford University Press, 1984).

what seemed to him a law of history, enacted first in Europe, and to be re-enacted all over again.

It was, perhaps, the stubborn rationalism of Roy's thinking which made him incapable of understanding the cultural power of Gandhism, its ability to fashion weapons of political struggle out of unorthodox material. This led him to misconstrue what, in retrospect, was the strength of Gandhi's politics as an impotent mysticism. Surely, Roy also exaggerated Gandhi's indigenism. Behind his indigenism was a mind which could calculate the repertoire of response open to his enemies with great precision, and posed him questions which he would be least likely to handle. And this could not be done without an intimate and shrewd acquaintance with British law, and administrative ethic. Gandhi's politics were formed out of an irreducible combination of cultural and political strategies—in which what you do and the way you do it are inextricably mixed—which resisted analysis into its elements in the way Santi Devi did in her *Imprecor* analysis. Resolved into its parts, it appeared laughable and simplistic; as a totality, it was, after all, the only strategy that worked against British imperialism. Roy did not see that a serious analysis of Gandhi was a precondition not merely for a critique of Congress politics, but also for understanding what sort of political action had chances of success, even if his kind of action was replaced. He never relented in his incomprehension of the primordial strengths of Gandhi's alphabet of political action. Indian culture is, in many ways, a culture of inflections. It has an enormous repertoire of gestures symbolizing actions, from insults to defiance, gestures of great subtlety and inflection. Subtlety of a culture is not a matter of literacy alone; and Gandhi's political style consciously tried to gather up these elements from other aspects of Indian life, in which their effectiveness had been tried for centuries, and apply them to the untried field of politics.

Seen in these terms, Gandhi's politics were not wholly mystical; rather, even its mysticism was often deliberate, its irrationalities carefully thought out. Surely, a part of Gandhi's critique of colonial culture was a deliberate counterposition of Westernized crudeness with an inherently subtle indigenous style, a cultural style which does not give an account or justification of what it is doing in the other's terms. Gandhi used the Indian cultural repertoire with great success. His style was a condensed introduction, and a breaking down of the barrier between the political interlocutor and his audience. He began to be understood before he began to speak, where others discoursed endlessly with little effect. Perhaps in a culture like India's, there is a reversal of the normal rationalist relation between acts and discourse, of the primacy of the intellectual. Of course, acts are a part of discourse in a sense, and discourse itself is an act. But it is still true that the way in which Gandhi used political discourse was fundamentally different from the normal rationalist way of looking at it.

A combination of literacy and subtlety made for a peculiar cultural mode in which few knew how to play with Gandhi's sureness of touch. He created a political culture which relied heavily on what can be called the *prediscursive*, a play on symbols and meanings which already said a great deal to an audience before the actual speaking began. Its use was double-edged as it put not only the British on the wrong foot but also his Indian political adversaries. The elaborate theatre of simplicity was not a matter of personal idiosyncracy; they constituted small but wholly credible everyday gestures of belonging, which formed, in their totality, a deeply political act.[25] It did through a personal symbolic style what a purely rationalist discourse could have imperfectly accomplished. It dispensed with the need of every urban politician to introduce himself to his rural constituency, arguments to establish his authenticity. Gandhi's metaphysics crossed this barrier implicitly.

Roy systematically underestimated the power of cultural elements in politics, which was merely the obverse of his belief in the effectiveness of economic revolutions. Despite the ceremonial importance given to the idea of contradiction, he did not see the contradictory character of Gandhian politics. Roy's theoretical consciousness belonged to the centre of the rationalist world—the external, the overt, the discursive in which all issues were loudly debated and intellectually settled. He mistrusted the other culture which placed more reliance on tone than on sense. He converted them into his own kind of language, in which they appeared pathetically incoherent, and then decisively destroyed these effigies.

After his break with the Comintern, Roy's political fortunes sank decisively. He appears increasingly as a tragic figure, standing forlorn and alienated from the mainstream of Indian nationalism. It was both a personal and political tragedy. When he broke with the Comintern, Roy was still a comparatively young man. But the boundaries of his political life would become steadily narrower. After a brief period of uneasy collaboration with left elements within the Congress, he assumed the role of an increasingly solitary critic of everyone else. His hostility towards Gandhi remained undiminished; and he would add to the list of those he disapproved of—Nehru, Bose and of course the CPI. In retrospect, his criticisms often do him credit. His general criticisms of Indian nationalism were largely justified; often his short-term judgements on political events were remarkably prescient. His intellectual skills were still powerful. He continued to polemicize with great incisiveness, with a single-mindedness of purpose and narrowness of mind which characterizes the successful polemicist. Yet, politically, he became increasingly peripheral to the Indian nationalist movement. He had begun his political career as an

[25] For a concise presentation of his later views, see his lecture, M.N. Roy, *The Philosophy and Practice of Radical Humanism* (lecture delivered in 1949), (New Delhi: Radical Humanist Association, 1970).

international politician. He ended it as a savant of a small and ineffective sect which could not quite make up its mind whether it was a political group or not. Such a decline must have been tragic for a man for whom, from the first, the whole world was the stage. In his later life, Roy moved decisively away from communism to what he called a 'new' or 'radical humanism,' but which could be seen as a resuscitation of the rationalist humanism of the European renaissance, and which perhaps explains his fascination for the renaissance motifs. He retained his optimism of the intellect, but abjured all forms of party politics, and advocated relying entirely on an uncompromising, if somewhat unpractical, individual critical consciousness, as an instrument for the creation of the good society.[26]

But why did this happen? Why did this man who debated with Lenin, who made the first Marxist analysis of Indian society, who produced some of the most important arguments against Gandhi, who was admired like younger radicals, lapse into political insignificance when he returned to India? Why did events pass him by? It is, of course, difficult to answer such questions, so difficult that some historians would rule them out of court. But part of the reason behind this strange ineffectivity of Roy's life perhaps lay in some deeper characteristics of his theoretical beliefs. If we analyze them, we may find a surprising continuity between his Marxist and anti-Marxist periods. On the political plane his position changed dramatically; but were there others on which it did not?

Some Methodological Aspects of Roy's Marxism

I have discussed Roy's political doctrines, or what he thought about important political issues; I will now turn to his conceptual apparatus which will show why he thought the way he did. Roy's Marxism had a straightforwardness which was, paradoxically, both its strength and weakness. Men often turn to theories which promise to resolve the apparent heterogeneity of historical facts into manageable explanations. Early Marxism in India, and indeed Roy's Marxism as a part of it, seemed to proffer this powerful inducement of intellectual resolution. Of course, in retrospect, this mode of thinking may appear simplifying; but it is important to remember that it saw simplifying as the major purpose of scientific analysis. Science simplifies; and thus makes data understandable. It reduces them into the comparative order of some recognized general rules. But Roy's kind of simplification also arose from the fact that he viewed Marxism in a strongly rationalist fashion.

In political analysis, Roy applied Marx's analyses straight, as I have argued in the foregoing, expecting the same classes to figure and to play largely the same roles in the contemporary history of India This is the

[26] Majid H. Siddiqui, 'Marxist and Popular Protest Historiography,' in Ravinder Kumar, ed., *Philosophical Theory and Social Reality* (Delhi: Allied Publishers, 1984), pp. 116 ff.

meaning of the claim that there are laws in history. Events belonging to a particular type tend to follow the same trajectory. Thus Marxists have the critical advantage over others of knowing the script in advance. This would, if true, give them an ineradicable advantage over all contenders. For the application of this model Roy needed some initial simplifying premises, which he asserted with characteristic assurance—for example, the decisive declaration, which forms the logical foundation of the whole argument in *India in Transition*, that Indian society should be seen as capitalist and not feudal. Given this premise, he could apply the entire model of late capitalism found in Marx's writings on Germany, or Lenin's on Russia, directly to India. It is characteristic that this, the most fundamental belief in the book, the one in most need of a demonstration, is simply asserted.

This could have been part of the reason for Roy's initial and undoubted success. He had a strongly positivistic notion of what science was, and his Marxism was always strongly coloured by this idea. In positivism science means primarily a reduction—a showing of a determining causality in the apparent complexity of historical events; of an underlying direction where there is no apparent drift. The undertaking of science is seen clearly in these terms. To create a science of history is to be able to make categorical judgements about what causes historical events, and about where history is going. A whole gamut of infelicities in Roy's Marxism (along with others of his times) could be traced to this positivistic residue. An analysis of Roy's errors may prove useful for understanding the nature of the claim that Marxism is a science.

When Marxists make this claim, it involves some crucial concepts of social theory: laws, their relation to historical occurrences, relations between regularity and precedents. These questions are quite clearly implicit in the basic conceptual and political judgements of Roy's Marxism. For instance, the questions 'Would the Indian bourgeoisie behave as the Chinese bourgeoisie has done?' and 'In what sense can we speak of there being laws in history?' are, though not identical, deeply interconnected. An answer to the first question would be governed by an answer to the second one. One can, therefore, suggest that Roy's judgements about political events were determined by his views about the nature of historical laws. It will be grotesquely unfair to imply that these methodological faults marked only Roy's understanding of Marxism, and not of others of his generation. On the contrary, these became the stock methods of political analysis of some Comintern writers in its 'third period'. By the mid-twenties, the experience of China was already determining Comintern policy towards all colonial nationalist movements. The behaviour of the Chinese bourgeoisie seemed to bear out Roy's doubts about their political trustworthiness; and political analysis, for some time at least, bestowed on this precedent the sanctity of an 'historical law'. But, if this was to be invested with the majesty of a law, a more general first premise was required. Among occurrences of a given type, first incidents would be given a precedental quality. It was not to be seen as one of the many forms in which a certain class of events could occur, out of a comparison of which a law was to be posited. The law was there in the privileged event. It was an event in which, because it was the first law of history, it announced itself and showed its tendencies in a pure form.

This relates to the question of the realist (or ontological) and constructivist views about historical laws, one of the most contentious questions in social theory. The realist view would assert that what a law 'describes' is an empirical state of affairs; a law merely declares the existence of an event which tends to happen with regularity. It is the same event, described in terms of its antecedents, which is typified by the law. It will be commonly granted that historical events cannot be regarded as repeating themselves in a strict sense of the term. The notion of regularity, when applied to history, must mean something weaker than what it means in the natural sciences. A constructivist view, by contrast, will claim that socio-historical laws are regularities of real occurrences. but in mental constructs, at a higher level of abstraction. A law, therefore, helps us understand historical occurrences, but they cannot be actually met in real events.

According to the first view, laws are simple summaries of events, or even events of a certain type; therefore, a knowledge of these gives us a strong power to predict. If I find a causal sequence—if a then b—I can confidently predict about this class of events, provided, of course, my identification of the class is right. Roy's conception of historical laws belonged to this type; and this gave him the confidence with which he predicted the imminent decline of Gandhian politics, or the eventual betrayal of nationalism by the bourgeoisie.

A Hidden Element of Heteronomy

But this is not a simple theoretical point. To a large degree, this determined Roy's politics in handling nationalism and the uses he put his analysis to. Perhaps there was an even deeper application of this precedental thinking in Roy's historical vision. Precedents reigned in history; thus the moves and rhythms of Indian history were bound to follow the European. As a basic premise, this was at work in both phases of Roy's intellectual development. It was this subtle Eurocentricity of his historical vision which nationalists instinctively, rather than consciously, opposed. This alienated nationalist opinion from him as surely in his second period as in the first, and this might go some way in explaining why, although he broke with communism, average nationalists did not find his thinking congenial. In his Marxist phase, Roy regarded India as a theatre for the kind of revolution that had occurred in Europe, a re-enactment of what he considered at that time the most important episode in European history. Later, his priorities and his way of looking at history changed—in what he considered most valuable in the European tradition. Now he thought renaissance humanism rather than proletarian revolution Europe's most abiding historical achievement. Accordingly, India was to be seen as a theatre of re-enactment of this altered ideal. But whether it was rationalist humanism or socialist transformation, it was to be an ideal of re-enactment all the same.

This might show us some subtle and surprising lineages of Roy's political thought. Early publicists of Indian nationalism sometimes showed this tendency in a pure form. They tried obstinately, singlemindedly, with a tragic idealism to live other peoples' histories, to re-enact the roles of great enlightenment figures of Europe. They thought crises and achievements would both have to be converted in European terms before they started becoming meaningful. One can see in their works the gradual emergence of a quintessentially heteronomous way of thinking. Naoroji shows something of its character, though he came at a time when it was already turning into a more authentic anti-imperialism. But the hesitations and inconsistencies in Naoroji's position are symptomatic. He works within a discourse in which moments of defiance and dependence are still indistinguishable. Criticism uses a language to which habits of colonial cultural deference still cling.

It will be unfair to view Roy as a simple inheritor of this tradition; but it would be wrong not to see some of the more complex continuities. His anti-colonialism is, of course, never in doubt; but in the context of colonial nationalism it is important to know which accents his discourse used for presenting itself to its audience. Roy saw leaders like Tilak and Gandhi as more alien to Marxists, and presumably himself, than the moderates. In his order of significance, the political is subordinate to the socio-economic; and though Gandhi is more radical than the moderates, in his social theory he seemed to Roy to be more reactionary. Roy's mental world was closest, as a type, to the rationalism of early enlightenment in Europe. He shared their strengths and prejudices. He had the same optimism of reason, also the same intolerance of complexity. Complexity was not a quality that inhered in historical things but was always a result of error. He was a mechanical materialist of the eighteenth century placed, incongruously, in the middle of Indian nationalism. Of course, in the surrounding atmosphere of chauvinism and celebration of irrationality, his adherence to this ideal was no mean achievement. He was, apart from Nehru, one of the few consistent rationalists the national movement produced. His work shows the aggression, historical optimism and the willingness to believe in hard-egded certainties characteristic of rationalists of an happier age. But there was, at the bottom of it all, also a gigantic inappropriateness: a mistaking of Asia for Europe, of Asian history as a theatre of re-enactments, not the original drama. This heteronomy was stamped on all of Roy's work, on all his enthusiasms and despair. He often called the leaders of Indian nationalism by evocative names of French revolutionary legend, and not surprisingly, found them equally often inadequate and inauthentic. With him this was perhaps more than a rhetorical flourish. He was excited when events in Indian history seemed to resemble some illuminated passages of the French revolution; when it diverged, this meant—not that it had a logic of its own—that it was straying into meaninglessness. It is surprising how European culture had occupied not only the conclusions of his mind, but also its essential meanings.

M.N. Roy was perhaps the most radical among the Indian nationalists of his generation, in political terms. But the story of his life shows that the political criterion is not the only criterion of judgement of nationalist thought. Other criteria sometimes have as much claim to application. The historian of ideas must, somehow, personally adjudicate between their often contrasting claims, and the picture he constructs is a result of the exact way in which he judges them. To interpret an author is to reduce his works into an order. Sometimes it can be the showing of an order which was there, but which eluded the author's consciousness. Roy's radicalism was surely powerful and sincere; but it carried, at a deeper level, the guilt of this heteronomy, the tendency to see events through an overriding primacy of European history. Events do not remain simple events, they become allegories to the sacred events of another, more significant history. It is startling to find within the stridency of this nationalist discourse such deference to the idea of the primacy of Europe: to regard European history as the rule, and the rest of the world's history as the massive exception. This does not mean, of course, that what we generally know about M.N. Roy's thinking should be given up; rather, this means that what we know should be read through this element too—to construct a picture that is surely more complex but perhaps also more realistic. This does not make Roy's thought less radical, but his radicalism more complex. In any case, this existence of heteronomy, within aspirations for independence, is not peculiar to Roy. It was true of a strand of nationalism. In some ways perhaps it was the common and general tragedy of colonial history. Roy simply symbolized the 'unhappy consciousness' of colonialism—'the struggle against an enemy, to vanquish whom is really to suffer defeat'.[27] Colonial thought is not able to escape this contradiction: its greatest audacities are often marked secretly by a peculiar insidious dependence. Even to break with the other, it needs the other.

[27] Hegel, *The Phenomenology of Spirit* (trans. A.V. Miller), (Oxford: Oxford University Press, 1977), p. 127.

14

MANORANJAN MOHANTY

Ideology and Strategy of the Communist Movement in India

Analytical Issues

The ideological evolution of the Indian communist movement has been a complex process. Debates on the strategy, socio-political developments in the country and the impact of the international situation have shaped the course of the movement. Polemical party writings emphasize the correctness or incorrectness of a strategy. Some historians place it mainly in the immediate context of the domestic or national environment. Others see the international linkage more prominently. However, it has been increasingly realized that the course of the communist movement can be better understood as an interacting process involving ideological, environmental and international factors.[1]

There are three key questions which need to be asked in a study of Indian communism. First, how did the Indian communists perceive the anti-colonial struggle and their role in it? Second, how did they analyse Indian society and to what extent did they grasp the specific features of the Indian situation? Third, what has been their revolutionary strategy to capture state power and achieve socialist transformation in India? Though the first two questions pertain to ideology and the third to strategy, they are related to each other and have ideological as well as strategic dimensions.

In the context of studying political movements, we can define ideology as a statement of ends, means and an outlook.[2] We have to find out the long-term and the short-term goals of the Indian communists, their approach to methods of achieving them and their world view or mode of

Acknowledgements: The author is grateful to Sudipta Kaviraj for his comments on an earlier draft of this paper.

[1] Manoranjan Mohanty, *Revolutionary Violence: A Study of the Maoist Movement in India* (New Delhi: Sterling, 1977); Mohan Ram, *Indian Communism: Split within a Split* (New Delhi: Vikas, 1969); and Bhabani Sengupta, *Communism in Indian Politics* (New Delhi: Young Asia, 1978) reflect this trend. So does Sudipta Kaviraj, *The Split in the Communist Movement in India* (unpublished Ph.D. dissertation, Jawaharlal Nehru University, 1979). Among the scholars who have overemphasized the international factor are G.D. Overstreet and Marshall Windmiller, *Communism in India* (Bombay: Perennial Press, 1960); and John Kautsky, *Moscow and the Communist Party of India* (New York: John Wiley, 1956). Studies which partly follow the contextualist approach include Bipan Chandra, ed., *The Indian Left: Critical Appraisals* (New Delhi: Vikas, 1983).

[2] The notions of ideology and strategy used in this essay are elaborated in Mohanty, *op. cit.*, Ch. 1.

understanding society and history. Ideology is by nature a dynamic and developmental concept rooted in historical practice. Therefore, we have to explain the course of ideological change and examine whether there is a basic continuity of the core postulates of the ideology or a deviation and consequently the birth of a new ideology. It is extremely important to distinguish between creative development of ideology and its erosion. Every observer has to choose certain standards for himself/herself to judge the nature of ideological change. One's interpretation of classical Marxism would determine what one considers to be the core postulates. Similarly, one's understanding of Bolshevik and Chinese revolutions and later experiences would influence one's judgement on ideological and strategic questions. In the case of the Indian communist movement, the differences of opinion are very wide. The rightward deviation is dubbed as revisionism and the leftward deviation as dogmatism. In this essay we shall try to understand each viewpoint on its own terms.

Strategy is a plan formulation to realize definite objectives in a specific time period in a particular country or region. Strategy is related to both ideological goals and environmental pressures. If it is merely deduced from ideology it is likely to be dogmatic; if it is merely a response to the environment it is likely to be opportunist and temporarily successful. In order to meet the challenges of the environment and move towards the cherished goals, a strategy has to be a dialectical synthesis on both ideological and environmental factors. Keeping this notion in view, we shall examine the nature of the revolutionary strategy of the Indian communists.

Two other preliminary points should be made: there are various shades of Marxism and not all Marxists have been in the communist party or parties in India. However, our focus in this essay will be on the organized communist movement. Second, the organizational history of the communist movement in India is intimately tied with its ideological history though, in this essay, we are mainly concerned with the latter. Prior to the first major split in the CPI in 1964, the ideological debates took place within the party and the leadership of a particular time reflected the winning line. Serious dissenters sometimes left the party. The birth of the CPI(M) in 1964 and the post-1967 emergence of the CPI(ML) groups presented a different picture. New ideological and strategic positions were now put into practice simultaneously. Earlier, the defeated line was more or less out of action. This also caused a change in the international linkage. While prior to 1964 a relationship of solidarity with the CPSU was considered significant by the CPI, the new communist parties had the option to judge the state of the international movement from time to time and decide their position accordingly. Thus, while the CPI continued to have fraternal relations with the CPSU, the CPI(M) was close to the CPC until the latter chose to side with the Marxist-Leninist movement in India till the early 1970s. In post-Mao China, however, things changed and the CPC and CPI(M) re-established their party-to-party relationship in 1983. By then most of the CPI(ML) groups had come out denouncing the new policies in China under Deng Xiaoping's leadership as revisionist.

Anti-colonial Struggle

The ideology of the Indian communist movement has been deeply influenced by its experience during the struggle against British colonialism. The communists' analysis of the nature of British rule in India, their attitude towards the Indian National Congress and its leaders, their method of linking up the peasants and workers' struggle with the freedom struggle and, above all, the communists' mode of reconciling nationalism with internationalism have left an indelible mark on the course of communist politics in India.

In discussing these issues, we have to keep in mind the fact that the communist movement was born in India under the inspiration of the Bolshevik Revolution. Therefore, the CPI was closely linked with the Third Communist International (Comintern), which was set up on the initiative of the CPSU in March 1919 with headquarters in Moscow. In fact, some Indian Marxists on their way to Moscow proclaimed the formation of the CPI at Tashkent in 1921. The First Congress of the CPI was held in 1943 during the people's war phase of World War II. The relationship between the CPSU and the CPI has been a critical factor in the history of the communist movement. On the one hand, it made the anti-colonial struggle in India a part of the wider Asian-African struggle against European colonialism and facilitated coordination among the revolutionary movements throughout the world. On the other hand, it was sometimes so greatly concerned with defending the interest of the first socialist state (namely, the Soviet Union) that it caused misunderstanding in India as to the validity of such policies in the interest of Indian nationalism. Besides, this relationship was often used as a substitute for ideological creativity. Instead of seriously analyzing the Indian conditions and their own practice, the Indian communists often accepted the formulations of the Comintern either directly or through the channel of the Communist Party of Great Britain (CPGB). This is where the Communist Party of China (CPC) learnt its lessons much earlier than the CPI did. After following the Comintern strategy till 1927, the CPC started groping for an appropriate strategy on its own while maintaining its link with the Comintern at the same time; after a process of trial and error, it evolved its line of people's democratic revolution. The CPI, however, remained an adherent to the CPSU-sponsored line for a long time. Only in the 1960s did this situation change.[3]

---

[3] Among the useful studies of the international relations of the Indian communist movement are Narahari Kaviraj, *October Revolution and National Liberation Movement* (Calcutta: K.P. Bagchi, 1978); and Sada Nand Talwar, *Under the Banyan Tree: The Communist Movement in India* (New Delhi: Allied, 1985).

The CPI's analysis of British rule in India was based upon Lenin's theory of imperialism as the highest stage of capitalism and Marx's notes and articles on India published in the *New York Daily Tribune* (1853). M.N. Roy's *India in Transition*, which was published in 1922, gave a general picture of how imperialism had plundered India's raw materials and, in response, how a general awakening had begun in India. By far the most comprehensive analysis of modern Indian society was attempted by Rajni Palme Dutt, the CPGB leader, in *India Today*, first published in 1940. Dutt followed Marx's clue to show how the stagnant Indian society underwent a process of turbulence in the course of the imperialist rule. These books, together with the documents of the CPI, presented the overall understanding of British colonial rule in India which formed the basis of the communists' anti-colonial strategy.

In retrospect, communist analysis has been found wanting in two respects, even though their basic understanding of the nature of colonialism was vindicated. It was correct to stress that the Indian economy had been integrated with the British colonial economy to exploit the raw materials of India for processing in the metropolitan country and to market them in the colonies. How industrial capitalism was intertwined with finance capitalism was also clearly demonstrated in the case of British rule in India. But where the communists' understanding was inadequate was in fully appreciating the dimensions of the colonial state apparatus, on the one hand, and the social structure of modern India, on the other. In these respects the Congress leadership, particularly Gandhi and Nehru, proved to be more astute analysts who succeeded in marginalizing the communist party by a careful strategy and paved the way for capitalist development.

The British colonial state was essentially a police state to guard colonial trade. But it gradually developed a two-pronged strategy of legitimation. In the first place, it created an educated elite to participate in the bureaucratic management of the state. This elite, drawn from the local landlords and upper castes, was now exposed to liberal ideas emanating from Europe. Second, the British did not wish to directly disturb the social structure of India. They had a complex strategy to maintain the structures of caste, religion and tribe while, at the same time, making occasional concessions to the pleas of the social reformers. This policy was used to build bridges between the colonial regime and the traditional elites of India. The communists were correct to point out that India's feudal society presented a vulnerable situation for imperialist exploitation. They were also right with Marx in noticing the stirring effects of colonial intervention in traditional Indian society. But the fact that the British had assiduously built up a system of multi-dimensional control was not fully reflected in Indian Marxist writings. This system not only consisted of the army, police and bureaucracy but also a legal system ostensibly symbolizing liberal values. The princes, tribal chiefs and landlords got legal recognition under the British while all of them were exposed to the new liberal ideas and institutions. All challenges to British supremacy were severely repressed while gradual concessions were made to associate Indian elites with the government. The cultural policy of the colonial state consciously projected the superiority of Western culture, but, at the same time, allowing Indian cultural movements to grow. The British turned India into 'Hindustan' emphasizing the culture of the religious majority of India, but simultaneously encouraged a process of alienation of the various communities from each other.[4]

British colonial rule in India was thus a complex system of multi-dimensional control. In fact, colonialism everywhere devised its own strategy of coercion and manipulation. The Indian communists did not show a sophisticated understanding of this complex process of colonial domination. All this can be said only with hindsight, on the basis of recent researches on the anti-colonial struggle in India.[5]

When communist groups appeared on the Indian political scene soon after the Bolshevik Revolution, the freedom struggle was already under the leadership of the Indian National Congress. Hence, one of the first decisions they had to take was to define their role vis-a-vis the Congress. This situation was not unique to India; in China too the communists had to relate themselves to the Kuomintang, the nationalist party then led by Sun Yat-sen. So this problem was taken up at the Second Congress of the Comintern in 1920. There the famous debate between Lenin and M.N. Roy took place on the question of the communists' participating in the bourgeois-led national struggle. Lenin pointed out that since the working class movements were weak in these countries and the main task in the agrarian societies was to organize the peasant movement, the communist parties should join the united front to carry on the national struggle under the leadership of the bourgeoisie. Roy, on the other hand, felt that the workers' movement was on the rise and if the communists accepted the leadership of the bourgeoisie the gains of the working class struggle would be lost. Especially in countries like India where the bourgeoisie had acquired a degree of maturity and was leading mass movements, it could obstruct the growth of the workers' movement. Lenin's line was accepted with a minor amendment that in specific situations the communist parties could try their independent strategy.[6]

---

[4] The 'divide and rule' policy of the British imperialist government has been emphasized by most scholars. But we have also to understand this two-pronged policy of the colonial state.

[5] Bipan Chandra, ed., *op. cit.*, throws some light on this complexity. But this book exaggerates the role of the non-coercive component in the strategy of the colonial state

[6] Sobhanlal Dattagupta, *Comintern, India and the Colonial Question* (Calcutta: K.P. Bagchi, 1980); P. Ulyanovsky, ed., *The Comintern and the East* (Moscow: Progress, 1979). See also S. Kaviraj, *op. cit.*, Ch. 2.

The Indian communists' attitude towards the Congress was determined partly by their assessment of the Congress leadership of the freedom struggle from time to time and partly by the line formulated by the Comintern. After 1919 the communists welcomed the trend of mass politics under Gandhi's leadership. As directed by the Second Congress of the Comintern, the communists were expected to join the bourgeois-led national struggle. But the sudden withdrawal of the non-cooperation movement by Gandhi after it turned violent at Chauri Chaura disappointed the communists. M.N. Roy (who had reluctantly accepted the Second Congress line) now cited this as evidence of the bourgeoisie's betrayal of the national revolution. In the meantime, the repression of the communists was heightened by the British government. The Kanpur Conspiracy Case was instituted in 1923. The organizers of the trade union movement in Bombay and Calcutta became targets of the British administration. The Congress leadership lay low, groping for new ideas. At this time, the massive suppression of communists in China in 1927 raised fresh questions about the united front line. In these circumstances, the Sixth Congress of the Comintern met in 1928 and revised its earlier approach. It now favoured the view that the national revolution should be led by the proletariat. The communists should independently organize workers and peasants for anti-colonial revolution rather than join the united front led by the bourgeoisie.

The new line of the CPI immediately invited a major crackdown on them by the British government in the form of the institution of the Meerut Conspiracy Case in 1929. Interestingly enough, the communists functioning within the Congress had some positive effects particularly on ideological debates. Jawaharlal Nehru wrote a glorious account of the Soviet Union after his visit there in 1928. Congress had to debate its attitude towards the wave of strikes in the late 1920s in various parts of India. Slowly a socialist group emerged in the Congress which crystallized into the Congress Socialist Party (CSP) in 1934. The communists remained a part of it until 1940. Nehru chose to remain out of the CSP, though in his 1935 booklet *Whither India*, he presented a socialist viewpoint on India's freedom struggle. Organizationally, Nehru stayed out of the CSP so that he could be with Gandhi and the majority in the Congress, but ideologically he often spoke the radical language of socialism.

With the outbreak of peasant struggles in different parts of the country and the growth of the trade union movement, the communists reviewed their overall strategy again. The experience of the CSP in its initial phase was encouraging. In 1935 the Comintern met in its Seventh Congress to chalk out a strategy to meet the twin challenges of imperialism as well as fascism. Dimitrov, in his report, spelt out the new line of the anti-imperialist national front. Within this framework, Bradley and R.P. Dutt (of the CPGB) in an article in the Comintern journal *Imprecor* (February 1936) worked out the new line for the CPI asking it to work with the Congress to strengthen it as an anti-imperialist force. The outbreak of World War II brought this collaboration to a virtual halt. When the communists described the war as an imperialist war, the Congress and the socialists accused them of being spokesmen for the CPSU.

The experience of 1942, when the socialists led the underground struggle and the communists opposed the 'Quit India' campaign, kept them divided for years to come. That also created a breach between the CPI and the Congress, which lasted till the early 1950s when the CPI began to evolve its 'unity and struggle' approach towards the Congress which was then in power in independent India. Throughout its existence, the CPI had been banned by the colonial government except during the 1942–45 period when the former supported the war efforts of the latter. The ban was reimposed by the Congress government after the CPI's Second Congress but was lifted in 1951 to enable it to take part in the forthcoming parliamentary elections.

The communists regarded the Congress as the organization of the Indian capitalists and landlords which Gandhi had transformed from an elite assembly into a mass movement.[7] When the Congress was fast acquiring the support of large sections of the common people, especially the peasantry, the communists joined it. They thought that they could ideologically influence the Congress by emphasizing the demand for complete independence and propagating the rights of the workers and peasants. To some extent they succeeded in doing this, as was reflected in the decisions of the Lahore and Karachi Congress sessions. Congress forums were also used by capitalist and landlord interests to counter some of the radical ideas from time to time.

Gandhi was the grand reconciler of interests within the Congress. The communists saw in Gandhi not only a master strategist of a mass movement but also a compromiser who was determined to stem the rising militancy of the anti-colonial struggle. His withdrawal of the non-cooperation movement after the Chauri Chaura incident, his ambiguous stand on peasant struggles in different parts of the country, his views on the revolutionary terrorist struggles of the Hindustan Socialist Republican Association of Bhagat Singh were some indications of his approach. Moreover, the communists were appalled by Gandhi's willing acceptance of the support extended by the capitalists and landlords in carrying out the freedom struggle.[8]

[7] The communists' statements in the Meerut trials indicated their approach to the Congress. *Communists Challenge Imperialism from the Dock* (Calcutta: National Book Agency, 1967).

[8] The critical Marxist studies include E.M.S. Namboodiripad, *The Mahatma and the Ism* (New Delhi: PPH, 1958) and Hiren Mukerjee, *Gandhiji: A Study* (New Delhi: PPH, 1960). Beginning in 1969, the Gandhi centenary year, Marxist assessment of Gandhi began to

Gandhi, the compromiser who was not willing to use violence in the fight against British imperialism, was the target of communist criticism. Gandhi's use of religious symbols in his methods of struggle also irked the communists. Though they recognized his hold over the Indian masses, they refused to accept his leadership right up to the dawn of independence. In the Congress, they often preferred to side with Nehru who appeared more modern, used the vocabulary of socialism, praised the Soviet Union and pleaded for progressive policies within the Congress. The communists had a positive view of Subhas Chandra Bose as well, since he emerged as a relatively radical alternative to Gandhi. But when he left India to organize the INA with the help of the Axis powers, the communists severely criticized him.

The communist critique of Gandhi during the latter's lifetime was somewhat one-dimensional. Gandhi's links with the Indian bourgeoisie and the traditional elites of India were exposed fairly well by the communists. But they never fully understood the basis of his unquestioned popularity among the Indian masses. Gandhi appealed to the Indian masses successfully because he accurately measured their level of democratic consciousness. He thought that the peasantry could be as much mobilized for the anti-colonial struggle as the urban workers and middle classes. So he consciously used traditional idioms and symbols in communicating with the common people. What the communists regarded as feudal images, Gandhi used effectively to carry people with him. At the same time, he made it clear to the landlords and capitalists that unless they stood by him they would invite the wrath of the common people. Thus the united front of otherwise antagonistic classes and sections of people actually materialized under his leadership which the communists failed to appreciate.

With mass support behind him, Gandhi dealt with British colonialism by unleashing a series of diverse pressures. Initially the British were reluctant to take Gandhi seriously. But when he emerged as the most powerful figure in the freedom struggle, they began to respond to his pressures. The final withdrawal of the British from India was the outcome of a number of developments, namely, the experience of World War II which had weakened the British, the surging nationalism in Asia and the multi-stranded, anti-imperialist struggle in India and so on. In this, besides the contribution of the Congress-led freedom struggle, the contribution of the revolutionary terrorists, the INA of Subhas Bose, the

---

change. See M.B. Rao, ed., *The Mahatma—A Marxist Symposium* (New Delhi: PPH, 1969). Gandhi was considered a positive populist by the Soviet scholar, V. Khoros, in his *Populism: Its Past, Present and Future* (Moscow: Progress, 1984). However, CPI(M-L) writings still treat Gandhi as the one who contained the militancy of the Indian revolution. See, for example, D.V. Rao, *People's Democratic Revolution in India* (Hyderabad: Proletarian Line Publications, 1982).

peasant struggles led by the CPI and the scattered incidents of rebellion by units of the British armed forces were also significant. But the Congress emerged as the most effective carrier of Indian nationalism. It was the best bet of the Indian ruling classes as well and the British found in it an acceptable organization to transfer power to. The communists were not convinced that Gandhi and the Congress had indeed become symbols of Indian nationalism. They only saw the social base of the Congress among the upper classes of India and attacked their compromising attitude towards British colonialism. This one-dimensional understanding inhibited the communists from looking for alternative nationalist and democratic strategies for the Indian revolution which could be equally authentic and mass-based. It was, perhaps, possible for the communists to pay more attention to peasant movements as well as to the democratic movements in the princely states and integrate them with the freedom movement.

The strategic line of the CPI had been defined according to the Comintern formulation as one of national liberation movement. The main area of struggle was the urban industrial sphere where the communists had built up trade unions. The model of the Bolshevik Revolution as a working class struggle inspired this line of development in India. Among the textile workers of Western India, the jute workers of Bengal and the railway workers, the CPI had secured a good deal of support. From this trade union base the communists tried to influence Congress politics both from inside and from outside. In addition, the communist influence had begun to grow among students in some cities as well. But not until the 1940s did the communists pay serious attention to peasant struggle. The Telengana people's armed struggle and the Bengal tenants' movement for a two-thirds share of the harvest, known as the Tebhaga movement, added new dimensions to the ideology and strategy of the Indian communists.

In the princely state of Hyderabad, a people's movement against the despotic rule of the Nizam was already going on. This merged with the campaign of the Telugu-speaking people for a separate province for their nationality. The Andhra Mahasabha, a broad democratic front, spearheaded this movement. Communists of the area played a key role within the Mahasabha mobilizing the peasants against the Nizam and the local landlords (known as Deshmukhs). In Nalgonda, Warangal and Khammam districts, peasants campaigned for debt relief, abolition of bonded labour, redistribution of land, and so on. The movement, which had started in 1945, gathered momentum in 1946 and invited severe repression by the Nizam's forces and the landlords' hirelings. The armed peasant squads succeeded in repelling these attacks and set up peasant committees to be in control of several villages and carry out reforms in them. By 1948 they had liberated nearly 16,000 square miles covering about three million people in 3,000 villages.[9] The Indian army carried out its Hyderabad operation to integrate the kingdom with the Indian union in September 1948 and, thereafter, had a massive mopping up campaign to crush the armed guerrillas of Telengana. The latter's resistance continued till the middle of 1951 when the CPI officially withdrew the movement.

The Telengana people's struggle was a local anti-feudal movement which grew into a typical struggle of the people's democratic revolution. The Indian communists were aware of Mao's theory of new democratic revolution. But it would not be correct to describe the Telengana movement as a conscious application of the Chinese revolutionary path by the CPI. It was, on the other hand, an indigenous peasant struggle led by local communists who later on theorized this experience as a people's democratic revolution. Indeed, it had some of the essential characteristics of such a revolution, namely, the united front of the poor, middle and rich peasants against the landlords and the use of agrarian armed revolution as the main form of the anti-colonial revolution.

The Tebhaga movement in Bengal did not lead to the establishment of new political power in the villages. However, it was a militant anti-feudal struggle as well. After the 1943 Bengal famine, the rural poor realized that the zamindars and jotedars were not their good protectors after all. The Bengal Pradesh Krishak Sabha, which had been working for tenancy reforms and better rights for the sharecroppers since 1936, started organizing them in several districts of Bengal. The Krishak Sabha demanded abolition of several special levies on the tenants by the land-lords and launched a series of campaigns for this purpose. The movement for a two-thirds share of the harvest gained momentum in nine districts in 1946. In some places the poor peasants occupied the landlords' land, burnt land deeds and raided grain stores. Peasant women played a significant role in this, sometimes as the frontline of the campaigners. Issues of social oppression by the jotedars on women and the oppressed castes were highlighted besides the demand for a two-thirds share in the harvest. The campaign continued to grow until it was met with severe

[9] For a detailed account of the Telengana struggle, see P. Sundarayya, *Telengana People's Struggle and Its Lessons* (Calcutta: CPI(M) Publication, 1972). He gives a generally authentic account while, at the same time, using the Telengana experience to condemn individual terrorism of the M-L groups. Another view justifying the CPI's withdrawal of the movement is of Ravinarayan Reddy, *Heroic Telengana* (New Delhi: CPI, 1973). See also C. Rajeswara Rao, *The Heroic Telengana Struggle* (New Delhi: CPI, 1972), For its comparison with the ideology and strategy of the democratic revolution see Mohanty *op. cit.*, n. 1, pp. 63–67. Among the academic studies on Telengana are Berry Pavier, *Telengana Movement 1944–1951* (New Delhi: Vikas, 1981) and D.N. Dhanagare, *Peasant Movements in India, 1920–1950* (New Delhi: Oxford, 1983).

police measures and the jotedars' offensive aided by the political campaign of the local Congress organization.[10]

The experience of agrarian armed struggle added a qualitatively new dimension to the Indian communist movement which was, until then, based on the trade union movement of the industrial workers. During the 1940s, the communists took the initiative in launching a progressive cultural movement as well. The Indian People's Theatre Association popularized new plays on anti-feudal and anti-colonial themes by using experimental folk forms.[11] Thus the scope and dimensions of revolutionary struggle vastly expanded during this decade.

Yet the communist strategy of national liberation movement did not make enough advance as an autonomous movement. Its course was determined by its attitude towards the Congress-led movement. This was mainly because of the inability of the communists to challenge the framework of the Congress which had subordinated social revolution to nationalism. Gandhi, the architect of this framework, sought to unite all classes to achieve freedom. His constructive programme, the programmes for Harijan welfare and communal harmony, were important but never seen as an overarching strategy of social revolution outflanking the freedom struggle. The communists were more or less drawn into this dichotomous framework of subordinating the peasant question to the question of nationalism. Hence the autonomous development of the workers' movement was thwarted for a long time. When militant peasant struggles did break out they were not integrated with the process of anti-colonial struggle. This is why the communist handling of nationalism also suffered from a handicap. Had they built up an organic link between agrarian revolution and the national revolution, they could have staked their claim to champion the cause of nationalism on behalf of the Indian masses. After they saw clear signs of the Congress being identified with the capitalists and landlords, they could have presented an alternative in the form of people's nationalism. Thus, the CPI's inability to build a dialectical, mutually reinforcing link between nationalism and agrarian revolution adversely affected their performance on both fronts. Their claim to the leadership of Indian nationalism was effectively contained by the Congress while their advance on the path of agrarian revolution remained slow. The post-independence experience illustrates the latter point. As to the former, the CPI's stand on the 1942 Quit India movement is a good example.

The CPI took the stand that the Indian freedom struggle was going to be seriously affected by the outcome of World War II. Anti-fascist fronts had emerged throughout the world in response to the call given by the

---

[10] Sunil Sen, *Agrarian Struggle in Bengal 1945–1947* (New Delhi: PPH, 1972).

[11] After a gap of thirty years or so, the people's theatre movement was revived in various parts of India in the 1970s.

Comintern Congress of 1935. When the war started, the communists characterized it as an inter-imperialist war. From 1939 to 1941, the Congress as well as the communists in India were not enthusiastic about supporting the British war efforts. After Germany invaded the Soviet Union in July 1941, the CPI reassessed the situation which had further deteriorated with the Japanese advance towards the Indian borders. In this situation, the CPI took the line that the anti-fascist war efforts of the British government should be supported to contain the Japanese advance into India.

The CPI was anxious to intervene in a situation where the first socialist state was in danger. Hence it called the present stage of the war a people's war. They insisted that this line would be eventually helpful to the cause of freedom in India. From this perspective, they opposed the AICC Quit India resolution of August 1942 while supporting its Preamble which set out the objective of the struggle. Thereafter, they campaigned for united anti-fascist resistance while the Congress organized popular protest against the British. The underground struggle, particularly of the Congress socialists, generated enormous mass support throughout the country. The subdued mass movement was suddenly unleashed into an upsurge.

The Congress leadership at this time accused the communists of having betrayed the cause of Indian nationalism. From that time on, the anti-communists, time and again, refer to the 1942 experience as the anti-national act of the CPI to serve the cause of a foreign country (namely, the Soviet Union). Some even branded the CPI as having worked as a collaborator with British imperialism in its war efforts between 1942–45. The British took full advantage of the situation without ever entertaining any doubt that the communists were their greatest enemy in India.[12]

Here one finds two different strategies applied by two political parties in a specific situation. The communists thought that the anti-colonial revolution would be adversely affected if they did not fight against fascism. The Congress thought that this was the opportune moment to pressurize the British to concede independence. In fact, the communist formulation of the line was theoretically both anti-fascist and anti-imperialist. It also demanded that the British allow the formation of a national government in India. The Congress maintained that an independent India could fight more effectively against the axis powers. The 'do or die' call of the Quit India movement caught the imagination of the

---

[12] One of the early documents which clarified the CPI stand on the issue was P.C. Joshi, *Congress and the Communists* (Bombay: PPH, 1944). In March-April 1984, Arun Shourie revived the debate with a series of four articles entitled 'The Great Betrayal' in the *Illustrated Weekly of India*. Responses to them came from both the CPI and the CPI(M). See Gautam Chattopadhyay, *Arun Shourie's Slanders Rebutted: History has Vindicated the Communists* (New Delhi: CPI, 1984) and M. Basavapunnaiah, *Quit India Call and the Role of Communists* (New Delhi: National Book Centre, 1984).

people and aroused Indian nationalism to an unprecedented extent. The communists offered very little to match it. If they had worked out the organic link between the worker-peasant movement and the anti-colonial struggle they would have implemented their own line differently.[13] They had the option of organizing a people's defence movement which could be anti-fascist as well as anti-imperialist. Later developments in independent India have brought increasing mass support for the communists in some regions of India and the charge of anti-patriotism has lost its appeal, except as a periodic propaganda weapon for the opponents; however, the discordance between nationalism and agrarian revolution (which characterized the CPI's role during the freedom struggle) had enormous consequences for the future.

Communists and Democratic Revolution

After the transfer of power in August 1947, the formulation of strategy was the subject of intense inner-party debate within the CPI. Swift changes in the party line took place during the next decade. The central issues of the debate were the nature of Indian independence, the character of the Nehru government, and the strategy of the Indian revolution. There were four high points of strategic shift by the CPI. At the Second Congress at Calcutta in 1948, the election of B.T. Ranadive as the General Secretary demonstrated the victory of the Titoist line of one-stage revolution. In 1950 the Telengana line of people's democratic revolution got official recognition when C. Rajeswara Rao became General Secretary. The following year when the crucial documents, namely, *Programme, Statement of Policy* and *Tactical Line*, were finalized by the CPI, Rao was replaced by Ajoy Ghosh. This line was formally proclaimed at the CPI's Third Congress at Madurai in 1953. The next major shift took place at the Fourth Congress at Palghat in 1956 when the 'unity and struggle' perspective took shape (which was fully developed at the Party Congress at Amritsar in 1959). From 1951 till 1959 Ajoy Ghosh had worked out a centrist compromise formulation jointly with E.M.S. Namboodiripad to reconcile the two opposite lines within the party—one advanced by P.C. Joshi and S.A. Dange and another by M. Basavapunniah and P. Sundarayya. After 1959 the intensifying tensions in Indo-Chinese relations and the growing rift between China and the Soviet Union accentuated the differences within the CPI leading to the first major split in 1964 which gave birth to the CPI(M).

At the dawn of independence the CPI General Secretary, P.C. Joshi, strongly felt that the transfer of power was real and the Nehru government

[13] Elements of an alternative formulation within the CPI were suggested by K. Damodaran's counter-thesis. See his 'Memoirs of an Indian Communist,' *New Left Review*, No. 93 (September-October 1975).

showed signs of representing an anti-imperialist force. Therefore, he argued, the CPI should reassess its understanding of the Congress. This did not find enough supporters in the party. At this time, two alternative lines were propounded within the party. One was the view that mass upsurge in India had gained momentum and the CPI could combine the democratic and socialist stages of revolution into one nation-wide armed uprising of workers and strive to seize power. Upholding this line, Ranadive cited the successful experience of post-war Yugoslavia. The second alternative was put forward by the Andhra leaders who theorized on the Telengana experience in terms of Mao Zedong's formulation on people's democratic revolution. They maintained that India had to first experience the people's democratic stage of agrarian revolution before moving into the socialist stage. During the former stage, a four-class united front of workers, peasants, petty bourgeoisie and national bourgeoisie should be built up on the basis of worker-peasant alliance to fight imperialism and feudalism. According to these 'Andhra Theses,' there had to be a people's war against the Indian state.[14]

At the Calcutta Congress in 1948, the Ranadive group was able to muster majority support. But both the national and international situation changed fast. The Nehru government ordered army action in Hyderabad and took strong measures to suppress the Telengana rebellion. The Tebhaga movement was also crushed with an iron hand. In October 1949, the CPC victoriously proclaimed the birth of the People's Republic of China. This turned the party debates in favour of the Andhra line. The Chinese path was now proclaimed internationally, not only by the Chinese leadership itself but also by the Soviet leadership as the appropriate path of revolution by the colonial peoples. In this situation the Andhra leader, C. Rajeswara Rao, took over the party leadership in 1950.

However, the CPI's adherence to the China path did not last long. It was subjected to a severe inner-party attack by the P.C. Joshi group which accused it of left deviation. They said that it dogmatically applied the Chinese model to India ignoring the crucial differences in the historical conditions of the two countries. The Joshi group maintained that the non-alignment policy of the Nehru government had an element of anti-imperialism and that the refusal of the same government to toe the U.S. line in the Korean War should be judged favourably. Promulgation of the Indian Constitution and the government's proclamations on zamindari abolition and planned economy were also to be considered as positive factors.

To resolve this serious inner-party controversy, a CPI delegation

[14] The various lines debated during this period are contained in M.B. Rao, ed., *Documents of the History of the CPI*, Vol. 7 (1948–50) (New Delhi: PPH, 1976). See also V.B. Karnik, ed., *Indian Communist Party Documents 1936–1956* (Bombay: Democratic Research Centre, 1957).

consisting of Rajeswara Rao, Basavapunniah, Ajoy Ghosh and S.A. Dange went to Moscow at the end of 1950. They had a party-to-party discussion with the CPSU delegation (consisting of Stalin, Molotov, Malenkov and Suslov). The three documents of 1951 were the products of this effort. To regard them merely as a Moscow-dictated line would be superficial because they were actually a compromise among the contending Indian lines.

The 1951 documents affirmed the concepts of the two-stage revolution, four-class united front and partisan warfare as in the case of the Chinese revolution. It regarded India as a dependent and semi-colonial country and the Nehru government as serving the interests of the landlords, big monopoly bourgeoisie and British imperialism. Clarifying the nature of the Indian bourgeoisie, Stalin suggested that there was a non-collaborative and nationalist element in the Indian bourgeoisie though it was primarily dependent on the imperialist bourgeoisie.[15]

The 1951 documents remained the guiding framework till the Palghat Congress of 1956 when the line of peaceful struggle and cooperation with the Nehru government began to emerge. But its implementation on the field was yet to unfold. Rao was replaced by Ajoy Ghosh, the centrist leader in the CPI, in 1951. After 1956 the Dange group steadily moved away from the 1951 line while the Sundarayya group stuck to its basic framework. After 1964 the CPI(M) partially modified the 1951 framework, particularly in respect to the nature of Indian independence and the assessment of the Indian bourgeoisie. These issues were further debated within the CPI(M) which caused its split in 1967 leading to the birth of the M-L groups. They stood by the 1951 framework in its essential components. But they too debated among themselves about the nature of the state and society in India since 1947 and the issues of revolutionary strategy. Thus the seeds of later ideological debates in the Indian communist movement lay in the 1951 line itself.[16]

Views on State and Society

How real was India's independence? Whose interest did the Indian state represent in the course of its development after 1947 under the leadership of Nehru and Indira Gandhi? What were the growing trends in the class

[15] The 1951 *Programme* was last published by the CPI in 1953. *The Statement of Policy* has been published several times by the CPI(M) since 1968.

[16] For the evolution of the new line, see Mohit Sen, ed., *Documents of the History of the CPI*, Vol. 8 (1951–56) (New Delhi: PPH, 1977). Bipan Chandra provides a critical assessment of the debate in 'A Strategy in Crisis—The CPI Debate 1955–1956,' in B. Chandra, *op. cit.* He asserts that the 1951 paradigm was empirically unsound and laments that the centre faction led by Ajoy Ghosh, which had made 'the most creative effort to come to terms with the reality,' did not succeed and the party became the battleground for the right pro-Nehru line and the militant anti-government approach of the left factions (pp. 262–63).

relations in India? These were the issues of ideological debate within the united CPI and among the communist parties after the splits. Correspondingly, there were divergent strategic and tactical formulations. The 1951 documents had described India as a semi-colonial country. A left faction within the CPI maintained this position throughout. The Joshi group, on the other hand, regarded the Indian state as an independent state which had emerged in 1947 as a result of the national liberation struggle led by the Congress. The CPSU position slowly shifted in the latter direction. During the Korean war, India's independent stand against the U.S. bloc was taken as an evidence of this trend. Stalin's original formulation that the world was divided into two camps—imperialist and socialist—was modified during his last years to recognize the existence of an intermediate group of anti-imperialist countries. The Bandung Conference of Afro-Asian countries in April 1955 convinced Stalin's successors of the magnitude of this trend. The visit of Bulganin and Khrushchev to India at the end of 1955 signalled the beginning of the new Soviet policy towards India in general and the Nehru government in particular. The Soviet Union now treated India as an independent country though vulnerable to imperialist pressures. This was not convincing enough for the two other groups in the CPI. Thus the formulation at the Palghat Congress was a cautious one. However, it gave up the 1951 characterization of India as semi-colony. It said that India had achieved political freedom, but economically it was still dependent a d intimately linked with the Western imperialist system.

The 1964 split saw a further differentiation on this issue. The CPI did not have any reservations about the reality of Indian independence. The CPI(M) was initially ambiguous and spoke of the collaboration between the Indian monopoly bourgeoisie and imperialism. But when they were challenged by the M-L factions within its ranks in 1967–68, they came out clearly stating that India had emerged as an independent country even though the transfer of power had taken place as a compromise between the Congress and the imperialists. But the CPI(M) emphasized that the economic linkages between the Indian bourgeoisie and Western imperialism was a constant challenge to the political independence of India.[17]

The CPI(M-L) of Charu Majumdar rejected the above view and regarded India's independence as sham, reiterating that India was a semi-colony.

[17] *Stand on Ideological Issues* (Calcutta: CPI(M), 1969)—Mohan Ram does not think that the CPI(M) had sufficiently clarified its ideological stand. See his *Indian Communism: Split within a Split*, p. 211. Bhabani Sengupta, however, thinks otherwise (*The CPI-M: Promises, Prospects and Problems*, New Delhi: Young Asia, 1980). The CPI(M)'s view of the Indian state as being independent and of the bourgeoisie as being collaborationist and dependent has remained unchanged. See Documents of the Eleventh Congress of the CPI(M) held in Vijayawada in January 1982 which talked of 'increased dependence' (p. 18).

During the 1967–72 period, according to the CPI(M-L), both the U.S. and the U.S.S.R. were imperialist powers subjugating countries like India. After the CPI(M-L) stream split into various groups, they began to re-examine this view. While all of them emphasized the dependent characteristics of the Indian bourgeoisie, some refrained from describing India as a semi-colony.[18] India's role as a leader of the non-aligned movement, Indira Gandhi's manipulative capacity to tilt in one or the other direction and the development of a national sector of the economy now complicated the earlier M-L formulation.

While recognition of the arena of independence of the Indian state became more pronounced, there was an increasing realization of newly arising areas of dependence on the Western powers in modern technology and capital. Thus the 1980s presented an altogether new set of issues of dependency which the earlier framework of colonialism and neo-colonialism could not adequately explain. The new mix of independence and dependence posed new questions which none of the communist groups have fully grappled with.[19]

As for the class character of the Indian state, the 1951 documents had said that the Congress to which power had been transferred by the British represented the interests of the landlords, the big bourgeoisie and the imperialists. In the early 1950s, there was a debate on the nature of the Indian bourgeoisie. How strong was the nationalist element in it? How deeply was it linked with the imperialists? In case of China, the CPC had made a differentiation between the compradore bourgeoisie, which was the agent of imperialism, and the national bourgeoisie, which was basically anti-imperialist. They also analysed the dual character of the national bourgeoisie which generally participated in the anti-colonial movement but sometimes also vacillated.[20] By the time of the Palghat Congress of the CPI, the Joshi line had become more pronounced. According to it, the Congress was the organization of the Indian bourgeoisie which had both a monopoly, pro-imperialist element and a non-monopoly, anti-imperialist element. The latter was represented by Nehru, who should be

---

[18] For the 1969–70 formulation, see *CPI(M-L) Programme* in *Liberation*, Vol. 3, Nos. 7–9 (May-July, 1970). Also T. Nagi Reddy, *India Mortgaged: A Marxist-Leninist Appraisal* (Anantapuram: Tarimala Nagi Reddy Memorial Trust, 1978).

[19] In the 1980s, the various M-L groups were engaged in re-examining many of the issues relating to the nature of the Indian state, the principal contradiction and revolutionary strategy. See *Lessons of History* (Varanasi: CC, CPI(M-L), 1981), i.e., of the Chandra Pulla Reddy group; 'Problems of Indian Revolution, Their Nature and Resolution,' in *Red Star*, No. 2 (March 1985), edited by Ram Nath for the Communist League of India; *Debates on Party Line* (Liberation Publication, 1985) put out by the Vinod Mishra group. Views of the people's war group can be found in their journal *Vanguard*.

[20] Mao Zedong, 'On New Democracy,' *Selected Works*, Vol. LL (Beijing: Foreign Language Press, 1965). See also Manoranjan Mohanty, *The Political Philosophy of Mao Tse-tung* (New Delhi: Macmillan, 1978), Ch. 1.

supported by progressive forces like the CPI. This viewpoint was clearly asserted by the CPI after the 1964 split. S.A. Dange, Ajoy Ghosh's successor as the CPI leader and designated as Chairman since 1961, steadfastly pursued this line during both Nehru's regime and Indira Gandhi's. Thus according to the CPI: 'The state in India is the organ of the class rule of the national bourgeoisie as a whole, in which the big bourgeoisie and landlords, led by the big bourgeoisie, who are increasingly landlords.'[21] The pressures from the big bourgeoisie, on the one hand, and the feudal forces, on the other, explained the periodic reactionary policies of the Congress which, according to the CPI, was otherwise an anti-imperialist and anti-feudal political organization. Hence the CPI's political line is geared towards the programme of national democratic revolution, according to which the national bourgeoisie should be supported to carry out the democratic revolution. Within this framework the CPI supports what it deems to be the progressive policies of the Congress. This orientation is different from the programme of people's democratic revolution of the CPI(M) and the CPI(M-L).

The CPI(M) programme of 1964 gave a different ideological assessment: 'The present Indian state is the organ of the class rule of the bourgeoisie and landlords, led by the big bourgeoisie, who are increasingly collaborating with foreign finance capital in pursuit of the capitalist path of development.' This characterization has been reiterated consistently afterwards.[22] The CPI(M) has emphasized the dominant position of the big bourgeoisie in the Indian society and says that over the years this trend has grown further. It is not compradore in character, but has a collaborative relationship with foreign capital. According to the CPI(M), the feudal forces still remain powerful and share state power with the bourgeoisie. The CPI(M) acknowledges the existence of the national bourgeoisie sharing state power, but only as a junior partner. Hence the Congress of Nehru or Indira represented the interest of the big bourgeoisie and the landlords and was not sufficiently anti-imperialist and should, therefore, be opposed.

The CPI(M-L) *Programme* of 1970 described state power in India as being in the hands of 'feudalism, compradore-bureaucrat capitalism, imperialism and social imperialism'. They drew a parallel with the Chinese revolution, with the only additional fact that besides U.S. imperialism, Soviet control over India was also significant. Some M-L groups later modified their understanding of the Indian bourgeoisie and dropped the reference to compradore bourgeoisie while at the same time emphasizing

[21] *Documents Adopted by the Eighth Congress of the CPI* (New Delhi: CPI, 1968), p. 297. This has been reiterated in successive party congresses. See *Documents of the 12th Congress of the CPI* held at Varanasi in 1982.

[22] *CPI-M Programme* (Calcutta: CPI(M), 1964). The formulation has been uniformly reaffirmed till the Eleventh Congress of 1982.

the dependency relationship of the Indian capitalists. Another point of debate among the various M-L groups was the relative position of the landlords vis-a-vis the capitalists in the exercise of state power. While some M-L groups maintained Charu Majumdar's line that the landlords were the dominant force in Indian society as well as in the state power, others admitted that the situation was more complex. They argued that the hold of the bourgeoisie on the state apparatus was becoming stronger day by day.[23]

Unlike what was stipulated by the 1951 documents, both the CPI and the CPI(M) believe that the Congress was taking India on the path of capitalist development. While the CPI regards this as a process of national, independent development, the CPI(M) sees in this process compromises with foreign capital. From the acceptance of the PL-480 food aid in the 1960s to the five billion dollar I.M.F. loan in the 1980s, there were many symptoms of this linkage with serious political and economic consequences. While the CPI underlines the growth of the national and non-monopoly bourgeoisie, though it also attacks the growth of monopolies, the CPI(M) sees the growth of the monopoly bourgeoisie as the main trend. After the shift in the CPI strategy began in 1978, they began to reassess this aspect and came closer to the CPI(M) view of the national situation. However, a section within the CPI continues to support the Congress while the splinter group of Dange, working under the name of the All India Communist Party, vociferously advocates the pre-1978 line of the CPI. At the other end of the spectrum, the CPI(M-L) groups not only talk about the massive growth of the monopoly bourgeoisie, but also point out their dependency relationship with foreign capital.

On the agrarian front, the CPI sees a clear trend of capitalist development, which was facilitated by the abolition of zamindari and land reforms and accentuated by the green revolution. The political process of the elections and Panchayati Raj have contributed to this process. The rural development schemes of the government (including the anti-poverty programmes) have induced this process further.[24] The CPI(M) is, however, cautious in its formulation. According to them, there are pockets of capitalist development in agriculture due to land reforms and the green revolution, but the vast areas of rural India continued to have semi-feudal relations. Even in the regions of green revolution, inequalities had been sharpened. There is also the deployment of migrant and bonded labour.[25]

[23] This view is forcefully presented by the Shramik Mukti Dal (based in Maharashtra) and the Communist League of India which operates in U.P. The C.C. of Vinod Mishra also recognizes this trend. This view is contested by the Chandra Pulla Reddy group as well as the people's war group of K. Sitaramaya. See Note 19 above.

[24] Besides the CPI's political resolutions see A.I. Medovey, *The Indian Economy* (Moscow: Progress, 1984).

[25] In addition to their political resolutions, see E.M.S. Namboodiripad, *Indian Planning in Crisis* (New Delhi: National Book Centre, 1982).

The CPI(M-L) groups, by and large, do not think that there has been any significant development of capitalist relations in Indian agriculture. What has happened in some areas is utilization of modern technology and other inputs by feudal and semi-feudal forces in the villages to carry on their exploitation of the lower peasantry, landless labour and particularly of people of the oppressed castes. They point out that in the case of the tribal people, the persistence of semi-feudal oppression is evident even as capitalist penetration into those areas is taking place.

Alternative Strategies

On the basis of their analyses of the character of state power and the ruling classes, the communist parties have evolved their revolutionary strategies. Three issues were constantly debated among the Indian communists while formulating a strategy for democratic revolution. First, to what extent did the Telengana experience present a model for carrying out an agrarian armed struggle? Second, to what extent did participation in parliamentary elections provide opportunities to advance the people's struggle? Third, what kind of mass organizations should be built up?

The CPI's centrist leadership in the 1950s led the party to fight the general elections. They cited the example that Lenin favoured participation in the elections for the Russian Duma. The understanding was that all the political opportunities available in a bourgeois democracy should be utilized fully to propagate the politics of the working classes. In the 1957 elections, the CPI and its allies in fact were elected to power in Kerala state. Very soon, however, the Congress mobilized anti-communist sentiments, staged large demonstrations and thereafter the ministry was dismissed by the central government.[26]

The Twentieth Congress of the CPSU advanced the formulation that in certain conditions a peaceful transition to socialism was possible. The CPC rejected this thesis. In India, the left faction of the CPI also questioned it. When the CPI(M) was formed, it asserted the classical Marxist idea that the ruling classes defend their power by force and that, therefore, they cannot be overthrown by peaceful means. This affirmation of the notion of armed revolution was one of the ideological issues which differentiated the CPI(M) from the CPI.

In the 1967 elections, a non-Congress front led by the CPI(M) was elected to power in West Bengal. In May that year, when the peasants rose in arms against the jotedars in the Naxalbari area, they hoped to be protected by the government. When the police suppressed their revolt, several leftists in the ranks of the CPI(M) questioned the CPI(M)

[26] See E.M.S. Namboodiripad, *Twenty-eight Months in Kerala—A Retrospect* (New Delhi: PPH, 1959) and Victor M. Fic, *Peaceful Transition to Communism in India* (Bombay: Nachiketa, 1969).

credentials as a revolutionary party. That is how the second major split in the communist movement began and the CPI(M-L) stream emerged. They rejected the line of electoral politics saying that it corrupts the revolutionaries by compelling them to accept the framework of parliamentary politics, its expensive election campaigns and its preoccupations. They emphasized the need to organize the peasantry for an anti-feudal movement. In 1968 several CPI(M) legislators resigned their offices to join the peasant struggle. In Srikakulam, Mushahari and Debra-Gopiballavpur armed mass campaigns of peasants were launched against the local landlords, some of whom were killed. When police measures against the M-L activities were intensified, Charu Majumdar advocated the line of squad action to annihilate the landlords. This invited even harsher repression by the state forces and was abandoned by most of the M-L groups in the mid-1970s.[27]

The CPI's electoral politics as an ally or near-ally of the Congress after 1969 landed it in a situation when it had to defend the emergency imposed by the Indira government in 1975. After the defeat of Indira Gandhi in the 1977 election, the CPI reassessed its policy and started taking a partially critical posture against the Congress. Without the support of the Congress, its electoral strength declined fast to reduce it to the status of a small, scattered political force. On the other hand, in both West Bengal and Kerala the CPI(M) steadily improved its strength by sustained work among the peasantry. In 1977, the CPI(M)-led left front was voted to power in West Bengal and Tripura to be returned again five years later.

The CPI(M-L) groups point out that the CPI(M) has become a parliamentary party operating the bourgeois-landlord state apparatus in the two states. According to them, the Marxist legislators and party cadres had been trapped by the corrupt system and can hardly demonstrate their commitment to the path of agrarian revolution. They cite the trend of declining popular support for the CPI(M) in Kerala as well as West Bengal to predict that they might one day be defeated by the Congress at the hustings. The CPI(M) argues in return that they had no illusions regarding carrying out revolutionary transformation through the government. They had used their limited power to protect the rights of the sharecroppers through 'Operation Barga' or the workers' rights by defending their just struggles and popularizing progressive ideas by various means. Thus the debate goes on among the communists about the options between parliamentary and non-parliamentary politics.

[27] For CPI(M)'s critique of the M-L line, see *On Left Deviation* (Calcutta: CPI(M), 1967) and Prakash Karat, 'Naxalism Today at an Ideological Deadend,' *The Marxist*, Vol. 3, No. 1 (April-June 1985). For the CPI(M-L) critique of the CPI(M), see Charu Majumdar, *Selected Writings* (Calcutta: Mass Line, n.d.).

New Challenges

While the totality of the Indian communist movement presents the full spectrum of revolutionary politics (ranging from electoral participation to armed struggle) there is a clear absence of sufficient links among them. Practitioners of electoral politics seem to be fully occupied with the overbearing pressures of the parliamentary system. Those who engage in armed struggle are still groping for a viable strategy that can overcome the mounting repression by the capitalist state. Others who refrain from either but concentrate on militant mass organization among the agricultural workers or tribals for their just rights get stuck with the struggles which may not advance steadily but invite the same level of terrorization by the government. Yet others have focused their attention on cultural activities, with or without any relationship with political parties.

While the CPI stream has continued to be almost an ally of the Congress led by Nehru and Indira Gandhi, the CPI(M) has taken the initiative in organizing an alternative to the Congress. The CPI(M-L) streams primarily operate in an alternative framework of politics and only secondarily participate in an oppositional role in the political system. Thus the post-independence period presents an expanded realm of creative experiments in the Indian communist movement.

To what extent do communist strategies reflect a deep understanding of the Indian environment? Are they derived from purely ideological formulations? The spilt of 1964 compelled a process of inquiry into the reality of Indian conditions. Earlier the CPSU Congress of 1956 had asserted that the reality of the modern world made it possible to strive for a peaceful transition to socialism. The Chinese sharply questioned this formulation. In India, the CPI(M) stream sided with the Chinese position. This debate forced the Indian communists to analyse the Indian conditions carefully. The CPI stream took the Congress party's agrarian measures seriously and saw evidence of a widespread capitalist development. The CPI(M) saw the large-scale persistence of pre-capitalist forms. Thus the split of 1964 put back the programme of agrarian revolution on the agenda. But the CPI(M-L) stream accused the CPI(M) of not doing enough on the front of agrarian revolution. They asserted the need for a more militant programme of anti-feudal revolution. Thus, paradoxically, the splits had the effect of constantly focusing attention on the issue of agrarian revolution as the main form of India's democratic revolution.

However, several new political trends emerged in Indian society, which got intensified from the late 1960s, to which the communists have not paid adequate attention. The politicization of caste, the recurrence of communal violence and the growth of nationality movements are the most significant among them. The communists had assumed that since caste was a pre-capitalist formation, it would break down as capitalism grew and revolutionary movements made progress. But the newly emergent intermediate peasantry which had benefited from zamindari abolition got mobilized on the plank of 'backward classes' or the middle level castes. At the same time, the Scheduled Castes have formed their own organizations. Modernization has strengthened the upper castes as well. Yet the issue of treating caste as an autonomous force has not been taken seriously by the communist parties, though Marxist scholarship has begun to debate this issue.[28]

Communists generally dismiss the occurrence of inter-religious violence either as an engineered act by religious obscurantists or as a manifestation of economic disparities in the region. Even if these two aspects are unexceptionally present in most situations, the phenomenon of increasing politicization of religion in the country and its inter-mix with modern infrastructure, election process and developmental experience is a much more complex phenomenon than the communist parties admit. The CPI's assessment of Nehru and Indira Gandhi as secularists has been under question as well.[29] The failure of the communists to see the social roots and operational dynamics of religion continues to create problems for their movement. Yet the experience of communist-led struggles amply indicates the possibilities of secular struggle.

On the nationality question, too, there has been debate among the communists. A party which had opposed partition and had blamed the imperialists and the Congress for it, slowly moved away from its theory of the multinational state. The CPI apprehended that this notion would weaken India and make it vulnerable to imperialist pressures. In 1967–69, the CPI(M) briefly asserted this concept and pleaded for decentralization of political power in India. But since the late 1970s, the CPI(M) has not reiterated this idea. Though it is for political decentralization which would give greater power to the states, it hesitates to characterize India as a multinational state. Some CPI(M-L) groups have underlined the importance of the nationality question and the need to emphasize the multinational character of India. They point out that the Indian ruling classes seek to consolidate their power through a centralized state apparatus since they find that they face challenges from the struggles of the nationalities. The long-drawn movement of the Nagas and Mizos in the north-east, the movement of backward regions like Jharkhand and

---

[28] Reluctance to treat caste as a relatively autonomous category is seen in B.T. Ranadive, *Caste, Class and Property Relations* (Calcutta: National Book Agency, 1982). For an alternative set of studies recognizing the autonomy of caste within a class framework, see Gail Omvedt, ed., *Land, Caste and Politics in Indian States* (New Delhi: Authors' Guild, 1981).

[29] With increasing communal violence in India and the explosive situation in Punjab, the strategy of secularization pursued by the CPI and the Congress has been proved ineffective.

Chhatisgarh, the rise of regional forces like the AIDMK, Akali Dal and Telugu Desam and the Assam and Punjab problems demand a great deal more attention to the nationality question than what the communist parties have given so far.[30]

The eighties saw the emergence of newer issues. The liberation of women, the problem of technology, the question of environmental pollution and the larger issue of human rights have become important issues. The communist parties, however, are not in the forefront of these movements. Needless to say, in all these spheres, the tasks of the struggle against neo-colonialism and the struggle for democratic revolution converge.

Thus, even though the communists have made significant advances in creatively developing their ideology and strategy, they have to grapple with these new problems even more seriously in the coming decades.[31]

---

[30] New ideas on the nationality problem in India began to be debated in the 1980s when the autonomy movements began to acquire momentum. See *Nationality Question in India* (Seminar Papers), (Hyderabad: Radical Students Union, 1981).

[31] For the level of creativity warranted by the contemporary challenges, see Sumanta Banerjee, 'The Island of Dr Marx,' *Economic and Political Weekly*, Vol. 17, No. 4 (23 Jan. 1982).

15

R.C. PILLAI

The Political Thought of Jawaharlal Nehru

Jawaharlal Nehru is widely acclaimed as one of the architects of modern India. His remarkable personality was an unusual combination of an intellectual and a practical political leader. The role that he played in the long struggle for national freedom, and later as the greatest political leader of free India, has had a profound effect on Indian political thinking. He belonged to that group of Western-educated Indian elites who drew their inspiration mainly from the intellectual currents of the nineteenth and twentieth centuries. If in the early part of his career he had absorbed many of the ideas and impulses of modern democratic thought, in his later years 'he acquired a deeper appreciation of Indian history and philosophy, and enriched the basis for subsequent thought and action.'[1]

Nehru had a long span of public life stretching for more than forty-five years. After his education at Harrow and Cambridge, he returned to India in 1912 when the national political scene was at a low profile. He was not inspired by the politics of the moderate group although his father, Motilal Nehru, was a vocal supporter of it. He believed rather strongly that individual and national self-respect required a more aggressive attitude to foreign rule. By nature he was an intense nationalist and an open rebel against authoritarianism. As he disliked the politics of prayer and petitions, he was naturally inclined to accept the programme of the extremist group, headed by B.G. Tilak, who was then the embodiment of militant nationalism in India. But though the aggressive nationalism of Tilak appealed to Nehru emotionally, it contained deep religious motivations which he totally disliked. His demand for a more fighting attitude towards foreign domination was a purely psychological urge and he continued to express it even after Gandhi's emergence on the political scene.

Liberal Nationalism

Nehru was aware that nationalism, particularly as it existed in the colonial world, was both a composite and a living force and could make the strongest appeal to the spirit of man. He also knew of its many-sided contributions to the development of modern civilization. It had, all along, been a driving force for freedom and independence. It gave a certain degree of unity, vigour and vitality to many people all over the world.

---

[1] Michael Brecher, *Nehru—A Political Biography* (London: Oxford University Press, 1959), p. 181.

But he was also conscious of the fact that Indian nationalism, though mainly rooted in the universal virtues of 'pacifism, liberalism and rationalism,' was not free from limitations. According to him, Indian nationalism did lack certain vital elements although it was free from violence and hatred. He wanted Indian nationalism to be limited, liberalized and balanced as he thought it would be harmful if it ever made the people conscious of their own superiority or aggressive expansionism. Nehru's intense nationalism, coupled with his urge for effective political action, made him a constructive critic of the Indian National Congress. What he demanded was the introduction of a secular, rational and scientific, international outlook as the essential ingredients of Indian nationalism. In other words, he was the most vocal critic of the religious, metaphysical and revivalist outlook which, according to him, was greatly harmful to the cause of national liberation as well as to the growth of nationhood.

Anti-imperialism

Nehru was a crusader against imperialism. His anti-imperialist attitude found its first open expression at the Brussels Congress held in February 1927. There he stressed the common element in the struggles against imperialism in different parts of the world. His close contact with European revolutionaries and movements created in him a new awareness of the forces which were shaping the destiny of mankind. His association with the 'League Against Imperialism'[2] and his short visit to the Soviet Union later in November 1927 brought about a radical change in his political perception. The Indian nationalist movement, according to him, was part of the world-wide movement and its serious impact would naturally be felt in most other countries. He, therefore made it a point to appeal to all progressive forces all over the world to lend their support to the Indian struggle.

Nehru's anti-imperialism was largely the product of his own understanding of the historical evolution of the laws of social change. His partial acceptance of the Marxist interpretation of history gave him an insight into the facts of social evolution. Though he made no deeper analysis, he believed that the dominant class—the class which controlled the means of production—was the ruling class and that class conflicts in an exploitative and oppressed society could not be avoided. As an intellectual, he diagnosed the social maladies and understood their socio-economic consequences. But on the practical side of his politics he remained extremely cautious.

Nehru was clear in his mind that so long as imperialism was not rooted out, mankind would continue to suffer both exploitation and oppression.

[2] In February 1927, Nehru was elected one of the five honorary presidents and a member of the Executive Committee.

Therefore, he asserted that 'the nationalist movement had to be un-compromisingly anti-capitalist, anti-feudal, anti-bourgeois, ... and of course anti-imperialist', and its sole objective should be the establishment of a democratic socialist republic in a free and independent India.[3] Nehru was fairly in agreement with Lenin's ideas on imperialism and the Soviet Union's firm anti-imperialist position. 'So I turned inevitably with goodwill towards communism,' wrote Nehru in his autobiography, 'for whatever its faults, it was at least not hypocritical and not imperialistic.'[4] Here his political outlook seemed to be that of a 'self-conscious radical' and throughout his life his sympathy lay broadly with the socialist countries.

Uncompromising Stand Towards Complete Independence

Nehru's new radicalism reaffirmed his enthusiasm for more purposeful political action. His whole effort during the twenties was to redefine the concept of *swaraj* in terms of complete independence. The content of *swaraj* as demanded by the nationalists remained largely vague and insufficient and so he had made up his mind to move in a different direction. As a first step, he tried to persuade the Congress for an open commitment to the goal of complete independence. With a deep sense of courage and determination, Nehru moved a resolution on complete independence at the Madras Session of the Congress held in 1927 and it was formally adopted there.

Though the resolution on independence was formally adopted by the Congress, Nehru had a genuine fear whether the Congress would follow it in both letter and spirit. The doubt arose because of the Congress' refusal to incorporate it in the constitution. Nehru, therefore, took immediate steps to form two new organizations. 'The Republican League' and the 'Independence for India League'. The former was mainly intended to work for the establishment of complete national independence while the latter was to carry on a vigorous campaign for the same cause.

At the Calcutta Session of the Congress held in 1928, Nehru noticed that some attempts were being made to obscure the issue of independence. He immediately stepped in and accepted the secretaryship just 'to prevent, as far as I could, the swing back to moderation and to hold on to the independence objective.'[5] In a sharply-worded rejoinder to all those who were still harping on Dominion Status, Nehru said, 'If India has a message to give to the world, it is clear that she can do so more effectively

---

[3] B.N. Pande, *Nehru* (London: Macmillan, 1977), pp. 122–23.

[4] Jawaharlal Nehru, *An Autobiography* (London: The Bodley Head, 1955, reprinted), p. 163.

[5] *Ibid.*, p. 168.

as an independent country than as a member of the British group.'⁶ Despite the pulls and protests from many of his colleagues, he was able to hold on to the independence objective and, in a sense, he had the satisfaction that the pressure that he built in the Congress in favour of complete independence had a positive effect.

Socialist Ideas

The beginning of Nehru's interest in socialist ideas can be traced to his Cambridge days when the Fabianism of Bernard Shaw and the Webbs attracted him. But that was, as he confessed, purely an academic interest. He was also influenced by the ideas of Bertrand Russell and John Maynard Keynes, in the sense that he used to regularly attend their lectures although his own university curriculum contained only science and not economics.⁷ The vague ideas of socialism which he had nurtured during his student days were subsequently revived and sharpened in the light of the sweeping political, social and economic changes taking place throughout the world.

Nehru was not a pioneer in the field of socialism in India; compared to others, he was certainly not in the forefront of the socialist movement. Some kind of a vague socialist thinking was already a part of the political process right from the early twenties. Marxian theory was increasingly influencing many individuals and this tendency was further strengthened by the developments in the Soviet Union. The workers' trade union movement and a majority of the youth leagues and socialist leanings. However, it was entirely at the instance of Nehru that the Congress committed itself very vaguely to the principle of socialism in 1929. In 1931, the Congress under his influence took a more definite step in that direction by adopting an economic programme at the Karachi Session. As he had occupied a high position in the Congress, he had the advantage of making his influence felt much more than others. He was also looked upon by the youth and the weaker sections of the masses as a symbol of their hopes and aspirations. Moreover, as the Congress began to enlist the active support of the masses for its political programme of national liberation, the organization felt more and more compelled to take up economic issues for consideration. As a matter of fact, Nehru continuously kept up his pressure on the organization in favour of socialism and, consequently, a number of vague socialist resolutions were adopted by the Congress from time to time.

⁶ Jawaharlal Nehru, 'Statement on the Independence Resolution,' *The Tribune*, 27 January 1928, in S. Gopal, ed., *Selected Works of Jawaharlal Nehru*, Vol. 3 (New Delhi: Orient Longman, 1972), pp. 22–23.

⁷ Frank Moraes, *Jawaharlal Nehru—A Biography* (New York: Macmillan Co., 1956), p. 42.

Socialism was not a mere economic doctrine for Nehru. 'It is a vital creed which I hold with all my head and heart,' he stated in 1936.[8] His early radicalism convinced him that there was no other way of ending the appalling mass poverty and sufferings in India except through socialism. He was, therefore, determined not only to work for that cause but was keenly interested in making the Congress an effective instrument of social and economic change. Nehru declared:

> I work for Indian independence because the nationalist in me cannot tolerate alien domination; I work for it even more because for me, it is the inevitable step to social and economic change. I should like the Congress to become a socialist organization and to join hands with other forces in the world who are working for the new civilization.[9]

More than most of his colleagues, Nehru had a clear understanding of the character of the National Congress and the movement it was piloting then. The Congress, during the pre-independence period, was a great movement; but that movement was neither a proletarian nor a peasant movement. It was purely a bourgeois movement whose objective was not of changing the social structure but of winning political freedom. However, there were quite a few in it who could think far beyond their surroundings. They stood for drastic socio-economic transformation and were quite enthusiastic about it. This group was asserting itself within the Congress with the sole aim of persuading others to accept socialism and Nehru was undoubtedly the spokesman of that group. In all his speeches and writings during this period, Nehru repeatedly stressed the need for *swaraj* and socialism as the joint objectives of the movement and he firmly believed that India could not have one without the other. It was also his conviction that political freedom could no longer be separated from economic freedom since world events were forcing the issue to the forefront.

Nehru's vigorous campaign for socialism continued for long, even after independence, and the Congress, under his undisputed leadership, adopted official resolutions to that effect. But his concept of socialism remained largely undefined throughout. He had no rigid adherence to any brand of socialism as such. He was solely guided by the practical considerations of Indian society and its concrete situation as it appeared before him. His approach to the fundamental problem of social transformation was, therefore, extremely cautious. He was aware that the Congress, constituted as it was, could hardly accept any revolutionary programme of social action. Had the issue been forced on it, the Congress,

[8] Jawaharlal Nehru, Presidential Address to the National Congress in 1936, in *India and the World* (London: George Allen and Unwin Ltd., 1936), p. 83.

[9] *Ibid.*, pp. 83–84.

being a loose organization, would have probably split. Even in the years of power, Nehru paid no serious attention to reorganizing the Congress into a cadre-based party with a deep sense of commitment to socialism. Inside the organization he was not unwilling to cooperate, even with those who did not accept his socialist ideas. He had no intention either of forming a new party or group in order to carry out his socialist objective.

However, in the pursuit of his 'vague-socialist ideal' Nehru had to face certain serious problems. The question of providing social justice without sacrificing individual freedom was certainly uppermost in his mind. It was, therefore, in the choice of method and general approach that Nehru revealed his pragmatism more apparently than anything else. Unlike the communists, Nehru chose the method of persuasion or peaceful democratic pressures as against the 'methods of destruction and extermination'.[10] He was critical of both the communists and the socialists who, according to him, were largely influenced by the literature on European socialism. In India, Nehru argued, nationalism and rural economy constituted the core of the problem and, as such, it could not be dealt with in terms of the industrial proletariat. European socialism had never dealt with such conditions. Nehru was, therefore, convinced that if socialism was to be established in India, it would have to grow out of Indian conditions.

Nehru did not subscribe to the Marxian theory of class-war and the dictatorship of the proletariat. His admiration for the finer aspects of Marxism (as evident both in his works as well as in his numerous speeches) was never uncritical or unqualified. He totally disliked the communist policy of 'ruthless suppression' of political dissent and the 'wholesale regimentation'. Moreover, he was completely opposed to the methods of violence and hatred. He honestly believed that it was possible to liquidate poverty and ensure a minimum standard of life for all without any violent overthrow of the existing order. Even if conflicts did exist between classes, the best way of resolving that conflict, according to him, was to put an end to it by peaceful methods.[11]

It was Nehru's political conviction that India would have to march gradually in the direction of socialism, but that march, he asserted, would be on different lines, different from a violent overthrow of the existing social order. 'Nothing is so foolish,' he argued, 'as to imagine that exactly the same process takes place in different countries with varying backgrounds.'[12] India, therefore, will have to find her own way to socialism which would avoid unnecessary sacrifice and the possibility of chaos.

Nehru's political ideas were conditioned by some of the liberal democratic

---

[10] Jawaharlal Nehru, *The Basic Approach*, a note published in *A.I.C.C. Economic Review* (New Delhi: All-India Congress Committee, 15 August 1958).

[11] *Jawaharlal Nehru's Speeches*, Vol. 3 (Delhi: Publications Division, Govt. of India, 1958), pp. 136–37.

[12] Jawaharlal Nehru, *Where Are We?* (Allahabad and London: Kitabistan, 1939), p. 60.

traditions of the nineteenth century. The brand of socialism which he advocated could be achieved only through the democratic process. He strongly believed that democracy and socialism were not contradictory but complementary to one other. His concept of social democracy did not amount to any serious infringement of individual freedom and civil liberty. 'I do not see why under socialism there should not be a great deal of freedom for the individual, indeed far greater freedom than the present system gives . . . .'[13] His tremendous respect for human freedom and individual rights, on the one hand, and his total opposition to authoritarianism and regimentation, on the other, and above all his practical considerations arising out of his desire to carry the bulk of the people with the system, possibly prevented him from accepting an ideologically rigid position.

'Nehru was a practical idealist.'[14] He did not want to rely on idealistic principles while dealing with the massive problems of an amorphous plural society with a clear semi-feudal background. The problem with Nehru was that the intellectual in him prompted him to be a critic of both communism and capitalism. He was aware of the inherent limitations of both and he wanted to avoid them in the developmental model that he initiated. His lip service to some of the fundamental tenets of Marxism was a mere intellectual exercise. But Nehru the political man, faced by the appalling socio-economic conditions of a semi-feudal society, with all his awareness of the actual character of the Indian National Congress, found favour with liberal democracy. Also looking at the mass poverty, illiteracy and social backwardness in the country, Nehru could not think of anything other than a socialist solution to that gigantic problem. But revolutionary socialism was neither feasible nor inevitable because the human values of a free society had to be preserved. His concept of socialism could be achieved only through a full democratic process, through the consent of a majority.

The task before Nehru was, therefore, to continuously educate the people in the spirit of democratic socialism in order to win them over to that cause. This was obviously a pragmatic approach based on political expediency and compromise and not on any ideological conviction. Choosing the method of persuasion rather than that of coercion, he said: 'I do not want India to be drilled and forced into a certain position, because the costs of such drilling are too great; it is not worthwhile; it is not desirable from my point of view . . . .'[15] In any case, the freedom and dignity of the individual was well preserved in Nehru's model which, if analysed objectively, was nothing but welfare capitalism.

[13] *Ibid.*, p. 59.

[14] Willard Range, *Jawaharlal Nehru's World View—A Theory of International Relations* (Athens: University of Georgia Press, 1961), p. 16.

[15] Jawaharlal Nehru, *India and the World* (London: George Allen and Unwin Ltd.), p. 259.

On Planning and Development

Another significant aspect of Nehru's model of economic development was the creation of a consciousness of economic planning. Since the early forties, it became quite apparent that his bitter antagonism to capitalism was being modified. By that time, in several countries of the West, 'capitalism had been civilized, tamed and toned down, and many of its old evils extricated by the insistent demand of the masses . . . .'[16] These countries were working vigorously to provide a better life for the masses. Nehru who was aware of these developments, however, continued to stress the importance of socialism for tackling contemporary economic and social problems. But, finally, he threw himself in favour of a mixed economy as the most suitable and most practicable for India. It would be an economy, he asserted, in which socialist principles and ideals would prevail generally, along with a fair share of capitalism. Thus the concept of a welfare state, on the basis of a mixed economy, in place of a completely socialized economy, became Nehru's political creed and model of economic development.

Much before the advent of freedom, Nehru realized the need for planning for the modernization and development of society. Insistence on planning for socio-economic reconstruction ius became a cardinal feature of his thought. He was also deeply ir ·pressed by the Soviet economic development through planning which, according to him, caught the imagination of the world. In 1938, when the Congress decided to set up a 'National Planning Committee' with Nehru as its Chairman, he boldly accepted the challenging task. He took up the work in all earnestness and the statement of objectives made by him as Chairman of the Planning Committee became a significant document on economic planning in India.

To Nehru, planning was an inevitable process of a socialist economy in a democratic structure. But he had no intention of frightening away any section of the people by stressing the socialist aspect. He, therefore, chose to remain vague and imprecise while formulating the aim of planning. His concept of planning was not based on any dogmatic or doctrinaire considerations. He was guided more by the desire for quick results than by any ideological adherence. His only interest was to put the people on the road of steady economic and social progress. 'I do not care what ism it is that helps me to set them on that road, if one thing fails, we will try another.'[17] It was this uncommitted and flexible attitude that led him to believe that a mixed economy was the most suitable for India.

[16] Willard Range, *op. cit.*, p. 71.

[17] Jawaharlal Nehru, *Independence and After*, p. 191, quoted in D.E. Smith, *Nehru and Democracy: The Political Thought of an Asian Democrat* (Calcutta: Orient Longman, 1958), p. 121.

Nehru's concept of a mixed economy envisaged the simultaneous participation of the public and private sectors in developmental activities. Key sectors of the economy were to be wholly under state control while the private sector would operate in other spheres. However, the private sector must be subject to state control so as to make it function within the objective of the national plan. While commenting on the role of the private sector, Nehru observed: 'The control over the private sector will relate not only to its. dividends and profits but will extend to all the strategic points in the economy of the country.'[18] He envisaged gradually more and more state control over the private sector in order to make the mixed economy sufficiently capable of adapting itself to changing conditions.

Nehru's arguments in favour of a mixed economy might sound logical in the peculiar Indian conditions. According to him, the choice before the country lay essentially between the socialist and capitalist systems. But he was not prepared to exercise the choice in view of the limitations inherent in both. Argued Nehru:

Western economics, though helpful, have little bearing on our present-day problems. So also have Marxist economics which are, in many ways, out of date even though they throw considerable light on economic progress. We have thus to do our own thinking, profiting by the example of others, but essentially trying to find a path for ourselves suited to our own conditions.[19]

Thus it was clear that Nehru did not want to imitate any economic model of other countries. India must evolve a system which suited her own requirements and genius. The ideal of a mixed economy was thus considered to be the best. Stressing this point rather heavily, Nehru declared:

. . (economic) change will have to be in the direction of a democratically planned collectivism . . . . A democratic-collectivism need not mean an abolition of private property, but it will mean the public ownership of the basic and major industries . . . . In India especially it will be necessary to have, in addition to the big industries, cooperatively controlled small and village industries. Such a system of democratic collectivism will need careful and continuous planning and adaptation to the changing needs of the people.[20]

[18] Jawaharlal Nehru's Speeches (1949–53), (Delhi: Publications Division, Govt. of India, 1957), p. 97.
[19] Jawaharlal Nehru, The Basic Approach, in Nehru's Speeches, Vol. 4 (Sept. 1957 to April 1963), (Delhi: Publications Division, Govt. of India, 1964), p. 123.
[20] Jawaharlal Nehru, The Discovery of India (Calcutta: Signet Press, 1946). pp. 635–36.

Nehru was quite sincere and earnest in his efforts to develop an Indian model of planning and development. However, the fact of the situation is that his efforts could not produce the desired results. Despite his best intentions, a certain minimum standard of living was still a far cry for a sizable section of the masses. The alarming growth of private capital and the colossal waste of the national resources resulting from misplaced national priorities in planning have all contributed to the ever-widening gap between the rich and the poor.

Liberal Democratic Ideas

Jawaharlal Nehru was the greatest champion of liberal democracy in India. Throughout his life, he stressed the importance of democracy and passionately desired that free India went along the full democratic process. His sensitive mind had absorbed much of the dominant concepts of modern democratic thought. In fact, the intellectual and social influence of the West appeared to have largely moulded his liberal democratic ideas. This he confessed when he wrote: 'My roots are still perhaps partly in the nineteenth century and I have been too much influenced by the humanist liberal traditions to get out of it completely.'[21]

Nehru's concept of democracy had certain specific implications. In the early years of the struggle for independence, democracy meant the ideal of self-rule or responsible government. During the later years, his socialist ideas altered his views on democracy, stressing more and more its economic aspect. In an ultimate analysis, democracy implied a mental approach applied to political and economic problems. Broadly, democracy emphasized equality of opportunity for all in the political and economic field and freedom for the individual to grow and develop to the best of his personality. It also involved a high degree of tolerance and a certain inquisitive search for the truth. Democracy was thus the dynamic concept for Nehru.

Nehru had tremendous respect for the freedom of man. He firmly believed that the creative and adventurous spirit of man could grow only in an atmosphere of rights and freedom. To promote and preserve the human values, both society and the individual must enjoy freedom. Explaining the reasons for accepting the democratic process in India, Nehru observed:

It is not enough for us merely to produce the material goods of the world. We do want a high standard of living, but not at the cost of man's creative spirit, his creative energy, his spirit of adventure, not at

[21] Jawaharlal Nehru, *An Autobiography, op. cit.*, p 591.

the cost of all fine things of life which have ennobled man throughout the ages. Democracy is not merely a question of elections.[22]

His concept of individual freedom necessarily implied freedom of speech and expression, of association and many other fields of creative activities. The general health of a society, he believed, was largely determined by the freedom of its people.

In Nehru's democratic thought, there was an integrated conception of political, economic and social freedom which could not be separated from one another. Realizing that the danger to democracy lay essentially in the economic structure of society, Nehru pointed out that democracy could grow and flourish only in an equal society. A serious weakness of Western democracy, according to him, was that political power there became the monopoly of the dominant class. The democratic machinery was often exploited to perpetuate class privileges and interests. It also failed to solve the burning problem of inequality. 'The spirit of the age is in favour of equality though practice denies it almost everywhere,' said Nehru, explaining the democratic principle of equality in the Indian context.[23]

One of the reasons for Nehru's fascination for democracy (as against authoritarianism) was that the former was based on rationalism while the latter relied on dogmatism. Free discussion and an inquisitive search for the truth, which found no place in authoritarianism, constituted the essence of democratic theory. Nehru had a tremendous faith in the spirit of man. The dismal failures of mankind never depressed him. Being a liberal by taste and temperament, he believed in the potentiality of human reason and man's ability for survival. However, he was very clear about his social objective of establishing an economic democracy, which, in his terminology, was to be a socialistic pattern of society. Such a society was to be based on cooperative effort providing equal opportunity for all.[24] It is, however, significant to note that when Nehru defined democracy in terms of individual freedom, popular government, or social self-discipline, he was speaking of the realities of the actual life. When he defined democracy in terms of economic and social equality, he was speaking of an ideal, a distant goal to be achieved in due course.

Nehru frequently referred to the Gandhian doctrine of ends and means; he obviously seemed to be under its impact when he stressed the importance of social self-discipline. It was his strong belief that

[22] Jawaharlal Nehru, 'Away from Acquisitive Society,' in Nehru's Speeches (March 1953–August 1957), Vol. 3 (Delhi: Publications Division, Govt. of India, 1958), p. 53.

[23] Jawaharlal Nehru, The Discovery of India, op. cit., p. 634.

[24] Jawaharlal Nehru's Broadcast, 13 December 1952, Building New India (New Delhi: A.I.C.C., 1958), p. 53.

social and political objectives must be sought only by non-violent methods. If democracy was to ensure individual liberty, Nehru held, then that liberty was to be considered in the larger context of social responsibility.

Science for Modernization

Gifted with a fascinating scientific temper, Nehru recognized from the beginning the supreme importance of science and technology for the modernization of Indian society. One of the most striking characteristics of Western civilization, according to Nehru, was its rational and scientific temper. By virtue of these, the Western mind was able to free itself from the shackles of medievalism, from 'unreason, magic and superstition'. Rationalism and scientism seem to have had a profound impact on Nehru's thinking. His persistent demand for them was based on his conviction that India must break with much of her past and not allow the past to dominate the present. In other words, India must get out of her traditional ways of thought and action.

During the long course of human history, Nehru observed, science revolutionized the conditions of human life more than anything else. Man secured considerable relief from the burden of miseries by the application of science and the scientific approach. The conquest of the physical world by the mind of man was so remarkable that nature was no longer regarded as something apart or distinct from himself.[25] But science must have a social objective apart from being an individual's search for truth and knowledge. Its objective should be to ward off the ills and evils of the community. In a country like India, 'science must think in terms of the suffering millions'.[26] 'It was science alone,' Nehru asserted, 'that could solve these problems of hunger and poverty, of insanitation and illiteracy, of superstition and deadening custom and tradition, of vast resources running to waste, of a rich country inhabited by starving people.'[27]

Nehru insisted that a scientific approach be accepted as a way of life, as a guiding principle, as a process of thinking. This was absolutely essential, according to him, to build the foundation of modern India. The scientific temper was exceedingly manifest in Nehru when he said, 'We have to build India on a scientific foundation to develop her industries, to change that feudal character of her land system, and bring her agriculture in line with modern methods to develop the social services which she lacks so utterly today.'[28] He strongly believed that national progress could be

[25] *Jawaharlal Nehru's Speeches* (Sept. 1957–April 1963), *op. cit.*, p. 114.

[26] Jawaharlal Nehru, 'Presidential Address at the 34th Indian Science Congress' (Delhi, 3 January 1947), in S. Gopal, ed., *Selected Works of Jawaharlal Nehru*, Vol. 1 (Second Series), (New Delhi: Nehru Memorial Fund, Teen Murti House, 1984), p. 372.

[27] J.S. Bright, ed., *Before and After Independence* (A Collection of Important Speeches), Vols. 1 & 2 (1922–50), (New Delhi: Indian Printing Works, n.d.), p. 292. [28] *Ibid.*, p. 293.

achieved neither by a repetition of the past nor by its denial. New patterns must be developed and integrated with the old. This was all the more necessary for India because, instead of relying on the present, India had heavily depended upon the past. She must get out of her obsession 'with the supernatural and metaphysical speculations'. Religious, ceremonial and mystical emotionalism not only crippled the mental discipline in India but also stood in the way of understanding ourselves and the world at large.[29] People in India will have to come to grips with the present, Nehru said, because there was only a one-way traffic in time and progress.

Secularism as a Social Ideal

It was mainly due to Jawaharlal Nehru's efforts that India emerged as a secular state in the mid-twentieth century. Much before independence, he played a heroic role in the development of a secular basis for Indian polity. For him, secularism was essentially a social ideal to be promoted in the interest of national unity and progress. He used every single opportunity to impress upon the people the danger of mixing religion and politics. Communalism, he believed, could not only weaken the very fabric of a society but also threaten its very existence.

Nehru's secularism found expression officially for the first time in the resolution drafted by him on 'Fundamental Rights and Duties' which was adopted by the Karachi Congress in 1931. Clause (1)(ix) of the resolution read: 'The State shall observe neutrality in regard to all religions.'[30] The secular state did not in any sense imply that religion ceased to be significant in the life of the individual. It only meant the separation of the state from religion—a cardinal principle of modern democratic practice. Nehru was vehemently opposed to the idea of a theocratic state which, in his view, was both medieval and anti-democratic in character and had no place in the mind of a modern individual.

Nehru favoured a strong secular base for the state primarily for the maintenance of social stability and religious harmony among diverse groups. It was his firm conviction that a secular state alone could better serve a community divided by diverse religious creeds and faiths. With the state pledged to a secular way of life, the Constitution of India guaranteed the right to freedom of religion as a fundamental right. Nehru was specially interested in the enumeration of the 'Directive Principles of State Policy' which suggested the creation of a uniform civil code for all in India. In order to maintain national unity and thereby to ensure orderly progress, a secular approach was considered to be an imperative need. Nehru's achievement in this direction was most praiseworthy and was acclaimed by even his critics.

[29] Jawaharlal Nehru, *The Discovery of India, op. cit.*, p. 633.
[30] Jawaharlal Nehru, *The Unity of India* (London: Lindsay-Drummond 1948, third impression), p. 406

World Outlook

Long before independence, Nehru realized that national isolation was neither desirable nor possible in a world which was fast changing and becoming more of a unit. He had a deep sense of history. What he did observe in history was the strong urge in man to come together, to cooperate and work out their problems in common. It was from that cooperation, Nehru felt, that man was able to progress from barbarism to civilization. In that ever-growing spirit of cooperation, nations too were becoming interdependent and none could go against that historical tendency. India, therefore, Nehru argued, 'must be prepared to discard her narrow nationalism in favour of world cooperation and real internationalism.'[31]

Nehru had all along possessed a rare ability to analyse the international situation by placing the national problem in the wider world context. It was he who persuaded the Congress to realize that the Indian struggle for freedom was part of a global struggle and that its strategy and tactics should be such as would fit into the context of world developments. 'If we claim independence today,' Nehru said, 'it is with no desire for isolation; on the contrary, we are perfectly willing to surrender part of that independence in common with other countries to real international order.'[32]

Time and again Nehru insisted that the states should maintain a reasonable balance between nationalism and internationalism. Every state should strive for an adjustment of her national interests with those of the other states in order to promote international harmony and cooperation. He probably visualized the emergence of a world federation in which India was to become an active member after independence. But it must be, according to Nehru, a world republic and not an empire for exploitation.[33]

When the Constitution of India was framed, Nehru was keenly interested in incorporating in it some basic guidelines for the country's foreign policy. This was provided under Part IV dealing with the Directive Principles of State Policy (in the enumeration and drafting of which he was specially interested). Apart from many other things, the Directive Principles enjoined that the country's foreign policy shall be directed with a view to promoting international peace and security. The state should strive for maintaining just and honourable relations between nations, by fostering respect for international law and treaty obligations, and by encouraging the settlement of international disputes by arbitration. In fact, the policy of non-alignment initiated by Nehru after independence

---

[31] Jawaharlal Nehru, 'Whither India,' in *Recent Essays and Writings* (Allahabad: Kitabistan, 1934), pp. 23-24.

[32] Jawaharlal Nehru, *An Autobiography*, op cit , p. 419.

[33] Willard Range, *Jawaharlal Nehru's World View—A Theory of International Relations*, op. cit , p. 54.

was mainly aimed at the attainment of the same objective. It is a great tribute to him that 'he insisted that India should be non-aligned in the insane struggle for power which has preoccupied the United States and the Soviet Union at the expense of the welfare of mankind.'[34]

Nehru had a deep sense of cosmopolitanism. He believed that his policy of democratic collectivism would ultimately lead to political and economic internationalism and India would inevitably play a leading role in international affairs. His optimism sounded well during his lifetime, although his hopes were belied by the events that followed.

Scientific Humanism

Nehru had a deep sense of respect for India's heritage. He was visibly moved by its past glory and present predicament. He passionately desired that the Indian people liberate themselves from the shackles of the past. At the same time, he urged them to recondition their mind, equipping themselves with the problems of the present and a perspective on the future. This, according to him, was possible only when the people tried to imbibe the highest ideals of the present age—humanism and scientific spirit. Despite an apparent conflict between the two, there was 'a growing synthesis between humanism and scientific spirit, resulting in a kind of scientific humanism.'[35] What Nehru wrote in his *Discovery of India* probably revealed much of his mind. Here he stated: 'The modern mind, that is to say the better type of the modern mind, is practical and pragmatic, ethical and social, altruistic and humanitarian. It is governed by a practical idealism for social betterment . . . . Humanity is its god and social service its religion.'[36]

Nehru was a multi-faceted personality. As a political leader, he did create in the Indian mind an awareness of the movements and the significance of events in the outside world. As an intellectual he could think far ahead of his surroundings, and his ideas did influence the progressive forces in and outside the country. As a humanist he championed the cause of humanity and devoted himself to the ideas of social progress. More than most of his contemporaries, Nehru had a clear vision of modern India emerging as an integral part of a free world community. He aspired to build a political order based upon the universal values of freedom and social justice.

[34] Bertrand Russell, 'The Legacy of Nehru,' *Illustrated Weekly of India* (Bombay, 27 May 1984), p. 44.

[35] Jawaharlal Nehru, *The Discovery of India. op. cit* , p. 681.

[36] *Ibid.*, p. 680.

16

DENNIS DALTON

The Ideology of Sarvodaya: Concepts of Politics and Power in Indian Political Thought

> If political theory is affected, let political theorists worry;
> if theories of politics tumble, political life will go on as
> before. I believe this to be a mistaken and shortsighted
> view . . . . What the political philosopher believes and
> teaches today will in some measure mould what politicians
> believe and do tomorrow.[1]

The purpose of this essay is to examine how most of modern India's major political theorists conceived of politics and power. The analysis will seek to demonstrate the conceptual consensus that exists among them in their interpretations not only of these two ideas, but of the conceptual clusters that they represent. These clusters, it will be argued, form the basis of modern India's ideological tradition, a cohesive school of thought that was initially defined by Swami Vivekananda, and in this century came to include a rich variety of theorists.[2]

Why a given civilization manages to produce and clarify an ideological tradition is uncertain, but when and where this does occur seems to be identified with two phenomena. First, in a social sense, the traditions emerge as responses to social crises which theorists perceive as fundamental challenges to established sets of values. Second, in an intellectual sense, the traditions have been clearly marked by the logical manner in

---

[1] W.H. Morris-Jones, *Politics Mainly Indian* (Bombay. Orient Longman, 1978), p. 9.

[2] The terms 'ideological tradition' and 'school of thought' in this context are used to suggest a number of political and social thinkers from India in the last one hundred years. These men may appear quite dissimilar in terms of their styles of thought, but they exhibit a clear consensus in their common commitment to ideas about human nature and the good society, the nature of authority and the relationship of the individual to the state, the values of freedom and equality, emphasis on consensus rather than conflict, cooperation rather than competition as social ideals, and on a method of change that relies on moral example and suasion rather than violent revolution or legislative reform. The concepts of politics and power are used here to focus the analysis on their agreement. These theorists include Swami Vivekananda, Aurobindo Ghose, Rabindranath Tagore, M.K. Gandhi, Vinoba Bhave and Jayaprakash Narayan among those examined in this article; but also included in the school are M.N. Roy and Deendayal Upadhyaya. For an analysis of the last two, see the author's 'Gandhi and Roy: The Interaction of Ideologies in India,' in S.N. Ray, ed., *Gandhi, India and the World* (Melbourne: The Hawthorn Press, 1970). pp 156–70 and 'Unity in Diversity,' Memorial Lecture in Upadhyaya Memorial Lecture Series. September 1980 (forthcoming)

which they form constellations or clusters of ideas, commonly centring on the key concepts of politics and power. The example of India's ideological tradition fits this pattern: it emerged in response to the crisis of values introduced by British imperialism in the nineteenth century and it soon formed into a cohesive cluster of ideas.

Traditions of political thought have conceptualized politics and power in at least three distinct ways. First, there was the theory, best set forth by classical Greek thought, of politics as an all embracing activity. The political community, Aristotle announced in the opening chapters of *The Politics*, is 'the most sovereign and inclusive association,' 'the final and perfect association,' in that it represents the natural, teleological fulfilment of all other communities, and the individual may therefore achieve his highest moral attainment, the realization of law and justice, only within the political order, for 'man is by nature an animal intended to live in a *polis*.'[3] This classical view of politics was revived in modern Europe by Rousseau and Hegel, and it remains the dominant stream of Western political theory today, primarily found in the ideology of nationalism. The classical conception of power was allied to its view of politics. For Plato, power must be employed in an enlightened way, by leaders with philosophical insight, but when it is employed wisely there are no limits on its use.[4] For the formation of the ideal *polis*, then, the sovereignty and broad scope of politics is matched by a sweeping justification of power. In his resurrection of Plato, Rousseau argued that the legislator should apply power in a majestic manner to inaugurate that all inclusive political order, the civil state.[5]

The second theory of politics and power has some antecedents in earlier Western traditions, but it is chiefly a modern European development that finds its best expression in the thought of John Locke and John Stuart Mill. This conceptualization sees society, not the state, as primary, and stresses the sanctity of the private rather than the political sphere of human conduct. This is the 'liberal tradition' of political philosophy that believes in 'the minimal character of the political order'.[6] It seeks to place 'absolute' or 'inviolable' limits on the political authority of the state and its sphere of legitimate action.[7] The corresponding view of power is that if

---

[3] *The Politics of Aristotle*, translated by Ernest Barker (London: Oxford University Press, 1958), pp. 1, 4–5.

[4] *The Republic of Plato*, translated by F.M. Cornford (London: Oxford University Press, 1958). The creation of the Republic, which is 'difficult but not impossible' (p. 208), can occur only when there will be 'power in the hands of men who are rich, not in gold, but in . . . a good and wise life' (p. 235). These are the Guardians who will have complete command of political power.

[5] Rousseau, *Political Writings*, translated and edited by F. Watkins (London: Nelson Philosophical Texts, 1953), *Social Contract*, Book 1, Ch. 8, pp. 19–20.

[6] Sheldon Wolin, *Politics and Vision* (London: George Allen and Unwin, 1961), p. 308.

[7] Isaiah Berlin, *Four Essays on Liberty* (London: Oxford University Press, 1969), pp. 165–66.

it invades the private, personal realm in the name of politics, then both politics and power will be corrupted: 'politics is a necessary and important part of human life but it is not the whole of it and it becomes diseased if it aspires to more than its share.'[8]

The third conception of politics and power is a logical extension of the second and a direct refutation of the first. This is the anarchist perception, systematized first by William Godwin and then developed by a wide variety of thinkers in Europe, Russia, and America in the nineteenth century. It reasoned from Locke's premises about the primacy of society and the need for placing limitations on the power of the state that the best community would be purged of the excesses of political authority. However, anarchism went beyond Locke and liberalism in its vision of a social order without government, and in its attack on the law. Henry Thoreau wrote:

> I heartily accept the motto—'That government is best which governs least'; and I should like to see it acted up to more rapidly and systematically. Carried out, it finally amounts to this, which also I believe—'That government is best which governs not at all'; and when men are prepared for it, that will be the kind of government which they will have. Government is at best but an expedient; but most governments are usually, and all governments are sometimes, inexpedient .... Law never made men a whit more just; and by means of their respect for it, even the well-disposed are daily made the agents of injustice.[9]

For Thoreau, as for all anarchists, politics and power are everywhere suspect not merely because they may tend to 'become diseased,' rather, they are themselves the source of the worst social disease, authoritarianism, and so they threaten society, like a contagious virus.

Strong parallels exist between the Western anarchist and modern Indian conceptions of politics and power. These similarities begin with Vivekananda who, more than any other nineteenth century Indian theorist, shaped and inspired his country's ideological tradition. In each area of thought that he touched, Vivekananda placed his indelible stamp, but nowhere more dominantly than in his teaching about the relation of nationalism to politics and power. In 1897, when he returned to India from four years in America and England, he discovered that 'the Nation had already accepted him as its Guru,'[10] and he eagerly embraced the role. He began by making a series of conceptual distinctions that starkly

---

[8] W.H. Morris-Jones, *op. cit.*, p. 26. See also pp. 25, 27–44.

[9] Henry David Thoreau, 'Civil Disobedience' in *Walden and Civil Disobedience* (N.Y.: Norton and Norton, 1966), pp. 224–25.

[10] *The Life of Swami Vivekananda* by His Eastern and Western Disciples (Calcutta: Advaita Ashrama, 1960), p. 452.

separated the cultures of India and England. 'The backbone, the foundation, and the bedrock' of India's 'national life,' he declared, was its spiritual genius. 'Let others talk of politics, of the glory of acquisition' or of 'the power and spread of commercialism'; these cannot inspire India. Look at 'the Western and other nations, which are now almost borne down, half-killed, and degraded by political ambitions' and the futility of that existence will be clear.[11] Anyone who knows India must understand that 'politics, power, and even intellect form a secondary consideration here. Religion, therefore, is the one consideration in India.'[12]

Vivekananda's indispensable role in the conceptualization of politics and power in modern India was to establish, with extraordinary precision, the central assumptions and lines of argument. Just as later ideologists, from Gandhi to J.P. Narayan, would attack Western political institutions and practices, so Vivekananda, decades before them, characterized 'parliaments' as 'jokes'[13] and 'party politics' as degenerate 'fanaticism and sectarianism'.[14] Preoccupation with political power was part of a distinctly Western 'vanity,' a reflection of the 'material tyranny' which tyrannized over both colonized and colonizer, a terrible evil, for 'by this power they can deluge the whole earth with blood.'[15]

One of the key premises in the Indian conceptualization of politics and power lay in its attitude towards law, especially in the relationship of law to individual morality and social change. Here, again, Vivekananda's voice was early and decisive. 'The basis of all systems, social or political,' he argued, 'rests upon the goodness of men. No nation is great or good because Parliament enacts this or that, but because its men are great and good.' The aim is to promote a sound body of individual ethics, and this must not be a political task, for 'men cannot be made virtuous by an Act of Parliament. ... And that is why religion is of deeper importance than politics, since it goes to the root, and deals with the essential of conduct.'[16] Too often, the state 'tries to compel all men through rigid laws and threats of punishment to follow that path with unconditional obedience' but this is disastrous for it means that 'the destiny of mankind becomes no better than that of a machine'.[17] The political history of India records 'a thousand years of crushing tyranny of castes and kings and foreigners,'[18] but the spiritual tradition of Hinduism calls for resistance to this legalized oppression. 'The very word Sannyasin means the divine outlaw'[19] and

[11] Swami Vivekananda, *Complete Works*, Vol. 3 (Calcutta: Advaita Ashrama, 1960), p. 148.
[12] *Ibid.*, p. 204.
[13] *Ibid.*, p. 158.
[14] *Ibid.*, Vol. 6, p. 8.
[15] *Ibid.*, Vol. 3, p. 158.
[16] *Ibid.*, Vol. 5, p. 200.
[17] *Ibid.*, Vol. 4, p. 435.
[18] *Ibid.*, Vol. 3, p. 244.
[19] *Ibid.*, Vol. 5, p. 193.

since 'it is freedom alone that is desirable. . . . It is not law that we want but ability to break law. We want to be outlaws. If you are bound by laws, you will be a lump of clay.'[20] Vivekananda concludes, therefore, that 'our aim should be to allow the individual to move towards this freedom. More of goodness, less of artificial laws'[21]

If the threat of India's contamination by political power came from the West, then the antidote is found in her own tradition, and especially in the idea of spiritual power. The Western notion of power was corrupted by an obsession with its 'material,' 'external' forms, while the Indian theory of power understood the superiority of its spiritual, 'internal' aspects.[22] Vivekananda's extensive discussions of the Indian concept of spiritual power clearly anticipate Gandhi's development of the idea of 'soul-force'. Like Gandhi, Vivekananda found this approach to power a unique, special component of the Indian genius, far superior in potential to what Gandhi called the Western idea of 'brute force'.[23] 'What power is there in the hand or the sword?' Vivekananda asked. 'The power is all in the spirit.'[24]

> Political greatness or military power is never the mission of our race; it never was, and mark my words, it never will be. But there has been the other mission given to us, which is to conserve, to preserve, to accumulate, as it were, into a dynamo, all the spiritual energy of the race, and that concentrated energy is to pour forth in a deluge on the world.[25]

Finally, Vivekananda signalled a crucial and prophetic departure from his classical tradition, by arguing that this spiritual power inhered in the masses. 'All knowledge is in every soul' regardless of caste or class, 'the same power is in every man.' This means, first, that Hinduism really promotes a 'wonderful state of equality'[26] but equally important for the future of the country, that 'the only hope of India is from the masses. The upper classes are physically and morally dead.'[27] To his disciples he repeatedly urged, 'You must have a hold on the masses,' 'We must reach the masses.'[28] If only the people could unite, that would mean 'infinite power. . . . Therefore, to make a great future India, the whole secret lies

[20] *Ibid.*, p. 289.
[21] *Ibid.*, Vol. 6, p. 100.
[22] *Ibid.*, Vol. 2, p. 65.
[23] M.K. Gandhi, *Collected Works*, Vol. 10 (Delhi: Publications Division, Government of India, 1963), pp. 42–47.
[24] Vivekananda, *Works*, Vol. 2, p. 21.
[25] *Ibid.*, Vol. 3, pp. 108–9.
[26] *Ibid.*, Vol. 1, p. 426.
[27] *Ibid.*, Vol. 5, p. 105.
[28] *Ibid.*, pp. 36, 114.

in organization, accumulation of power, co-ordination of wills. . . . That is the secret of power in India.'[29] Emphatically, it was a power that could be summoned forth not from the imposition of alien forms of government and law but only from the cultivation of India's own inspired cultural and religious tradition.

In one sense, Vivekananda's ideas powerfully influenced not only the political theory but also the political practice of twentieth century India, if one considers the application of his thought to the Indian nationalist movement for independence. His aggressive nationalism, which attacked Western culture as inferior and emphasized the need for establishing a mass base of action, with corresponding stress on social equality and reforms, all inspired the independence movement. Yet, in another sense, his conceptualization of politics and power suggested a marked divergence between main currents of Indian political theory and the practice of Indian politics after 1947. The divergence occurs between a theory that is essentially anarchist in orientation and a practice that after independence sought to integrate the nation under a centralized system of government. It is rather extraordinary that throughout this century India has produced a rich body of political theory, yet not a single major theorist of centralized authority. All of India's leading political thinkers have followed Vivekananda's conceptualization of politics and power. The first to accept him was also the most systematic political philosopher of this century—Sri Aurobindo Ghose.[30]

Among Aurobindo's most influential tracts was *The Spirit and Form of Indian Polity*.[31] The ideas on politics and power set forth here follow closely those of Vivekananda. 'The master idea that has governed the life, culture, social ideals of the Indian people has been the seeking of man for his true spiritual self and the use of life.' In this quest, politics cannot perform a significant role, for it inevitably belongs to the 'imperfect,' 'grosser' area of human conduct, and 'the effort at governing political action by ethics is usually a little more than a pretence.'[32] Throughout its political history, Indian polities have approached spiritual realization in only a very limited sense, but even at its worst

> Indian polity never arrived at that unwholesome substitution of the mechanical for the natural order of the life of the people which has been the disease of European civilisation now culminating in the monstrous artificial organisation of the bureaucratic and industrial State.[33]

[29] *Ibid.*, Vol. 3, p. 299.

[30] Sri Aurobindo has been rightly called 'the real intellectual heir of Vivekananda'. In Romain Rolland, *Prophets of the New India*, translated by E.F. Malcolm-Smith (London: Cassell and Co., 1930), p. 499.

[31] Sri Aurobindo, *The Spirit and Form of Indian Polity* (Pondicherry: Sri Aurobindo Ashram, 1966).

[32] *Ibid.*, pp. 20–21.   [33] *Ibid.*, p. 28.

This kind of state comes at an 'advanced stage of corruption of the Dharma marked by the necessity of the appearance of the legislator and the formal government of the whole of life by external or written law and code and rule.'[34] The ideal society, dictated by the spirit of Indian polity, is where

> there is no need of any political government or State or artificial construction of society, because all then live freely according to the truth of their enlightened self and God-inhabited being and therefore spontaneously according to the inner divine Dharma.[35]

A much fuller statement of these ideas is given in Aurobindo's two major works of political philosophy, *The Human Cycle* and *The Ideal of Human Unity*. In the latter book, he vigorously attacks the idea and reality of the modern state. 'The State principle leads necessarily to uniformity, regulation, mechanisation; its inevitable end is socialism.'[36] Not only the socialist state, though, has deprived individuals of their freedom. The democratic state has failed, too, and 'we see today the democratic system of government march steadily towards such an organised annihilation of individual liberty as could not have been dreamed of in the old aristocratic and monarchical systems.'[37] The central problem lies in the very principle of the state, which in its fascist, socialist, or democratic forms promotes not merely 'tyranny of the majority,' but worse, 'tyranny of the whole, of the self-hypnotised mass over its constituent groups and units,'[38] usually orchestrated by a small elite of demagogic politicians. Aurobindo saw this in 'Fascist Italy and Soviet Russia' alike,[39] and in those states (like Britain and America) who claim to enjoy representative government 'legislators and administrators do not really represent their electors. The Power they represent is another, a formless and bodiless entity, which has taken the place of monarch and aristocracy, that impersonal group-being . . . the huge mechanism of the modern State.'[40]

In successive chapters entitled 'The Drive Towards Economic Centralisation' and 'The Drive Towards Legislative and Social Centralisation and Uniformity,' Aurobindo condemns in the 'history of the growth of the State . . . the development of a central authority and of a growing uniformity in administration, legislation, social and economic life and

---

[34] *Ibid.*, p. 31.

[35] *Ibid.*, p. 30.

[36] Sri Aurobindo, *The Ideal of Human Unity* in *The Human Cycle, The Ideal of Human Unity (and) War and Self-Determination* (Pondicherry: Sri Aurobindo Ashram, 1962), p. 673.

[37] *Ibid.*, p. 677.

[38] *Ibid.*, p. 678.

[39] *Ibid.*

[40] *Ibid.*, p. 679.

culture.'[41] This is wrong because no centralized political authority can represent or promote the realization of individual interests. Diversity, not uniformity and over-centralization, is the 'law of life'; while order is necessary, it must be understood that 'the truest order is that which is founded on the greatest possible liberty.'[42] A society that achieves this ideal will be 'perfectly spiritualised . . . as is dreamed of by the spiritual anarchist' in which 'each man will be not a law to himself, but *the* law, the divine Law. . . . His life will be led by the law of his own divine nature.'[43] This vision, from the ideal of an anarchist society free of state authority to the promise of spiritual freedom that transcends the artificial regulation of politics, power and law, comes from Vivekananda.

At the same time that Aurobindo was writing, in the first quarter of this century, two other intellectual giants emerged on the national scene—Rabindranath Tagore and Mohandas Gandhi. As in the case of Vivekananda and Aurobindo, their contribution to Indian life ranged far beyond their theories of politics and power, yet their controversy over these two ideas deserves to be regarded as an unusually rich component of India's ideological tradition. Their debate was perhaps so fruitful because they shared so many basic attitudes on politics and power.

Before Gandhi had formulated his own political ideology, Tagore published in 1904 an important essay entitled 'Society and State'. Tagore emulates Vivekananda's formulation, first in the sharp demarcation drawn between society and the state, and, second, by associating the former with Indian civilization, and the latter with the British.

The vital strength in different civilizations is variously embodied. The heart of a country lies wherever the people's welfare is centred. A blow aimed at that point is fatal for the whole country. In England the overthrow of the State might mean peril for the nation—that is why politics there is such a serious affair. In our country there would be danger only when the social body, *samaj*, becomes crippled. . . . England relies on the State for everything, from the relief of the destitute to the religious education of the public; whereas our country depends on the people's sense of duty. Therefore, England has to exist by keeping the State alive while we exist by preserving our social consciousness . . . . The government in our country has no relationship with our society and no place in the social organization, so that whatever we may seek from it must be bought at the expense of a certain freedom.[44]

[41] *Ibid.*, p. 615.
[42] *Ibid.*, p. 685.
[43] Sri Aurobindo, *The Human Cycle, ibid.*, p. 347.
[44] Rabindranath Tagore, 'Society and State,' in *Towards Universal Man* (London: Asia Publishing House, 1961), pp. 51–52.

Five years later, in *Hind Swaraj* (1909), Gandhi accepted the basic distinctions made between society and state, and India and the West, set forth by Vivekananda and Tagore. Indeed, if anything, he drew the dichotomies between the spiritual, moral fabric of Indian society, and the violent, politically corrupt nature of the European state even more dramatically than any of his predecessors. He reserved his harshest language for the English parliamentary system,[45] and described all Western political power as 'brute force'.[46] Ancient Indian society was idealized, where 'kings and swords were inferior to the sword of ethics,' and people enjoyed an organic social existence in small villages independently of the abuses of political institutions.[47]

As Gandhi became increasingly involved in politics, he maintained his view of its corrupt nature in the West, and seemed often ambivalent about whether it might be practised rightly in India. At best it was an impure, threatening activity: 'If I seem to take part in politics, it is only because politics encircle us today like the coil of a snake from which one cannot get out, no matter how much one tries. I wish therefore to wrestle with the snake.'[48]

Later, Gandhi would conclude his autobiography (1928) with his famous defence that he had been drawn into politics irresistibly in his pursuit of truth,[49] but the overriding tone in Gandhi's discussions of politics is of its subordinate, inferior status. Thus, shortly after his most successful political campaign, he could write:

> My work of social reform was in no way less or s .bordinate to political work. The fact is, when I saw that to a certain extent my social work would be impossible without the help of political work, I took to the latter and only to the extent that it helped the former. I must, therefore, confess that work of social reform or self-purification of this nature is a hundred times dearer to me than what is called purely political work.[50]

For both Gandhi and Tagore, *swaraj* meant more than mere political independence; it meant India's spiritual liberation through a fundamental change in each individual's moral perception. This could hardly be achieved through legislative reforms. Tagore's comment on this reflects as well his generally poor view of the potential force of law:

[45] M.K. Gandhi, *op. cit.*, p. 16.

[46] *Ibid.* Compare Gandhi's use of 'brute force' in Ch. 16, pp. 42–47 with his conceptualization of 'soul-force or truth force' in Ch. 17, pp. 47–53, and his identification of 'brute force' as a weapon of the extremists (p. 50). It is clear that the extremists have been infected by British methods.

[47] *Ibid.*, pp. 37–38.

[48] M.K. Gandhi, 'Neither a Saint nor a Politician,' in *Works*, Vol. 17, p. 406.

[49] *Ibid.*, Vol. 39, p. 401.

[50] *Ibid.*, Vol. 47, p. 246.

Our woes, we fondly imagine, can be ended by legislation and we can
become full-fledged human beings when we obtain seats in the legislature. But a nation's progress is not achieved mechanically. It cannot
be achieved until we are prepared to pay the price.[51]

Politics and law were inevitably 'mechanical,' 'external' and 'artificial,'
and usually corrupt and degraded. The 'price' for both Tagore and
Gandhi must be paid in self-sacrifice, for that alone could produce the
internal self-purification required for *swaraj*.

In all these respects, Tagore and Gandhi were in profound agreement.
Their differences came over the issue of power. Gandhi believed that
'power is of two kinds,'[52]—one based on physical force, the other rooted
in *satya* and *ahimsa*, 'truth-force'. Tagore, conversely, argued in his
classic letter to Gandhi of 12 April 1919, at the outset of the Mahatma's
first national campaign in India: 'Power in all its forms is irrational, it is
like the horse that drags the carriage blind-folded . . . . The danger
inherent in all force grows stronger when it is likely to gain success, for
then it becomes temptation.'[53] At the end of the letter, Tagore grew more
conciliatory by acknowledging Gandhi's struggle against an 'overwhelming
material power' that 'scoffs at the power of the spirit,' and the rightness of
his attempt to 'purge [India's] present-day politics of its feebleness'.[54] Yet,
Tagore's suspicion of politics and power increased as Gandhi pursued his
aim of independence, and at the height of Gandhi's non-cooperation
campaign of 1921, Tagore launched a salvo entitled 'The Call of Truth'
which is, perhaps, unparalleled in Indian political literature for its
eloquence. In it, Tagore concedes that 'to make the country our own by
means of our creative power is indeed a great call.'[55] But the use of this
power must be purely moral and not political, for politics and truth will
not mix. Gandhi's supreme difficulty in responding to this charge was that
he had himself set truth as his highest goal, and had acknowledged that
the practice of politics meant 'wrestling with the snake,' that power can be
deadly poisonous, and even the best of men may be bitten. He could only
seek to justify his leadership with the assertion that 'my politics are not
corrupt, they are inextricably bound up with truth.'[56] It is Tagore who
gets the better of this debate; for Gandhi is arguing with not only
Rabindranath, but against a tradition, and ultimately with a part of
himself.

[51] R. Tagore, *op. cit.*, p. 172.

[52] M.K. Gandhi, *Works*, Vol. 25, p. 563.

[53] R. Tagore in R.K. Prabhu and R. Kelkar, eds., *Truth Called Them Differently*
(Ahmedabad: Navajivan Publishing House, 1961), p. 14.

[54] *Ibid.*, p. 16.

[55] Tagore, *Towards Universal Man*, p. 260.

[56] Gandhi, as quoted in D.G. Tendulkar, *Mahatma*, Vol. 3 (Delhi: Government of India,
Publications Division, 1961), p. 113.

However, perhaps Gandhi's best response to Tagore came not within the context of this debate but, rather, in another aspect of his conceptualization of politics and power. This came with his development of a theory of decentralization, which his ideological tradition lacked before him. The theory was based, in part, on one main theme in the tradition, and idea that had been set forth first by Vivekananda, and then expanded by Aurobindo and Tagore. This was the concept of 'unity in diversity,' which Tagore called 'the inmost creed of India'.[57] Aurobindo had explained that human communities should be formed on 'one essential principle of nature—diversity in unity'[58] and we must seek to realize the free play of interests and ideas that necessarily permeate all human relationships. Vivekananda and Aurobindo insisted that this free exchange need not give way to conflict and competition, as so often happened in the West, but could be grounded in an enlightened sense of spiritual unity. For if individuals are allowed the freedom to express and pursue their interests, they will gradually discover their identity of interests, as part of a spiritual oneness, that transcends all sense of separateness.[59]

Gandhi believed that he had discovered the essence of this principle early in his career, in South Africa, when he succeeded in resolving a legal dispute by discovering a common interest. This, he said, 'taught me to appreciate the beauty of compromise. I saw in later life that this spirit was an essential part of Satyagraha.'[60] On the basis of this insight, he constructed a theory of human nature which stressed people's capacities for compromise and mutual aid if these are allowed to develop freely.

In agreement with others in his ideological tradition, as well as with Western anarchists like Kropotkin and Tolstoy, Gandhi argued that the state represented the greatest obstacle to our realization of both individual freedom and social harmony. 'The State represents violence in a concentrated form. The individual has a soul, but as the State is a soulless machine, it can never be weaned from violence to which it owes its very existence.'[61] In the ideal society, 'there is no political power because there is no State,' but in striving towards that ideal we may decrease the scope of violence and political power and increase the sphere of individual freedom and voluntary action by decentralizing the state's authority. Gandhi says that he views 'with the greatest fear' the increasing centralization of power in most states because this 'does the greatest harm to mankind by destroying individuality which lies at the root of all progress.'[62] Therefore, 'if India is to evolve along non-violent lines, it will have to decentralize,'

[57] Tagore, *Towards Universal Man*, p. 65.
[58] Aurobindo, *Ideal of Human Unity, op. cit.*, p. 560.
[59] Vivekananda, *Works*, Vol. 2, p. 153; Vol. 5, pp. 278, 536.
[60] Gandhi, *Works*, Vol. 39, p. 122.
[61] *Ibid.*, Vol. 59, p. 318.
[62] *Ibid.*, p. 319.

because 'centralization as a system is inconsistent with a non-violent structure of society.'[63] Gandhi does not delineate the precise functions that would be retained by the central government; the important point is that Gandhi advocated for independent India 'the maximum possible decentralization of the political and economic power and resources of the state . . .'[64] Equally important, this position places Gandhi squarely in line with the thought of Vivekananda, Aurobindo, and Tagore, who share with him suspicion of state authority and a firm desire for its decentralization based on thier common attitudes towards politics and power.

So far in this analysis, the examination of modern India's ideological tradition has been drawn from examples in the pre-independence period. From one perspective, the strong antipathy which Vivekananda, Aurobindo, Tagore, and Gandhi demonstrate towards state authority might be attributed to their historical situation, that their thought understandably developed in opposition to the British raj and the oppressive nature of that imperial authority. It is obvious from their 'East vs. West' theory that this was the case. However, as we move now to theorists of independent India and observe how they continue this ideological tradition, it can be seen that the presence of the British is not a necessary condition for the survival of this particular line of thought. Indeed, the tradition not only survives, it flourishes in independent India, enjoying the support of the country's foremost theorists since 1947. The enduring spirit and content of this tradition in the last three decades may be attributed, first, to the strength of its development during the nationalist period, second, to the continuing presence of a centralized state authority, and third, to the high quality and independent spirit of those theorists who have perpetuated it.

As a theorist and activist during the 1940s, 1950s and 1960s, Vinoba Bhave ably articulated attitudes towards politics and power that were representative of his ideological tradition. Vinoba was the first to use the term 'total revolution,' in the sense of a movement of change that must transform 'all aspects of life'.[65] The goal was nothing less than 'to mould a new man . . . to change human life and create a new world.' For Vinoba, the departure of the British had not brought Indian society any closer to the realization of *sarvodaya*, and the main obstacle remained the same: centralized government. 'Sarvodaya does not mean good government or majority rule, it means freedom from government, it means decentralisation of power.'[66] Gandhi had correctly defined the value of *swaraj* as

[63] M.K. Gandhi, *Harijan*, 18 January 1942, p. 5.
[64] J. Bandyopadhyaya, *Social and Political Thought of Gandhi* (Bombay: Allied Publishers, 1969), p. 89.
[65] Vinoba Bhave, *Revolutionary Sarvodaya* (Bombay: Bharatiya Vidya Bhavan, 1964), p. 1.
[66] Vinoba Bhave, *Democratic Values* (Kashi: Sarva Seva Sangh Prakashan, 1962), p. 3.

necessary for *sarvodaya*. *Swaraj* meant 'ruling your own self,' which implies 'not to allow any outside power in the world to exercise control over oneself' and 'not to exercise power over any other. These two things together make *swaraj*—no submission and no exploitation.' Government, with all its supposed services and benefits, inevitably violates this value of *swaraj* because it demands obedience. 'That is why my voice is raised in opposition to good government . . . . People know very well that bad government should not be allowed, and everywhere they protest against it. But what seems to me to be wrong is that we should allow ourselves to be governed at all, even by a good government.'[67]

Vinoba distinguishes three theories of government to better clarify his own. The first desires the eventual, 'withering away' of the state, but sanctions the present use of maximum state power in order to achieve its goal. 'Those who accept this theory are totalitarians in the first stage and anarchists in the final stage.' The second theory argues that government has always existed and must remain. The best course is to organize it so that everyone will receive some benefit. The third, Vinoba's theory, shares with the first the ultimate goal of a 'stateless society,' but refuses to accept its means of attaining it. 'On the contrary, we propose to proceed by decentralising administration and authority.' It may take a while to 'advance from good government to freedom from government,' but it is urgently necessary to begin this movement to the 'final stage' where 'there would be no coercion but a purely moral authority.'[68] Vinoba argues further that those who advocate the second theory (e.g., those on the Indian Planning Commission) rely heavily on centralization of power. However, this leads the Indian people in the wrong direction for 'centralised arrangements will never bring us nearer to a stateless society,' they only foster an addiction to politics and power. The immediate aim of the *sarvodaya* movement, therefore, is that 'production, distribution, defence, education—everything should be localised. The centre should have the least possible authority. We shall thus achieve decentralisation through regional self-sufficiency . . . . We must therefore start at once to introduce decentralisation, and this will be the basis of all our planning.'[69]

At the centre of Vinoba's conceptualization of politics and power lies his basic distinction between '*raj-niti*, the politics of power and *lok-niti*, the ethics of democracy.'[70] Vinoba believes that 'the world is at present in the clutches of centralised [state] power,'[71] and people must learn that there is another source of change at their disposal, that 'non-violence is a great power,' the 'power of the Self,'[72] and this can be found through

[67] *Ibid.*, pp. 12–13.   [68] *Ibid.*, p. 29.

[69] *Ibid.*, p. 30.

[70] *Ibid.*, p. xi.

[71] *Ibid.*, p. 117.

[72] Vinoba Bhave, *Revolutionary Sarvodaya*, pp. 49–50.

pursuit of *lok-niti*, which strives to use 'the potential powers of the citizen'.[73] *Raj-niti* is enamoured of the wrong kind of power and, in its lust for acquisition of it, there ensues 'constant struggle' among parties and politicians, elections marked by a 'ceaseless rivalry for power'. *Lok-niti* would abandon political parties and elections, arrive at decisions through consensus, and forge an identity of interests that would ensure continuing social harmony.[74] Vinoba calls the power of *lok-niti*—which, following Gandhi is necessarily non-violent—a 'third force,' distinguished from both violent coercion and 'the force of law'.[75] For Vinoba, as with others in his tradition, the impersonal force of law must be inferior to the personal influence of dedicated social workers who 'maintain the purity of their own personal lives,' and shape a *sarvodaya* society with a 'third force' that is legitimate not because it has legal sanction, but rather because it is 'uncontaminated by any lust for [political] power'.[76]

A striking aspect of Vinoba's ideal society is the emphasis which he places on consensus rather than conflict. He repeatedly states that people must transcend 'sects, castes, parties, groups or isms' and deplores the fact that India, at present, is 'fragmented by innumerable divisions of race, caste, colour, religion, and political ideologies. We need social integration if Swaraj is to survive.'[77] This spirit of integration and consensus cannot be imposed by law or state power; it is attainable through the kind of voluntary effort exemplified by *sarvodaya* workers who encourage a genuine transformation of values. 'Every individual has to learn to put the interests of the village before his own' and hence foster an organic conception of society so integrated that 'if every limb were to function smoothly, the whole body would function properly.'[78] The aims of *lok-niti* can never be to 'produce conflict' but always to achieve social harmony because 'cooperation is an eternal principle of life'.[79] This argument for an organic society and social consensus runs consistently through the Indian ideological tradition. It parallels directly positions taken in the West by anarchists, such as, Kropotkin and Tolstoy. But because it is essentially an anarchist conception, attacking state authority and championing natural, spontaneous forces of social harmony, it is directly opposed to the kind of political consensus advocated by apologists of a centralized state such as Rousseau and Hegel. Like the Western anarchists, the Indian theorists connect their idea of consensus with a

---

[73] Vinoba Bhave, *Democratic Values*, p. xi.

[74] *Ibid.*, pp. 86–88.

[75] *Ibid.*, pp. 212–13.

[76] *Ibid.*, p. 223.

[77] Suresh Ram, *Vinoba and His Mission* (Rajghat, Kashi: Akhil Bharat Sarva Seva Sangh, 1962), p. 208.

[78] Vinoba Bhave, *Revolutionary Sarvodaya*, p. 45.

[79] Vinoba Bhave, *Swaraj Sastra* (Rajghat, Varanasi: Sarva Seva Sangh Prakhashan, 1963), p. 63.

vision of small communities, free from coercive political institutions, precisely because people are inherently capable of organizing themselves without a strong government. It is not surprising, then, that Vinoba uses Aurobindo's term, 'spiritual anarchism' to identify his political philosophy.[80]

Because Jayaprakash Narayan articulates the essential values of modern India's ideological tradition with exceptional clarity and directness, and exposition of his theory may be used as a summation of that tradition, not only with respect to its concepts of politics and power but also of the entire cluster of ideas that it has developed. Jayaprakash (J.P.) begins, like all anarchists,[81] with a theory of human nature as benign: capacities for destructive behaviour obviously exist, but if motives of compassion and non-violence, creativity and cooperation, are cultivated and reinforced by society, then people can unquestionably realize the essential spirit of goodness that lies within them. With the proper example and education to encourage them, individuals will choose to follow 'good men' and 'noble efforts'.[82] This, in turn, will lead to the evolution of the kind of non-violent community that Gandhi first called *sarvodaya*.

Methods of change commonly used by political or military regimes cannot create a *sarvodaya* social order. The example of the Russian revolution and the Soviet state demonstrates the bankruptcy of violence, which only tends to 'ensure the victory of the party that is more skilled in its use,' establishing an 'iron grip on the people,' undermining all attempts at democracy and the attainment of social justice or equality.[83] Parliamentary democracies, on the other hand, are ineffective in their reliance on legislation. As the case of India's political system shows, legislation for the redistribution of land has failed because there has not occurred a corresponding change in moral values to enforce it. 'Law cannot come into effect without public opinion' to enforce it; 'legislation without conversion [first] is a dead letter.'[84] Echoing attitudes toward law and social change that hark back to Vivekananda, J.P. writes:

It is not institutions, not laws, not political systems, not constitutions which create good people. For that you require a widespread process

[80] Vinoba Bhave, quoted in Vishwanath Tandon, *The Social and Political Philosophy of Sarvodaya After Gandhiji* (Rajghat, Varanasi: Sarva Seva Sangh Prakashan, 1965), p. 124.

[81] James Joll, *The Anarchists* (London: Eyre and Spottiswoode, 1964). 'The fundamental idea that man is by nature good and that it is institutions that corrupt him remains the basis of all anarchist thought' (p. 30). Joll is one of the few analysts of anarchist thought who includes recognition and comment on Indian anarchism. See his brief mention of Gandhi, Vinoba, and J.P. (pp. 277–78).

[82] Jayaprakash Narayan, *A Picture of Sarvodaya Social Order* (Tanjore: Sarvodaya Prachuralaya, 1961), p. 6. J.P. says: 'Man is essentially good and not bad.'

[83] *Ibid.*, pp. 4–5.

[84] *Ibid.*, p. 9.

of education understood in the widest sense of the word. Education does not mean academic education; but the improving of human beings through service, love, examples, preaching, reasoning and argument.[85]

J.P. consolidates many of the ideas of his tradition in his most important work, *Reconstruction of Indian Polity*. This book has been given close scrutiny by commentators in and outside of India,[86] and the analysis of it here will be confined to the respects that it serves to clarify or enlarge India's ideological tradition. J.P., like all the others of his tradition, is concerned with reconstituting his past, deriving enduring truths from the lessons of 'ancient Indian polity'. This was, as noted above, precisely the task that Aurobindo undertook, and J.P. borrows extensively and explicitly from Aurobindo's work, praising 'that extraordinary, intuitive sweep of his vision [which] has laid bare the true nature of the foundations of Indian polity.'[87] On the basis of Aurobindo's work, J.P. contends that in ancient India the political order was founded on the system of the self-governing village community which lasted with remarkable 'sufficiency and solidity' until it was 'recently steamrollered out of existence by the ruthless and lifeless machinery of the British bureaucratic system.'[88] Classical India had discovered the key 'principle of an organically self-determining communal life,' and today it is only 'a question of an ancient country finding its lost soul again'.[89]

Gandhi had contended in *Hind Swaraj* that Britain had seduced India into selling its soul to the demonic spirit of modern civilization, which included the false charms of parliamentary government. J.P. extends this line of argument, observing that independent India institutionalized a form of government that lacks both traditional sources and theoretical support from any major Indian political theorist. J.P.'s condemnation of parliamentary democracy is as sweeping and categorical as any made by an anarchist, Eastern or Western. He draws from a variety of political commentators, European, American, and Indian, to indict the intrinsic defects of the parliamentary system. The electoral system pretends to represent the wishes of an informed public, but instead serves only to fragment the body politic, confusing voters who are cynically 'manipulated by powerful, centrally controlled parties, with the aid of high finance and

[85] *Ibid.*, p. 151.

[86] See, for example, W.H. Morris-Jones, 'The Unhappy Utopia—J.P. in Wonderland,' in *Politics Mainly Indian*, pp. 97–106. This critique of J.P.'s *Reconstruction* first appeared in *Economic Weekly*, 25 June 1960, and prompted an exchange between William Carpenter and W.H. Morris-Jones, published in *The Economic Weekly Annual*, 4 February 1961.

[87] Jayaprakash Narayan, *A Plea for Reconstruction of Indian Polity* (Rajghat, Kashi: Akhil Bharat Sarva Seva Sangh, 1959), p. 22.

[88] *Ibid.*, p. 22.

[89] *Ibid.*, p. 26.

diabolically clever methods and super media.' Consequently, only the 'forces and interests behind the parties and propaganda machines' are represented, while the masses are subjected to continuing exploitation, and the society becomes increasingly atomized. But, perhaps the most serious fault of parliamentary democracy lies in its 'inherent tendency toward centralism'. Just as Gandhi had believed that 'centralisation as a system is inconsistent with a non-violent structure of society,' so J.P. saw centralized authority as invariably fostering vast impersonal bureaucracies and huge interest groups that made 'organic integration' impossible. The main remedy for this is to scrap the parliamentary system, and replace it with a 'communitarian democracy' and decentralized political economy.[90]

In his conceptualization of this communitarian democracy, J.P. consistently recapitulates the central attitudes of his ideological tradition. He wants to avoid 'competitiveness' because it is necessarily exploitative, and achieve instead a 'cooperative and co-sharing,' 'integrated' social order in which there would be a true 'harmonization of interests'. Only a 'deliberate and bold process of devolution and decentralization,' shaping all aspects of social development, may attain this goal. It needs to be initiated by 'hundreds of thousands of voluntary workers' who understand that the basic task is one 'of moral regeneration to be brought about by example, service, sacrifice and love.'[91] Although J.P. is more specific about the structural organization of his decentralized system than any of his predecessors,[92] the ideology that underpins it goes straight back to Vivekananda

Among those ideas that link J.P. most conclusively with his ideological tradition are his preoccupations with the corrupting influence of political power and the compelling need for finding a path of pure moral action. He says, for example, that he soured on Russian communism for reasons that might have been felt by Gandhi, on the one hand, or M.N. Roy, on the other. For J.P., Marxism among the Soviets quickly degenerated into 'a struggle for power among the ruling class,' which assumed the familiar 'pattern by which a party comes to power with high and noble ideals,' and then eventually crashes into a state of 'demoralisation'.[93] In 1952–53, J.P. explained his departure from Marxism partly as a result of his 'shock' over the international experience of communism, and especially with the Soviet example. He denounced 'the totalitarian distortions of socialism in

[90] *Ibid.*, pp. 66–68.

[91] *Ibid.*, p. 107.

[92] J.P.'s ideas on the organization of his polity, often referred to as *panchayati raj*, are contained in the best collection of his writings, *Socialism, Sarvodaya and Democracy*, edited by Bimla Prasad (London: Asia Publishing House, 1964), especially the essay 'Swaraj for the People,' pp. 239–74.

[93] J.P. Narayan, *Towards Total Revolution*, Vol. 1 (Surrey: Richmond Publishing Co., 1978), p. 153.

Russia,' and blamed them on 'not only the heavy concentration of political but also of economic power.'[94] From his knowledge of world politics, he drew this lesson in November 1952: 'With the ghastly spectacle of the growth of totalitarianism with its leviathan state on a world scale we realised that decentralisation and devolution of economic power must be accepted as the essential tenet of democratic socialism.'[95]

As a national leader perpetually in opposition to the Congress government throughout the 1950s, J.P. remained primarily concerned with the abuse of political power in India. In February 1957, on the eve of the second general election, J.P. issued 'an appeal to the voters,' warning them that 'the most important issue this time is that of the absoluteness of Congress power.' He cited Lord Acton's dictum on power as 'one of the most profound political truths,' and declared that 'concentration of every form of power must be destroyed.'[96] Eighteen years later, a month before Indira Gandhi declared the emergency and imprisoned J.P., he was still citing Lord Acton, and still convinced that 'the present all-pervading corruption has its roots in politics and power.' The chief task before the Indian people was to discover a way 'to prevent power from being corrupted in the future.'[97]

J.P. never saw this task as impossible. He reiterated that the worst evils of power come only when it is centralized. 'The problem,' he insisted, is always with 'concentration of too much power in the hands of a small group of persons,' with 'more and more power concentrated in the hands of the executive, which in reality means one person, the Prime Minister.'[98] The first aim of the *sarvodaya* worker, therefore, must be to 'diffuse political and economic power and decentralise the politico-economic structure.'[99] In December 1974, during his leadership of the student movement in Bihar, he asserted that he did not advocate the disappearance of all political power but, rather, the placement of it where it belongs, in the hands of the people. Following Vinoba, J.P. distinguished between legitimate and illegitimate forms of power:

> What you see happening in Bihar is a struggle between 'chhatra shakti' (student power) and 'jan shakti' (people's power) on the one hand and 'rajya shakti' (state power) on the other. And the struggle is not for the capture of power . . . but for the purification of government and for fashioning instruments and conditions for taming and controlling power . . .[100]

[94] *Ibid.*, Vol. 2, pp. 218–19.
[95] *Ibid.*, p. 180.
[96] *Ibid.*, pp. 253, 255.
[97] *Ibid.*, Vol. 4, p. 127.
[98] *Ibid.*, Vol. 4, pp. 133, 135.
[99] *Ibid.*, Vol. 3, p. 79.
[100] *Ibid.*, Vol. 4, p. 110.

J.P.'s conceptualization of power defines with commendable lucidity the attitudes of his ideological tradition, a tradition that may surely be Utopian in spirit, but its theoretical premises are at least the most clear and consistent that India has produced in this century. Its central concerns are familiar to Western political theory; they deal with the crucial issue of finding a legitimate basis for the exercise of power. J.P. was not a systematic philosopher.

Fundamental criticisms have been made of J.P.'s thought by many of those familiar with his work, and these have been best expressed by W.H. Morris-Jones. A main concern running through Morris-Jones' critique is that there are elements in J.P.'s thought, such as his insistence on 'systematic mass participation' and 'identification of rulers and ruled,' that some political theorists have tended to 'prepare the way for totalitarianism'. In the case of Rousseau:

> Satisfied with nothing less than each man retaining his 'freedom' by taking full part in the laying down of laws he is to obey, he ends by asserting that some men will obtain their 'freedom' by being coerced; ordinary language and ordinary people both suffer when such violence is done to them.[101]

It is fair to ask if there is any explicit evidence in J.P.'s writings that he has either defined freedom in a manner similar to Rousseau, or shown himself insensitive to the dangers of totalitarianism. The answer must be 'no' on both counts. J.P. consistently defines freedom in the traditional, Indian sense as *swaraj*, and claims that it was his own quest for freedom in this sense that drove him away from Marxism.[102] Moreover, his writings are alive with warnings against totalitarian government, and in his last eloquent yet tragic writing, *Prison Diary*, he inveighs throughout against his main foe, a Prime Minister who destroyed democracy, substituting for it a 'totalitarian system'.[103] Here he argues for liberty in the fullest sense, and especially for freedom of the press.[104]

Yet Morris-Jones believes that there is an inescapable and intrinsic danger to freedom and liberal democracy in J.P.'s ideal of mass participation:

> Men want many things from governments and they may want to be governed in certain ways, but they do not want to do the governing. The dogmatic democrat who insists that they shall do so is bound to become a tyrant—or pave the way for one.[105]

---

[101] W.H. Morris-Jones, *Politics Mainly Indian*, p. 102.

[102] J.P. Narayan, *Picture of Sarvodaya Social Order*, p. 112.

[103] J.P. Narayan, *Prison Diary*, edited by A.B. Shah (Seattle: University of Washington Press, 1977), p. 1.

[104] *Ibid.*, pp. 105–6.   [105] W.H. Morris-Jones, *Politics Mainly Indian*, p. 103.

Then Morris-Jones returns to his theme of J.P.'s parallels with Rousseau by linking his critique of the ideas of freedom and mass participation in J.P.'s thought with his concept of consensus:

> Moreover, the stress on consensus seems to imply a peculiar view of the common good. It is thought of as something single and simple—discernible to men of insight and goodwill, attainable (as Rousseau again believed) through the silencing of particular or selfish interests.
>
> But is this really our experience? Is the position not rather that the common good is something towards which we can approximate only through a forthright expression of all relevant clashing interests and their reconciliation so far as is possible? The pretence that interests do not clash, that a common interest is somehow always present and only needs to be uncovered, is likely to yield a good that is far from common. And there is no community, however organic it may be, without different interests . . . . Consensus is a fair name for what could be an ugly reality.[106]

At the outset of this paper, it was suggested that when J.P. and other Indians of his ideological tradition are compared with Western political theory, they are allied not with the school of thought that links Plato and Rousseau, but rather with Western anarchists, and that the Indian ideological tradition itself constitutes a significant body of anarchist thought. The central differences between the Plato-Rousseau school and the anarchists hinge on the concepts of politics and power. Rousseau, following Plato, envisaged his political leaders or 'law-givers,' attaining an advanced stage of consciousness, and then ruling with 'sublime reason, which is beyond the understanding of the vulgar...in order to compel by divine authority those whom human prudence could not move.'[107] No anarchist, Eastern or Western, could ever justify such a conception of leadership. This is largely because for Plato and Rousseau the unique capacity of the state was to create and nurture a life of virtue. Outside the realm of politics, justice and morality could not exist, and the role of legitimate authority was sanctified. This is at the opposite pole from the anarchists' perception, for whom politics and power remained not only inherently suspect but also singularly incapable of producing the virtuous individual or society. If there is a 'politics' of *lok-niti*, it represents a kind that Plato and Rousseau would certainly regard as anaemic or impotent; they would be even less satisfied with the Indian view of the necessary limitations on law as a force in shaping human behaviour.

The emphasis which Plato and Rousseau place on the unique role of politics is decisive, and nowhere more than in their view of the individual.

---

[106] *Ibid.*, p. 105.
[107] Rousseau, *Political Writings*, pp. 44–45.

For Rousseau, each individual 'puts in common his person and all his powers under the supreme direction of the general will' and so each becomes 'an indivisible part of the whole'.[108] The 'civil state' is thus born, with 'natural liberty' replaced by 'civil liberty'. For all J.P.'s stress on mass participation and the organic community, there is no language anywhere in his writings or in any of the others in his tradition, that compares with Rousseau's description of the supremacy of the general will, the sovereignty of the civil state, or his contention that 'anything which breaks the unity of society is worthless'.[109] On the contrary, the writings of those in the Indian ideological tradition are replete with statements like Vivekananda's that 'any system which seeks to destroy individuality is in the long run disastrous'[110] or Gandhi's that 'no society can possibly be built on a denial of individual freedom'.[111] Within the context of this ideological tradition, then, there would seem to be no theoretical justification for the creation of the 'ugly reality' that Morris-Jones fears. That sort of sanction comes from other traditions of thought, alien neither to India nor to the West, which rationalize political dictatorship.

These are not the only critical concerns that W.H. Morris-Jones has expressed about J.P.'s thought and those theorists related to it. He levelled a major criticism at this whole line of thought first in an essay called 'India's Political Idioms,' where the idiom or language in India of 'saintly politics' was described and examined:

... saintly politics is important as a language of comment rather than of description or practical behaviour . . . . Its influence is rather on the standards habitually used by the people at large for judging the performance of politicians. In men's minds there is an ideal of disinterested selflessness by contrast with which almost all normal conduct can seem very shabby...it contributes powerfully to several very prevalent attitudes to be found in Indian political life: to a certain withholding of full approval from even the most popular leaders; to a stronger feeling of distrust of and disgust with persons and institutions of authority; finally, to profoundly violent and desperate moods of cynicism and frustration.[112]

---

[108] *Ibid.*, p. 16.

[109] *Ibid.*, p. 148.

[110] Vivekananda, *Works*, Vol. 4, p. 82.

[111] M.K. Gandhi, 'Plain Thinking and High Living,' in *Harijan*, 1 February 1942, p. 27. See also Vinoba Bhave, *Democratic Values*, p. 116: 'Every person must enjoy the fullest liberty for the propagation of his ideas.'

[112] W.H. Morris-Jones, 'India's Political Idioms,' in *Politics and Society in India*, edited by C.H. Philips (London: George Allen and Unwin, 1963), pp. 140–41. This analysis is placed in a larger context in W.H. Morris-Jones, *The Government and Politics of India*, third revised edition (London: Hutchinson University Library, 1971), pp. 59–61.

Morris-Jones reinforced this criticism recently in his new preface to his essay on J.P. with the comment:

> . . . very many people in India who are far too sceptical to embrace J.P.'s full doctrines nevertheless continue to adopt his norms, so that although they do not follow him in striving towards Utopia they use his utopian vision to look upon the functioning reality of everyday Indian politics with scorn and despair. The paradoxical consequence of the idealist is furtherance of cynicism.[113]

He concludes that it may be more constructive for a political theorist to advocate 'instead more modest versions of democracy and emphasising some of the neglected virtues of the system, imperfect but capable of improvement, which we have with us . . . .'[114] This is an especially important criticism because it returns us to the view expressed in the opening quotation of this article from Morris-Jones concerning the purpose and impact of political theory. Since the dawn of political philosophy, its purpose has been to project a 'transcending form of vision' which meant 'thinking about the political society in its corrected fullness, not as it is but as it might be.' This essential character of vision served a function for human behaviour. 'Precisely because political theory pictured society in an exaggerated, 'unreal' way, it was a necessary complement to action. Precisely because action involved intervention into existing affairs, it sorely needed a perspective of tantalizing possibilities.'[115]

The Indian theorists examined here were, above all, visionaries in that they persistently posed the great Socratic question: 'Which course of life is best?' In their responses, they envisioned human nature gifted with such a panoramic range of capacities that a community based on mutual aid and non-violence truly offered 'a perspective of tantalizing possibilities'.

It is surely debatable whether their vision is the right one, especially if it encourages cynicism, frustration and despair. Yet, it is not debatable that India needs a vision, for since independence the nation has been strong on power politics but weak on those ideals that Mohandas Gandhi showed could inspire and mobilize the masses. Visions are sometimes difficult to conceive; and even then they are easily lost. India has been markedly unable to produce many in this century outside of those conceived by the theorists examined here. Instead, the nation has been integrated not only *sans* vision, but against a prevailing anarchist ideology that has persistently called for decentralization of political power. It remains to be seen how long this unusually wide gap between political practice and theory can prevail and whether 'what the political philosopher believes and teaches today will in some measure mould what politicians believe and do tomorrow.'

---

[113] W.H. Morris-Jones, *Politics Mainly Indian*, p. 97.
[114] *Ibid.*   [115] Sheldon Wolin, *Politics and Vision*, pp. 20–21.

17

INDIRA ROTHERMUND

Gandhi's Satyagraha and Hindu Thought

Gandhi had an abiding faith in the unfailing power of non-violence and the ultimate victory of truth. It is out of this faith that Gandhi evolved his satyagraha, which continues to be relevant to this day. For instance, the achievements of the Polish Solidarity, though very limited, serve to revive our hopes in the efficacy of satyagraha movements in resisting authoritarianism. While the potency of the Gandhian satyagraha is thus recognized, the stringent requirements of, or demands on, the satyagrahis are seldom appreciated. From what follows, it would seem that nothing short of a form of 'religious' or spiritual commitment on the part of the satyagrahis would suffice.

Satyagraha (truthful action), Gandhi's enduring contribution to political thought and practice, is derived from the Vedic concept of binding truth. He used the word God as standing for Truth (*satya*). His concept of satyagraha emphasized not only *satya* but also the means of holding on to it. In this, he draws upon the entire Indian tradition, from the vow (*vrata*) as implied in the invocation of *Rta* of the *Vedas* to the *Sat-Brahman* of Vedanta, from the detached action of the *Bhagavad Gita* to the *ahimsa* of the Buddha.

In Gandhian thought and practice, religion and politics are inseparable. In *Hind Swaraj*, in reply to a question, he writes:

> Your argument tends to show that there must be complete divorce between politics and religion or spirituality. This is what we see in everyday life under modern conditions. Passive resistance seeks to rejoin politics and religion and to test any one of our sections in the light of ethical principles.[1]

In order to understand Gandhi's satyagraha, therefore, we must try to understand his relationship to Hinduism because he considered himself a Hindu, although he did not approve of everything that was taught in the name of Hinduism. Gandhi says he is a Hindu because Hinduism gives him all that he needs and because it signifies a 'relentless search after Truth'. He writes:

Acknowledgements: I would like to acknowledge the helpful comments and suggestions received from Dr. Ram Bapat of Poona University and Thomas Pantham of M.S. University of Baroda.

[1] *Young India*, 3 September 1925. Also in *The Collected Works of Mahatma Gandhi*, Vol. 10, p. 248.

Hinduism is not an exclusive religion. In it there is room for the worship of all the prophets of the world. It is not a missionary religion in the ordinary sense of term. It has absorbed many tribes in its fold, but this absorption has been of an evolutionary imperceptible character. Hinduism tells everyone to worship God according to his own faith or Dharma and so it lives at peace with all the religions.[2]

His political thought is suffused with his religious faith which maintains a symbiotic unity in his apparently fragmentary statements. He builds his thought on his faith in the unbroken validity of the Indian tradition and claims 'to throw new light on many an old truth'. Consequently, he thinks, speaks and works in terms of what he believes to be the essence of this tradition.

Gandhi's approach to the Hindu tradition is an intuitive one. He is steeped in folk-tradition which has preserved the essentials of Indian religion. His mind reproduces these essential features clearly. He says: 'Hindu Dharma is like a boundless ocean teeming with priceless gems. The deeper you dive, the more treasures you find.'[3] However, since he is not concerned with a reconstruction of the Hindu tradition he never attempts to give a systematic account of his insights. Therefore, the coherence of his thought and its relationship to the fundamental precepts of Hindu religion have tended to be overlooked. Here, an attempt is made to place Gandhian thought in the perspective of the Hindu tradition.

Gandhi intuitively grasped the 'existential' content of the *Vedas* as well as the later achievement of Hindu thought. He pitted them against the petrified social customs of contemporary Hinduism. We may say that he is able to do this because he derives his insight into the Hindu tradition not from the study of numerous commentaries but from the living folk tradition. This is the source of his inspiration and, at the same time, the basis of his intimate communication with the common people, which enabled him to transform the constitutional reform movement into a mass struggle for freedom.

Gandhi defines Hinduism as a 'search after truth through non-violent means'.[4] It is, therefore, important to discuss the full meaning of truth. The common Indian word for truth is *satya*, a word that has its origins in the Vedic language. Central to the Vedic concept of truth, however, is the word *Rta*, which according to modern research can be translated as 'truth'. For a long time the word *Rta* has been interpreted in varying ways by different scholars. Most of these interpretations projected the essentialism of later Hindu philosophy back into the *Vedas*. They translated *Rta* by the words 'law' or 'cosmic law'. In recent years, however, Luders

[2] *Young India*, 12 October 1921, p. 1059.
[3] *Harijan*, 2 June 1946.
[4] *Young India*, 24 April 1924.

has shown that *Rta* means truth and that this meaning makes the best sense when consistently applied to all passages of the *Vedas* in which *Rta* is mentioned.[5] The concept of truth begs the question of verifiability, against which it must be qualified. We may, therefore, take *Rta* to mean 'binding truth'. By 'binding' we mean to convey the existential obligation which ties man, God and the world together in a very direct way. It is the invocation of this bond which seems to characterize most passages in the *Vedas* which mention *Rta*.

In order to find out this binding quality of truth, it is important to take a look at the chief guardians of *Rta*, the gods Mitra and Varuna. As Dumezil has shown, Mitra and Varuna are a pair, with divided functions.[6] Mitra is a god of contract, Varuna a god of oath. Mitra has a positive and protective task, Varuna a punitive and restrictive one. Thus, while Mitra would stand for truth, Varuna stands for the binding. Mitra later merges with the Brahman-idea and with the essential of *sat* and *satya*, which we shall discuss later. Varuna, however, has the existential task of binding those who deviate from the path of truth. The binding power of *Rta*, which Varuna administers, is largely automatic insofar as any invocation of *Rta* contains implicitly a grave risk for the man who invokes it. This point is made very explicit in the case of the oath, because every oath is nothing more than the invocation of a curse upon the man who takes it, in the event that he does not fulfil his promise. Varuna is only a witness to this act, being usually represented by his favourite element, water; and in the case of the breaking of the oath he becomes the administrator of the curse—thus he 'binds' the man. Oaths and invocations are the responsibility of the man who invokes them: the initiative is his, the invocation then brings God, man, and world together; and herein lies its strength and its danger. Invocation is, therefore, an act of existential significance. The risks are not to be avoided; they must be taken. Truthful invocation in song and praise strengthens the Gods, who are described as *rtavrdh* ('one who increases in strength by *Rta*'). In invocation, man asserts his truthful bond ('religio') to the Gods.

Gandhi recovers the meaning of *Rta* in his own 'experiments with truth'. Seen in this light, these experiments lose their casual pragmatic appearance and reveal their true character as grave risks taken at the cost of relapse into bondage. This problem of bondage as the result of untruthful action looms large in the Mahatma's thought, and we shall discuss this concept later with regard to his interpretations of the *Bhagavad Gita*.

In the Upanishads, *sat* or the essence, the being within, is the transindividual self, the Brahman. *Tat tvam asi* (that thou art) is the famous

[5] Heinrich Luders, *Varuna* (Goettingen, Vandenhoeck and Rupprecht, 1951), Vol. 1, pp. 40, 55; Vol. 2, p. 411.
[6] George Dumezil, *Mitra-Varuna* (Leroux: Universitaires de France, 1940, Bibliotheque de l'ecole des Hautes Etudes, 56), pp. 79–146.

principle of identification of the *Chhandogya Upanishad*. Gandhi sums
up this philosophy as 'Truth (*satya*) is God.' He believes in the essential
unity of God and man and, for that matter, of all that lives. This parallels
the ontological equation *Satya-Brahman* of the Upanishads.[7] *Satya*,
however, was not an exclusively ontological term. It was more than the
philosophical truth of the Vedanta philosophers. It retained its magical
connotations which it had inherited from the defunct term *Rta*. The
magical tradition of *satya* was kept up by the 'heterodox' schools of Indian
thought like Buddhism, Jainism, and Tantrism.

The invocation of truthful action brings us to the term *dharma*, which
assumes more and more importance as Indian thought developed through
the centuries. *Dharma* is derived from *dhr*—to be firm, to uphold,
support, sustain. In Vedic times, the term *dharma* referred to 'benefits
accrued from sacrifices'.[8] Monier Williams points out that the older form
in the *Rigveda* is *dharman*, meaning 'that which is firmly established,
steadfast; decree, . . . ordinance, law, virtue, morality, religion.'[9] The
word would thus imply not only righteousness or duty, but also the
universal ordinance by which the cosmos is governed and sustained.[10]
From the term *Rta*, *dharma* inherited the element of obligation, while
satya inherited the element of truth. In other words *Rta* is *satya-dharma*.
In the Vedic philosophy of *Rta*, ontology and ethics are one. With the
advance of philosophical speculation, these two realms received special
treatment. Their common root, however, remains the dominant feature
of Indian philosophy.

We can characterize *dharma* as ontological ethics. This is clarified by
Radhakrishnan thus: 'Dharma gives coherence and direction to the
different activities of life . . . . It is the complete rule of life, the harmony
of the whole man who finds a right and just law of his living. Each man
and group, each activity of soul, mind, life, and body, has its dharma.'[11]

Implicit in the terms *dharma* and *swadharma* is the notion of life as a
yajna (offering or sacrifice) to God. This sacramental view of life is typical
of ontological ethics. The ontological character of this ethic becomes
particularly evident when the principle of *dharma* is applied to society or
humanity. Since *dharma* is trans-individualistic, no social contract is
necessary; harmony is attained when everyone follows his own *dharma*.
The individual *swadharma* cannot be in conflict with social ethics unless

---

[7] R.E. Hume, *The Thirteen Principal Upanishads* (London: Oxford Press, 1921), Taittiriya
Upanishad I-1: 'He who knows Brahma as the real (*satya*) . . . obtains all desires.'

[8] S. Dasgupta, *Indian Idealism* (Cambridge: University Press, 1933), p. 2.

[9] Sir Monier Williams, *Sanskrit-English Dictionary* (Oxford: The Clarendon Press, 1894),
p. 510.

[10] Henrich Zimmer, *Philosophy of India* (New York: Meridian Books, 1956), p. 163.

[11] S. Radhakrishnan, *Eastern Religion and Western Thought* (London: Oxford University
Press, 1939), p. 353.

dharma as a whole disintegrates. Consequently, *dharma* will be at its best when it is in accord with *satya*. The Golden Age in India has, therefore, the name '*Satyayuga*,' the Age of Truth, 'when all live freely according to the truth of their enlightened self and God-inhabited being; and, there- fore, respond spontaneously according to the inner divine dharma.'[12]

Accordingly, Gandhi asserts in his autobiography that *dharma* and politics (*rajaprakarna*) cannot be considered in isolation.[13] He says: 'I do not believe that the spiritual law works in a field of its own. On the contrary, it expresses itself only through the ordinary activities of life. It thus affects the economic, the social, and political fields.'[14] Again:

> To see the universal and all-pervading spirit of Truth face-to-face one must be able to love the meanest of creation as oneself. And a man who aspires after that cannot afford to keep out of any field of life. That is why my devotion to Truth has drawn me into the field of politics; and I can say without the slightest hesitation, and yet in all humility, that those who say that religion has nothing to do with politics do not know what religion means.[15]

Thus far we have seen how, in Hindu philosophy, *dharma, satya* and *Rta* are related to each other. We have also seen how Gandhi finds the way back to the Vedic roots of Indian thought by asserting that the search for truth is the *dharma* of Hinduism and that truth is God. He has, thus, recaptured the divine quality of the 'binding truth' in his concept of satyagraha which binds one to truth. From here we have to turn to the problem of right action, the kind of action which is compatible with this system of ontological ethics.

The problem of right action, as embodied in satyagraha, is funda- mental to Gandhi's political thought. As Albert Schweitzer says: 'The Bhagavadgita continued what the Buddha began . . . . The supreme inactivity it teaches is when one performs actions as if one did not perform them . . . . If God himself practises activity in creating and maintaining the Universe, then man also must devote himself to action.' This activity, according to the *Bhagavad Gita*, must be based on *dharma* with no attachment to the results of action, or any desire for reward. The spirit of detachment advocated is 'self-surrender to God'. 'The charm of the Bhagavadgita,' Schweitzer goes on to say, 'is due to this idea of spiritualised activity which springs only from the highest motives.'[16]

[12] Sri Aurobindo, *The Spirit and Message of Indian Culture* (Pondicherry, 1946).

[13] M.K. Gandhi, *My Experiments with Truth* (Ahmedabad: Navajivan Publishing House, 1956), p. 453.

[14] Quoted in N.K. Bose, *Studies in Gandhism* (Calcutta: Nishan, 1947), p. 304.

[15] M.K. Gandhi, *An Autobiography: The Story of My Experiments with Truth* (London: 1949), pp. 370–71.

[16] Albert Schweitzer, *Indian Thought* (Boston: The Beacon Press, 1936), pp. 186–87.

This spirit of detachment, however, raises some philosophical issues. Underlying it are the Indian ideas of *advaita* (non-duality) and *avidya* (ignorance or false consciousness) in its relation to *karma* (action). The early Upanishads had arrived at a philosophy of non-dualism by identifying subject and object, man and Godhead. The clarification of this idea, however, posed a problem since it became necessary to explain why duality and diversity are perceived by us. This was similar to the Western philosophical problem of the One and the Many. However, while Western philosophy was concerned with the unifying factors of perceived diversities, Indian philosophy was concerned with the diverse manifestations or appearances of the one (*Brahman-Sat-Atman*). *Avidya* (false consciousness) was postulated as the source of the manifoldness of perception. All appearance is only an epiphenomenon. But what is the cause of *avidya*? What falsifies the consciousness? *Karma*, action, falsifies the consciousness in the sense that man cannot distinguish appearance from reality.

> Since doers of deeds (*karmin*) do not understand, because of passion (*raga*)
> Therefore, when their worlds are exhausted, they sink down wretched .
> . . .
> They re-enter this world, or a lower.[17]

Here we have the whole doctrine in a nutshell; the relation between *karma* and ignorance, the relation between *karma* and passion, the doctrine of rebirth, and the additional manifoldness of a hierarchy of worlds. This fits well into the general system, since it is easy to reason from the manifoldness of appearance to an ever greater manifoldness beyond appearance (multiplicity of births, worlds, etc.), once the direction from the one to the many (rather than from the many to the one as in the Western philosophy) is accepted.

The statement that there is a lower and a higher world and that action becomes the cause of ignorance because it is accomplished by passion, leads to the conclusion that only dispassionate action—if any action at all—would lead into a higher world, or is the end to the true awareness of identity with the Godhead.

Shankarcharya, as a Vedanta monist, has interpreted the dispassionate activism of the *Gita* to fit in with his monistic essentialism. He accomplishes this by maintaining that the *Gita* presupposes a higher and a lower level of 'Brahman'. The device of the two levels is, of course, not without support in the *Gita* itself, since Lord Krishna presents himself for the greater part of the time as a human incarnation, but once, on Arjuna's request, reveals his awe-inspiring form as a Godhead, which is unbearable to human

[17] R.E. Hume, *op. cit.*, p. 369.

finitude. The hypostasis of the two respective levels of perfection is, however, Shankara's own contribution to the reading of the *Gita*. From there he can go on to point out that for the man who has overcome '*avidya*' there can be neither 'action' nor 'non-action'. Accordingly, the action prescribed in the *Gita*—including the personal God—is only an epiphenomenon; the true, the higher message of the *Gita* is that of renunciation in general, the ideal type towards which it is aimed is the *sannyasin*, the ascetic.

Once action is advocated, the question of the standards of right action arises. In a spiritual sense, action can be right action only if it does not land the soul into bondage by clouding the spirit with *avidya* and chaining it to the wheel of rebirth by the accumulation of *karma*. Action, therefore, must be not only dispassionate but also *yajna*, an offering to God.

The controversy about right action acquired great importance in the struggle for national independence. Tilak, the orthodox nationalist, wrote a great commentary on the *Bhagavad Gita* while he was in prison. He wrote, 'Action alone must be necessary for such action.'[18] Whatever a man does must be taken to have been done by him for the purpose of sacrifice (*yajna*). According to the *Gita*, he says, 'Actions performed for the purpose of *yajna* do not create bondage.' For him, *karmayoga* (the path of action) is the path to self-perfection.

While Tilak emphasized the importance of non-attachment to the results of action, Gandhi sought to find the root of non-attachment. He perceived that there must be an attachment to something else in order to sustain detachment from the results of actions. This attachment, he finds, should be to truth and *ahimsa*. *Ahimsa*, however, means non-violence. It is the first step to self-mastery. This creates a new problem of interpretation, since after all, in the *Bhagavad Gita*, Krishna exhorts Arjuna to fight on the battlefield. Gandhi therefore accept·, like Tilak, the *karmayoga* of the *Bhagavad Gita*, but, unlike the latter, Gandhi refuses to take the text of the *Bhagavad Gita* simply at face value. He says that, on a closer study of religion and the *Bhagavad Gita*, he discovered how there is no reference to any physical warfare and that non-violence rather than violence is the central theme.[19]

Thus, according to Gandhi, Arjuna never discusses war with Krishna, who merely recoils from killing his own kith and kin. Therefore, Krishna says to Arjuna: 'Thou hast already done the killing. Thou canst not all at once argue thyself into non-violence. Finish what thou hast already begun.' Krishna thus advises Arjuna to follow his *swadharma*, the essential duty of the warrior (Kshatriya). Non-violent Krishna could give Arjuna no other advice. 'But to say that the Bhagavadgita teaches or justifies war is as wrong as to say that *himsa* (violence, killing) is the law of life,' says

[18] B.G. Tilak, *Gita Rahasya*, Vols. 1 and 2 (Bombay, 1935).

[19] M.K. Gandhi, *Hindu Dharma* (Ahmedabad: Navajivan Publishing House, 1950), p. 155.

Gandhi.[20] And then he transposes the teaching of the *Bhagavad Gita* to a higher level and points out: 'The field of battle is our own body. An eternal battle is going on between the two camps (of higher and lower impulses). Krishna is the Dweller within, ever whispering in a pure heart.' In this context, Gandhi also recognizes the merits of *Abhaya*, freedom from fear, which the *Bhagavad Gita* teaches. He says:

> He who fears, who saves his skin . . . must fight the physical battle, whether he will or not, but that is not his Dharma . . . . *Himsa* (violence) will go on eternally in this strange world. The Bhagavadgita shows a way out of it. But it also shows that the escape out of cowardice and despair is not the way. Better far than cowardice is killing and being killed.[21]

Gandhi boldly declares that the *Bhagavad Gita* tries primarily to prove the futility of physical warfare and that it shows an excellent way for man to become 'like unto God' through renunciation of the fruits of action. Renunciation leads to self-purification and a perception of the reality. Gandhi maintains that if only the first verse of the *Isha Upanishad* were left intact in the memory of the Hindus, Hinduism would live forever. The verse reads thus: 'All that we see in this great universe is pervaded by God. Renounce it and enjoy it or enjoy whatever he gives you, do not covet anybody's wealth or possessions.'[22] Gandhi tries to read this verse in the light of the *Bhagavad Gita* which he finds to be a commentary on the essence of this verse. The act of renunciation which is stressed here is not merely a physical act but 'represents a second or new birth. It is a deliberate act—not done in ignorance. It is therefore a regeneration . . . . Do not covet anybody's possessions. The moment you carry out these precepts you become a wise citizen of the world living at peace with all that lives.'[23]

Two major foundations of detachment, as emphasized by Gandhi, have been mentioned in the foregoing—truth and *ahimsa*. The concept of truth has been described earlier. Since truth constitutes the highest being (*Sat-Brahman*), it follows that attachment to truth can be considered as complete freedom or perfect detachment. Being bound by truth means freedom from all other bondage, as implied in what Gandhi says: 'Truth is the Law of our being.'[24]

Ahimsa is mentioned as another foundation of detachment. Here Gandhi draws on the Buddhist and Jainist traditions. Lord Buddha says:

[20] *Ibid.*, p. 155.
[21] *Ibid.*, p. 156.
[22] *Ibid.*, pp. 41–42.
[23] *Ibid.*
[24] D.G. Tendulkar, *Mahatma*, Vol. 5 (Bombay, 1951–54), p. 380.

'Never in this world does hatred cease by hatred—hatred ceases by love . . . let a man overcome anger by kindness, evil by good.'[25] And the highest sacrifice, according to Buddha, is 'love of humanity and moral life'. Practising non-violence step-by-step we learn how to make friends with all and thus realize the fundamental oneness of all. According to Gandhi, there is an inviolable connection between Truth and *ahimsa*. He says: 'Truth or *satya* is God and *ahimsa* is God's love, and,Truth is hurt by every evil thought about anyone, therefore, *ahimsa* is fundamental to the discovery of Truth.'[26]

Gandhi adopts the well-known Buddhist tenet '*ahimsa parama dharma*' (non-violence is the highest duty). He gives a more universal meaning to *ahimsa* and points out that *ahimsa* 'may entail continuous suffering and the cultivating of endless patience.' Any evil thought, undue haste, hatred and wishing ill to anybody, and not killing alone, have to be avoided by the votary of *ahimsa*. Finally, Gandhi widens the meaning of *ahimsa* to the general meaning of love, and tries to incorporate the essence of Christ's 'Sermon on the Mount' into *ahimsa* as well.

Truth and non-violence, however, have to be achieved by the discipline of mind and body. This discipline is described as *tapas* (the equanimity of mind and soul) in which the state of mind is completely at rest; it increases man's control over himself and his environment. This implies restraint which is the most important foundation of detachment leading us to the core of *yoga*. Since Vedic times, it has been maintained that one can obtain supranatural powers through *tapas* or the practice of austerities.[27]

The Upanishads speak of *tapas* as capable of producing great inner strength. It is this inner strength that Gandhi stresses as power. Fasting, celibacy and other aspects of bodily discipline are only outward means of attaining this strength. In this way he refers to the ethical preparation, which he also terms the 'eternal guides of conduct' as the essentials for the realization of truth. He enumerates them as (*i*) *ahimsa*, (*ii*) *satya* (here, verifiable truth), (*iii*) *asteya* (non-stealing), (*iv*) *aparigraha* (non-possession), (*v*) *brahmacharya* (celibacy).[28] He describes them as the 'five restraints'. It is clear that these controls are set up voluntarily, in the same way as a scientist sets up his controls for an experiment.

In Gandhi's satyagraha, the vow is the starting point; it constitutes a 'bulwark of strength,' as he says. And he insists on purificatory vows (such as, fasting and celibacy) which demand self-control, since voluntary discipline and restraint are the essential prerequisites of satyagraha.

[25] S. Radhakrishnan, *Indian Philosophy*, Vol. 1 (New York: Macmillan Company, 1923), p. 475.

[26] M.K. Gandhi, *For the Pacifists* (Ahmedabad: Navajivan Publishing House, 1949), pp. 4-5.

[27] S. Dasgupta, *op. cit.*, pp. 2–10; also Luders, *op. cit.*, Vol. 2, p. 644. Luders points out that in RV.X-190–91, *Rta* and *satya* are said to be born out of *tapas*.

[28] M.K. Gandhi, *Hindu Dharma*, pp. 291-92.

Gandhi resorted to the vow of fasting whenever he felt a need for self-purification, and he called such a fast *tapas* (austerity). His fasts on behalf of the Harijans were intended to purify the hearts of the higher castes from the evil of untouchability. He had the 'faith that it must lead to the purification of self and others and that workers [his cooperators] would know that true Harijan-service was impossible without inward purity.'[29]

In short, satyagraha itself assumes the character of a vow. And it also assumes the character of *ahimsa*, since non-violence was another prerequisite; it commanded action, since the '*karmoyoga*' as recommended by the *Bhagavad Gita* was also a prerequisite. The Mahatma sums up these prerequisites by saying that the satyagraha-leader must be a 'man of God who will compel reverence and love even of the opponent by the purity of his life, the utter selflessness of his mission and the breadth of his outlook.'[30]

This character of satyagraha implies certain lines of procedure, and thus Gandhi demands of the satyagrahi: 'All his actions must be transparent through and through. Diplomacy and intrigue can have no place in his armoury.'[31] Consequently, satyagraha cannot be conducted secretly: the satyagrahi's intentions have to be clearly stated and publicly announced. The satyagraha campaign can also become a mass movement only to the extent to which every participant is willing to comply with the prerequisites which have been mentioned earlier.

From the foregoing analysis, it would seem that Gandhi's satyagraha made of resistance against untruth or injustice had its roots in the living Hindu folk tradition. Nehru grasped this when he said that Gandhi is the 'link between all the past and all the future revolutions of Asia'.[32] Tagore made a similar assessment when he wrote, 'India has created a new technique in the history of revolution, which is in keeping with the spiritual traditions of our country, and if maintained in its purity, will become a true gift of our people to civilization.'[33] As in the recent case of the Solidarity Movement in Poland, non-violent and peaceful methods can be an effective mode of affirming the moral autonomy of individuals against authoritarian regimes.

[29] M.K. Gandhi, *Hindu Dharma* (Ahmedabad: Navajivan Publishing House, 1950), p. 109.

[30] M.K. Gandhi, *Satyagraha* (Ahmedabad: Navajivan Publishing House, 1951), p. 203.

[31] *Ibid*.

[32] Tibor Mende, *Nehru: Conversations on Indian and World Affairs* (New York: Braziller. 1956).

[33] Quoted in S. Radhakrishnan, *Mahatma Gandhi* (London: Allen and Unwin, 1939), p. 281.

18

RONALD J. TERCHEK

Gandhi and Democratic Theory

Gandhi is best known for his theory of non-violence. Throughout his writings, he emphasized that everyone must be respected as a free moral agent and that violence degraded both its objects and subjects. When we turn to some of the other themes in his writings, however, his teaching may not always be clear. In large part, this stems from Gandhi's emphasis on particular institutional solutions to promote non-violence and freedom in India. In writing about spinning, rural economics, or village democracy, Gandhi offered concrete recommendations for a particular historical situation: the India of his time. But if too much attention is given to Gandhi's specific recommendations about specific solutions, there is a danger we might lose sight of his overall goals which were not to develop institutional arrangements for everyone everywhere but to pursue freedom and non-violence.

To leave Gandhi's democratic writings at the descriptive level, then, means we miss much of his commitment to the democratic process, the importance he gave to democracy in promoting a non-violent, free society, and his insistence that democracy fostered tolerance and growth. In this essay, I will distinguish the core of his work from the secondary features of his writing. Plato is important today not because we want to construct the small polity he envisioned in *The Republic*, but because we want to know what he had to say about justice. By the same token, Rousseau's simple society is not what attracts the modern reader to *The Social Contract*, but rather a concern about legitimacy and civic virtue. In a similar vein, Gandhi needs to be read with the intention of finding what he wanted to accomplish rather than concentrating on some of his suggested institutional solutions.

Democracy was instrumental to his larger goals of non-violence and freedom, and did not receive more attention in Gandhi's writings because he did not believe that political solutions could be understood apart from social and economic relations. If the institutional foundations of society promoted inequalities, dependency, and fear, then the political system would reflect these defects. The reason for this conclusion in Gandhi's works is not the Marxist rationale that the political system merely reflects the interests of the ruling class. The problem was more complicated for Gandhi, who was willing to acknowledge the potency of concentrated wealth but who insisted that economic inequality was not the sole or even the most important challenge to freedom. Modernization, stratification, industrialization, and urbanization presented obstacles to a sustained non-violent society where freedom was respected. And they could be important obstacles to the democratic prospect as well.

To see what Gandhi meant by democracy, the first section of this essay is devoted to a brief sketch of Gandhi's own writings on this topic. To help put his theories about democracy in perspective, the second section considers carefully some of Gandhi's basic goals and then examines some of the major Western theories of democracy. The first exercise allows us to place Gandhi's views about democracy in his own normative framework; the second enables us to see how his democratic society coincides with and differs from some other Western models of democracy. The final section of the essay draws the implications of Gandhi's theory for democratic theory in general.

Gandhi and Democracy

Arbitrary rule was antithetical to the goals Gandhi had set for himself. He realized that no single political system could guarantee non-violence or freedom, but that democratic government coupled with an equitable society appeared to offer the greatest prospects to achieving his goals. Democratic rule fostered a diffusion of power and increased the prospects that equality and freedom would be pursued. Moreover, democratic government meant that people must bear the mistakes they made rather than pay for the mistakes that others made. If a majority were wrong, then they had themselves to blame rather than some governing elite. However, Gandhi saw that this justification can be carried too far because sometimes majorities expected the minority to pay as well and because democratic majorities sometimes enacted policies which benefited them but not the rest of the community. Recognizing that majority rule was not infallible Gandhi argued:

> The rule of the majority has a narrow application, i.e., one should yield to the majority in matters of detail. But it is slavery to be amenable to the majority, no matter what its decisions are . . . . Under democracy individual liberty or opinion and action is jealously guarded. . . . What we want, I hope, is a government not based on coercion even of a minority but on its conversion.[1]

For Gandhi, democracy was not merely procedural but also substantive. The real purpose of democracy, he argued, 'is that under it the weakest should have the same opportunity as the strongest. This can never happen except through non-violence.'[2]

[1] Nirmal K. Bose, ed., *Selections from Gandhi* (Ahmedabad: Navajivan, 1948), pp. 110–11.

[2] M.K. Gandhi, ed., *Non-Violence in Peace and War*, Vol. 1 (Ahmedabad: Navajivan, 1948), p. 269.

Gandhi placed his ideal democracy in the village where life was simpler, power diffused, and the economy decentralized. Consuming only what they produced themselves, the villagers would be self-sufficient.[3] Work in the village would revolve around handspun cloth or *khadi* and provide everyone with useful labour. Gandhi laid considerable emphasis on direct labour in the fields and handicraft industries and insisted the worker must be able to control the machinery and not become so dependent on mechanized work that he could not earn his livelihood without it.[4] Work would be localized in cottages, not in factories because, according to Gandhi, 'distribution can be equalized when production is localized; in other words, when the distribution is simultaneous with production.'[5]

By concentrating all activity in the villages, Gandhi believed 'the means of production of elementary necessaries of life would remain in the control of the masses.'[6] The villagers would work cooperatively, pooling their labour and goods and dividing their profits.[7] Gandhi expected that the competition of capitalism would be replaced by the cooperation engendered by manual labour with 'the struggle for mutual service for the struggle for mutual existence.'[8] He projected an agrarian-based society in which each village would be largely economically and politically self-contained.[9]

Government would be locally controlled by the people; and *panchayats*, or village councils of five persons elected by the people, would resolve conflicts and try to teach the other members of the community how to avoid disputes. Although Gandhi admitted that he could not specify all of the elements of his non-violent villages, he expected that they would have no traditional armed forces, their power would be diffused, and their governments would rest on a popular base.

Non-violence would be the ordering principle in Gandhi's democracy. Majority rule based on the Western model would be inappropriate, however, because Gandhi believed it ignored the great mass of the people. And majority rule based on violence was 'terrorism' and 'worse and really more godless' than minority British rule.[10] Decision-making would be highly diffused and there would be few 'political' issues, as such. He believed some of the problems which confronted the village could be solved through discussion and agreement rather than through the edicts of political authorities or specialists who buttressed their solutions with

---

[3] See M.K. Gandhi, *Rebuilding Our Villages* (Ahmedabad: Navajivan, 1952), pp. 31–37.
[4] *Young India*, 26 June 1924 and *Harijan*, 18 August 1946.
[5] *Harijan*, 2 November 1934.
[6] *Young India*, 15 November 1928.
[7] *Young India*, 17 June 1926 and *Harijan*, 14 September 1935.
[8] M.K. Gandhi, *Gita—My Mother*, p. 123.
[9] M.K. Gandhi, *Rebuilding Our Villages*, pp. 31–37.
[10] Bose, *op. cit.*, pp. 193–94. Cf. *Harijan*, 3 September 1938.

the threats of violence.[11] But the best way for the political system to practise non-violence was to be relatively inactive. Following Jefferson and Thoreau, Gandhi held, 'that state is perfect and non-violent where the people are governed the least.'[12]

The Philosophical Foundations of Gandhi's Thought

The two central features of Gandhi's thought are non-violence and 'truth'. Of the two terms, non-violence is a relatively straightforward concept, but 'truth' represents special problems of interpretation. First, I will turn to a brief discussion of non-violence and then take up the second topic in this section. I will then turn to two other goals that were central to Gandhi's moral and political thought—the concepts of freedom and equality.

For Gandhi, violence meant exploitation, which, he insisted, represented a denial of individual integrity. As moral beings, we had a right to expect our integrity to be respected by others and also a responsibility to respect the integrity and freedom of others. Such a moral posture meant that individuals must be treated as ends in themsleves, even if we judged their actions as immoral, unethical, or unjust. Violence, Gandhi saw, treated other people as means and we were willing to excuse violence as justified because of some higher standard. Our opponents were seen as impediments to the good, the just, the virtuous and, therefore, could be approached violently to force them to change their own ways and accept our standards. Such a position meant that we thought we had somehow discovered the absolute truth, a position Gandhi was unwilling to accept, and that our claims of having discovered justice or equality were superior to the actual freedom and dignity of others. Such a stance was antithetical to Gandhi, who held that only in respecting the individual moral worth of ourselves and others could we achieve justice. In this respect, he argued that 'means are after all everything. As the means, so the end. There is no wall of separation between means and end.'[13]

Violence not only treats others instrumentally and degrades them, it also makes the users of violence less human. The violent person is at war with the world and believes the world is 'at war with him and he has to live in perpetual fear of the world.'[14] But such violence leads to helplessness, isolation, and incompleteness and builds barriers to a full social life.[15]

Not all violence is personal, with one individual inflicting physical

[11] Bose, *op. cit.*, p. 292.
[12] *Young India*, 27 August 1925.
[13] *Young India*, 17 July 1924.
[14] *Young India*, 6 October 1921.
[15] Ronald J. Terchek, 'The Psychoanalytic Basis of Gandhi's Politics,' *Psychoanalytic Review*, Vol. 62, No. 2 (1975), p. 226.

coercion on others. Much of it is institutional, negating the autonomy of others. Gross poverty, unemployment, and discrimination are recurring themes in Gandhi's writings that are presented as destructive to free choice and result in violence, either directly or indirectly, to control others. Unfortunately, these institutional forces are often incomprehensible and uncontrollable; many 'hugged the chains that bound them'.[16] And so it would become necessary, Gandhi argued, to look at new institutional arrangements that would promote non-violence and freedom.

The Status of Truth

To admit that we do not know the absolute truth means that we cannot impose our partial vision of the truth on others. Gandhi's approach to the subject of truth must be understood in this light. He attempted to provide a direction to approaching answers rather than to produce solutions that admit of no change. For Gandhi, truth may be absolute, but knowledge is relative.[17] In this regard, he held:

> It has been my experience that I am always true from my point of view and often wrong from the point of view of my honest critics. I know that we are both right from our respective points of views. And this knowledge saves me from attributing motives to my opponents or critics . . . . I very much like the doctrine of the manyness of reality. It is this doctrine that has taught me to judge a Mussulman from his own standpoint and a Christian from his.[18]

A relativity about knowledge and respect for differing points of view diminishes claims to absolute power. Like Camus' existential stance about absolute power corrupting liberating ideas in violent revolutions, Gandhi held that absolutism destroyed the truth we tried to reach.[19] Any insistence by someone that he possessed absolute truth gave that person, in his own mind at least, the justification to impose that truth on others, to force others to be free. But, as suggested earlier, Gandhi believed that the exercise of such power negated any recognition of the integrity of those who would be hurt in the quest for truth. Power holders who think they own the truth see no need to enter into a dialogue to convince others and close themselves from the possibility of learning more.

[16] *Young India*, 11 August 1920.
[17] Raghavan Iyer, *The Moral and Political Thought of Mahatma Gandhi* (New York: Oxford University Press, 1973), p. 244.
[18] *Young India*, 11 August 1920.
[19] In this regard, Gandhi held 'that if the state suppressed capitalism by violence, it will be caught in the coils of violence itself and fail to develop non-violence at any time.' Bose, *op. cit.*, p. 42.

One reason we cannot justify violence is that we can never absolutely justify any project as solving all problems once and for all and liberate everyone now and forever. Moreover, we must recognize our own inevitable fallibility and egoism. No one, Gandhi claimed, can attain perfect detachment from his own ego, 'for the simple reason that the ideal state is impossible so long as one has not completely overcome his ego, and ego cannot be wholly gotten rid of.'[20]

Because we cannot be absolutely sure about our actions, we need to act in ways which are true to or honest with our best intentions and knowledge without forcing our solutions on others. Indeed, Gandhi held that our humanity comes from trying to improve ourselves morally and from respecting the worth of others, even though we know we cannot be completely successful in this task. According to Gandhi, we should be sure of our ideal but know we 'shall ever fail to realize it, but never cease to strive for it.'[21] According to Gandhi, 'that constant striving, that ceaseless quest after the ideal,' represents the best of the human condition.[22]

Gandhi's political theory and politics emphasized dialogue as a way of discovering truth. Dialogue implies an openness between moral equals. In hierarchical power relations, openness is difficult to achieve and superiors are unlikely to see their inferiors as equals. Dialogue opens the possibility that others might be converted to our position rather than coerced. In this regard, Gandhi insisted: 'We must try patiently to convert our opponents. If we wish to evolve the spirit of democracy out of slavery, we must be scrupulously exact in our dealings with opponents . . . . We must concede to our opponents the freedom we claim for ourselves.'[23]

Gandhi's position about the relativity of knowledge gives rise to the need for tolerance, a civic virtue that virtually all schools of democracy hold is essential. Tolerance implies a mutual regard for others; and if it is missing, the dialogue of the democratic process is diminished, if not destroyed. Gandhi in India, like Dewey in America, saw dialogue as necessary to both individual growth and to the democratic prospect. Indeed, democracy received one of its primary justifications from Dewey because it promoted tolerance and fostered development. Dewey held that open communication enlarges and changes experience. 'One shares in what another has thought and felt and insofar, meagerly or amply, has his own attitude modified.' But, Dewey went on, our position 'requires getting outside of it, seeing it as another would see it, considering what points of contact it has with the life of another so that it may be got into

---

[20] Bose, *op. cit.*, p. 6.

[21] *Speeches and Writings of Mahatma Gandhi* (Madras: Natesan, 1934), 4th ed., p. 363. Cf. *Harijan*, September 1939.

[22] Iyer, *op. cit.*, p. 100.

[23] Ronald Duncan, *Selected Writings of Mahatma Gandhi* (Boston: Beacon Press, 1951), p. 79.

such form that he can appreciate its meaning.'[24] Through open dialogue, people not only test their own ideas, they also learn, and in the process, advance in tolerance and non-violence. 'Intolerance,' writes Gandhi, 'is itself a form of violence and an obstacle to the growth of a true democratic spirit . . . . When self-satisfaction creeps over a man, he has ceased to grow.'[25]

Freedom and Responsibility

To talk about morally autonomous agents means we must talk about free agents. And this is what Gandhi pursued in his politics. 'No society,' he insisted, 'can possibly be built on the denial of individual freedom. It is contrary to the very nature of man. Just as man will not grow horns or a tail, so will he not exist as a man if he has no mind of his own.'[26] For Gandhi, free choice meant that men and women should not be constrained by physical coercion, economic power, government, or social position. But more than choice is involved with freedom; Gandhi continually connected duty with freedom and held that everyone was responsible for the choices he made.

Gandhi's position on freedom departs from the major approaches in the Anglo-American liberal tradition in important respects. That tradition generally insists that individuals are the authors of their own desires and aversions and it is only natural that they pursue their interests.[27] From this perspective, freedom is defined as the absence of restraints. But such an approach presents conceptual difficulties which their authors have recognized. The more apt we are to define freedom as the lack of restraints and the ability to pursue our interests, the more apt we are to find that complete freedom leads to the Hobbesian state of war where life is 'nasty, brutish, and short'.[28] However, such a consequence leads us to seek ways to limit freedom. Unrestricted freedom gets in the way of enjoying freedom, and government, in the liberal tradition, is justified as providing us with a manageable, protected environment to pursue our interests. For most liberal writers, government must restrain citizens from interfering with specified rights and may use force against those who abridge those rights.

From a Gandhian perspective, however, there are several flaws in such an approach to freedom. In the first and most obvious place, it sanctions violence by the government. The state is given authority to use coercion to enforce rights. Apart from the central Gandhian concern that these

---

[24] John Dewey, *Democracy and Education* (New York: Free Press, 1966), pp. 4–5.
[25] *Young India*, September 1921 in Iyer, *op. cit.*, p. 314.
[26] *Harijan*, 1 February 1924.
[27] Hobbes, Locke, and Bentham are taken as representative of the liberal tradition.
[28] Thomas Hobbes, *Leviathan*, Ch. 13.

sanctions demean the moral autonomy of individuals, such a solution does not recognize the prospect of rights in conflict. As times change and the idea of rights expand, a clear agreement about what is a valid claim and what is not is not always easy to discover. Moreover, when several claims are recognized, it is difficult to find liberalism supplying a clear understanding of which rights have priority over others.[29]

Liberalism found that the greatest dangers to freedom came from the state, a position Gandhi would find acceptable but incomplete. Unlike the classical liberal writers, particularly the liberal economists, Gandhi would insist that freedom is assaulted by many forces, not just the state. Gross economic inequality made some destitute and dependent on others, industrialization created unemployment and impersonalized social relations, a rigid caste system and untouchability denied people their autonomy, and colonialism minimized the prospects for free choice.[30] To produce such a list indicates that Gandhi believed freedom is socially located and the obstacles to freedom come from numerous sources. Indeed, one reason why the ideals of moral integrity and human freedom are elusive is that everyone is subject to potential, constant assault, even in the best of situations. The task Gandhi set for himself was to minimize the obstacles to freedom and eliminate situations in which institutions contracted choices.

The liberal justification of freedom tends to ignore human needs at the expense of rights. For Gandhi, to be human requires meeting certain basic needs, particularly the need for work. It was through work that Gandhi believed that people would gain some measure of autonomy, breaking their dependency on others for their very existence. He insisted, 'I must refuse to insult the naked by giving them clothes they do not need, instead of giving them work which they sorely need.'[31] For Gandhi, work gives people control over their lives and eliminates dependency on others for basic needs.

Although no conscious plan may be responsible for people being out of work, Gandhi insisted a lack of intentionality did not reduce the actual restrictions placed on the choices of the unemployed. This emphasis on consequences of action, whether intentional or unintentional, separates Gandhi from much traditional liberal thought which did not consider impersonal forces in the market or society as major barriers to freedom. He feared that the institutions of modern life imposed such barriers on freedom and sponsored a set of 'wants' that removed people further from their roles as moral agents.[32] In satisfying their newly-created wants, Gandhi believed, people would forget they were moral actors responsible for their actions.

[29] Roberto Unger, *Knowledge and Politics* (New York: Free Press, 1965).
[30] Terchek, *op. cit.*
[31] Bose, *op. cit.*, p. 50. Cf. pp. 66–68.   [32] *Young India*, 2 January 1927.

The liberal formulation of freedom is also defective from Gandhi's perspective because it is self-maximizing and refuses to recognize the social basis of human life. From Gandhi's view, what we do affects others, we are affected by them, and we cannot make claims for ourselves at the expense of others. In other words, we have a responsibility for our actions. He insisted that rights and responsibilities are reciprocal. Without the one, the other is impossible to justify. 'Every duty performed confers upon one certain rights, whilst the exercise of every right carries with it certain obligations. And so the never-ending cycle of duty and right goes ceaselessly on.'[33]

Responsibility as a topic is most pronounced in Gandhi's discussion about obligation and disobedience. We cannot deny our role in society and cannot avoid responsibility when social and political agents act in our name or on our behalf. In this regard, Gandhi insisted that people needed to be aware of the consequences of their own actions. Only when they realized that they were responsible for what they did and what they tolerated could they be said to be free. To allow others responsibility for our actions meant that we were only partially free; to suggest that the cost of our freedom on others was accidental or unintended and imposed no responsibility on us was to deny the real nature of freedom. According to Gandhi, freedom meant that we made free choic s about those things that seemed important to us and that we accep' :d the costs of those choices. In this regard, Gandhi held:

> . . . most people do not understand the complicated machinery of the government. They do not realize every citizen silently but nonetheless certainly sustains the government of the day in ways of which he has no knowledge. Every citizen therefore renders himself responsible for every act of his government. And it is quite proper to support it so long as the actions of the government are bearable. But when they hurt him and his nation it becomes his duty to withdraw his support.[34]

Gandhi's insistence that freedom and responsibility are linked is hard on narrow individualism: it acknowledges that freedom is essential but Gandhi then logically concludes that if we are free, we must account for our own action. Freedom without responsibility is a contradiction in terms for Gandhi. We may not want to join the two together, but Gandhi condemns us to recognize the realities of freedom, that is, the responsibilities of freedom. Someone cannot be free, from Gandhi's perspective, who does not account for his actions or who dismisses unintended consequences.

[33] *Ibid.*, 29 August 1929.
[34] *Ibid.*, 28 July 1920.

Equality and Inequality

Freedom and dialogue, so central to Gandhi's thought, are not values that come easily. In societies with great differences in background, resources, occupations, and power, it is difficult for people to see how they are affecting others. One reason for this is that we do not always understand the position of those who differ radically from us. As distance grows between groups because of their social position, their common experiences become more diverse. But it is shared experience that helps us understand the concerns and needs of others. Without some common experiences, the happiness and pain of others tend to be ignored or, at best, become abstractions, and consequently, we respond with moral indifference to the distant and isolated experiences of others. What seems important to the doctor may be irrelevant to the farmer and what is critical to the labourer may be incomprehensible to the bureaucrat. In such a setting, it becomes easy to ignore or misread the consequences of our actions on others or to find that dialogue with those in different groups is unrewarding. Communication, if it is to be more than a mere exchange of words, must convey meaning as well. This is one reason Gandhi was so concerned about equality. Only when the range of differences separating people are relatively narrow can people appreciate the consequences of their actions on others. And even when they do not anticipate the effects of their behaviour on others, shared experiences will open dialogue as a potential corrective.

In talking about equality, Gandhi did not mean absolute economic equality which applied to everyone in the same way. At the economic level, he insisted, equality 'simply meant that everybody should have enough for his or her needs.'[35] Although this kind of equality could be achieved through government ownership of all property, Gandhi rejected such a solution because it rested on centralized power. He feared that centralized governments, and particularly socialist governments, do 'the greatest harm to mankind by destroying individuality.'[36] But for Gandhi, equality should enhance individual freedom, not retard it. Accordingly, he wanted the range of economic differences significantly narrowed. Limited differences would not only promote responsibility and fruitful, comprehensible dialogue, they would also, as in Rousseau, assure that no one was so rich as to be able to buy someone else and none would be so poor as to be forced to sell himself to someone else.

Gandhi also expected that his goal of equality would be promoted if everyone worked with his hands. Indeed, in Gandhi's ideal village, the franchise was restricted to those who spun cloth, something he insisted

[35] *Harijan*, 3 March 1946.
[36] D.C. Tendulkar, *Mahatma: Life of Mohandas Karamchand Gandhi*, Vol. 4 (Bombay: Jhaveri and Tendulkar, 1951–54), p. 15.

everyone could do. Not surprisingly, he considered 'labour to be a powerful unifying agent. It is a great equalizer.'[37] And the reason it was the great equalizer was that it gave everyone the same range of experiences to judge their conduct and appreciate its effects on others. It gave everyone something in common and in so doing facilitated the prospects for a community. Finally, work for everyone meant that no one was inherently dependent on others for survival and that everyone would have a recognized dignity. Gandhi's view of equality is similar to John Scharr's who held:

> . . . the heart of equality is its affirmation of equality of being and belonging. That affirmation helps identify those sectors of life in which we should all be treated in a common or average way, so that the minimal conditions of a common life are available to all . . . . It also stresses the greatest possible participation in and sharing of the common life and culture while striving to assure that no man shall determine or define the being of any other man.[38]

Equality, like democracy, is really instrumental to the goals of non-violence and freedom and is not an end in itself. And, as with democracy, Gandhi believed equality could thrive only in societies which diminished their reliance on materialism and large, impersonal institutions.

The Current Status of Democratic Theory

The dominant model of democracy today emphasizes competitive elections and interest group pluralism. Voters choose who will represent and govern them for a period of time, and if satisfied will return the incumbents, if dissatisfied will turn to alternative candidates. Between elections, organized groups are expected to represent the interests of their members before various government agencies to influence public policy.[39]

Gandhi's departure from this model at the institutional level is obvious. He wanted a small setting with a relatively simple economy, while the pluralists have been concerned with the problems of representation in large, highly diversified societies. But what is theoretically more interesting than the question of scale is the difference between the pluralists and

---

[37] *Harijan*, 12 August 1933.

[38] John Scharr, 'Equality of Opportunity and Beyond,' in J. Roland Pennock and John W. Chapman, *Equality (Nomos, IX)*, (New York: Atherton Press, 1967), pp. 228–49.

[39] The thesis that democracies rest on competitive elections is presented by Joseph Schumpeter, *Capitalism, Socialism and Democracy* (New York: Harper, 1950), pp. 250–73. The classic position of the pluralist view is advanced by Robert Dahl in several books including *Who Governs?* (New Haven: Yale University Press, 1961) and *After the Revolution* (New Haven: Yale University Press, 1970).

Gandhi over the matter of interests. The pluralists hold that politics is based on pursuit of interests which invariably leads to disagreements and conflict. You have your set of interests and I have mine. Sometimes I can satisfy what I desire without affecting you; but at other times we may both want the same thing, or I want something and expect you to pay for it, and conflict develops. From the pluralist perspective, interests are individualistically generated and consequently not in some automatic harmony. To put it more simply, interests are natural and conflict is inevitable. Accordingly, politics should be structured in ways which allow the freest expression of interests, and institutions should be devised which hold conflict to manageable levels.

The byplay of interests in pluralist thought leads to the politics of bargaining and compromise. According to pluralist theory, there are many different kinds of resources that can be used to mobilize political power; no single individual, group, or class monopolizes all of these resources. Money, time and numbers are among the more common resources, and those who have much money may not have a large following. Because of the dispersal of resources, no single side can dominate the political process and even the stronger must take account of the weaker participants. What emerges as public policy in pluralist politics results from bargaining and the dispersal of power and takes the form of a compromise, that is, a policy that is tolerable to each of the major participants. While this does not lead to perfect policies, the pluralists argue that policies based on compromise assure that no one is an absolute loser and that the stakes of politics do not lead to intense cleavages which lead to constant conflict.

As everyone in the pluralist model goes about the business of defending his own interests, little attention is paid to how this affects the rest of society. Gandhi clearly hoped to define political life in ways that emphasize the community rather than individual interests. He began from the premise that social life required both freedom and interdependence and that we needed the appropriate social setting to pursue these values effectively. He also insisted that many of the things we would call interests were really artificial and that as some people pursued their interests they deprived others of their real needs. Unlike much contemporary pluralism, Gandhi did not hold that one interest is as good as another or that we could say with Bentham that poetry is as good as pushpin.

Gandhi believed we could differentiate needs from interests and that politics should be institutionally structured to give priority to basic needs. From this perspective, interest group politics endangered the very purpose which any government should be designed to serve—to provide for the common good.

Gandhi would also deny that interests are really natural in the sense the pluralists defined interests. We are more than the interests which stem from our jobs, status, or region. For Gandhi these characteristics are incidental to our human nature and if they become the defining characteristics of men and women, the accidental features of our lives become central and most basic and shared elements are lost. But it is not enough to say to someone, 'Do not be worried about your property, income, or job.' People do live in the real world and there they must be concerned about a variety of needs as well as how they adjust to the requirements of their society. To be indifferent to such questions seems to invite others to take advantage of us or to fail to advance in our own societies.

Gandhi was well aware of this problem, and his suggested solution, much in the spirit of Rousseau, has been especially difficult for many to accept. Because interests do come from our particular situations in society and because contemporary society both generates inequalities as well as introduces new needs, the solution comes not simply by asking people to restrain themselves. On the contrary, Gandhi argued that the social and economic institutions of society must be restructured to diminish the causes of diverse, contentious interests. In a society patterned on Gandhi's concept of equality, many of the interests which seem so important in highly diversified, hierarchical societies would become less important or would disappear. The Gandhian formula for dealing with interests, in or outside of democratic societies, is to eliminate the causes of interests as much as possible.

Classical republican theory was also concerned about the role of interests in democratic politics and writers as diverse as Cicero, Machiavelli, and Rousseau attempted to deal with the prospects of restraining the egoistic element in politics. Some, like Rousseau, reached for the small, simple society to reduce interests; others, like Machiavelli, attempted to introduce necessity (or crisis) into their societies to emphasize the common interest and overwhelm the private interests; and many used a kind of civil religion to condemn private desires and praise service and sacrifice. Self-interest, which was natural to the liberal and pluralist writers, was the problem the republicans thought they must solve before they could talk about freedom and a just political order.

The republicans believed that freedom could be secured only if people restrained themselves. For them, the worst society, the corrupt society, occurred when everyone became a free rider. In such an environment, no one's freedom was secured and the need for restraint became particularly important. Accordingly, the republicans attempted to disperse power, institutionalize cooperation, emphasize service, and promote widespread participation. However much they differed in their specific recommendations about the structures of their ideal republics, they were of one mind that self-interest must be contained.

Another common theme in much republican thought as well as in early American democratic theory and practice was concerned with full and free participation, on the one hand, and dependency relationships, on the other hand. It was thought that people who were dependent on others could not be autonomous citizens and that a democracy required free citizens if it were to fulfil its promise of a government resting on the will of the people and responsive to the people. Gandhi was critically aware of the dependency problem and set about formulating programmes which assured autonomy. For him, however, the solution was not primarily political in nature but social and economic. Dependency was created by unemployment, poverty, and gross discrimination, and his various economic and social programmes were all designed to reduce dependency relationships and increase autonomy. From Gandhi's point of view, the proper social and economic relationships were preconditions for an effective democracy.

It is in this light, for example, that his insistence on *khadi* or hand-spinning as a precondition for franchise in his village democracy should be read. According to Gandhi, *khadi* provided everyone with a chance to contribute to his own welfare and survival and reduced dependency on others. What is important about *khadi* is not the specific activity but its functional or metaphorical value. That is, Gandhi's use of spinning introduced some measure of autonomy and reduced dependency.

One other feature of much early democratic theory needs to be emphasized because of its departure from the contemporary voting/pluralist model. The early Americans and Rousseau insisted that the character of society and democracy were closely linked and the underlying structure of society and the economy would open some political possibilities and close others. For these early democrats, concentrated economic power was especially troublesome because vast wealth tended to be converted into political power which could subsequently influence politics, including democratic politics. Accordingly, many of the early democrats were preoccupied with the economy and some, such as Jefferson and Rousseau, were particularly suspicious about modernization. For them, modernization tended to weaken old institutions, create inequalities, and introduce new dependency relationships; all these consequences were seen as dangerous to the vitality of the democratic process.

Models of democracy which link democracy and freedom, promote moral growth, and tie political structures to the economic and social foundations of society differ from modern pluralist conceptions of democracy in important ways. In modern pluralist theories of democracy, participation outside of voting and interest group activity have generally been discounted and emphasis has been given to the primacy of interests. However, as I have tried to show, pluralism is not the only available model of democracy. And it is with these alternative forms of democracy that Gandhi's own theories of democracy are, in many ways, compatible.

The Implications of Gandhi for Democratic Theory

Gandhi's contribution to democratic theory is not that he offers specific institutional alternatives to representative democracy and pluralism, although he does that. Rather, his importance comes from offering alternative ways of thinking about politics in general and democracy in particular.

He hoped to devise a system of government which secured freedom and individual integrity and which also promoted non-violence. And it is non-violence that is perhaps Gandhi's most original legacy to democratic theory. To the extent that any government relied on violence, Gandhi believed, it lost its legitimacy, whether it was a democracy or another form of regime.

One of the great tasks of political philosophers has been to make government legitimate and their solutions have included rights, justice, or equality. These approaches held that a government which upholds these ideals was legitimate and could use coercion to protect its values and security. For Gandhi, violence represented a failure by the government to convince others about the justice of its position. And so the challenge posed by Gandhi is to discover some of the reasons why people refuse to acknowledge a government's claims to obedience. To deal with the problem of disagreement requires dialogue and tolerance which encourages the members of society to find the common ground they share, to settle their differences without physical conflict, and to respect one another's worth while they worked towards a solution.

Of course, not all conflicts would disappear, and Gandhi believed that the role of political leadership in a democracy should be to promote non-violence and conciliation rather than to mobilize power in conflict situations. To act as an advocate for one or another side only increased the chances for conflict and violence and to assert the right of the state to use violence diminished the legitimacy of the state according to Gandhi. For Gandhi, the test of leadership was not winning but avoiding conflict, and in failing that, avoiding violent solutions to conflict.

A second implication of Gandhi's work is the importance of equality in a democratic society. The problem with economic inequality is not so much that great wealth in the hands of a few generally deprives the many of their livelihood. To expropriate the wealth of the very rich and distribute it to the very poor will not probably lead to the continued improvement of the new beneficiaries, particularly in a place like India where millions of people live in dire economic conditions. But concentrated wealth is, nevertheless, important because it can readily be translated into political resources to influence public policies. Inequalities in wealth tend to lead to other kinds of inequality, including political inequality.

The democratic commitment, however, is that everyone should

politically count the same, a position best summarized by the slogan 'one man, one vote'. Assuring an equal vote to all adults has been relatively easy to effect. Today, the once commonplace practice of weighted voting (which favoured property holders and university graduates with more than one vote) has largely been abolished. And people who were denied a vote because of their sex, race, and absence of property have been included in the franchise. As important as these reforms have been, Gandhi wanted to call attention to gross disparities in resources that can easily be converted into political influence. If such resources are concentrated in the hands of a few people, then a small part of the population has an extraordinary potential to influence policy and decision-makers while the rest of the citizens occupy an inferior place in the democratic process.

Gandhi recognized this problem and saw that political equality was essential for any working democracy. To repair the imbalance of political resources did not require economic equality, and Gandhi showed a keen appreciation that economic inequalities were bound to exist, even in an ideal society. For him, the task was to limit the range of inequalities, and his various economic programmes were designed to assure employment for everyone and disperse concentrated industrial and political power. Gandhi believed that his reforms in the economy would not only have important distributive and psychological effects, they would have important political consequences in establishing the conditions for political equality.

Another implication of Gandhi's theory comes from the relationship between dependency and democracy. Some of the early democratic writers in the West were so concerned about the problem of dependency that they wished to restrict the franchise to those who were property owners or freeholders.[40] The pressing fear of the Levellers that servants and wage earners would be controlled by their employers no longer seems important to us, particularly with the introduction of the secret ballot. And even when we can identify dependency relationships, we are not about to claim that the best way of solving the problem is to restrict the franchise to those who are economically independent.

Dependency has not received much attention in modern democratic theory in part because some of the worst forms of dependency have been eliminated, such as, with the abolition of slavery. Not denying that these correctives have been important to the operation of any democratic society, the question remains whether we need to think about other forms of dependency which can retard full and equal participation or which can deprive individuals of the autonomy required to be full citizens in a democratic polity. As with the previous point about equality, Gandhi's

[40] See Don Wolfe, *Leveller Manifestos of the Puritan Revolution* (New York: Nelson, 1944).

real contribution does not so much lie in his specific solutions as it does in the questions he posed about the meaning of full and effective citizenship in a responsive democracy. Gandhi's programme for spinning and the village economy were offered as ways of reducing dependency. The point to be emphasized is that he saw dependency as a brake on full participation and a restriction on freedom. To pretend that dependency is unimportant or that it can be effectively solved by giving the vote to everyone does not solve the problem.

A fourth implication of Gandhi's theory concerns the relationship between responsive government and active citizens. Whatever variant of contemporary democracy may be under consideration, each is becoming increasingly bureaucratic. As modern democratic society becomes more complex and its diverse parts grow increasingly interdependent, the need for coordination and efficiency have increased. Not surprisingly, the explosion of bureaucratic control has not been restricted to government operations: increasingly, the private sector is becoming more bureaucratic, as modern corporations, universities, and trade unions amply demonstrate. Bureaucracy gains its efficiency because of its hierarchical structure, its minute division of labour, its heavy reliance on specialists, and its impersonality. No longer playing favourites, the modern bureaucracy theoretically treats everyone the same way. The irony of modern bureaucracy is that in attempting to rationalize diverse operations and introduce greater efficiency, it has become more removed from its constituencies and less responsible and responsive.

Elected officials have frequently lost control of the very government they were charged to govern and much of the business of governing is done by the bureaucracy. If it were possible to do away with bureaucracy in modern, technological society, the effort would have been seriously made long ago. But those who frequently complain about bureaucracies do not really plan to dismantle this vast network of specialized personnel doing technical tasks. On the contrary, they usually want to dismantle part of the bureaucratic structure and keep the rest.

Modern democratic theory and contemporary political science have been least helpful in solving the anti-democratic features of bureaucracy. In calling attention to the danger posed by centralized bureaucracies, Gandhi held that bureaucratic norms could not be reconciled with democracy. Gandhi's contribution in this area, I think, comes not so much from his insistence that all modern institutions must disappear but that we may often have to choose between efficiency and coordination or autonomy, citizen participation, and equality.

To move in this direction, Gandhi would insist, it is also necessary to examine the vast centralization in the private sectors of society, particularly in the economy. Vast corporations, and for that matter, unions and other private institutions, have become commonplace, frequently diminish choice, and add to inequalities in society. A less complex government in a world where power and wealth are hierarchically ordered would only compound the problems facing those at the bottom. Those with private resources would only fill the vacuum left by an inactive government. In talking about the diffusion of government power, it is also necessary to consider the dispersal of private power as well if the goals of freedom and equality are to have any chance of succeeding.

In talking about the problems of modern democracy, it is easy to concentrate on the institutional and distributive aspects of politics and society. As important as these matters are, it is misleading to think that if they were set right, democracy would flourish and freedom would be respected everywhere. The individual also plays an important role in the future of the democratic prospect. To the extent that people emphasize only their own interests and ignore their responsibilities to the broader community, politics becomes a struggle for benefits that others must support. And political community becomes a fatality in the process.

Gandhi attempted to reintroduce political culture and political psychology as vital elements in the theory and practice of democracy. A restructured society, where no one saw responsibilities and everyone attempted to pursue his own interests, would be no great improvement for Gandhi. Those who had been at the bottom would have additional resources to enter the political conflicts of the day. The formula of politics would not change, but new winners and losers would appear. Accordingly, Gandhi emphasized structuring a community of common purpose and individual responsibility to the community.

As Western democracies move towards the prospect of slower growth and increasing scarcities, the old model of interest group politics may lead to phenomenal cleavages. To meet these new challenges, the need for restraint, responsibility, and community becomes more important than in easier, carefree times, and Gandhi's theory of democracy may help to understand and meet these challenges.

19

THOMAS PANTHAM

Beyond Liberal Democracy: Thinking with Mahatma Gandhi

Gandhi's case against the West looks . . . infinitely stronger than it looked, to us Westerners, thirty years ago.

–G.D.H. Cole[1]

Purna Swaraj or Integral Democracy

There is an increasing recognition by political theorists that contemporary liberal democracy is in a crisis that is not confined to the politico-economic sphere, but which has permeated the socio-cultural sphere.[2] The remedy, according to Jurgen Habermas, lies not so much in the critique of political economy as in the critique and supersession of the scientization of politics. In Sheldon Wolin's view, what is needed is 'nothing short of a long revolution, aimed at deconstituting the present structure of power.'[3] In the present article, I shall try to show that such a project of deconstitution is contained in Gandhi's social theory and praxis. I shall try to demonstrate that Gandhi's theory—far from being 'all fine Ruskin-Tolstoyan rodomontade by a lawyer with a printing press,'[4] or the primitivist yearnings of a withdrawn mystic—offers guidance in transforming what he called the 'nominal' democracy of the modern Western type into a truer or fuller democracy, which he referred to as *purna swaraj* (complete or integral democracy), *ramarajya* ('sovereignty of the people based on pure moral authority'), or *sarvodaya*

[1] G.D.H. Cole, *Reflections on 'Hind Swaraj' by Western Thinkers* (Bombay: Theosophy Company, 1948), p. 17. See also note 5 below.

[2] Jurgen Habermas, *Legitimation Crisis*, tr. Thomas McCarthy (Boston: Beacon Press, 1975); William Connolly, *Appearance and Reality in Politics* (Cambridge University Press, 1981); Christian Bay, *Strategies of Political Emancipation* (University of Notre Dame Press, 1981, and Bombay: Somaiya, 1982); Alan Wolfe, *The Limits of Legitimacy: Political Contradictions of Contemporary Capitalism* (New York: Free Press, 1977); Daniel Bell, *The Cultural Contradictions of Capitalism* (New York: Basic Books, 1976); George Kateb, 'On the "Legitimation Crisis"', '*Social Research* (Winter 1979); and Richard Lowenthal, 'Political Legitimacy and Cultural Change in West and East,' *Social Research* (Autumn 1979).

[3] Sheldon Wolin, 'The People's Two Bodies,' *Democracy* (January 1981), p. 24. That 'the world needs cultural alternatives to the dominant Western paradigm of development' is argued in Rajni Kothari, 'Symposium on a New International Development Strategy: A Report,' *Alternatives*, Vol. 5 (1979–80).

[4] George Catlin, *In the Path of Mahatma Gandhi* (Macdonald, 1948), p. 245, as cited in Raghavan N. Iyer, *The Moral and Political Thought of Mahatma Gandhi* (Delhi: Oxford University Press, 1973), p. 30.

(a social order promoting the good of all).[5] I shall argue, moreover, that the Gandhian project is aimed at resolving a fundamental contradiction in the theory and practice of liberal democracy, namely, the contradiction between the affirmation of the freedom of the individual in the so-called private sphere of morality and its curtailment in the allegedly amoral or purely technical public/political sphere. I shall try to show that Gandhi repairs this contradiction by de-reifying the objectified state through *swaraj* (participatory democracy combining 'self-rule and self-restraint') and by integrating politics and morality through the *satyagraha* process of socio-political action.

Beyond Utilitarian Ethics

For a proper understanding of 'Gandhi's case against the West,' it is useful to note some of its parallels with Habermas' contemporary critique of the late capitalist state.[6] Both Gandhi and Habermas were reacting to the untruth of the legitimacy claims of the late capitalist state, whose imperialist and fascist manifestations revealed to them the false foundations of Western liberal democracy. Looked at from the bottom up, the contradictions of the late capitalist state were seen earlier in the periphery than at the centre of the world capitalist system.[7] In other words, the untruth of the state's claims to democratic legitimacy, which Habermas sees today in the advanced capitalist countries, was seen earlier by Gandhi in the peripheral states of South Africa and India, which were the arena of his 'experiments' with truthful or authentic politics.

State intervention in the economic, social, and cultural spheres in support of the private appropriation of public wealth is the common feature of the colonial societies and the present-day advanced capitalist

[5] Gandhi's most significant tract on political thought is his *Hind Swaraj* (Ahmedabad: Navajivan, 1938). Three anthologies particularly useful for the present article are M.K. Gandhi, *Democracy: Real and Deceptive*, comp. R.K. Prabhu (Ahmedabad: Navajivan, 1961); M.K. Gandhi, *Nonviolence in Peace and War*, Vols. 1 and 2 (Ahmedabad: Navajivan, 1942); M.K. Gandhi, *Sarvodaya* (Ahmedabad: Navajivan, 1954). Among the secondary sources, the most comprehensive and penetrating is R.N. Iyer, *Moral and Political Thought*. Special mention may also be made of Joan Bondurant, *Conquest of Violence: The Gandhian Philosophy of Conflict* (Bombay: Oxford University Press, 1959); Buddhadeva Bhattacharyya, *Evolution of the Political Philosophy of Gandhi* (Calcutta: Calcutta Book House, 1969); and Arne Naess, *Gandhi and Group Conflict* (Oslo: Universitatforlaget, 1974).

[6] Habermas, *Legitimation Crisis*. I have benefited from the treatment of Habermas' theory in Thomas McCarthy, *The Critical Theory of Jurgen Habermas* (Cambridge, MA: MIT Press, 1978).

[7] Some of the implications of the world-system perspective for comparative political analysis are spelt out in Immanuel Wallerstein, 'The Rise and Future Demise of the World Capitalist System: Concepts for Comparative Analysis', *Comparative Studies in Society and History* (September 1974), pp. 387–415. See also Thomas Pantham, 'Integral Pluralism—A Political Theory for India?' *Indian Quarterly*, Vol. 36, Nos. 3–4 (July-December 1980).

countries. Such an interventionist state needs cultural legitimation because it is not engaged in maintaining the natural or inherent 'justice' of the exchange of equivalents as was believed to have been done by the invisible hand of the market in the early, liberal phase of capitalism. But, as Habermas has shown, what it actually experiences is a legitimation deficit; such culturally sanctioned norms of legitimation as possessive individualism, achievement ideology, and utilitarian ethics are offset by the political and administrative considerations, which, under state-managed capitalism, determine the social production and private appropriation of surplus value. Moreover, since such a state is not engaged in promoting 'the greatest good of all' (Gandhi) or 'the generalizable interests' of the people (Habermas), it lacks any basis for a truly democratic legitimation of its actions. To quote Habermas: 'Genuine participation of citizens in processes of political will-formation, that is, substantive democracy, would bring to consciousness the contradiction between administratively socialized production and the continued private appropriation and use of surplus value.'[8]

Gandhi too believed that the capitalist ethos and utilitarian principles militate against participatory or substantive democracy. He realized that 'this age of awakening of the poorest of the poor' is the 'age of democracy' and that 'the states that are today nominally democratic have either to become frankly totalitarian or, if they are to become truly democratic, they must become courageously nonviolent.'[9] According to him, violence is antithetical to democracy because a social system based on the former 'cannot provide for or protect the weak,' while democracy requires that 'under it the weakest should have the same opportunity as the strongest.'[10] He therefore maintained that a truly democratic or non-violent social order 'is clearly an impossibility so long as the wide gulf between the rich and the hungry millions persists.'[11]

Early in his public life, Gandhi realized that he was a 'pariah untouchable' of the imperialist system, whose claims to be bearing the burden of 'civilizing' and 'democratizing' the colonies he found to be untrue or 'hypocritical'. For instance, taking the meaning of the Gujarati equivalent of 'civilization' as 'good conduct,' he found that what British imperialism did in the colonies was the opposite of it.[12] Similarly, he argued that the electoral democracies of Europe and America are only 'nominal

---

[8] Habermas, *Legitimation Crisis*, p. 36. For a related treatment of the relationship between participation and legitimacy, see Dennis F. Thompson, *The Democratic Citizen* (Cambridge University Press, 1970), pp. 62–64.

[9] Gandhi, *Democracy: Real and Deceptive*, p. 68.

[10] Gandhi, *Nonviolence in Peace and War*, Vol. 2, p. 269.

[11] Gandhi, *Democracy: Real and Deceptive*, p. 68.

[12] *The Collected Works of Mahatma Gandhi*, Vol. 10 (Government of India, Ministry of Information and Broadcasting), p. 37.

democracies,' belonging to 'the same species' as fascism; both are exploitative systems and 'resort to ruthlessness to the extent required to compass their end.'[13] The only differences he saw between liberal democratic and fascist systems were that the violence of the latter was much better organized than that of the former, and that these 'have the backing of their peoples who imagine that they have a voice in their own government.'[14]

In an article in *Young India* in 1925, he clarified the deceptive, 'hypocritical,' one-dimensional nature of liberal democracy:

> The people of Europe have no doubt political power but no *Swaraj*. Asian and African races are exploited for their partial benefit, and they, on their part, are being exploited by the ruling class or caste *under the sacred name of democracy*. At the root, therefore, the disease appears to be the same as in India. The same remedy is, therefore, likely to be applicable. Shorn of all the camouflage, the exploitation of the masses of Europe is sustained by violence.[15]

As exploitative aspects of Western democracy, Gandhi referred to the British conquest of India 'not through democratic methods,' the white race's domination over the native and coloured people of South Africa, and the oppression of the Blacks in the United States. In an interview with an American journalist at Sevagram in April 1940, Gandhi said:

> My notion of democracy is that under it the weakest should have the same opportunity as the strongest. That can never happen except through nonviolence. No country in the world today shows any but patronizing regard for the weak. The weakest, you say, go to the wall. Take your own case. Your land is owned by a few capitalist owners. The same is true of South Africa. These large holdings cannot be sustained except by violence, veiled if not open. Western democracy as it functions today is diluted Nazism or Fascism. At best it is merely a *cloak to hide the Nazi and the Fascist tendencies of imperialism*.[16]

At the outbreak of World War II, Gandhi reiterated his contention that fascism and nazism belonged to 'the same species as the so-called democracies' and that the end of the war 'will mean also the end of the rule of capital.'[17] He declared that the 'great powers will have to give up the imperialistic ambitions and exploitation of the so-called uncivilized

---

[13] Gandhi, *Democracy: Real and Deceptive*, p. 78.
[14] *Ibid.*, p. 9.
[15] *Ibid.*, p. 76. Emphasis added.
[16] *Ibid.*, p. 11. Emphasis added.
[17] Gandhi, *Nonviolence in Peace and War*, Vol. 1, p. 373.

or semicivilized nations of the earth and *revise their mode of life.*[18] By this 'revision,' he meant the revision of the capitalist ethos. In an article published in 1925 under the title 'What of the West?' he clarified the nature of the needed revision as follows:

From what will the masses be delivered? It will not do to have a vague generalization and to answer from 'exploitation and degradation'. Is not the answer this, that they want to occupy the status that capital does today? If so it can be attained only by violence. But *if they want to shun the evils of capital*, in other words, *if they would revise the view point of capital*, they would strive to attain a juster distribution of the products of labour. This immediately takes us to contentment and simplicity, voluntarily adopted. *Under the new outlook, multiplicity of material wants will not be the aim of life*, the aim will be rather their restriction consistently with comfort. We shall cease to think of getting what we can, but we *shall decline to receive what all cannot get.*[19]

On another occasion, Gandhi defined his conception of true democracy as a post-capitalist social order in which 'inequalities based on possession and nonpossession, colour, race, creed or sex vanish' and 'land and state belong to the people'.[20]

In Gandhi's scheme of transcending the capitalist system, trusteeship is of central importance. That Gandhi envisaged trusteeship as a post-capitalist arrangement may be gathered from the following 'formula,' which he approved:

Trusteeship provides a means of transforming the present capitalist order of society into an egalitarian one. It gives no quarter to capitalism, but gives the present owning class a chance of reforming itself. It is based on the faith that human nature is never beyond redemption. It does not recognize any right of private ownership of property, except inasmuch as it may be permitted by society for its own welfare.[21]

This 'new outlook' of 'declining to receive what all cannot get' was Gandhi's alternative to the utilitarian norms of social organization. He said that the utilitarian, unlike the votary of sarvodaya, takes happiness 'to mean only physical happiness and economic prosperity' and is never willing to sacrifice himself.[22] Gandhi wrote:

[18] *Ibid.*, pp. 158–59. Emphasis added.

[19] Gandhi, *Democracy: Real and Deceptive*, pp. 76–77. Emphasis added.

[20] M.K. Gandhi, *Towards Lasting Peace*, ed. A.T. Hingorani (Bombay: Bharatiya Vidya Bhavan, 1956), p. 217.

[21] This is the final version of a trusteeship formula which was originally drafted by Professor M.L. Dantwala and modified by Gandhi. See Pyarelal, *Mahatma Gandhi: The Last Phase*, Vol. 2 (Ahmedabad: Navajivan, 1958), pp. 633–34.

[22] Gandhi, *Sarvodaya*, pp. 4, 7.

I do not believe in the doctrine of the greatest good of the greatest number. It means in its nakedness that in order to achieve the supposed good of 51 per cent the interest of 49 per cent may be, or rather, should be sacrificed. It is a heartless doctrine and has done harm to humanity. *The only real, dignified, human doctrine is the greatest good of all, and this can only be achieved by uttermost self-sacrifice.*[23]

The Objectification of the State and the Curtailment of Freedom

The 'post-liberal' or post-capitalist thrust of Gandhi's theory of democracy, which I have highlighted above, has not been given sufficient emphasis by Gandhian scholars.[24] This is not without any justification. For, in Gandhi's writings, the main target of attack is the amoral, coercive state, and not any particular class. Not that Gandhi was oblivious of, or tolerant toward, the class conflicts of modern times. He did recognize the reality of class conflicts between capital and labour, and between landlords and landless labourers.[25] He also maintained that capitalism and *zamindari* should be 'sterilized' and that in a truly democratic society, class conflicts would be transcended.[26] He, however, not only opposed the class war approach to social transformation but also regarded the domination by any particular class to be a lesser evil than the violence and oppression of the state. He believed, in other words, that human liberation from 'the evils of capital' is hampered by the fact that the class conflicts of the capitalist-imperialist system have become enmeshed with and transformed by a basic conflict between the individual and the state, which, he said, 'represents violence in a concentrated and organized form'.[27] As if in anticipation of the Habermasian diagnosis of the crucial role of state intervention in the maintenance of the late capitalist system, Gandhi wrote that 'the violence of private ownership is less injurious than the

---

[23] *The Diary of Mahadev Desai*, Vol. 1, tr. V.G. Desai (Ahmedabad: Navajivan, 1953), p. 149. Emphasis added.

[24] Some notable exceptions are Ashis Nandy, 'From Outside the Imperium: Gandhi's Cultural Critique of the "West",' *Alternatives*, Vol. 7 (1981), pp. 171–94; J.D. Sethi, *Gandhi Today* (New Delhi: Vikas, 1978); and V.R. Mehta, *Beyond Marxism* (New Delhi: Manohar, 1978). On the notion of post-liberal democracy, see C.B. Macpherson, *Democratic Theory: Essays in Retrieval* (London: Oxford University Press, 1973), Ch. 9; and Alan Wolfe, *Limits of Legitimacy*.

[25] See A.K. Das Gupta, 'Gandhi on Social Conflict,' *Economic and Political Weekly*, Vol. 3, No. 49 (7 December 1968); Abha Pandya, 'Gandhi and Agrarian Classes,' *Economic and Political Weekly*, Vol. 13, No. 26 (1 July 1978); and V.K.R.V. Rao, 'Gandhi and Social Change,' *Mainstream*, Vol. 18, No. 11 (10 November 1979).

[26] Gandhi, *Sarvodaya*, pp. 95–97.

[27] *Ibid.*, p. 74.

violence of the State.'[28] While he recognized the need for mankind to move beyond the capitalist utilitarian system of social organization, he was convinced that 'if the State suppressed capitalism by violence, it will be caught in the coils of violence itself and fail to develop non-violence at any time.'[29] True to his belief in the integral nature of the means-ends continuum, he maintained that through violent means we cannot break out of 'the vicious circle of violence and exploitation'. He wrote,

> The whole reason why labour so often fails is that instead of sterilizing capital, as I have suggested, labour . . . wants to seize that capital and become capitalist itself in the worse sense of the term. And the capitalist, therefore, who is properly entrenched and organized, finding among labourers also candidates for the same office, makes use of a portion of these to suppress labour.[30]

Gandhi's objection to the organized and concentrated violence of the state had to do with his commitment to individual freedom. 'The individual,' he said, 'is the one supreme consideration.'[31] 'If the individual ceases to count,' he asked, 'what is left of society?'[32] In fact, Gandhi's entire social theory and praxis were aimed at using and *extending* civil liberties for the democratization of 'the whole social structure'.[33] He shared the liberal concern for individual freedom. But he found the liberal and liberal-democratic method of securing social order through the supposedly amoral, objectified state to be at the expense of the political dimension of the freedom of the individual. He, therefore, sought to redeem individual freedom even in the political sphere without endangering social harmony. He, in other words, attempted to resolve the contradiction in the theory and practice of liberal democracy between the *affirmation* of individual freedom in the so-called private sphere of morality and its *curtailment* in the allegedly amoral or purely technical public/political sphere. Let me explain this.

Unlike the pre-liberal world-views, the modern, liberal ideology recognizes the individual's freedom of judgement, choice, contract, and possessions. This has historically been 'a vast emancipatory achievement for mankind.'[34] But the ensuing inequalities in property and the clash of

---

[28] *Ibid.* According to Habermas, 'State-regulated capitalism, which emerged from a reaction against the dangers to the system produced by open class antagonism, suspends class conflict.' Habermas, *Toward a Rational Society* (Boston: Beacon Press, 1970), p. 107. In *Legitimation Crisis* (p. 57), he speaks of 'a partial class compromise' under state-managed capitalism.

[29] Gandhi, *Sarvodaya*, p. 74.   [30] *Ibid.*, p. 92.

[31] Gandhi in *Young India* (13 November 1924), p. 378.

[32] Gandhi in *Harijan* (1 February 1942), p. 27.

[33] Gandhi, *Nonviolence in Peace and War*, Vol. 1, p. 353, and Vol. 2, p. 61.

[34] Christian Bay, *Strategies of Political Emancipation*, p. 21.

individual, private interests and judgements, which were unleashed by the liberal revolution, endangered social order. The liberal and liberal-democratic answer to this problem of social order was the invention of a *political* form of government, which excluded individual *private* judgements.[35] That is, the 'rule of one man' (i.e., rule through an individual's private judgement) was replaced by the republican form of government, which, with the eventual democratization of the franchise, became the liberal-democratic state. This state of the 'political' is supposed to be autonomous from, or external to, the rest of social life; the standards of expediency or effectiveness of the former are assumed to be divorced from private, moral standards. That the constitution of the liberal-democratic state is based on this artificial dichotomization of social life into the public (i.e., the political) and the private, the amoral and the moral, is argued by Carole Pateman:

> The liberal answer to the problem of social order inherent in such a society was to divide social life into two spheres and to substitute for shared principles a 'political method' or procedure for arbitrating between the conflicting individual interests and deciding on the 'public interest'. In the private sphere of social life, individuals' non-political natural rights are given actual expression; this is the proper sphere for individuals to exercise their private judgement and pursue their interests. In the political sphere individual private judgement is excluded, the natural political right is given up and decisions are made on behalf of individuals by specially chosen representatives.[36]

These representatives, as Pateman goes on to point out, are supposedly engaged in representing 'the political or public interest, not the separate, conflicting interests of individuals.'[37] Political decisions are thus assumed to be value-neutral, procedural, or technical decisions. Similarly, democracy is *reduced* to an allegedly amoral 'political method,' which, unlike integral or participatory democracy, only gives the people 'the opportunity of accepting or refusing the men who are to rule them.'[38] These rulers or representatives are supposed to embody 'the political selves, the citizen selves, of the members of the community.'[39]

[35] Carole Pateman, 'Sublimation and Reification: Locke, Wolin and the Liberal Democratic Conception of the Political,' *Politics and Society* (1975), p. 451.

[36] *Ibid.*, p. 454.   [37] *Ibid.*, p. 456.

[38] For a critique of this democratic methodism, see Thomas Pantham, 'On the Theory of Democracy: A Critique of "the Schumpeter Dahl Axis",' *Journal of the M.S. University of Baroda* (Social Sciences), Vols. 25–26, 1976–1977.

[39] Pateman, 'Sublimation and Reification,' p. 456. Similarly, Benjamin R. Barber writes: 'The chief obstacle to political participation is, paradoxically, the chief instrument of political participation in the United States—representation. Representation, intended by the Founders to mediate the value conflict between active local citizenship and effective central administration, has been far too efficacious; it has made citizens unnecessary.' Barber, *Political Participation and the Creation of Res Publica* (Bloomington, IN: Poynter Center, 1977), p. 10.

Thus, in liberal democratic theory and practice, the political is reified and objectified into the representative state, which becomes the bearer of the alienated political rights of the citizens. This is what I meant when I said above that there is a fundamental contradiction in liberal democratic theory and practice between the affirmation of individual freedom in the private sphere and its curtailment in the public/political sphere.

Actually, the objectification of the political into the state and its privatization and hierarchization by the technocrats of power, which militate against the requirements of participatory or substantive democracy, serve the requirements of the capitalist-industrial system for state intervention in the process of capital accumulation.[40]

It needs to be emphasized that this technocratization of politics has been going on even in the liberal democracies. Under favourable socio-historical conditions, liberal democracy has indeed served as a peaceful mechanism of securing formal democratic legitimacy for the state. But when the masses have used or threatened to use their civil liberties for pushing the electoral or formal democracies in the direction of a substantive or participatory democracy, which would have offset the state-managed private accumulation of socially produced surplus value, the technocrats of power have raised the cry of 'governability crisis' and have used coercive methods to depoliticize the mass public, thereby further objectifying the state and privatizing it as a purely technocratic enterprise.[41]

Gandhi, as we saw in the foregoing, attacked the late-modern capitalist state for its fascist proclivities. He believed that the de-reification of the objectified state was necessary for redeeming the political dimension of individual freedom: 'I look upon an increase in the power of the State with the greatest fear, because, although while apparently doing good by minimizing exploitation, it does the greatest harm to mankind by destroying *individuality which lies at the root of all progress.*'[42]

He maintained that the state is a 'soulless machine' and that amoral polities 'encircle us like the coils of a snake.' He therefore sought to repair the liberal democratic one-dimensionalization of freedom and democracy without endangering social harmony by combining *swaraj* (participatory democracy) with the satyagraha mode of integrating politics and morality. He professed his aims in the following words, in which, as he himself clarified elsewhere, 'religious' is used interchangeably with

    [40] See Brian Fay, *Social Theory and Political Practice* (London: George Allen & Unwin, 1975), p. 46. Alvin Toffler writes: 'Representative government—what we have been taught to call democracy—was, in short, an industrial technology for assuring inequality.' Toffler, *The Third Wave* (Bantam Books, 1981), p. 77.
    [41] See Walter Dean Burnham, 'Thoughts on the "Governability Crisis" in the West,' *Washington Review of Strategic and International Studies* (July 1978), pp. 46–57; and Jurgen Habermas, 'The Public Sphere,' *New German Critique*, Vol. 3 (1974), pp. 49–55, as cited in T. McCarthy, *Critical Theory of Jurgen Habermas*, p. 382.
    [42] Gandhi, *Sarvodaya*, p. 74. Emphasis added.

'moral' or 'spiritual': 'I could not be leading a religious life unless I identified myself with the whole of mankind and that I could not do unless I took part in politics. The whole gamut of a man's activities today constitutes an indivisible whole.'[43] As we see in this quote, the two parts of Gandhi's redemptive project are participatory democracy and the spiritualization of politics.

Swaraj or Participatory Democracy

On several occasions, Gandhi criticized the liberal-democratic reification, objectification, and technocratization of the political and the alienation of the people's political rights. He also put forward the alternative of participatory democracy, which ruptures the positivist disjunction between subject and object, means and ends. To quote him:

> A superficial study of British history has made us think that all power percolates to the people from parliaments. The truth is that power resides in the people and it is entrusted for the time being to those whom they may choose as their representatives.[44]
>
> Let us not push the mandate theory to ridiculous extremes and become slaves to resolutions of majorities . . . . Swaraj will be an absurdity if individuals have to surrender their judgement to majority.[45]
>
> The very essence of democracy is that every person represents all the varied interests which compose the nation. It is true that it does not exclude, and should not exclude, special representation of special interests, but such representation is not its test. It is a sign of its imperfection.[46]
>
> True democracy cannot be worked by twenty men sitting at the Centre. It has to be worked from below by the people of every village.[47]

While admitting that the necessity of a 'central government administration' cannot be ruled out, Gandhi maintained that it need not and ought not be patterned after 'the accepted Western form of democracy'.[48] His objection was to the central government administration becoming the bearer of the alienated political rights of the citizens. 'Under my plan,' he said, 'the State will be there to carry out the will of the people, not to

---

[43] D.G. Tendulkar, *Mahatma: Life of Mohandas Karamchand Gandhi*, Vol. 4 (Bombay: 1951–1954), pp. 387–88.

[44] Gandhi, *Constructive Programme* (Ahmedabad: Navajivan, 1945), pp. 8–9.

[45] Gandhi, *Democracy: Real and Deceptive*, p. 45.

[46] *Ibid.*, p. 7.

[47] *Ibid.*, p. 7.

[48] As told to Louis Fischer. See Fischer, *A Week With Gandhi* (Bombay: International Book House, 1944), p. 44.

dictate to them or force them to do its will.'[49] While he did caution us against converting democracy into mobocracy, he insisted that 'democracy is an impossible thing until the power is shared by all.' He said, 'Most people do not understand the complicated machinery of the government. They do not realize that every citizen silently but nonetheless certainly sustains the government of the day in ways of which he has no knowledge.'[50] Elsewhere he added,

> real swaraj will come not by the acquisition of authority by a few but by the acquisition of the capacity by all to resist authority when it is abused. In other words, swaraj is to be attained by educating the masses to a sense of their capacity to regulate and control authority.[51]

As I said earlier, Gandhi recognized the need for a 'central government administration'. But he said it should be structured not as a pyramid but as an oceanic circle:

> In this structure composed of innumerable villages, there will be ever-widening, never-ascending circles. Life will not be a pyramid with the apex sustained by the bottom. But it will be an oceanic circle whose centre will be the individual always ready to perish for the village, the latter ready to perish for the circle of villages, till at last the whole becomes one life composed of individuals, never aggressive in their arrogance but ever humble, sharing the majesty of the oceanic circle of which they are integral units.[52]

Politics and Ethics

Gandhi's project of the redemption of political freedom by the individual from the objectified state through participatory democracy is not to be taken to mean that he was unconcerned with the problem of social order. Paradoxic though it may seem, Gandhi, who, compared to the liberal democratic theorists, had a greater concern for individual freedom, also had a greater concern for social harmony. He felt that the liberal democratic scheme of securing social order through the supposedly amoral machinery of government not only curtailed individual freedom, but also failed to bring about any lasting or authentic social harmony. He believed that the observance of social norms 'consciously and as a matter of duty' not only was a more secure foundation for social order than their observance for reasons of legality or out of fear of external sanctions but

---

[49] Gandhi, *Democracy: Real and Deceptive*, p. 70.
[50] *Ibid.*, p. 30.
[51] *Ibid.*, pp. 4–5.
[52] *Ibid.*, pp. 73–74.

was also conducive to individual freedom. According to him, therefore, both individual freedom and social harmony could be ensured if the participatory process of reclaiming political freedom from the objectified state was *eo ipso* a process of the spiritualization of politics or the reintegration of politics with morality. Anticipating Habermas' contention that the technocratic model of politics is at the expense of democracy and that a society can be ordered democratically 'only as a self-controlled learning process' of communicative ethics,[53] Gandhi said his conception of true democracy was one of 'the reign of the self-imposed law of moral restraint.'[54] He held that 'by learning to adjust his individualism to the requirements of social progress' man could move in the direction of a truly democratic order.[55]

In fact, it was the divorce of politics from morality that Gandhi found most objectionable in the 'modern civilization,' which arose in, and spread out from, the West. In his famous book, *Hind Swaraj*, which he wrote on board the *S.S. Kildonan* during his return voyage to South Africa from England in 1908, he declared, 'This civilization takes note neither of morality nor of religion.'[56] In a lecture he gave at the Muir Central College, Allahabad, in December 1916, he said that it was his 'firm belief that there is little to gain from Britain in intrinsic morality' and that 'if we copy her because she provides us with rulers, both they and we shall suffer degradation.'[57] He therefore proposed and experimented with an action project, namely, satyagraha, for superseding the modernist, amoral, elitist paradigm of government. That action project, it may be noted in passing, ruptures the modern, positivist dichotomies between subject and object, means and ends, politics and morality. Regarding the last mentioned dichotomies, Gandhi wrote that social life 'is not divided into water-tight compartments, called social, political and religious' and that 'every act . . . has its . . . spiritual, economic and social implications.'[58] He referred to his ideal of true democracy as 'the square of *swaraj*,' whose four sides are the political, the economic, the social, and *dharma* (i.e., universal morality).[59]

The morality or spirituality, which, according to Gandhi, is to be reintegrated with politics, is not any revealed, sectarian religion, but sarvodaya ethics or universal morality. 'The highest moral law,' he said, 'is that we should unremittingly work for the good of mankind.'[60]

[53] Habermas, as cited in T. McCarthy, *Critical Theory of Jurgen Habermas*, p. 331.
[54] Gandhi, *Towards Everlasting Peace*, p. 217.
[55] Gandhi, *Democracy: Real and Deceptive*, p. 32.
[56] Gandhi, *Hind Swaraj*, p. 27.
[57] Gandhi, *Economic and Industrial Life and Relations*, Vol. 2 (Ahmedabad: Navajivan, 1957), p. 8.　　　　　　　　　　[58] *Young India*, 2 March 1922, p. 131.
[59] *Harijan* (2 January 1937), p. 374. Emphasis added.
[60] M.K. Gandhi, *Ethical Religion*, tr. A. Ramaiyer (Madras: S. Ganesan, 1922), p. 7. Emphasis added.

He singled out truth and non-violence as the most important moral norms, which, he pointed out, 'are no cloistered virtues' but are to be discovered and formed through 'the ordinary activities of life' in the economic, social, and political spheres.[61] Moreover, according to him, an action to be moral has to be done 'consciously and as a matter of duty'; actions that are 'dictated by fear or coercion' or 'promoted by hope of happiness in the next world cease to be moral.'[62] So, instead of withdrawing from politics, he, as I mentioned earlier, introduced and experimented with an emancipatory political project, namely, satyagraha, whose assumptions and action implications are different from those of liberal democracy.

Liberal political thought is based on a pessimistic, one-dimensional conception of man as a brutish and selfish being. It is this conception of man that lies behind the preoccupation of the pre-democratic and democratic liberal thinkers with political devices or machinery rather than with action techniques for the resolution of social conflicts. The reified and objectified state is their answer to man's brutishness and selfishness. Their reasoning is that because men are brutish and selfish, social order can be secured, not through any action by the individuals, but through the structure of political machinery. This structure is meant to facilitate the process of bargaining and compromise in situations of conflict over relatively minor issues and to impose order through violent force when the conflict is of a fundamental nature. Thus, liberal democratic theory provides no technique of action for avoiding violent revolution in the face of fundamental social conflicts, for example, conflict over the legitimacy claims of the state.

Gandhi argued that if we adopt the pessimistic, one-dimensional conception of man and rely only on the structure of political machinery for securing social harmony, the stronger among the selfish will use that machinery as an additional means of domination or oppression. It is to avoid this vicious circle of violence and exploitation that Gandhi made an inversion of the Hobbes-to-Lenin approach to political theorizing. He based his theory and practice of democracy on a realistic, integral conception of human nature, which, while not denying man's selfishness, acknowledges his potential for rationality and goodness. Accordingly, Gandhi's action project of satyagraha has the twin objectives of enabling humanity to realize its potential for rationality and goodness, and thereby securing a moral or democratically legitimate social order. He wrote that 'the desire to improve ourselves for the sake of doing good to others is truly moral.'[63] He discussed the distinctiveness of his assumptions in the following words:

    [61] *Harijan*, 8 May 1937, p. 98.
    [62] Gandhi, *Ethical Religion*, pp. 8–11
• [63] *Ibid.*, p. 7.

Socialism and communism of the West are based on certain conceptions which are fundamentally different from ours. One such conception is their belief in the essential selfishness of human nature. I do not subscribe to it for I know that the essential difference between man and the brute is that the former can respond to the call of the spirit in him, can rise superior to the passions that he owns in common with the brute, and, therefore, superior to selfishness and violence, which belong to the brute nature and not to the immortal spirit of man. That is the fundamental conception of Hinduism.[64]

In the application of the method of non-violence, one must believe in the possibility of every person, however depraved, being reformed under human and skilled treatment. We must appeal to the good in human beings and expect response.[65]

While the pre-democratic liberal theorists assumed the brutishness of man and justified the role of the Leviathan in maintaining social order, the liberal-democratic theorists assume that men are atomistic beings and that their interests are to be regarded by the political sphere as being morally neutral. For the liberal democrat, all the interests of all the people are of equal worth; he does not discriminate between morally justifiable and immoral interests. For him, the task or 'business' of the 'democratic method' is to accommodate or adjust the supposedly amoral interests of the people or, at least, of those who take part in politics.[66] Accordingly, as Immanuel Kant wrote, the problem of securing social order is a problem of arranging

the powers of each selfish inclination in opposition . . . so that one moderates or destroys the ruinous effect of the other. The consequence for reason is the same as if none of them existed, and *man is forced to be a good citizen even if not a morally good person.* The problem of organizing a state, however hard it may seem, can be solved even for a race of devils if only they are intelligent. The problem is: 'Given a multitude of rational beings requiring universal laws for their pre-servation, but each of whom is secretly inclined to exempt himself from them, to establish a constitution in such a way that, although their private intentions conflict, they check each other, with the result that their public conduct is the same as if they had no such intentions.'[67]

Gandhi, as I pointed out earlier, repaired this modern scientistic/

[64] M.K. Gandhi, *Socialism of My Conception* (Bombay, 1957), p. 270.

[65] Gandhi, *Democracy: Real and Deceptive*, p. 64.

[66] Alvin Toffler says that the votes are the atoms of the Newtonian mechanism of representative government. Toffler, *The Third Wave*, p. 72.

[67] 'Perpetual Peace,' in L.W. Beck, ed., *Kant on History* (New York: 1963), p. 112. Emphasis added.

positivist divorce of morality from politics. He argued that if the stuff of politics is taken to be the atomistic, amoral conception of human interests, there would necessarily ensue the vicious circle of mindless competition, hierarchy, overcentralization and violent coercion. In his view, therefore, we cannot escape the inherent contradictions of liberal democracy without abandoning the liberal-individualistic conception of humanity and the atomistic, amoral conception of its interests. He argued that the promotion of human freedom and fulfilment and the building of human community depend on our ability and willingness to adopt a new conception of humanity *and* act on the basis of that new conception. That new conception is that humans are essentially social beings, that not all their interests or wants are of equal moral worth, and that they can be educated to discover and pursue their morally justifiable interests.

Satyagraha or Communitarian Ethics

Gandhi argued that we, as *isolated individuals*, are not the sufficient judges of the truth or moral worth of our interests, if they are to be embodied in socially binding norms, claiming democratic legitimacy. In his weekly, *Harijan*, of 31 March 1946, he wrote: 'Individual liberty and interdependence are both essential for life in society.' Again:

> I value individual freedom, but you must not forget that man is essentially a social being. He has risen to the present status by learning to adjust his individualism to the requirements of social progress. Unrestricted individualism is the law of the beast of the jungle. We have learnt to strike the mean between individual freedom and social restraint. Willing submission to social restraint for the sake of the well-being of the whole society enriches both the individual and the society of which one is a member.[68]

According to Gandhi, therefore, only if our interest positions are capable of receiving the uncoerced acceptance of all those who are affected by them, can we advance any truthful or moral claim for their inclusion in socially binding norms. In other words, for Gandhi, as for Habermas, the critical principle of democracy is the principle of uncoerced, consensual or communitarian truth. Gandhi believed that even in situations of fundamental social conflict there is a potential harmony of the essentially human interests of the parties to the conflict.[69] It is for the discovery and

---

[68] Gandhi, *Democracy: Real and Deceptive*, p. 32.

[69] C.B. Macpherson has argued that an optimistic assumption about the potential harmony of the essentially human interests has always been at the root of the democratic vision. Macpherson, *Democratic Theory*, pp. 54–55. See also the discussion of Habermas' theory of communicative ethics in Thomas McCarthy, *Critical Theory of Jurgen Habermas*, and Stephen K. White, 'Reason and Authority in Habermas: A Critique of the Critics,' *American Political Science Review*, Vol. 74 (1980), pp. 1007–17.

formation of such communitarian truth that he developed his satyagraha mode of action.

In a satyagraha movement, the contested truth of a social 'system' or norm is sought to be validated through three steps: (*i*) persuading the opponents through reasoning and being open to, and inviting, the counter-persuasive efforts of the opponents; (*ii*) appealing to the opponents through the self-suffering of the *satyagrahis*; and (*iii*) non-cooperation and civil disobedience.

The various methods of satyagraha are: (*a*) purificatory or penitential actions by the satyagrahis, such as pledges, prayers, and fasts; (*b*) acts of non-cooperation, such as boycott, strikes, *hartal*, and the like; (*c*) acts of civil disobedience, such as picketing, non-payment of taxes, and defiance of specific laws; and (*d*) works of constructive programmes, such as the promotion of intercommunal unity, the removal of untouchability, adult education, and the removal of economic and social inequalities. At each stage of the programme, the satyagrahis, while holding on to the truth as they see it, assume their own fallibility and give the opponents every chance to prove that the satyagrahis' position is erroneous. Satyagraha 'excludes the use of violence because man is not capable of knowing the absolute truth and therefore not competent to punish.' The ideal to be kept in mind is that of a self-regulated society of communitarian truth, in which every one 'rules himself in such a manner that he is never a hindrance to his neighbour.'[70] 'The claim for satyagraha,' writes Joan Bondurant, 'is that through the operation of non-violent action the truth as judged by the fulfilment of human needs will emerge in the form of a mutually satisfactory and agreed-upon solution.'[71] Hence the important operative principles to be observed by the satyagrahis are the admission of truths as relative, non-violence and toleration, and the self-suffering of the satyagrahis. Gandhi justified these operative principles in the following passages:

> In the application of satyagraha, I discovered in the earliest stages that pursuit of Truth did not admit of violence being inflicted on one's opponent, but that he must be weaned from error by patience and sympathy. For what appears to be Truth to the one may appear false to the other.[72]
>
> The golden rule of conduct, therefore, is mutual toleration, seeing that we will never all think alike and we see truth in fragment and from different angles of vision. Conscience is not the same thing for all. Whilst, therefore, it is a good guide for individual conduct, imposition of that conduct upon all will be an insufferable interference with everybody's freedom of conscience.[73]

[70] Gandhi, *Sarvodaya*, p. 73.　　　　　[71] Bondurant, *Conquest of Violence*, p. 195.
[72] Gandhi, *Satyagraha* (Ahmedabad: Navajivan. 1958), p. 6.
[73] *Young India*, 23 September 1926, p. 554.

People's conceptions of true interests and just laws differ. That is the main reason why violence is eliminated and a satyagrahi gives his opponent the same right of independence and feelings of liberty that he reserves to himself and he will fight by inflicting injuries on his person.[74]

Evolution of democracy is not possible if we are not prepared to hear the other side. We shut the doors of reason when we refuse to listen to our opponents, or having listened, make fun of them. *If intolerance becomes a habit, we run the risk of missing the truth.* Whilst, with the limits that Nature has put on our understanding, we must act fearlessly according to the light vouchsafed to us, we must always keep an open mind and be ever ready to find that what we believed to be truth was, after all, untruth. This openness of mind strengthens the truth in us.[75]

Regarding the third operative principle of satyagraha, namely, self-suffering, Gandhi believed that it was an extension of the non-violent method or, in other words, 'the chosen substitute for violence to others'.[76] He believed that through self-suffering, the satyagrahis could make extra-rational appeals to their opponents, who may thereby be moved to make the big change expected of them. 'I have found,' he wrote, 'that mere appeal to reason does not answer where prejudices are age-long and based on supposed religious authority. Reason has to be strengthened by suffering.'[77] Further,

Suffering is the law of human beings; war is the law of the jungle. But suffering is infinitely more powerful than the law of the jungle for converting the opponent and opening his ears, which are otherwise shut, to the voice of reason. Nobody has probably drawn up more petitions or espoused more forlorn causes than I, and I have come to this fundamental conclusion that if you want something really important to be done, you must not merely satisfy the reason, you must move the heart also. The appeal of reason is more to the head, but the penetration of the heart comes from suffering. It opens up the inner understanding of men. Suffering is the badge of the human race, not the sword.[78]

Another reason given for the principle of self-suffering was that it served as the proof of the truthfulness and courage of the satyagrahis.

Just as one must learn the art of killing in the training for violence, so one must learn the art of dying in the training for non-violence . . . .

---

74 *Young India*, 1919–1922, p. 18.
75 Gandhi, *Democracy: Real and Deceptive*, pp. 34–35. Emphasis added.
76 *Young India*, 8 October 1925, p. 345.
77 *Young India*, March 1925.
78 M.K. Gandhi, *India's Case for Swaraj* (Yeshanand, 1932), p. 369.

The votary of non-violence has to cultivate the capacity for sacrifice of the highest type in order to be free from fear . . . . He who has not overcome all fear cannot practise *ahimsa* to perfection.[79]

The Effectiveness of Satyagraha

Several critics of satyagraha have maintained that non-violence and self-suffering are impractical methods against violent oppression, and that self-suffering is too high a price demanded of the democratic emancipators. The Gandhian ideal, they argue, is 'other-worldly, anti-humanist'. For instance, George Orwell has argued that we 'must choose between God and Man,' and that 'Gandhi's teachings cannot be squared with the belief that man is the measure of all things and that our job is to make life worth living on this earth.'[80] Gandhi's great compatriot, Lokmanya Tilak, too believed that the Gandhian project of integrating politics and morality was unsuited to this-worldly concerns. In his famous letter to Gandhi, he wrote that politics 'is a game of worldly people and not of *sadhus*,' and that the approach of Sri Krishna is more suited to this world than the Buddhist approach.[81]

In his reply to the Lokmanya (Tilak), Gandhi averred that non-violence and self-suffering were 'not for the unworldly but essentially for the worldly'. He did admit that those principles were very difficult to practise but insisted that we need to, and can, keep on moving along those lines. 'Perfect non-violence whilst you are inhabiting the body,' he wrote, 'is only a theory like Euclid's point or straight line, but we have to endeavour every moment of our lives.'[82] He elaborated this analogy in the following manner: 'Euclid's line is one without breadth but no one has so far been able to draw it and never will. All the same it is only by keeping the ideal line in mind that we have made progress in geometry.'[83] Similarly, 'A government cannot succeed in becoming entirely non-violent, because it represents all the people . . . . But I do believe in the possibility of a predominantly non-violent society. And I am working for it.'[84]

Gandhi maintained that both in the liberal democracies and in dictatorships, satyagraha is an effective way of bringing about a truly democratic transformation of the society. He realized that both violent and non-violent resistance by the oppressed and the exploited become the objects

---

[79] *Harijan*, 1 September 1940. For a discussion of Gandhi's conception of self-suffering as an efficient instrument of social persuasion, see W.H. Morris-Jones, 'Mahatma Gandhi—Political Philosopher?' *Political Studies* (February 1970).

[80] George Orwell, 'Reflections on Gandhi,' *Partisan Review*, Vol. 16 (January 1949).

[81] For Tilak's letter and Gandhi's reply to it, see *Young India*, January 1920.

[82] Gandhi, *Nonviolence in Peace and War*, Vol. 1, p. 292.

[83] Gandhi, *My Socialism* (Ahmedabad: Navajivan, 1959), pp. 49–50.

[84] *Ibid.*, pp. 50–51.

of state surveillance and repression. But he believed that satyagraha has a distinctive claim to ennobling consequences and to emancipatory effectiveness as it releases the forces of freedom and love for undermining the paradigm of violence. He pointed out that satyagraha, unlike violent resistance, is 'three-fourths invisible and only one-fourth visible,' and that even though it may appear to be ineffective in its visibility, it is 'really intensely active and most effective in ultimate result.' He illustrated and elaborated this argument as follows:

A violent man's activity is most visible, while it lasts. But it is always transitory. What can be more visible than the Abyssinians done to death by Italians? There it was lesser violence pitted against much greater. But if the Abyssinians had retired from the field and allowed themselves to be slaughtered, their seeming inactivity would have been much more effective though not for the moment visible. Hitler and Mussolini on the one hand and Stalin on the other are able to show the immediate effectiveness of violence. But it will be as transitory as that of Chenghis' slaughter. But the effects of Buddha's non-violent action persist and are likely to grow with age. And the more it is practised, the more effective and inexhaustible it becomes.[85]

Regarding the effectiveness of satyagraha against dictatorships, Gandhi wrote:

Even a Nero is not devoid of a heart. The unexpected spectacle of endless rows upon rows of men and women simply dying rather than surrender to the will of an aggressor must ultimately melt him and his soldiery. Practically speaking, there will be probably no greater loss in men than if forcible resistance was offered; there will be no expenditure in armaments and fortifications. The non-violent training received by the people will add inconceivably to their moral height.[86]

Aldous Huxley too believed in the effectiveness and practicality of the Gandhian approach. He wrote,

[85] Gandhi, *Nonviolence in Peace and War*, Vol. 1, pp. 128–29.
[86] Gandhi, *Democracy: Real and Deceptive*, p. 21. That the 'inner strength' of the satyagrahi and not the civility of the opponent is the crucial requirement of the Gandhian satyagraha is persuasively argued by Indira Rothermund in her paper, 'Gandhi's Satyagraha and Hindu Thought,' in this volume. Unlike Gandhi, John Rawls is reluctant to commend civil disobedience against dictatorships because they would use 'more repressive measures if the calculation of advantages points in this direction.' Rawls, *A Theory of Justice* (Oxford: Clarendon Press, 1972), p. 387. For an excellent comparison of Rawls' and Gandhi's views, see Vinit Haksar, 'Rawls and Gandhi on Civil Disobedience,' *Inquiry*, Vol. 19 (Summer 1976), pp. 51–92.

In the years ahead it seems possible that *satyagraha* may take root in the West, *not primarily as the result of any 'change of heart,' but simply because it provides the masses, especially in the conquered countries, with their only practicable form of political action.* The Germans of the Ruhr and Palatinate resorted to *satyagraha* against the French in 1923. The movement was spontaneous; philosophically, ethically and organizationally, it had not been prepared for. It was for this reason that it finally broke down. But it lasted long enough to prove that a Western people—and a people more thoroughly indoctrinated with militarism than any other—was perfectly capable of non-violent direct action, involving the cheerful acceptance of sacrificial suffering.[87]

The sceptic may still object to Gandhi's project on the ground that the individual freedom which he redeems from the objectified, amoral state is sacrificed on the altar of satyagraha, which demands the satyagrahis' self-suffering even unto death. Actually, this is not so.

An element of sacrifice is indeed involved in satyagraha. So also in the case of violent resistance against oppression. Sacrifice even unto death is thus the common element in both the violent and non-violent resistance against oppression. That is why Gandhi approved of the use of satyagraha only in cases of conflict over fundamental issues and only after all milder methods of non-violence have failed. 'I should be deeply distressed,' he wrote in 1921, 'if on every conceivable occasion every one of us were to be a law unto oneself and to scrutinize in golden scales every action of our future National Assembly. I would surrender my judgement in most matters to national representatives, taking particular care in making my choice of such representatives.'[88] But when a situation of violent oppression persists even after all milder methods of non-violent resistance have been tried, Gandhi maintained that the self-suffering even unto death of the non-violent fighter for communitarian truth is a truer assertion of individual freedom than is the death-in-defeat of the violent resister. Gandhi rejected the charge that the non-violence and self-suffering of the satyagrahis are 'a resignation from all real fighting against wickedness'. On the contrary,' he stated

The non-violence of my conception is a *more active and more real fighting against wickedness than retaliation whose very nature is to increase wickedness.* I contemplate a mental, and therefore a moral, opposition to immoralities. I seek entirely to blunt the edge of the tyrant's sword, not by putting up against it a sharper-edged weapon, but by disappointing his expectation that I would be offering physical resistance.[89]

[87] Aldous Huxley, *Science, Liberty and Peace* (New York: Harper Brothers, 1946), pp. 7–8. Emphasis added.

[88] Gandhi, *Nonviolence in Peace and War*, Vol. 1, pp. 22–23.

[89] *Ibid.*, p. 44. Emphasis added.

Gandhi's Audience

Gandhi did not theorize in any historical vacuum or for any atemporal audience. He and his addressees experienced the initial impact of the modern, technocratic, overorganized paradigm of politics. His audience was not confined to the East; it included the people of the West as well. What was needed for human emancipation, he argued, was not any 'revised edition' of the same technocratic paradigm of government (such as, the fascist and Leninist-Stalinist systems), but an alternative, non-violent, educative, mass-based approach to democratization. 'Satyagraha,' he asserted, 'is a process of educating public opinion, such that it covers all the elements of society and, in the end, makes itself irresistible. *Violence interrupts the process and prolongs the real revolution of the whole structure.*'[90] The method of violence, he said, not only fails to lead us out of 'the vicious circle of violence and exploitation' but also contributes to the culture of violence and thereby delays the start of the truly emancipatory process. He said:

> The socialists and communists say they can do nothing to bring about economic equality today. . . . They say, 'when they get control over the State they will enforce equality.' Under my plan, the State will be there to carry out the will of the people, not to dictate to them or force them to do its will. I shall bring about economic equality through non-violence, by converting the people to my point of view by harnessing the forces of love as against hatred. *I will not wait till I have converted the whole society to my view but will straightaway make a beginning with myself.* It goes without saying that I cannot hope to bring about economic equality of my conception, if I am the owner of fifty motor cars or even if ten *bighas* of land. For that I have to reduce myself to the level of the poorest of the poor.[91]

In the Gandhian approach, the oppressed masses are not to be made the objects of domination by their so-called emancipators. Also, the goal of the emancipatory process is not simply to raise the poor to the position of their oppressors, which Gandhi said would be a within-paradigm move, enhancing the forces of violence. The end pursued rather is 'removing the ignorance of the poor and teaching them to non-cooperate with their exploiters'[92] and thereby bring about a 'real revolution of the whole structure' so that all the members of the initial conflict situation may find their true or moral human interests in a new, communitarian

---

90 *Harijan*, March 1946. Emphasis added.

91 Gandhi, *Democracy: Real and Deceptive*, pp. 69–70. Emphasis added.

92 *Ibid.*, p. 67. Gandhi believed that 'the rich cannot accumulate wealth without the cooperation of the poor in society. If this knowledge were to penetrate to and spread among the poor, they would become strong and would learn how to free themselves.' *Ibid.*, p. 66.

synthesis. As Ashis Nandy has noted, 'All his life, Gandhi sought to free the British rather than the Indians from the clutches of imperialism and the Brahmins rather than the untouchables from the caste system.'[93]

Thus the Gandhian praxis of the quest for communitarian truth through non-violence and self-suffering shakes the foundations of both the pluralist-elitist and vanguardist-bureaucratic variants of the late-modern, amoral, technocratic paradigm of government. Hence, as Brian Fay has noted perceptively, Gandhi's praxis of 'educative transformation' through 'free and uncoerced communication' makes him 'the most significant political theorist . . . in the context of mass society.'[94] Gandhi himself believed that satyagraha was not only an effective and heroic mode of emancipation of the people of a weak country, but also

> a beacon light . . . for Europe with all its *discipline, science and organization.* If Europe but realized that, heroic as it undoubtedly is for a handful of people to offer armed resistance in the face of superior numbers, it is far more heroic to stand up against overwhelming numbers without any arms at all, it would save itself and blaze a trail for the world.[95]

[93] Ashis Nandy, 'Oppression and Human Liberation: Towards a Third World Utopia,' *Alternatives*, Vol. 4 (October 1978), p. 172.

[94] Fay, *Social Theory and Political Practice*, pp. 100–1.

[95] Gandhi, *A Pilgrimage for Peace* (Ahmedabad: Navajivan, 1950), p. 56. Emphasis added.

20

ASHIS NANDY

Oppression and Human Liberation: Towards a Post-Gandhian Utopia

> Alas, having defeated the enemy, we have ourselves
> been defeated . . . . The . . . defeated have become
> victorious . . . Misery appears like prosperity, and
> prosperity looks like misery. This our victory is twined
> into defeat.
>
> *The Mahabharata*[1]

Utopian or futurist thinking is another aspect of—and a comment upon—the here-and-now, another means of making peace with or challenging man-made suffering in the present, another ethic apportioning responsibility for this suffering and guiding the struggle against it on the plane of contemporary consciousness.[2] No utopia can, thus, be without an implicit or explicit theory of suffering. Particularly so in the peripheries of the world, euphemistically called the Third World. The concept of the Third World is not a cultural category; it is a political and economic category born of poverty, exploitation, indignity and self-contempt. The concept is inextricably linked with the efforts of a large number of people trying to survive, over generations, quasi-extreme situations.[3] A Third World utopia—the South's concept of a decent society—as Barrington

Author's Note: This is an abridged version of a much larger paper which has had a few previous incarnations. It was originally presented at the first meeting of the group of Alternative Visions of Desirable Societies at Mexico City in April 1978. The meeting was organized by Centre de Estudios Economicos y Sociales del Tercier Mundo and the project on the Goals, Processes and Indicators of Development of the United Nations University. Earlier versions of the paper have been published in *Alternatives*, Vol. 4, No. 3 (1978–79), and in Eleonora Masini and Johan Galtung, eds., *Visions of Desirable Societies*, Vol. 1 (London: Pergamon, in press). The latest version which is abridged here has gained much from the suggestions and criticisms by the participants in the Mexico meeting and by M.P. Sinha, R.A.P. Shastri, Rajni Kothari and Giri Deshingkar.

[1] *The Mahabharata*, Sauptik Parva: *10*; Slokas 9, 12, 13. Translated by Manmatha Nath Dutt (Calcutta: Elysium, 1962), p. 20.

[2] Such a utopianism is, of course, very different from the ones Karl Popper ('Utopia and Violence,' in *Conjectures and Refutations, The Growth of Scientific Knowledge*, London: Routledge and Kegan Paul, 1978, pp. 355–63) or Robert Nozick (*Anarchy, State and Utopia*, Oxford: Basil Blackwell, 1974, Part 3) have in mind.

[3] I have in mind the extremes Bruno Bettelheim describes in his 'Individual and Mass Behaviour in Extreme Situations' (1943), in *Surviving and Other Essays* (New York: Alfred A. Knopf, 1979), pp. 48–83.

Moore might call it—must recognize this basic reality.[4] To have a meaningful life in the minds of men, such a utopia must start with the issue of man-made suffering which has given the Third World both its name and its uniqueness.

This essay is an inter-civilizational perspective on oppression, with a less articulate psychology of survival and salvation as its appendage. It is guided by the belief that the only way the Third World can transcend the sloganeering of its well-wishers is (i) by becoming a collective representation of the victims of man-made suffering everywhere in the world and in all past times, (ii) by internalizing or owning up the outside forces of oppression and, then, coping with them as inner vectors, and (iii) by recognizing the oppressed or marginalized selves of the First and the Second Worlds as civilizational allies in the battle against institutionalized suffering.[5]

II

What resistance does a culture face in working through its remembered past and through the limits that past sets on its cognition? What are the psychological techniques through which the future is controlled or pre-empted by an unjust system or by the experience of injustice? What are the inner checks that a society or civilization erects against minimizing man-made suffering? What can liberation from oppression in the most utopian sense mean?

We cannot even begin to answer these questions without recognizing three processes which give structured oppression its resilience.

The first of these processes is a certain anti-psychologism which oppression breeds and from which it seeks legitimacy . . . .

. . . . [N]o vision of the future can ignore that institutional suffering touches the deepest core of human beings, and that societies must work through the culture and psychology of such suffering, in addition to its politics and economics. This awareness comes painfully, and each society in each period of history builds powerful inner defences against it. Perhaps it is in human nature to try to vest responsibility for unexplained suffering in outside forces—in fate, in history or, for that matter, in an objective science of nature or society. When successful, such an effort concretizes and exteriorizes evil and makes it psychologically more manageable. When successful, it at least keeps questions open. Predictably, every

---

[4] Barrington Moore, Jr., 'This Society Nobody Wants: A Look Beyond Marxism and Liberalism,' in Kurt H. Wolff and Barrington Moore, Jr., eds., *The Critical Spirit: Essays in Honour of Herbert Marcuse* (Boston: Beacon, 1967), pp. 401–18.

[5] Though this is not relevant to the issues I discuss in this essay, the three processes seem to hint at the cultural-anthropological, the depth-psychological and the Christian-theological concerns with oppression respectively.

other decade we have a new controversy on nature versus nurture, a new incarnation of what is presently called sociobiology, and a new biological interpretation of schizophrenia. Biology and genetics exteriorize; psychology owns up.

The second process is a certain continuity between the victors and the victims. Though some awareness of this continuity has been a part of our consciousness for many centuries, it is in this century—thanks primarily to the political technology developed by Gandhi and the cultural criticisms ventured by at least some socialist thinkers and some interpreters of Freud—that this awareness has become something more than a pious slogan. Though all religions stress the cultural and moral degradation of the oppressor and the dangers of privilege and dominance, it is on the basis of these three eponymic strands of consciousness that a major part of our awareness of the subtler and more invidious forms of oppression (which make the victims willing participants and supporters of an oppressive system) has been built. The most detailed treatment of the theme can be found in Freudian metapsychology. It presumes a faulty society which perpetuates its repression through a repressive system of socialization at an early age. Its prototypical victim is one who, while trying to live an ordinary 'normal' life, gives meaning and value to his victimhood in terms of the norms of an unjust culture. Almost unwillingly, Freud develops a philosophy of the person which sees the victim as willingly carrying within him his oppressors.

In other words, Freud took repression seriously. He did not consider human nature a fully open system which could easily wipe out the scars of suffering and could, thus, effortlessly transcend its past. Like all history, the history of oppression has to be worked through. This piercing of collective defences is necessary, Freud could be made to say, because human groups can develop exploitative systems within which the psychologically deformed oppressors and their psychologically deformed victims find a meaningful life-style and mutually potentiating cross-motivations. Such cross-motivations explain the frequent human inability to be free even when unfettered, a tendency which Erich Fromm, as early as the 1940s, called the fear of freedom.

The third process which limits man's vision of the future is his refusal to take full measure of the violence which an oppressive system does to the humanity and to the quality of life of the oppressors. Aimé Césaire says about colonialism that it 'works to *decivilize* the colonizer, to *brutalize* him in the true sense of the word . . . .'[6] And, that decivilization and brutalization one day come home to roost: '. . . no one colonizes innocently, . . . no one colonizes with impunity either.'[7] If this sounds like

[6] Aimé Césaire, *Discourse on Colonialism*, translated by Joan Pinkham (New York and London: Monthly Review Press, 1972), p. 11. Emphasis in the original

[7] *Ibid*, p. 170

the voice of a Black Cassandra speaking of cruelties which take place only outside the civilized world, there is the final lesson Bettelheim derives from his study of the European holocaust—'So it happened as it must: those beholden to the death drive destroy also themselves.'[8] Admittedly, we are close to the palliatives promoted by organized religions, but even in their vulgarized forms religions do maintain a certain touch with the eternal verities of human nature. At least some of the major faiths of the world have not failed to affirm that oppressors are the ultimate victims of their own systems of oppression; that they are the ones whose dehumanization goes farthest, even by the conventional standards of everyday religion. We have probably come here a full circle in post-modern, post-evolutionary, social consciousness. It now again seems obvious that no theory of liberation can be morally acceptable unless it admits that, in addition to the violence done to the obvious victims, there is the exploitation by imperfect societies of their instruments of oppression.

This general continuity between the slaves and the masters apart, there is the more easily identifiable penumbra of the oppressed in any organized system of oppression. In addition to the millions of direct victims, there are also millions of secondary victims of the oppressive systems. Their brutalization is planned and institutionalized,[9] so is the hostility these 'legitimately' violent groups often attract to protect those more central to the oppressive system. The ranks of the army and the police in all countries come from the relatively poor, powerless or low-status sectors of society. Almost invariably, imperfect societies arrive at a system of mobility under which the lower rungs of the army and the police are some of the few channels of mobility open to the plebians. That is, the prize of a better life is dangled before the socio-economically deprived groups to encourage them to willingly socialize themselves into a violent empty life-style. In the process, a machine of oppression is built; it has not only its open targets but also its dehumanized cogs. These cogs only seemingly opt for, what Herbert Marcuse calls, 'voluntary servitude'; actually they have no escape.

Though I belong to a society which was once colonized and ruled with the help of its indigenous population, and where the number of white men rarely exceeded 50,000 in a population of about 400 million, I shall give an example of this other oppression from another society in more recent times. The American experience with the Vietnam war shows that even anti-militarism, in the form of draft dodging or avoidance of military service, can become a matter of social discrimination. Pacifism can be

---

[8] Bettelheim, 'The Holocaust—One Generation Later,' *Surviving and Other Essays*, p. 101.

[9] See, for example, Chaim F. Shatan, 'Bogus Manhood, Bogus Honour: Surrender and Transfiguration in the United States Marine Corps,' *Psychoanalytic Review*, Vol. 66 (1977), pp. 585–610.

classy. The better placed dodge better and avoid the dirty world of
military violence more skilfully. In the case of Vietnam, this doubly
ensured that most of those who went to fight were the socially underprivileged, men who were already hurt, bitter and cynical. As is well
known, a disproportionately large number of them were Blacks, who
neither had any respite from the system nor from their progressive and
privileged fellow citizens protesting the war and feeling self-righteous.
They were people who had seen and known violence and discrimination—
manifest as well as latent, direct as well as institutional, pseudo-legitimate
as well as openly illegitimate. Small wonder, then, that in Vietnam many
of them tried to give meaning to possible death and mutilation by
developing a pathological overconcern with avenging the suffering of
their compatriots or 'buddies,' by stereotyping the Vietnamese and the
communists, or by being aggressive nationalists. The Vietnam war was, in
the ultimate analysis, a story of one set of victims setting upon another set
of victims on behalf of a reified, impersonal system.[10]

III

An insight into such processes helps us visualize utopias of the Third
World different from the ones which a straight interpretation of some of
the major civilizations can be made to yield. This does not mean that
cultural themes or cosmologies are unimportant. It means that the
experience of exploitation and suffering is a great teacher. Those who
maintain, or try to maintain, their humanity in the face of such experience
perhaps develop the skill to give special meaning to the fundamental
contradictions and schisms in the human condition—such as, the sanctity
of life in the presence of omnipresent death; the legitimate biological
differences (between the male and the female, and between the adult, the
child and the elderly) which become stratificatory principles through the
pseudo-legitimate emphases on productivity, performance and
'substance'; and the search for spirituality and religious sentiment, for
human values in general, in a world where such a search is almost always a
new sanctification of unnecessary suffering and status quo. Like Marx's
'hideous heathen god who refused to drink nectar except from the skulls
of murdered men,' human consciousness has sometimes used oppression
to sharpen its sensitivities and see meanings that would have been otherwise lost in the limbo of over-socialized thinking.

One important element in their vision (which many major civilizations
in the Third World have protected with care) is a certain refusal to think

[10] This issue has been approached from a slightly different perspective in Maurice Zeitlin,
Kenneth Lutterman and James Russell, 'Death in Vietnam: Class, Poverty and Risks of
War,' in Ira Katznelson, Gordon Adams, Philip Brenner and Alan Wolfe, eds., *The Politics
and Society Reader* (New York: David Mckay, 1974), pp. 53–68.

in terms of opposed, exclusive, clear, Cartesian dichotomies. For long, this refusal has been seen as an intellectual stigmata, the final proof of the cognitive inferiority of the non-White races. Today, it triggers debates on race and IQ and on the metaphors of primitivism and infantility. Arguments against such accounts of the non-West have ranged all the way from the empirical-statistical to the philosophical. (Césaire, for example, has mentioned the 'barbaric repudiation' by Europe of Descartes' charter of universalism: 'reason . . . is found whole and entire in each man.'[11]) Perhaps the time has come to work through this memory of intellectual racism, to admit that Descartes is not the last word on the intellectual potentials of humankind, and to acknowledge that what was once an embarrassment may some day become a hope.

. . . . [I]t is remarkable that in spite of all the indignities, and exploitation they have suffered, many of the Eastern civilizations have not drawn a clear line between the victor and the defeated, the oppressor and the oppressed, and the rulers and the ruled.[12] Unwillingly they have recognized that the gap between cognition and affect tends to get bridged outside the Cartesian world, whether the gap be conceived as an evolutionary trap or as a battle between two halves of the human brain. Often drawing inspiration from the monistic traditions of their religion, from the myths and folkways which have set some vague half-effective limits on inter-group violence and on the objectification of living beings, some civilizations have carefully protected the faith—now mostly lost to the modern world—that the borderlines of evil can never be clearly defined, that there is always a continuity between the aggressor and his victim, and that liberation is not merely the freedom from an oppressive agency outside, but also ultimately a liberation from a part of one's own self.[13] This can be seen as wishy-washy collaboration with the powerful and the victorious; it can also be seen as a more humane strain in political and social awareness.

Frantz Fanon's concept of the cleansing role of violence—and the implicit ideology of the drive to 'annihilate class enemies' in some Third World societies—sounds so alien and so Western to many sensitive

---

[11] Césaire, *Discourse on Colonialism*, pp. 35, 51–52.

[12] The post-Renaissance Western preoccupation with clean divisions or oppositions of this kind is, of course, a part of the central dichotomy between the subject and the object, what Ludvig Binswanger reportedly calls 'the cancer of all psychology up to now'. Charles Hampden-Turner, *Radical Man* (New York: Doubleday Anchor, 1971), p. 33. For 'psychology' in the Binswanger quote, one must of course read 'modern Western psychology'.

[13] See, for example, an interesting cultural criticism of Hinduism by even a person as humane and sensitive as Albert Schweitzer (*Hindu Thought and Its Development*, New York: Beacon, 1959) for not having a hard, concrete concept of evil. For discussions of the debate around this issue, see W.F. Goodwin, 'Mysticism and Ethics: An Examination of Radhakrishnan's Reply to Schweitzer's Critique on Indian Thought,' *Ethics*, Vol. 67 (1957), pp. 25–41 and T.M.P. Mahadevan, 'Indian Ethics and Social Practice,' in C.A. Moore, ed., *Philosophy and Culture: East and West* (Honolulu: University of Hawaii, 1962), pp. 476–93.

Afro-Asians mainly because of this awareness.[14] Fanon admits the presence of the oppressor within the oppressed, but calls for an exorcism, where the ghost outside has to be finally confronted in violence and annihilated because it carries the burden of the ghost inside. The outer violence, Fanon suggests, is only an attempt to make a painful break with a part of one's own self. Fanon fails to sense that such a vision ties the oppressed more deeply to the oppressor and to the culture of oppression than any collaboration can. Continuous use of the major technique on which an oppressive system is based (namely, the cultural acceptance of violence) gradually socializes the peoples fighting oppression to some of the basic values of the systems which oppress them. Violence converts the battle between two visions of the human society into a fight between two groups sharing some of the same values, for spoils within a permanently power-scarce and resource-scarce system. The groupings may change; the system does not. If Fanon had lived longer, he might have come to admit that in this process of internalization lies a partial answer to two vital questions about the search for liberation in our times—namely, why dictatorships of the proletariat never end and why revolutions always devour their children. Hatred, as Alan Watts reminds us at the cost of being trite, is a form of bondage, too.

In contemporary times, no one understood better than Gandhi this stranglehold of the history of oppression on the future of man. That is why his theory of conflict resolution is something more than a simple-minded emphasis on non-violence. It recognizes that the meek are blessed only if they are, in Rollo May's terms,[15] authentically innocent and not pseudo-innocents accepting the values of an oppressive system for secondary psychological gains. Gandhi acted as if he was aware that non-synergic systems, driven by zero-sum competition and search for power, control and masculinity, force the victims of oppression to internalize the norms of the system, so that when they displace their exploiters, they build a system in which the older norms covertly prevail. So his concept of non-cooperation set a different goal for the victims; he stressed that the aim of the oppressed should be not to become a first class citizen in the world of oppression instead of a second or third class one, but to become the citizen of an alternative world where he can hope to win back his human authenticity. He thus becomes a non-player for the oppressors—one who plays a different game, refusing to be either a player or a counter-player. Perhaps this is what a Western biographer of Gandhi means when he suggests that Gandhi's theory of

[14] Frantz Fanon, *The Wretched of the Earth* (Harmondsworth: Penguin, 1967) and *Black Skin, White Masks* (New York: Grove Press, 1967).
[15] Rollo May, *Power and Innocence: A Search for the Sources of Violence* (New York: Delta, 1972).

conflict resolution imputes that an irreducible minimum humanity could be actualized.[16]

The basic assumption here is that the oppressor in his state of dehumanization is as much a victim of the exploitative system as the oppressed; he has to be liberated, too. The Gandhian stress on austerity and pacifism does not come so much from the traditional Indian principles of renunciation and monism as from a deep-seated, early Christian belief in the superiority of the culture of the victims of oppression and from an effort to identify with the more humane cultural strain within an oppressive system. All his life, Gandhi sought to free the British as much as the Indians from the clutches of imperialism and the Brahmans as much as the Untouchables from the caste system. Such a position bears some similarity with certain forms of Marxism and Christianity. Father G. Gutierrez represents both these ideological strains when he says: 'One loves the oppressors by liberating them from their inhuman condition as oppressors, by liberating them from themselves. But this cannot be achieved except by resolutely opting for the oppressed, i.e., by combating the oppressive classes. It must be real and effective combat, not hate.'[17]

This other identification, which Gandhi so successfully made, is difficult for even those identifying with the victims. The temptation is to use a psychological mechanism more congruent with the basic rules of the exploitative system so as to have a better scope to express one's aggressive drives. The temptation is to equal one's tormentors in violence and to regain one's self-esteem as a competitor within the same system. Thus, identification with the oppressed has often meant identification with his world-view, not in its original form but as adapted to the needs of legitimizing an oppressive machine. Through this two-step identification, even the interpreters of oppression begin to internalize the norms of one exploitative system or another. As a result, the phantasy of the superiority of the oppressor gets even more deeply embedded in contemporary consciousness. We may openly attack the exploiters of the world, we may even speak of their loneliness, mental illness, or decadence, but we are unable to sympathize with them—as if a corner of our mind continued to believe that the privileged were superior to the underdogs we supported; that they were more powerful economically, politically or socially and, as powerful counterplayers, at least deserved to invite jealousy or hatred from us.[18]

[16] Erik H. Erikson, *Gandhi's Truth: On the Origins of Militant Nonviolence* (New York: Norton, 1969).

[17] G. Gutierrez, *A Theology of Liberation* (New York: Orbis Books, Maryknoll, 1973), p. 276.

[18] The obverse of this is of course the oppressors' search for the 'proper' worthy opponent among the oppressed. For an analysis of such a set of categories in an oppressive culture, see my 'The Psychology of Colonialism: Sex, Age and Ideology in British India,' in Ashis Nandy, *The Intimate Enemy: Loss and Recovery of Self Under Colonialism* (New Delhi: Oxford University Press, 1983, Part 1). See an earlier and briefer version in *Psychiatry*, 1982, Vol. 45 (1982), pp. 197–218.

I have tried to convey some idea of how Gandhi's future began in the present, why he constantly sought to convert the struggle against oppression from an inter-group conflict to a within-person conflict, and why his utopia was, to use Abraham Maslow's word, an eupsychia.[19] For better or for worse, this is the age of false consciousness; it is the awareness of the predicament of self-awareness which has shaped much of this century's social thinking and helped the emergence of the psychological man. In this sense, Gandhi's concept of self-realization is the ultimate product of an age which has been striving for the means of locating *within the individual* and *in action* the subject-object dichotomy (man as the maker of history versus man as the product of history; man as a product of biological evolution versus man as a self-aware aspect of nature; the ego or reality principle versus the id or pleasure principle; praxis versus dialectic or process).[20] Such a concept of self-realization is a 'primitive' corrective to the post-Enlightenment split in the vision of the liberated man. During the last two-and-a-half centuries—starting probably with Giovanni Vico—the Western sciences of man have worked with a basic contradiction. They have sought to make man the maker of his own fate—or history—by making him an object of the modern incarnations of fate—of natural sciences, social history, evolutionary stages and cumulative reason. This over-correction can only be remedied by world-views which re-emphasize man's stature as a subject, seeking a more humble participation in nature and society. There are world-views in which man is a subject by virtue of being a master of nature and society *within.* He acknowledges the continuities between the suffering outside and the suffering within and defines the self as consisting of both the suffering of the self and that of the non-self.[21]

Here lies the import of someone like Gandhi who, probably more than anyone else in this century, tried to actualize in practice what the more sensitive social thinkers and litterateurs had already rediscovered for the contemporary awareness—namely, that any oppressive system is only overtly a triad of the oppressor, the victim and the interpreter. Covertly

[19] As it happened, he was clearly influenced by important strands of Indian traditions which did stress such interiorization and working through. Being a critical traditionalist, he therefore had to do the reverse too, namely, exteriorize the inner attempts to cope with evil as only an internal state. His work as a political activist came from that exteriorization.

[20] I have derived this formulation from a set of somewhat casual comments made by Neil Warren in his 'Freudians and Laingians,' *Encounter* (March 1978), pp. 56–63. See also Philip Reiff, *The Triumph of the Therapeutic* (New York: Harper, 1966).

[21] Though some Western scholars like Alan Watts would like to see such a location of others in the self as a typically Eastern enterprise (Alan Watts, *Psychotherapy East and West*, New York: Ballantine, 1961), this has been occasionally a part of Western philosophical concerns, too. See, for instance, Jose Ortega y Gasset, *Meditations on Quixote* (New York: Norton, 1967). Within the Marxist tradition Georg Lukacs has argued that in the area of cognition and in the case of the proletariat at least, the subject-object dichotomy is eliminated to the extent self-knowledge includes molar knowledge of the entire society. Georg Lukacs, *History and Class-Consciousness* (London: Marlin, 1971).

the three roles merge. A complex set of identifications and cross-identifications makes each actor in the triad represent and incorporate the other two. This view—probably expressed in its grandest form in the ancient Indian epic on greed, violence and self-realization, *Mahābhārata*—is the flip side of Marx who believed that even the cultural products thrown up by the struggle against capitalism and created by the victim and enemies of capitalism were flawed by their historical roots in an imperfect society.[22] In fact, one may say that Gandhian praxis is the natural and logical development of radical social criticism because it insists that the continuity between the victim, the oppressor and the observer must be realized *in action*, and one must refuse to act *as if* some constituents in an oppressive system were normally pure or uncontaminated.

To sum up, a violent and oppressive society produces its own special brands of victimhood and privilege and ensures a certain continuity between the victor and the defeated, the instrument and the target, and the interpreter and the interpreted. As a result, none of these categories remain pure. So even when such a culture collapses, the psychology of victimhood and privilege continues and produces a second culture which is only manifestly not violent or oppressive. Not to recognize this is to collaborate with violence and oppression in their subtler forms, which in effect is what most social activism and analysis begin to do once the intellectual climate becomes hostile to manifest cruelty and exploitation.

IV

A **second example** of this consciousness of non-duality can well be the refusal of many cultures to translate the principles of bio-psychological continuities (such as sex and age) into principles of social stratification. Many of the major Eastern civilizations, in spite of all their patriarchal elements, have continued to see a certain continuity between the masculine and the feminine, and between infancy, adulthood and old age. Perhaps this is not all a matter of traditional wisdom. At least in some cases it is a reaction to the colonial experience which assumed clear breaks between the male and the female, the adult and the child, and the adult and the elderly, and then used these biological differences as the homologues of the secular political stratifications. In the colonial ideology, the colonizer became the tough, courageous, openly aggressive, hyper-masculine ruler and the colonized became the sly, cowardly, passive-aggressive, womanly subject. Or, alternatively, the colonizer became the

---

[22] It is one of the minor tragedies of our age that many of Marx's disciples sought to place Marx outside history and culture. He himself knew better. In another essay ('Evaluating Utopias,' presented at the Second Meeting on Alternative Visions of Desirable Societies, Mexico City, May 1979; briefer version in *Mazingira*, No. 12, 1980), I have briefly discussed how far any theory of salvation, secular or otherwise, can shirk the responsibility for whatever is done in its name.

prototype of a mature, complete, adult civilization while the colonized became the mirror of a more simple, primitive, childlike cultural state. In some cases, faced with their own ability to subjugate complex ancient civilizations, the colonial cultures defined the colonized as the homologue of the senile and the decrepit who deservedly fell under the suzerainty to become the responsibility of more vigorous civilizations.

Once again, I shall invoke Gandhi, who built an articulate model of political action to counter the models of manhood and womanhood implicit in the colonial situation in India.

It is an indication of how systems of oppression draw their strength from certain aspects of the 'mother culture' that British colonialism in India made an explicit order out of what they felt was the major strength of the Western civilization vis-a-vis the Indian. It went:

Masculinity > Femininity > Femininity in man

In other words, masculinity is superior to femininity which, in turn, is superior to effeminacy. (One major pillar of this cultural stratarchy was the British emphasis on the differences between the so-called martial and non-martial races of India. The other was—and this I venture as another instance of the continuity between the oppressors and the oppressed—the presence of a similar stratarchy in some Indian sub-traditions which acquired a new cultural ascendancy in British India.) As against this, Gandhi posited two alternative sets of relationships. In one, masculinity was seen to be at par with femininity and the two had to be transcended or synthesized for attaining a higher level of public functioning. Such 'bisexuality' or 'trans-sexuality' was seen as not merely spiritually superior both to masculinity and to femininity as it was in India (particularly Indian ascetic) traditions, but also politically so.

Gandhi's second model saw masculinity as inferior to femininity which, in turn, was seen as inferior to femininity in man. The following is a crude representation of the relationships:

androgyny > (masculinity ≃ femininity)

androgyny > femininity > masculinity

I have discussed the psychological and cultural contexts of these concepts in some detail elsewhere.[23] All I want to add is that the formal equality which is often sought by the various movements fighting for the cause of woman is qualitatively different from the synergy Gandhi sought. For the

[23] Ashis Nandy, 'Woman versus Womanliness: An Essay in Social and Political Psychology,' *At the Edge of Psychology: Essays in Politics and Culture* (New Delhi: Oxford University Press, 1980), pp. 32–46 and 'The Psychology of Colonialism'.

former, power, achievement, productivity, work, control over social and natural resources are seen as fixed quantities on which men have held a near-monopoly and which they must now share equally with women. In the Gandhian model, these values are indicators of a system dominated by the masculinity principle, and the system and its values must both be jettisoned for the sake of building a new world, unfettered by its history of sexual oppression. To fight for mechanical equality, Gandhi seems to suggest, is to accept or internalize the norms of the existing system, and pay homage to the masculine values under the guise of pseudo-equality . . . .

. . . . [This essay], I hope . . . will not be seen as an elaborate attempt to project the sensitivities of the Third World as the future consciousness of the globe or a plea to the First World to wallow in a comforting sense of guilt. Nor does it, I hope, sound like the standard doomsday 'propheteering' which often preface fiery calls to a millennial revolution. All I am trying to do is to affirm that ultimately it is not a matter of synthesizing or aggregating different civilizational visions of the future. Rather, it is a matter of admitting that while each civilization must find its own authentic vision of the future and its own authenticity in future, neither is conceivable without admitting the *experience of co-suffering* which has now brought some of the major civilizations of the world close to each other. It is this co-suffering which make the idea of cultural closeness something more than the chilling concept of One World which nineteenth century European optimism popularized and promoted to the status of a dogma.[24]

The inter-cultural communion I am speaking about is defined by two intellectual coordinates. The first of them is the recognition that the 'true' values of different civilizations are not in need of synthesis. They are, in terms of man's biological needs, already in reasonable harmony and capable of transcending the barriers of particularist consciousness. In other words, the principle of cultural relativism—that I write on the possibilities of a distinct eupsychia for the Third World is a partial admission of such relativism—is acceptable only to the extent it accepts the universalism of some core values of humankind. Anthropologism is no cure for ethnocentrism, it merely pluralizes the latter. Absolute relativism can also become an absolute justification of oppression in the name of scholarly commitment, as it often becomes in the apolitical treatise called the anthropologist's field report.

---

[24] As Fouad Ajami recognizes, 'The faith of those in the core in global solutions came up against the suspicions of those located elsewhere that in schemes of this kind the mighty would prevail, that they would blow away the cobwebs behind which weak societies lived . . . . In a world where cultural boundaries are dismantled, we suspect we know who would come out on top'. See Ajami, 'The Dialectics of Local and Global Culture: Islam and Other Cases,' paper written for the meeting of the group on Culture, Power and Transformation, World Order Models Project, 1980, mimeographed. Ajami rightly advises us to walk an intellectual and political tight rope, avoiding both the 'pit of cultural hegemony' and 'undiluted cultural relativism'.

The second coordinate is the acknowledgement that the search for authenticity of a civilization is always a search for the other face of the civilization, either as a hope or as a warning. The search for a civilization's utopia, too, is part of this larger quest. It needs not merely the ability to interpret and reinterpret one's own traditions but also the ability to involve the dominant or recessive aspects of other civilizations as allies in one's struggle for cultural self-discovery, the willingness to become allies to other civilizations trying to discover their other faces, and the skills to give more centrality to these new readings of civilizations and civilizational concerns. This is the only form of a dialogue of cultures which can transcend the flourishing inter-cultural barters of our times.

About the Contributors

Radharaman Chakrabarti is Director of the Netaji Institute of Asian Studies, Calcutta. He has previously been Professor and Chairman of the Department of Political Science at the University of Burdwan and a Post-Doctoral Visiting Fellow in the USA (1978–79). Apart from contributing articles to various journals, he has written three books including *The Theory and Practice of International Politics* (New Delhi, 1982) and *The Political Economy of India's Foreign Policy* (Calcutta and New Delhi, 1982).

Partha Chatterjee is Professor of Political Science, Centre for Studies in Social Sciences, Calcutta. He has published a number of books including *Arms, Alliances and Stability: The Development of the Structure of International Politics* (Delhi and London, 1975) and *Bengal 1928–1947: The Land Question* (Calcutta, 1984).

Dennis Dalton is Professor of Political Science, Barnard College, Columbia University. He has contributed articles to various journals and books and has published *The Indian Idea of Freedom* (Gurgaon, 1982) and co-edited (with A J Wilson) *The States of South Asia* (London and Honolulu, 1982).

Kenneth L Deutsch is Professor of Political Science at the State University of New York, Geneseo. He has been a Fulbright Senior Visiting Lecturer in Political Science at the universities of Rajasthan and Baroda (1979) and has received research grants from the National Endowment for the Humanities. He has contributed articles to various journals and books and has co-edited *Political Obligation and Civil Disobedience* (New York, 1972) and *Constitutional Rights and Student Life* (St. Louis, 1979).

Prabha Dixit is Senior Lecturer in History, Miranda House, Delhi University. She has been an Exchange Scholar at Sweet Briar College, USA, and has written three books including *Communalism: A Struggle for Power* (Delhi, 1974).

N R Inamdar is Lokmanya Tilak Professor of Politics and Public Administration, University of Poona. Among his numerous books are *Political Thought and Leadership of Lokmanya Tilak* (New Delhi, 1983) and *Inter-relationship between Bureaucracy and Political Leadership* (in press).

Sudipta Kaviraj is Associate Professor, Centre for Political Studies, Jawaharlal Nehru University, New Delhi. He has been a Fellow of St. Antony's College, Oxford (1981–83). Besides having contributed articles to various journals and books, he has co-authored *The State of Political Theory: Some Marxist Essays* (Calcutta, 1978).

Manoranjan Mohanty is Professor of Political Science, Delhi University. He has been a visiting scholar at the Institute of Far Eastern Studies of the USSR Academy of Sciences and at the University of California, Berkeley. He has contributed numerous articles to journals and edited books besides having authored *Revolutionary Violence: A Study of the Maoist Movement in India* (New Delhi, 1977) and *The Political Philosophy of Mao Tse-tung* (New Delhi, 1978).

Ashis Nandy is with the Centre for the Study of Developing Societies, Delhi. He is Chairman of the Committee for Cultural Choices and Global Futures, Delhi, and active in movements for peace, civil rights and alternative science and technology besides being associated with the United Nations University, Tokyo. Among his books are *Alternative Sciences* (New Delhi, 1980), *At the Edge of Psychology* (New Delhi, 1980), and *The Intimate Enemy* (New Delhi, 1983). His works have been translated into French, Spanish, Polish and several Indian languages.

Thomas Pantham is Professor of Political Science at the M.S. University of Baroda. He has been nominated UGC National Lecturer in Political Science (1985–86), has been a Visiting Fellow at the University of Essex (1973) and a Fulbright Senior Scholar at the universities of Princeton and Massachusetts (1981). He has contributed numerous articles to journals and edited volumes and has written *Political Parties and Democratic Consensus* (New Delhi, 1976).

Bhikhu Parekh is Professor of Political Theory at the University of Hull and Chairman of the Political Philosophy Study Group of the International Political Science Association. He has been Vice-Chancellor of the M.S. University of Baroda (1981–84) and Member of the University Grants Commission, New Delhi, besides having taught at the universities of London, Glasgow, McGill, Concordia, and British Columbia. A prolific writer, his publications include *Hannah Arendt: Search for a New Political Philosophy* (London, 1980), *Karl Marx's Theory of Ideology* (Baltimore and New Delhi, 1981), and *Contemporary Political Thinkers* (Oxford and Baltimore, 1982).

R C Pillai is Reader in Political Science at Deshbandhu College, Delhi University. He has been a guest lecturer at Jawaharlal Nehru University, New Delhi. Besides having contributed articles to journals, he has written *Nehru and his Critics* (New Delhi, 1986).

B R Purohit is Professor of Political Science at Sukhadia University, Udaipur. He has contributed articles on political theory and electoral politics and is the author of *Hindu Revivalism and Indian Nationalism* (Sagar, 1965).

Indira Rothermund is Professor at the Centre for Development Studies and Activities, Pune. She has lectured in several American colleges and was an Associate Professor at Heidelberg University for six years. She has also been an ICSSR Fellow at the Gokhale Institute of Politics and Economics, Pune. Apart from several articles in Indian and foreign journals, her publications include *The Philosophy of Restraint: Mahatma Gandhi's Strategy and Indian Politics* (Bombay, 1963), *The Split of the Communist Party of India* (Wiesbaden, 1969) and *Gandhian Grass-roots Democracy: The Aundh Experiment* (Bombay, 1984).

Moin Shakir is Professor of Political Science at Marathwada University, Aurangabad. Besides numerous articles in edited volumes and journals, he is the author of several books including *Khilafat to Partition* (New Delhi, 1983), *Politics and Society* (Aurangabad, 1976) and *Islam in Indian Politics* (New Delhi, 1983).

Ronald J Terchek teaches political philosopny and democratic theory at the University of Maryland. He has written *The Making of the Test Ban Treaty* (The Hague, 1970) and co-edited *Interactions: Foreign Policy as Public Policy* (Washington, 1983) besides having contributed to a large number of journals.

Rajendra Vora is at the Department of Politics and Public Administration, Poona University. Besides contributing to edited books and journals, he has authored research monographs on elections and political socialisation.

Eleanor Zelliot is Professor of History, Carleton College, Minnesota. She Chairs the South Asia Council, is on the Executive Committee of the Association of Asian Studies and has been Vice-President of the American Institute of Indian Studies. She has contributed to numerous journals and edited volumes, such as, D.E. Smith, ed., *South Asian Politics and Religion* (Princeton, 1966).